A CULTURAL HISTORY OF THE
MODERN AGE

A CULTURAL HISTORY OF THE MODERN AGE

By EGON FRIEDELL

TRANSLATED FROM THE GERMAN BY CHARLES FRANCIS ATKINSON

PLAN OF THE COMPLETE WORK

VOLUME I.

INTRODUCTION

BOOK ONE — Renaissance and Reformation: from the Black Death to the Thirty Years' War

VOLUME II.

BOOK TWO — Baroque and Rococo: from the Thirty Years' War to the Seven Years' War

BOOK THREE — Enlightenment and Revolution: from the Seven Years' War to the Congress of Vienna

VOLUME III.

BOOK FOUR — Romanticism and Liberalism: from the Congress of Vienna to the Franco-German War

BOOK FIVE — Imperialism and Impressionism: from the Franco-German War to the World War

ALFRED · A · KNOPF · PUBLISHER

A CULTURAL HISTORY
OF THE MODERN AGE

THE CRISIS OF THE
EUROPEAN SOUL

FROM THE BLACK DEATH
TO THE WORLD WAR

BY

EGON FRIEDELL

Translated from the German by
CHARLES FRANCIS ATKINSON

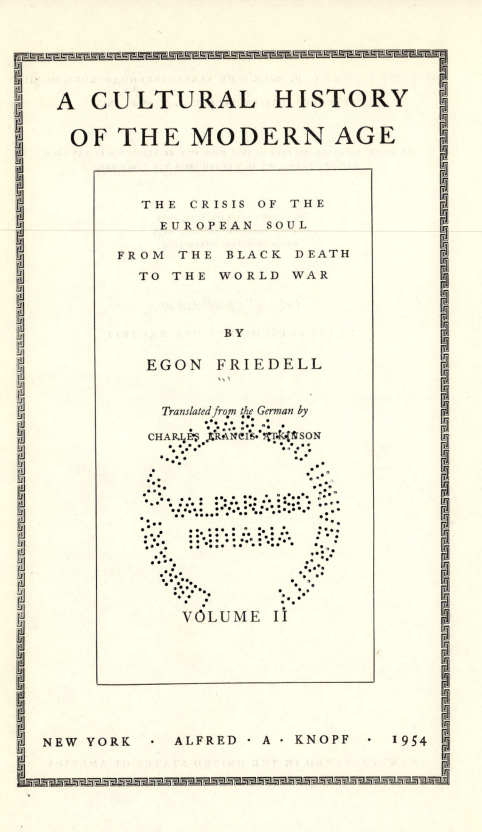

VOLUME II

NEW YORK · ALFRED · A · KNOPF · 1954

PUBLISHED SEPTEMBER 11, 1931
SECOND PRINTING, JANUARY 1933
THIRD PRINTING, MARCH 1954

Originally published as

KULTURGESCHICHTE DER NEUZEIT

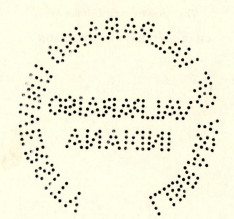

MANUFACTURED IN THE UNITED STATES OF AMERICA

"*In the examples brought forward herein, I have taken care not to alter the circumstances in the least: consciously I have not twisted an iota: unconsciously— well, that I don't know! But with an old tale it is not as with a prescription for a sick man: it is not so dangerous a matter whether some ingredient be precisely right or not.*"

MONTAIGNE

TABLE OF CONTENTS

BOOK II: BAROQUE AND ROCOCO

From the Thirty Years' War to the Seven Years' War

CHAPTER I: *Overture to the Baroque*

CHAPTER II: *Le Grand Siècle*

CHAPTER III: *The Death-Struggle of the Baroque*

vii

BOOK III: ENLIGHTENMENT AND REVOLUTION

From the Seven Years' War to the Congress of Vienna

CHAPTER I: *Common Sense and the Return to Nature*

BOOK II: BAROQUE AND ROCOCO

From the Thirty Years' War to the Seven Years' War

OVERTURE TO THE BAROQUE

" When we are born, we cry that we are come
To this great stage of fools. . . ."

King Lear

Just as the Baroque culture was on the point of opening its earliest dark blossoms, there flared up in an eastern corner of middle Europe a savage war, which, though set alight by sudden incidents, really issued from the deepest depths of the soul of the age. Then at once, ravenous and headlong, it ate its way unchecked into half the Continent, blazing up at hazard, now here, now there, reducing cities, forests, villages, fields, crowns, and philosophic systems to ashes, and finally becoming a law unto itself, controlled solely by the necessity of finding something on which to feed, until, one day, it vanished as mysteriously as it came, leaving in its wake nothing but a vast ghostly void: broken men, waste ground, destroyed homesteads, and a world orphaned of its God.

The Meaningless

Among the many long and senseless wars recorded in the world's history, the Thirty Years' War is one of the longest and most senseless — and probably so long simply because it was so senseless. For it had no clearly marked goal to reach or miss, no round, tangible " apple of discord " to win or lose. It is a matter of observation that, in general, it is the smaller wars that show a well-defined object of contention and in consequence a decisive result. To take only a few recent instances: the war of 1866 was concerned with the hegemony of Germany, that of 1870 with German unity; the Russo-Japanese war was fought for the possession of Korea, the Balkan wars for European Turkey. But the big world-wars, so-called, have for the most part very general intentions, such as " destroying the supremacy " of a particular world-power, " restoring the balance in Europe," " liberating the nations," and so on; and they end, almost always, in a draw.

Consider, for instance, the Spanish Succession War, the Seven Years' War, the Napoleonic wars (and the same would apply even to the latest world-war, which need not be discussed here). Such convulsive upheavals as these present themselves, when seen in the lump, from afar and from above, as nothing but obscure manifestations of vitality in the human race which take place automatically, vegetally, and without any apparent practical object; they are to be weighed up neither morally, politically, nor logically, but just physiologically. And they appear to us to be as senseless as everything else that transcends our senses. They are gigantic metabolisms which take place in our world-body, elemental events of which we ourselves can see only the catastrophic aspect. It may be that they are self-cleansing processes on a large scale, healing fever-phenomena, or cyclical disease processes — we cannot tell. But a certain periodicity they undoubtedly have, and we shall probably one day reach exact conclusions as to the dynamics of this mysterious vital phenomenon through a science that it is reserved for the future to create, one which will devote itself to investigating the *biology and pathology of the organism: " humanity,"* on the basis of its evolutionary and clinical history.

The Weed   Besides this quality of " senselessness," possessed by the Thirty Years' War in common with the other giants among wars, there was, however, another which had its roots in the peculiar character of the age: namely, the peculiar felted, wooden, woody, grasping, *weed-like* quality of all the cultural formations of this period, particularly in Germany. One of the basic characters of the generation was a clumsy intricacy, a combination of circuitous and tangential tendencies without real direction — that is, without a parallel — although (as we have seen) a state of chaos and spiritual lability is more or less typical of all the ages in which new ideas are germinating. Add to all this the wild desperadoism and boundless amorality which this generation also possessed — and in a rare degree — and it was inevitable that there should be born the grotesquely horrible monstrosity of this bestial, blindly furious war, without end or principle, which devoured for the sake of devouring, a whole generation through, and left no clue as to why it began, why it ended, or why it ever was at all.

For, long as it lasted, it might quite well have dragged on for years longer, though under increasingly wretched starvation conditions. Interminable negotiations preceded the peace-treaty and there was no reason why equally interminable ones should not have prolonged it. Neither on the Swedish-French nor on the Imperial-Bavarian side was there any absolutely compelling reason for stopping it. Nor was there any historical necessity for its breaking out in 1618 rather than earlier. The conflict which it set out to settle and, for all this powerful and prolonged effort, failed entirely to settle, had its roots in the question whether Germany was to be a Catholic or a Protestant country. Now, on the one hand the question was already a century old, and on the other hand a chance of ending the feud presented itself when no more than one year had elapsed. In the beginning of June 1619, Matthias Thurn stood in Vienna with a strong contingent at a moment when Ferdinand II had practically no troops. The Lower Austrian Estates could have captured him without more ado and thus forced the peace. But so straightforward, rapid, and clear a solution would have been contrary to Austrian and Baroque usage. Yet again, in the following year, after the battle of the White Mountain, the war was at an end, this time to the advantage of the Imperial party. The Estates of the whole of the Austrian hereditary lands, being entirely defeated, took an unconditional oath of allegiance, and the union of the Protestant German princes dissolved itself. But to have rested content with this unexpected and definitive victory would have been contrary to Habsburg and Catholic usage. Ferdinand carried the war into the Palatinate — that is, into Germany — and in a short time there was hardly a European state which was not participating in the war, whether wantonly or compulsorily, passionately or indifferently, militarily or only financially and diplomatically, permanently or sporadically: Poland, Sweden, Denmark, Holland, England, France, Spain, and Italy were all drawn little by little into the vortex. Once again, after Wallenstein's death, there was no excuse in any quarter for continuing the war, all the participators being both exhausted and heartily sick of it. And yet, although it had hardly any vitality, the war could not make up its mind to die; and it coughed through an agony of as many years as it had flourished, growing ever more asthmatic and anæmic. When at last it had worn itself out, it was found that everything remained essentially just as it had been. The Habsburgs had not been forced out of

5

their position of supremacy, but neither had the sovereign powers of the German hereditary princes been weakened — they had in fact been strengthened. The Papacy had forfeited none of its power, but it had been obliged to recognize once more, and more definitely, the equal rights of Evangelicalism. In fact, almost everyone must have asked his neighbour: "To what end did we fight and endure this war, and for thirty long years sacrifice everything we had power to sacrifice?" For some, it is true, the war had even so not been long enough. When General Wrangel heard that peace had been concluded he fell into a paroxysm of rage, flung his general's hat on the floor, stamped on it, and thrust out the messenger with curses.

In short, the Thirty Years' War was distinguished above all other wars by its fortuitousness. Everything concerning it was fortuitous: its beginning, its course, its spread, its end. But this fortuitousness was in itself anything but fortuitous: it flowed from the very nature of the epoch which bears its name. Long and lanky, empty and lame, disconnected and meaningless, it ambled on its way propelled by sheer inertia like the speeches and *carmina,* the documents and epistles, the poses and formalities of its time. Paradoxical as it seems, it had, in spite of its gigantic proportions and formidable destructive force, something amorphous and disjunct about it, something anecdotal.

Anecdotal — for it is a fact that posterity, though horrified for generations after it was all over, could only see it as anecdotal, without arriving at a true understanding of its nature — because there was nothing to understand. The Thirty Years' War has no real history. It consists of a number of histories which combine to form a more or less patchy mosaic and not a composed picture. We are left with a handful of original characters, a few engaging cultural curiosities, and a quantity of blood-curdling stories. As an instance take even the storming of Magdeburg, the most famous single incident of the war, made familiar to every German by the art of Schiller. The brilliant battle-cartoon that he displays before us rests on a fiction. Recent research has made it very probable that the fire was the work, not of Tilly's men, but of the leader of the defence, Hofmarschall Dietrich von Falkenberg, Gustavus Adolphus's emissary, who, when he saw that the city could not hold out, brought about this terrible catastrophe with the aid of a band of Evangelical fanatics. In any event the sack of Mantua was an equally terrible incident, yet it aroused little attention at the time and never found its Homer subsequently. All the same, although both here and elsewhere Schiller worked on insufficient or dubious material and, what is more, not seldom deliberately touched it up himself, his picture of the Thirty Years' War will always retain a lofty poetic sincerity. Similarly in writing *Wallenstein* the flair of genius enabled him to see that the "Camp"— that is, the *anecdote*—was the essential and historically significant feature of the war. There we have the witches' cauldron all complete with its dangers and its childishnesses, its delightful and its disgusting ingredients, its horrors and its absurdities — motley, crude, and cynical, like the costume of this riven world — all classes, nations, and life-forms thrown together in it pell-mell: nobility and coarseness, God's paladins and the Devil's own foolhardiness, and the bargain-driving fear of death and gallows-humour. And everywhere on this stage all the players are but genre figures, or supers, heads that at best have a profile or a good mask; nowhere a full man in the round. In the whole of this incredibly vast array of episodists, figurants, and auxiliaries, only two serious protagonists stand out who can with some degree of justification be called heroes of the Thirty Years' War: the King of Sweden and the Duke of Friedland.

But how strangely distorted, besmudged, and degraded even so seems a hero-figure in this incomprehensible age. Only the rôle of leader is left to him. Everyone's eyes are upon him, everyone follows him willingly, confident in his higher insight and far-sightedness, his power to act, and his firmness; but he can only lead them all to darkness and confusion, to defeats and abysses; no divine idea inspires him, and no earthly idea either — in fact, no idea at all. No sublime conviction drives him dæmonically on, not even a sublime prejudice, a pious error. He is merely cleverer than the herd, not wiser; stronger than they, not better. His heaven is astrology, and his Bible politics.

As statesmen Gustavus Adolphus and Wallenstein were *Wallenstein* equally matched. The Swedish King was a higher force as a field general, but the Friedlander was unique as an organizer. He possessed the talent, in that disjointed age, of raising armies literally with a stamp of the foot. Not his wealth, his adroitness,

7

and his military renown alone could have achieved this. There must also have been some subtle effect of his personality, which must have had for that age a fascination of which we can form almost no idea. He was the first to discover and effectively to develop the principle — ruthless but irresistible in its broad simplicity — that war must be self-sustaining. In other directions too he not infrequently surprises us by a clarity and soundness in his way of thinking, which was entirely foreign to the age. But on the other hand he proves himself the legitimate child of his century in the hesitating tentative character of his diplomacy and strategy, his weighing and postponing, the perpetual wavering between several alternative opportunities which prevented him from attaining any of his political aims, minimized his military successes more than once, and finally led to his downfall. With great perspicacity he recognized from the beginning of the war the point on which everything depended. This great war of religion, with all the internal political and territorial quarrels from which it derived constant nourishment, could only be definitely concluded by the Habsburg dynasty successfully setting up the complete absolutism that already existed in France and Spain and was the standing program of the Stuarts in England. Repeatedly he counselled the imposition of the same régime on Germany, and his own chosen rôle in it, according to all the indications, would have been that of military dictator — substantially a Mayor of the Palace in whom lay the real centre of power; for he who commanded the army commanded Germany. But for this very reason Ferdinand II, who had mistrusted his generalissimo from the first day, could not take kindly to the scheme, which would also have encountered a fatal opposition on the part of Maximilian of Bavaria, head of the Catholic League. Later Wallenstein conceived the idea of creating for himself, as Duke of Mecklenburg, a great Northern principality, with the dominion of the Baltic as a wider vision. But here the obstacle to realization would be not so much the Emperor as Gustavus Adolphus. Accordingly his next idea was an alliance with Sweden, and there is no doubt that he carried on negotiations to that end, although written documents are for obvious reasons not in existence. But the " Snow King " trusted him as little as the Habsburger had done. After Lützen he tried the same game with the Evangelical princes of the Empire, with a view presumably to obtaining the Bohemian crown. This would probably have been the best solution for him. His rule in Bohemia would have found a strong tradition already in existence, and he possessed there not only extensive properties, but a large and sympathetic following; it is fairly certain, in fact, that he would have made an excellent figure as head of a Czech realm. But he did not seize his chance promptly enough, and along a course of proposals and counter-proposals, in which neither side acted with entire sincerity and each kept an eye on its line of retreat, he came to his murder. (It is clear from the subsequent attitude of the Viennese Court that the order for his death was given with a bad conscience, for it made every effort to shift the responsibility.) In all these situations Wallenstein appears, not as an Imperial official, but as a potentate. And in fact that is precisely what he was, for at that time the only real sovereign among hundreds of apparent and titular rulers was the war-wielding condottiere with his power of money and troops and talent.

Around the figure of Wallenstein there hangs a strange gloomy splendour that makes it interesting and suggestive, but does not arouse human sympathy. Even in his lifetime he had grown to more than life-size. It was believed that he was bullet-proof, that he controlled troops of invisible horsemen and had made a pact with the Devil. Undoubtedly he belonged to that band of diplomatic-strategic geniuses who are endowed with a wide field of vision and pre-eminent capacity for synthesis, and of whom Napoleon was the greatest. But his icy egotism, his dark lust of power, and his entire lack of what we may call private characteristics place him outside the scope both of our comprehension and of our sympathy. It has, therefore, become usual to contrast him with Gustavus Adolphus, as presenting a complete foil to the limelight hero of the North who shed blessings when he landed, bearing tolerance, protection, and liberation on his sword-point. But that is a Protestant legend. Actually he was a close spiritual blood-relation of Wallenstein's, equally devoured by greed and ambition, equally full of the serpent's cunning, equally cold-hearted.

Gustavus Adolphus

Gustavus Adolphus's belief in the Lutheran doctrine was no doubt quite as genuine as Wallenstein's belief in astrology; but the Evangelical cause alone would no more have induced him to enter

9

the war than love of the stars would have set Wallenstein's plans in motion. Rather we may say that the Bible was for the one what the horoscope was for the other: namely, an instrument of policy. The domination of the Baltic, which Wallenstein had set before himself for a moment, was for Gustavus Adolphus a steady guiding idea. He came for the sake of helping hard-pressed Protestantism against the Emperor, but how could he have made his help of lasting effect without establishing himself permanently in Germany? The Reformation was to triumph over Rome; translated into Swedish this meant that Pomerania, Prussia, and half of northern Germany were to fall to the Vasas.

His victorious progress caused astonishment and consternation in all Europe. Within a year of his landing he had reached Munich. His successes he owed in part to his troops — who formed a real national army and were not, like other armies, a rabble brought together by desire for plunder, love of adventure, and superstition — but even more to his own genius. In almost every department of land warfare he introduced far-seeing reforms which were greatly in advance of their time. He improved firetechnique in replacing the complicated musket by a lighter weapon, and wooden cartridges by paper ones which could be carried in the pocket. Tactics he reformed by organizing infantry in three ranks, of which the first knelt, the middle one stood, and the third loaded. In strategy he achieved greater freedom in manœuvre for his troops, and he would carry out wheeling movements in the middle of a battle — an unheard-of thing in those days. Most important of all, he reinstated cavalry as the dominating arm. But his appetite grew with his success, and it cannot be denied that the end of his career found him determined not to be content with a strip of the north German coast, but to secure for himself much bigger and more durable gains. It is extremely probable indeed that he aimed at the throne of the German emperors, and also the dukedom of Bavaria, which in the case of a decisive Protestant victory would have been lost to the Catholic Maximilian: in this connexion it is significant that the Palatinate, which Bavaria had taken from the " Winter King " in the early part of the war, was not restored to the latter when reconquered. Small wonder, then, that even the Evangelicals began to be afraid of their liberator. But at Lützen all these plans and all these fears were crushed under Croat horse-hoofs — for Gustavus Adolphus, cool and steel-hard *Realpolitiker* though he was, had still so much of the romantic, the northern sea-king, in him that, although short-sighted and fat, he invariably fought out the battle in the midst of his troops; so that there came a day when he met his death in the thick of a *mêlée,* just as though he had been a mail-clad duke of the grey Middle Ages. He died not too early to have impressed the world with his superior power, and early enough to be put into Protestant text-books and festival plays as the selfless champion of liberty and faith.

The " Great War," as it was called, has always tempted later generations to indulge in criticisms which, whether favourable or unfavourable, have the common characteristics of complacency and exaggeration. It came to be habitually looked at through a magnifying-glass, and until quite recently its effects have been vastly over-estimated. This was the consequence of relying ex- *Exaggerated* clusively on contemporary narratives without taking into account *judgments* the fact that they were frankly polemical in character and no more represented the real proportions of things than, say, today's descriptions of White or Red rule in individual countries. More-over, a rage for distorting and puffing out everything to the point of abstruseness or monstrosity was one of the deep-rooted traits of the age. Even that most famous of contemporary documents, Grimmelshausen's *Simplizissimus,* has only the value of a coarse and powerful oleograph, of a fantastic although very impressive caricature, employing the poetic licence naïvely and without restraint to present things in a more compressed form than that which they bear in reality. Further, it was forgotten that this abortion of a war represented no connected action, but an amor-phous crowd of isolated war incidents, and, therefore, that only a few districts suffered permanently, most of them only tempo-rarily or at long intervals, and others not at all. It had also no similarity with the wars of today. These have as their most characteristic feature the straining of all available forces to the utmost. But in the Thirty Years' War there was no question at all of bringing in every section of the country, every class of the population, every physical and material means of fighting. The obligation to bear arms did not exist even for the citizens of a beleaguered city. One was a soldier only if one pleased and for as long as one pleased. Men went into the army from a sense of vocation, from depravity or greed or ambition, or as a sport; so that the war-folk consisted essentially of three sorts: professionals, *déclassés*, and sensation-seekers. As a result armies were, according to our ideas, very small; battles were very short, small-scale, and moreover, owing to the wavering character of war-policy in general, infrequent. Thus the formlessness and indiscipline of the age on the one hand made a " world-war " in our sense impossible, and on the other hand led, in particular cases, to the most shocking excesses — although, even so, one must not be content to assume that such events as Grimmelshausen describes were the rule. If we remind ourselves of the stories told of the gruesome deeds of the Russians in Poland and the " atrocities " of the Germans in Belgium, which were spread about at the time and are partially believed to this day, we shall be able to make the necessary allowances in this case also.

Of course, even after all deductions, the full extent of Germany's desolation after the war is beyond our imagination. And yet — here again we are confronted by the same confusion between cause and effect that we met more than once in the field covered by our first volume. It was not because trade and commerce began to flourish towards the close of the Middle Ages that a new material culture developed, but vice versa. It was because the race of men living at that time had this tendency that international intercourse was strengthened, finance was born, and production intensified. It was not the discovery of America, or the art of printing, or the Reformation that caused " modern times " to arrive; it was because at the turn of the fifteenth century a distinctive human variety, " modern man," appeared on the stage of history that West Indian coasts were explored, books printed, and the institutions of the Church of Rome opposed. Neither was the German nation brought low by the Thirty Years' War; the war happened because of the depths to which the nation had sunk.

The economic rout   This is best seen in the economic sphere. Already before the war Germany had lost her supremacy in the cloth trade through the superiority of her western competitors, in particular Holland, and while, throughout the sixteenth century, she had been the European mart for the luxury-products of arts and crafts, she was now outstripped in this field also by the French manufacturers, with whom she could not compete in either fashionableness or quality of goods. The Mediterranean traffic too, for which Germany had provided the natural route to the North, had long been ousted from its dominant position, partly through the improvement in navigation, and the great discoveries, but partly also by Germany's own fault: for the innumerable customs barriers, with their trickery and extortion, and the many varieties of coinage made landwise trading a positive torture. The lack of a uniform currency especially gave rise to a national scourge which proved more devastating to Germany than the war: this was the scandalous race, denounced in many a contemporary pamphlet, of coiners and clippers — "*Kipper und Wipper*," as the papers called them, appellations as flattering as that of "profiteer" to-day. It was these elements in the population that were blamed, and not without some justification, for the general misery. But the chief culprits were really the various sovereigns. They had soon discovered that the currency nuisance held a great advantage for them in that they could enforce the acceptance of their own baser money at face values, such being the primitive method of the time for enriching oneself through a government loan. At first the population raised no objection, for the old full-weight gold, of which nearly everyone had a store, went up in price. But in course of time a general crash became inevitable. Smuggling, receiving, fraudulent barter, and other disreputable practices took charge of finance; men paid out "light" money and bought good money much in the manner of speculators on the Stock Exchange today. The sovereign princes, caught in a vicious circle (for they were now having their taxes and interest paid to them in their own bad coinage), resorted to more and more desperate measures. Finally the coins were made merely of silvered copper, or even inferior material, and became simply counters. It happened very much as in our own day, with the difference that they used sheet metal and not paper. And the appropriate social phenomena followed as a matter of course: sudden wealth and extravagant luxury on the part of the lucky speculators, distress of the salaried class and brain-workers, poverty of those with small savings, rapid depreciation of all capital assets, endless strikes, wild tumults.

The ruin was made complete by the Peace of Westphalia, which reduced Germany almost to an inland country, by leaving her with practically no important river-mouth, that of the Rhine becoming Dutch, that of the Vistula Polish, those of the Oder, the Elbe, and the Weser Swedish. The Baltic was disputed by Danes, Swedes, and Poles; the North Sea by French, Dutch, and English — nowhere was there room for Germany. And at the same time this treaty perpetuated Germany's particularism by granting to all the states of the Empire the *superitas territorialis*, which gave them the right to form alliances among themselves and with foreign powers "except against the Emperor and the Empire" — this reservation being a mere form of words. The Swedish chancellor Oxenstierna, who is responsible for the wise saying: "*An nescis, mi fili, quantilla prudentia regatur orbis?*" ("Do you not know, my son, with how little understanding the world is governed?"), failed, it would seem, to find even that little in the German constitution, for he describes it as a confusion only maintained by Providence. Two hundred years later Hegel, still more candidly, called it a "constituted anarchy."

The Thirty Years' War, kindled originally as a war of beliefs, lost its religious character in the first decade and became ever more and more political as it went on. We have seen that Gustavus Adolphus's chief motive in intervention was in no wise the championing of a confusion. He was pursuing a great-power policy for Sweden, and a further (perhaps a chief) motive for setting himself in opposition to the Emperor's party was the fact that it supported his hereditary enemies the Poles in their claim to the throne of the Vasas. He was made uneasy also by the plans of Wallenstein, who had been nominated General of the Baltic by the Emperor and was using every effort to make this much more than an empty title. Wallenstein, for his part, never once in his whole career gave the Catholic cause a thought. So, too, after the second battle of Breitenfeld the Protestant King of Denmark by his threatening attitude prevented the Swedes from reaping the fruits of their victory. At the Peace of Prague, which occurred about the middle of the war, the Elector of Saxony, the bulwark of the Lutheran cause, went over to the Imperialists. The final phase upon which the struggle now entered was entirely under the influence of France, which continued the war against the

Catholic party by means of Protestant princes and generals. And the head and brain of this policy was a Cardinal of the Roman Church, the great Richelieu, who therein was carrying out the testament of Henry IV, Most Christian King of France. After Richelieu's death his life's work was continued and completed by Mazarin — likewise a Roman Cardinal. Only Ferdinand II, the soldier of his "Generalissima" the Mother of God, and Maximilian of Bavaria, the friend of his youth, fought for the Catholic Faith's sake. And life passed them by, and in the end everyone had forgotten the origins of the war: Catholics fought in the Swedish, Protestants in the Imperial, armies. The law of the age proved stronger than both parties: the will to secularize all human activities and relations, which we have seen to be the essence of the Reformation, now took possession of the Catholic world also. And whereas in the sixteenth century doctrinal convictions and passions still occupied the minds of men so exclusively as to drive out all national, social, and patriotic considerations and feelings, the exact opposite now took place: all Europe was completely politicalized, secularized, rationalized. The Middle Ages are at an end.

The first section of the genuine Modern Age, which may thus be said to begin simultaneously with the Thirty Years' War, reaches to about the year 1660 and may be described as a sort of pre-Baroque period. In it the new world-picture comes slowly into the field of vision, now too coarse and now too pale in features. It is an era of preparation, in which as it were the provisional plan, the first sketch, the rough draft of Baroque man is conceived. The beginning of the sixties makes a fairly distinct cæsura here. After the death of Cromwell comes the Restoration of the Stuarts in 1660; after the death of Mazarin, Louis XIV in 1661 becomes a self-sufficing personal ruler; in 1660 Velasquez dies, in 1662 Pascal. These four dates, around which are grouped numerous others of the second rank, but equally significant, close one stage in history and open another. *The Pre-Baroque*

The central political idea of this era, in which absolutism was to ripen, is the "reason of state," *ratio status,* of which Moscherosch, the German satirist, said: "*Ratio status* is from its origin a glorious, magnificent, and divine thing. But what is there the Devil cannot do? He has joined himself with the *ratio* *Ratio status*

status and turned it upside down, so that it is now nothing better than the biggest swindle in the world, and a ruler who pays his respects to it may do whatever he pleases in its name." And according to another contemporary writer: " It is an eye-powder or dust which the rulers sprinkle in the eyes of their subjects ; it is a most superior artifice to keep the common folk quiet." The leading political personage is now the all-powerful minister of state, familiar with every intrigue and feint and finesse of secret diplomacy ; in the place of the court theologian we now have the court lawyer, while the other, in so far as he is allowed to exercise any real influence, excels in a peculiarly ugly form of intolerance — most of all, in the Lutheran camp, where he is equally bitter against the Calvinist and the Roman doctrines. The Elector of Saxony's court divine, von Hohenegg, for instance, declared that to take up arms for the Calvinists was nothing but doing knight-service for the original founder of Calvinism — namely, the Devil ; that whoever should depart in the smallest detail from the Augsburg Confession was a Syncretist (this being in the eyes of strict Lutherans the most terrific of all reproaches). Even a man of such genuine human piety as Paulus Gerhardt could say: " I cannot consider the Calvinists *qua tales* as Christians." In short the prevailing state of mind was that described by Karl von Hase in his brilliant *Kirchengeschichte:* " In spite of all their subtlety, they really thought of God as a great Lutheran pastor who hit out in defence of his honour." The only exception was Angelus Silesius, originally a Protestant, but later a Catholic. In his *Cherubinische Wandersmann* German mysticism once more unfolded all its profundity and creative power. Yet even this pure, strong-minded thinker, who was able to write: " He who sayeth that God turneth away from the sinner doth clearly show that he doth not yet know God," flooded the world in his last years with bigoted writings, in which he attacked Protestantism with the same narrow and ruthless fanaticism that had so dishonoured Protestantism itself.

It was in those days that the word " political " came to have the subsidiary meaning of wary, cunning, diplomatic, knowing, that it still retains in the popular tongue. A " head for politics " was one that knew how to manage and make use of fellow-creatures skilfully, how to turn everything smartly to one's own advantage, how to insinuate oneself non-committally into people's affairs, and in fact how to make the most of that kind of ability which is always conducive to worldly success. *"Politesse,"* on the other hand, meant polished manners, social ease, fluent conversation — these again mere instruments to success in high life. Other words, too, acquired new meanings and very significant ones. What everyone shared in became "common," "vulgar." A man who bore himself courteously, who was presentable at court, counted as a man of moral values, and " *schlecht,*" up till then synonymous with " *schlicht* " (plain, straight), came to mean the same as " inferior," " mean."

Although people prided themselves in those days on their social forms and accomplishments, German life has never been so loose, slack, and uncontrolled as at this particular time. A society in the social sense, such as was almost always to be found in the Romance countries, had simply never existed in Germanic countries, and least of all in Germany. There was never on German soil a universal standard of refinement for public life; a universal art of behaviour, urbanity, conversation; a universal purity and agreeableness of the spoken and written word and of taste. This much-praised quality of the Latins had, however, its shady side: it was based on a lack of inward freedom and individuality. High development of collective culture presupposes something like uniformity, or at least a common determination to submit to certain conventions, traditions, statute-books, and regulations. In this respect a striking contrast becomes evident between the Germanic and Latin cultures. In Italy, Spain, and France there is a higher collective spirit, and, correspondingly, they hardly show an instance of the phenomenon of misunderstood genius. On the other hand we do not find any genius towering so often above his fellows as in England, Germany, or Scandinavia. These countries have a lower general level, and their great men have to wait long for recognition, sometimes until after they are dead. But it is more rarely that first-rank phenomena appear at all on Latin soil. It is uncommon, again, in the Romance lands to find a great man who looks down on his own nation, feels himself an exile in his fatherland, and looks abroad for his sympathizers — yet with Germanic genius this is almost the rule. Take Frederick the Great, Schopenhauer, Nietzsche, Handel, Beethoven, Strindberg, Ibsen, Shaw, Byron, and many more. All his life, even

17

in banishment, Dante was a Florentine; Voltaire looked longingly over to France day and night from his Swiss asylum; Descartes's meditations in his self-chosen "Dutch hermitage" were all for the benefit of his Paris friends; Victor Hugo in Guernsey wrote solely for France and about France — and, generally speaking, no Italian, Spanish, or French artist or philosopher would have conceived the crazy idea of wanting to live and create for anything but his country, his capital, his people, and his culture. This all arises from the fact (already noted in our section on the Italian Renaissance) that with the Latin races the great man is the collective expression and essence of his nation, whereas with the Germanic peoples it is not so. But just as, in nature and in history, the great law of action and reaction sees to it that apparent damages and attacks have always their compensations — and more than compensations — so in this case genius at times is stimulated, by the very obtuseness or hostility of the *milieu,* to rise to heights of achievement never attained in other circumstances. In Descartes, Calderon, Balzac, or Verdi we have peaks of their race; in Kant, Shakspere, Goethe, Beethoven, peaks of humanity.

" Alamod-ishness" It need hardly be said that in this period, the most sterile that Germany ever knew, all the leading ideas in literature, art, luxury, and manners came from abroad. The ideal of the age was the *homme du monde,* also called *homme de cour, honnête homme, monsieur à la mode.* The whole phase came to be known as "alamodishness" ("*alamodisches Wesen*"). In those days, however, it was Holland, and not yet France, which led the fashion, and the German's "grand tour" abroad, indispensable to all who wished to be in the swim, usually took him to the Netherlands. On the other hand we have even Moscherosch, so soon, complaining with all downrightness of a general Frenchification. "O more than foolish youth! What animal would be so senseless as to alter his speech and voice to please another? Did you ever hear a cat bark to please a dog, a dog mew to please a cat? Truly, a firm Teutsch nature and a slippery Welsch wit have no more in common than cat and dog: will you then display less sense than the animals, and ape them, and get no thanks for it too? Did you ever hear a bird moo, or a cow sing?" The epistolary style of the nobles was already completely French. And, when you look into it, practi-

18

cally everyone was of the nobility. For it was uncommonly easy to acquire a title, either by purchase or by services rendered to some pocket-edition of a prince. This paper nobility — against which the nobility of lineage waged a fight as strenuous as it was hopeless — gradually absorbed all the upper ten thousands. The custom (which still survives in Austria) of addressing every well-dressed man as Herr "von" So-and-so dates from this time. In Italy it was carried so far that everyone belonging to the best society became automatically a *marchese*. In this striving after outward nobility, unaccompanied by any shedding of inner vulgarity, we see the first symptoms of the servility which was soon to become the hall-mark of social life. "Reputation" and "*honnêteté*" became the sole criteria, and the reverse of these is tail-wagging, crawling before the court, the bureaucracy, and everyone a stage higher than oneself. Nice manners and elegances of speech were taught quite crudely and mechanically in "manuals of taste," and that which the French had arrived at doing naturally and with easy grace, Germany sought to imitate in a most clumsy, philistine, and tasteless fashion. It was the mode and the right thing to affect an aristocratic air, though no place in the world was less appropriate to it than this hole-and-corner society. Swords were worn by all. When the students at Jena were forbidden to wear them they amused themselves by having them carried behind on wheelbarrows. A constant use of the toothpick was also considered to be particularly good form.

Conversation was, in spite of all these means of education, extremely dry and dull. In large gatherings it was sustained by the uninspiring method of introducing a subject and hearing everyone's opinion on it in turn. Argument and counter-argument consisted chiefly in an exchange of rehearsed, high-faluting phrases by which thought was neither conveyed nor evoked. When a youth made the acquaintance of a girl, she became straight away a Pallas Athene, a goddess to be worshipped, a "virtuous and blessed nymph"; at the betrothal ceremony it was considered good form for both sides to protest in endless stereotyped phrases that they were not worthy of such honour. The effect of this deliberate formalism was that the most unimportant things took on vast significances. It was a great problem whether a particular guest should be offered a stool or an arm-chair to sit upon. For years there was a controversy on the question of whether the coaches of the great ambassadors were to have precedence, even when empty, over those of minor envoys when the latter occupied them in person. And in the Diet there were full houses for endless debates when the envoys of the princes challenged the claim of the representatives of the Electors to the exclusive right of placing their chairs on the carpet in the conference hall; finally it was decided that the former should be allowed at least to place the front legs of their chairs on the fringe of it. Even in the extraordinary twirly writing, too, which looks like nothing but a web of initials, and in the addresses and headings of letters, the character of the age discloses itself. The simple " Sir " no longer sufficed, it had to be " *dem hochwohlgeborenen Herrn Herrn*," and the official manner of addressing the Supreme Court of the Empire at Wetzlar was as follows: " To the high- and well-born, noble, stout, and most learned; likewise the high-born, and high- and well- and nobly born, active privy councillors of His Imperial and Royal Catholic Majesty: the official judges, presidents, and members of the venerable Imperial and Royal Supreme Court of Wetzlar in order appointed; our very dear Sirs, each and every one; also our most honoured and likewise well-beloved and highly esteemed Sirs and Cousins; also our highly and greatly esteemed, likewise especially gracious and most highly esteemed Sirs ! " The delight in foreign-sounding, rolled-out forms of speech is seen too in the Latinizing of names — once a mannerism of the Humanists, but now a general custom. " One cannot call a man Rosskopf (Horse's head) now; he has to be Hippocephalus, and Schütz is Sagittarius," says Moscherosch. And from this time date all the Textors, Molitors, Fabers, and Sartoriuses who were originally plain Webers (Weavers), Müllers (Millers), Schmidts (Smiths), and Schneiders (Tailors).

The Trumpeter of Säckingen

On costume the war naturally had a direct influence. Spanish dress, the tightness and stiffness of which has been described in our first volume, was useless for soldiers; and as in those days the military set the tone, dress in general became more comfortable, stouter, and more warlike. Wide sack-like trousers; high spur-clinking jack-boots; immense gauntlet gloves; big challenging felt hats with a flapping plume and a broad brim turned up at one side; flat white turned-down collars, and swords in rattling metal-mounted baldrics — this in essence is the costume which, worn even today by the officials of university-corps on festive occasions, is familiar to everyone from the twopence-coloured sentimental type of novel and opera which abounded in the eighties of the last century, and of which Nessler's *The Trumpeter of Säckingen* may be called the most famous example. It is truly remarkable, the way in which the transfiguring power of historical retrospect has succeeded in disguising one of the coarsest, most prosaic and banal of cultural epochs in the glamour of romance.

The hair, which had of necessity been kept short for the Spanish " millstone " ruff, was now again worn in flowing locks; the moustache was twisted upward as also for a time the whiskers, though these disappeared in the course of the war. There again the object was to appear provocative, dashing, martial; and in the pursuit of this end, moustache-binders and darkening dyes were used to enhance the gloomy threatening impression. In a word the ideal was Bramarbas, who soon, however, became a comic figure: Gryphius describes him, not without a certain heavy humour, in *Horribiliscribifax;* he is immortalized in French literature as " Capitaine Rodomont " (his birthplace being transferred to Spain — land of boasters and bravoes), and he is finally incorporated in the *commedia dell'arte* as the permanent mask of the *capitano,* who is in fact the perfectly truthful caricature, inwardly and outwardly, of the type of that day. He is bearded like the pard, armed with a gigantic rapier; wears spurs a hand's span long and a terrifying plumed hat; and talks incessantly of war, duels, seduced women, and lopped-off limbs, whereas actually he is only interested in kitchen odours and winebottles and makes off at the least suspicion of a disturbance.

Ladies wore steel-ribbed corsets, but dispensed with the crinoline, which was superseded by a skirt in heavy folds; to replace the crinoline several petticoats of different colours were worn on top of each other. Their hair was dressed similarly to men's, but divided into bunches of curls which fell right and left over the ears. But the details of hairdressing, such as the arrangement of curls on the brow and temples and the parting, underwent frequent changes. So also with the cut of men's beards: the moustache was at first thick and projecting, becoming later a mere dark line on the upper lip and finally consisting of two spots right and left of the nose. Hats changed their shape almost every three months, varying from a butter-pot, a Dutch cheese, a sugar-loaf to a cardinal's hat. Colours too underwent veritable revolutions, the violent early favourites being superseded by delicate and shaded hues such as *bleu-mourant* and " Isabella." Equally varied in their startling and adventurous forms were the buttons, braids, and rosettes and the rich lace insertions on collars and boot-legs.

Tobacco and potatoes Two other articles of fashion, if we may call them so, also became popular in Germany at this time — tobacco and potatoes. The " Tartuffel-fruit," of which the seed capsule was at first supposed to be the edible part, was brought by Sir Walter Raleigh to Ireland, where at first it was but little appreciated, though in the sequel it became the favourite (and only too often the sole) article of food among the peasants. In France the potato was long regarded as a delicacy — as indeed it really is. In Germany it made its way with less opposition and more speedily than elsewhere on account of the poverty caused by the war; since then it has become the favourite food of the Germans owing to its nutritive value (although it contains practically no albumen relatively to its starch content and can therefore only be regarded as a secondary food), its easy cultivation, and its inexhaustible uses in cookery. It is indeed for the German what the fig is to the Near Eastern, rice to the Japanese, and the tomato to the Italian. " Tobacco-eating," as chewing was called, " tobacco-drinking," as smoking was called, and snuff-taking, which was considered the most refined manner of enjoying the weed, came from England, via Holland and France, to Germany, where the pipe soon became an indispensable item in a soldier's, student's, or dandy's equipment and even began to be appreciated by ladies. Naturally the satirists seized upon it as a theme for their coarse bludgeon-humour, while doctors described the diseases, and preachers the hell-fire, to which the new vice was to lead — with precisely the amount of success which such admonitions against fashionable pleasures have had all down the ages. Pope Urban VIII even issued a bull against snuff-taking, and in Russia they had the bright idea of stopping it by slitting the noses of its devotees. But already in the first half of the seventeenth century there were tobacco cultures in Europe, and everywhere there sprang up " Tabagies " — places in which everything was staged for the undisturbed enjoyment of the desired weed, whether by chewing it or by inhaling it to exhale it again. Very soon even the strictest absolutisms were reconciled to the new " purveyors of hell " by the fat income which tobacco taxes and monopolies provided.

The literature of this period was likewise uncouth and affected, noisy and high-coloured, a mixture of coarseness and gentility. To cleanse the language of its numerous Spanish, Italian, and French ingredients two great literary societies were founded: in 1617 the *Fruchtbringende Gesellschaft* or Order of the Palm; in 1644 the *Pegnitzschäfer* or " Flower-Crowned " Order, from which there originated the famous " Nuremberg Funnel," for " pouring in the art of making German poetry and rhyme in six hours (*Poetischer Trichter, die Teutsche Dicht- und Reimkunst in sechs Stunden einzugiessen*)." But the purism which these reformers preached so vigorously was nothing but a new kind of gibberish. The most rabid of the company, Philipp von Zesen, not content with excommunicating foreign words, refused even to leave the Greek deities their honourable names — Pallas became *Kluginne,* Venus *Lustinne,* and Vulcan *Glutfang* — and would not allow such good German loan-words as " *Fenster* " (window) and " *Natur,*" which became respectively " *Tageleuchter* " (daylighter) and " *Zeugemutter* " (mother of production). " Cloister," even, became " *Jungfernzwinger* " (virgins' lock-up) — which was rough luck on the monks, though the foreign origin of their own name was sufficient anyhow to put them out of doors.

The poetry of this period is dominated by mere mechanical picture-making, void of ideas or art; a childish, primitive music or jig-saw puzzle. There arose in fact a kind of poetry-making in which each conception had its allotted " poetic " vocable, and each substantive its automatically provided " embellishing " adjectives, the result being a paper-pattern arrangement of words designed solely for the eye — conventional, superficial, empty and effect-seeking, a lifeless pattern-work of colour, finesse, and drapery. The rhymed couplets of Hans Sachs and the master-singers, which were a reasonably adequate expression of the relatively uncomplicated mental outlook of the day, were now scorned as doggerel; and in its stead came the French Alexandrine — impossible in German — moving on stilts like a flapping stork. The wooden solemnity and pomposity of these productions, the effort to be grandiose and exalted at any cost for the sake of effect, place the majority of them, for us, in the category of humorous literature. The smattering of learning that is in them makes these efforts still more ludicrous and robs them of their last remnant of spontaneity. Gryphius did well to call the separate portions of his dramatic works " treatises " (*Abhandlungen*). He took for his model Seneca (who was himself a frigid and academic imitator) and from him he acquired the taste, shared by all his contemporaries in drama, for things monstrous and ugly, for crude amphitheatre effects. In his " Murder Scenes " (*Mordspektakeln*), which, as the title indicates, is nothing but a string of filthy and preposterous scenes of bloodshed, he carries a mean realism to its extreme. When the hero is compelled to take his life, he chooses to run his head into a wall because this is the nastiest way to do it. The stage direction usually runs thus : " He becomes desperate and runs his head into the wall so that the blood comes through his hat (this can easily be managed by means of a bladder)." It is expected of Mars that he should " burst on to the stage with beating of drums and firing of guns, brandishing a bloody dagger, and yelling, with his mouth full of tobacco-smoke which he blows out." The famous Dutch scholar Vossius, who was regarded as an oracle in everything concerning art and science, went so far as to suggest that real criminals should be executed in tragic dramas. Comedy was dominated by the " pickled herring " — a Dutch scion of the English clown and forerunner of the German Hans Wurst — whose permanent repertory consisted in idiotic and commonplace antics which reached their climax when he lost his trousers. For the rest, comedy, according to Opitz's classification, dealt with " bad people and things, marriages, drinking parties, gaming, swindling, and mischievous servants, braggart landsknechts, intrigues, youthful indiscretion, stingy old age, procuring, and the like, as they occur daily among the common people," while tragedy was made up of " death-blows, desperations, infanticide and parricide, fire, incest, war, insurrection, wailing, howling, sighing."

This Opitz — the same who heads the list of dates and book-names detested of schoolchildren — was celebrated by his contemporaries as the *princeps poetarum Germaniæ*. He was, however, really no more than the chiefling of this guild of leathern, conceited, anæmic pedants, and even the ingenious and profound whitewashing recently attempted by Gundolf, though it has given us a finer and clearer understanding of his psychological anatomy, will hardly suffice to relieve him of his general bad reputation. He was first and last a preceptor (which no doubt accounts for the devotion of even present-day schoolmasters to him) : he demonstrated theoretically and practically how to make poetry, poetry being to him a delectable form of edification (although his own specimens are delectable only in so far as they are unconsciously funny) ; he was, therefore, doubly a schoolmaster, for he taught how to teach. But since real poets have from all time had an antipathy both to teaching and to being taught, we are compelled to see in him one of the most complete anti-poets who ever argued their way into poetry. It is possible that he has some significance in the history of the German language and metre, but European cultural history can pass him by without loss.

In the other branches of science, too, we find the same rigid *Comenius* intransigent doctrinairism. In the universities a theologian was sworn in on the dogmas, a lawyer on the *corpus iuris,* a philosopher on Aristotle. A figure such as the great educator Comenius is without parallel in this period. It sounds like a voice from another world when we hear him insisting that man should be led by his own and not by others' reason, that he should not gain his knowledge of things from books, but must create out of originals — the sky, the earth, the oaks, and the beeches, and all the everyday objects that meet his eye — that, in fact, the thing itself should come first and only then the conception ; that the alpha and omega of pedagogy is not the Bible, but Nature. His ideal was the " Pansophia," a synthesis of piety and nature-knowledge which was to unite all Christian sects within the free faith of an understanding humanity.

It was only in the domain of natural science that Germany pro- *Natural* duced anything of importance. The burgomaster of Magdeburg, *science* Otto von Guericke, invented the air-pump, the manometer, the electrifying machine, and the water barometer, and in addition proved that in an air-tight chamber a flame goes out, animals soon die, and sound is not propagated, whereas light-rays will pass through it unhindered. The Franconian doctor Johann Rudolf Glauber succeeded in producing sal-ammoniac and sodium sulphate (called after him " Glauber salts " and still used in our

25

time as a blood-purifier). These two men are, moreover, noteworthy as having come near to understanding the phenomenon of polarity: Guericke showed that electrified bodies of the same name repel each other; and Glauber set up the conception of chemical affinity, which is most clearly exhibited by substances differing in kind. Indeed this first half of the sixteenth century gives proofs on every hand that we are approaching the classic age of the natural sciences. The two outstanding scientists of this period are the Italian Torricelli and the Englishman Boyle. Evangelista Torricelli worked with great success in a branch of physics which had not hitherto been seriously considered, the dynamics of liquids; and in this field he discovered, among other things, the very important law that a jet which issues from a full containing vessel always takes the form of a parabola and possesses a velocity of outflow proportional to the square root of the head of pressure. Robert Boyle, called by his countrymen " the great experimenter," can be regarded as the founder of modern chemistry. His principal work, *Chymista scepticus*, is, as the very title indicates, a rejection of the existing chemical methods. In his preface he says that chemists had hitherto let themselves be guided by narrow principles which exclude the higher points of view. They had seen themselves as dispensers of medicine and transmuters of metals, whereas he sought to treat chemistry from an entirely different angle, not as a doctor, not as an alchemist, but as a natural philosopher. Chemistry was for him the knowledge of the constitutions of bodies. He succeeded in defining, for the first time really clearly, the concept of the element, he made experiments upon the constituents of the air and the relation between the pressure and the volume of gases, and he proved that when metals rust, there is an increase in their weight. Beside him worked William Harvey, who discovered the circulation of the blood, and set up the proposition: *Omne animal ex ovo*. In the domain of practical mechanics — the construction of ships, fortresses, and canals — the primacy was with Holland, which, generally speaking, led the world in matters of economics and culture at this time.

Holland's supremacy The bold and self-sacrificing struggle of the Netherlands against Spanish despotism had ended in the full recognition of their independence, and now this nation was at liberty to develop those special talents which evoke our admiration no less than they repel our sympathies. The Dutch are the first great commercial people of the Modern Age. They recall the Phœnicians in their hard matter-of-fact materialism, their crafty and unscrupulous acquisitiveness, and their turbulent decayed oligarchy. Like the Phœnicians they owed their economic supremacy to the circumstance that they were ahead of other nations in the developing of the mercantile idea. And it was for this same reason that they were unable to maintain that supremacy: for all its busy tenacity, their effort lacked a higher inspiration and, therefore, real vitality. Numerically, too, they were too few to be able for long to subdue and batten on half the world. It was the same maladjustment which turned Sweden's taste of world-power into an episode: the national basis was too small.

There is no doubt that the cultural level was at that time higher in Holland than in the rest of Europe. The universities enjoyed an international reputation. Leyden in particular was accounted supreme in philology, political science, and natural philosophy. It was in Holland that Descartes and Spinoza lived and worked, as also the famous philologists Heinsius and Vossius, the great jurist-philosopher Grotius, and the poet Vondel, whose dramas were imitated all the world over. The Elzevir dynasty dominated the European book trade, and the Elzevir publications — duodecimo editions of the Bible, the classics, and prominent contemporaries — were appreciated in every library for their elegant beauty and their correctness. At a time when illiteracy was still almost universal in other lands, nearly everyone in Holland could read and write; and Dutch culture and manners were rated so high that in the higher ranks of society a man's education was considered incomplete unless he could say that he had been finished off in Holland, " *civilisé en Hollande.*"

The colonizing activities of the Dutch set in practically with the new century, and fill the first two-thirds of it. They quickly gained a footing in all quarters of the world. On the north-east coast of South America they took possession of Guiana, and in North America they founded the New Amsterdam which was later to become New York: centuries afterwards the Dutch or " Knickerbocker " families still constituted a sort of aristocracy. They spread themselves over the southernmost tip of Africa, where they became known as Boers, and imported from there the excellent

Cape wines. One whole continent bore their name: namely, New Holland — the later Australia — round which Tasman was the first to sail. Tasman did not, however, penetrate to the interior, but supposed Tasmania (which was named after him) to be a peninsula. The Dutch were also the first to land on the southern extremity of America, which was named Cape Horn (Hoorn) after the birthplace of the discoverer. Their greatest acquisitions, however, were in the Sunda islands: Sumatra, Java, Borneo, Celebes, and the Moluccas all came into their possession. Extending out to Ceylon and Further India, by 1610 they had already founded their main base, Batavia, with its magnificent trade-buildings. In fact they ruled over the whole Indian archipelago. For a time they even held Brazil. With all this, they never, in the true sense of the word, colonized, but merely set up trading centres, peripheral depots, with forts and factories, intended only for the economic exploitation of the country and the protection of the sea routes. Nowhere did they succeed in making real conquests; for these, as we said before, they had not the necessary population, nor had they, as a purely commercial people, the smallest interest in doing so. Their chief exports were costly spices, rice, and tea. To the last-named Europe accustomed itself but slowly. At the English Court it first appeared in 1664 and was not considered very palatable — for it was served as a vegetable. In France it was known a generation earlier, but even there it had to make its way slowly through a mountain of prejudice. Moreover, its consumption was limited by the Dutch themselves, who, having a monopoly to export it, raised the prices to the level of sheer extortion. This was in fact their normal procedure throughout, and they did not shrink from the most infamous practices, such as the burning of large pepper and nutmeg nurseries and the sinking of whole cargoes. Their home production, too, dominated the European market with its numerous specialities. All the world bought their clay pipes; a fishing fleet of more than two thousand vessels supplied the whole of Europe with herrings; and from Delft, the main seat of the china industry, the popular blue and white glazed jugs, dishes, and table implements, tiles, stoves, and fancy figures went forth to all points of the compass.

One Dutch article that was in universal demand was the tulip bulb. It became a sport and a science to breed this gorgeous flower in ever new colours, forms, and patterns. Immense tulip farms covered the ground in Holland, and amateurs or speculators would pay the price of an estate for a single rare fancy breed. The get-rich-quick people threw themselves into the "option" game: that is, they sold costly specimens, which often existed only in imagination, against future delivery, paying only the difference between the agreed price and the price quoted on settling day. It is indeed the Dutch who may claim the dubious honour of having invented the modern stock-exchange system with all the manipulative practices that we know today. The great tulip crash of 1637, which was the result of all this bubble trading, is the first stock-exchange collapse in the history of the world. The shares of the Dutch trading companies, in particular the East Indian (floated in 1602) and the West Indian (1621), were the first stocks to be handled in the stock-broking manner (their par value speedily tripled itself, and the dividends rose to twenty per cent and higher) ; and the Amsterdam Exchange, which ruled the world, became the finishing school for the game of "bull" and "bear." Then, too, during the first half of the seventeenth century, the Dutch were Europe's sole middlemen: their mercantile marine was three times as big as that of all other countries. And although — or indeed because — the whole world depended on it, there arose a bitter hatred against it (contrasting strangely with the extravagant admiration accorded to their manners and comforts) which was intensified by the brutal and reckless extremes to which they went in maintaining their advantage. "Trade must be free everywhere, up to the gates of hell," was their supreme article of faith. But by free trade they meant freedom for themselves — in other words, a ruthlessly exploited monopoly. This was also the kind of freedom that Grotius meant when in his famous treatise on international law, *Mare liberum,* he stated that the discovery of foreign countries does not in itself give right of possession, and that the sea by its very nature is outside all possession and is the property of everyone. But as the sea was in fact in the possession of the Dutch, this liberal philosophy was no more than the hypocritical mask for an economic terrorism.

In this wise the "United States" became the richest and most prosperous country of Europe. There was so much money that the rate of interest was only two to three per cent. But although naturally the common people lived under far better conditions than elsewhere, the great profits were made by a comparatively small oligarchy of hard, fat money-bags, the so-called " Regent-families," who were in almost absolute control — since they filled all the leading posts in the government, the judicature, and the colonies — and looked down on the common man, the " Jan Hagel," as contemptuously as did the aristocrats of other countries. Opposed to them was the party of the Oranges, who by an unwritten law held the hereditary town governorships; their aim was indeed a legitimate monarchy, but they were nevertheless far more democratic in their ideas than the moneyed class, and were therefore beloved of the people. The best talent, military and technical, gathered about them. The first strategists of the age were on their staff. They nurtured a generation of virtuosi in siege warfare, privateering, artillery, and engineering science. The water-network created by them, which covered the whole of Holland, was considered a world marvel. They were masters, too, of diplomacy.

But in speaking of the culture of Holland in those days, one really thinks, at once and instinctively, of its painting. Dutch painting was rooted in the healthy matter-of-factness and unprejudiced breadth of view with which a world-embracing imperialism had endowed the whole nation. It must not be supposed, however, that its progress was materially assisted by any kind of organized and enlightened patronage. Prosaic aridity, lack of imagination and of generosity, wrote their signature over Holland as over every commercial country, and the art which grew up in this atmosphere became stamped with that grandiose commonplaceness which makes most of its representatives second-rate phenomena. Where it rose to the superhuman stature of true genius, it did so in an embittered struggle *against* the environment. The uninspired dullness and counting-house correctness of these sober and respected business men, who must have everything about them " proper " and handsome, but yet go in terror of " superfluity " and " extravagance," are reflected most clearly in the dreary commercial style of the architecture — for instance in the town hall at Amsterdam, long considered an architectural masterpiece. Frans Hals, Ruysdael, and Rembrandt — to mention only three important artists — died in poverty; and, after all, Belgium, we

30

must remember, has nearly as many great names to show as Holland.

In most art-histories a sharp dividing line is drawn between these two countries, but there is really no absolute necessity for this. It is true that Grotius himself said that north and south had nothing in common but their hatred of the Spaniards. But in actual fact the relation is almost the opposite of this, for it was precisely the inequality of these hatreds — far weaker in the south than in the north — that led to the division of the country into the Spanish Netherlands, which remained under Habsburg rule (and corresponded roughly to the Belgium of today) and the republican Union of the Northern Provinces; and on the whole there is a considerable degree of likeness between the two peoples. The northern half of Belgium is inhabited by the Flemings, who resemble the Dutch almost completely in speech, origin, character, and attitude towards life. After all, what is there in the Belgians, Jordaens, Brouwer, Teniers, and Snyders, that is not Dutch? The southern half, of course, is populated by the French-speaking Walloons, but these have had no influence to speak of on the art and culture of the country. In one point only does the northern part of Belgium differ essentially from Holland: it is Catholic throughout. But this very fact would be rather a stimulant than otherwise to art, for Dutch Calvinism, puritanic prudery, and almost Mosaic formlessness of worship robbed painting of its finest material and, by limiting it to portraits, domestic scenes, and nature studies, gave it the stamp of genre painting. How predominantly philistine the public's requirements in art were is shown by the small interest taken in historical painting, for which one would have supposed the country's past would have excited an urgent demand.

Dutch art is essentially bourgeois. The respectable citizen wants in the first place to see himself in paint — himself and all that makes his life worth living: his family, his business, his festivals, and his pleasures. Accordingly we get individual portraits and group portraits, in which all the family relatives pose, half bashful and half saucy, as models; " musketeer " pictures, in which the little shopkeeper plays at being a soldier; grave council-meetings, club meetings, and banquets; well-found interiors and inviting still-life, with the cosy furnishings, bright pot-plants, valuable table equipment, winebottles, fish, ham, game, and all the other things that served to make existence appetizing for this nation of gormandizers. Apart from such objects, which are all in prolongation of his own personality, the only thing that interests the bourgeois is the anecdote. And so we have juicy family scenes, brawls, records of sport; touching or comic or ghastly character paintings, all with special emphasis on the particular point which has to be made as broad and evident as possible. This is why in Holland the painters who had the greatest success with the public were those clever and banal enough to concentrate on producing a single article. Paul Potter specialized in cows, Philip Wouvermann in grey horses, Melchior Hondecoeter on poultry, William van de Velde on ships, Jan van Huysum on flowers, Abraham van Beijeren on oysters, lobsters, and fruit, Pieter Claesz on fine silverware. In short, the whole art of the brush in the Netherlands, except for the work of a few great ones whom no one understood, was one vast domestic picture-book and family album.

On the other hand, Dutch genre painting has a prodigal variety and richness, a lapidary factualness and impartiality, an impressive brutality and naked self-evidence, an exuberant strength and swelling fertility such as nothing else but Nature herself shows. What this painting described, exclusively, but with the sincerity of ravenous hunger, with a furious seething greed, was life unqualified and unadorned, without moral or fastidiousness, or teleological intrusions, life as an end in itself, one brief self-indulgent moment of effervescing unrestrained vitality.

Art has always an irresistible tendency to try to raise reality to a higher power, to ideology of one sort or another. But these Dutchmen were in a very unfortunate situation. The conventional idealism of the past — the Italian tradition, that is — was repellent to their deepest instincts, and in a cultural world which had the cleric and the pedlar as protagonists it was utterly impossible for them to produce a new idealism out of their own age and for their own people. The only outlet left to them was a naturalism worked up to a dæmonic intensity, and this course led them to the discovery of traits of eternity in the humblest things, symbolism in the most trivial, and divinity in the coarsest. They proved that man can be heroic even while he gormandizes, gets drunk, vomits, or thrusts his hand under a petticoat, provided that it is shown at the same time that creative nature is enthroned behind it all in mysterious majesty. By rendering Being in its full and overwhelming *life-size*, they achieved the miracle of creating a sort of mythology of the everyday.

Amidst this diligent noisy crowd there towers one giant, lonely in his supremacy and unrevealed to their earth-bound vision — Rembrandt. As Shakspere and Michelangelo in their own times, so he also stood, exile and stranger, avoided by all and truly known to none. With Michelangelo he has in common the quality of timelessness: he belongs everywhere and nowhere; for he might just as well have lived a hundred years sooner as an uncomprehended master-creator of the Renaissance, or two hundred years later as a leader of Impressionism. With Shakspere he has in common the character of anonymity; for he vanishes completely behind his life's work — the variety and profusion of figures that he creates leave the creator's own face indistinct and undefinable. And to both he has the profound kin-likeness that in the art of his last period he loses himself completely in the transcendental and brings forth inscrutable creations to which such crude and banal terms as "realism" and "idealism" are no longer applicable. That art which first he toiled to achieve and then, at the height of his creative power, handled with such consummate ease became at the end of his earthly career transparent to him: looking through it he realized its emptiness, its impotence, its superficiality, and saw that it was not the supreme thing he had all his life imagined it to be; and it fell from him, making room for something more profound, which, however, being no longer quite of this world, eludes men's comprehension.

Rembrandt

He was, therefore, as little an expression of his age as Michelangelo and Shakspere were of theirs; and just as we were forced to assign the rôle of "representative man" to an inferior in each of those ages — in the first to Raphael, in the second to Bacon — so do we select a far shallower master as the hero of this: namely, Peter Paul Rubens. In Rubens the drunken joy of life, the triumphant affirmation of the exuberant present, turned itself into colour. His work is one mighty hymn to the healthy power of enjoyment, the sturdy materialism of the Low-German type of humanity. As a Catholic and a Fleming he coloured and celebrated the double triumph of the Counter-Reformation and of

Rubens

Dutch commerce in flaming tints, heaped-up measure of composition, and Olympian figures of force. Man, as he sees him, is a sort of demigod, who has descended to earth to give play to his invincible powers and is never ill, never tired, never melancholy, serene in the bloodiest battles, athletic even when a Lazarus — in fact a magnificent beast of prey which hunts, fights, devours, begets, and one day dies ignobly with a roar at the height of its strength. His women are never virgins, never even mothers, but fat rosy pieces of flesh with exemplary pelvises, bosoms, and posteriors, existing solely for the purpose of being flung on to a bed after a savage, lustful struggle which only enhances the enjoyment. A massive revelling in every aspect of dissolute living forms the basic emotion of all his paintings; it is as if they were surrounded by the fragrant brood-warmth of a humming hive or the huge, white spawn-cloud of a shoal of herrings. In form, too, his figures are designed merely to enhance the pomp and the joy of life; they are parts of the *décor*, glowing with colour like rich fantastic tapestries. For the rest, his relation to the world of Classical legend, from which he takes the most elaborate of his allegories, is perfectly cool and academic; it equips him with a vocabulary, and that is all.

In times of economic boom Rubens has always been vastly admired. His buoyant pleasure-loving animality tells of the good conscience that comes with good business, the shallowness of the man favoured by fortune — for Rubens was a child of fortune all his days — and, above all, that profound atheism which was gradually taking possession of Europe and, as Holland was the most advanced country, first reared its head there. Rubens is certainly one of the most irreligious artists who ever held a brush, and for that reason he will always be the idol of those who regard God as tiresome or superfluous. But everyone of finer feeling will, if honest with himself, be forced to confess that in spite of his admiration for Rubens's proportion, his power as a colourist, and his magnificent gift of grasping the outer shell of a man, he was nothing but a royal animal-painter and the glorifier of a steaming super-healthiness which is as irresistible as it is barbaric.

King
Charles
Holland's blossoming was as luxuriant as it was brief, for it could only be a matter of time for the real great powers to drive this insolent parvenu from its factitious supremacy. It was inevi-

34

table that England in particular should find it intolerable to have all the North Sea shipping, and even its own trade, in foreign hands. It will be remembered that this country had leapt forward with an astonishing swiftness in all directions during the second half of the sixteenth century, and that the tide of progress had not been stemmed even under the rule of James I — who, though one of the narrowest, most ordinary and incompetent of men and a positive caricature of a king, had so extreme a conception of his kingship by the grace of God as has seldom been seen among his fellow-monarchs. In his speech from the throne on his accession he said that, as God has power to create and to destroy, to give life and death, and is the lord of soul and body, so also kings have the power to create and destroy their subjects, the command of life and death over them, and to direct them in all things; that kings are responsible to no one but God, can deal with their subjects as chess-men and raise or debase them like a coinage. His son Charles I was in many respects his opposite: clever, amiable, of gracious manners, a finished cavalier, and a discriminating patron of the arts and sciences. Van Dyck painted the whole Court of St. James's: the self-consciously elegant King, the decorative dreamy Queen, the gentle stiff princesses, and the anæmic feminine Crown Prince — and aristocratic decadent society in discreetly autumnal colouring.

But Charles I had one bad quality which outweighed all the good ones: he was incapable of speaking a straight word or doing a straight thing. The still popular King Charles spaniels are named after him — very blue-blooded, sensitive creatures, but distinctly treacherous and conceited. And this was the King's own character. It was absolutely impossible to treat with him; he cheated and lied to everyone, never kept his promises, and twisted his own words to mean their opposite. He was so foolish as to believe that the best fighting method was to deceive all parties so that he might dominate them all. It seems that in him this fundamental double-tonguedness and word-breaking had its basis not only in the hereditary perfidy of the Stuarts, but in the conviction that the king stood so high above his subjects that he could allow himself anything in his relations with them. And so, falling deeper and deeper into the net of feints and contradictions, he gradually lost the confidence of the whole country. All the same it is a tendencious untruth on the part of democratic historians to maintain that his execution was the will of the people. It evoked universal horror and was actually no execution, but a political murder, for the jury that decreed it was legally incompetent to do so and, even apart from that, acted only under pressure.

His position was at first anything but unfavourable. On coming to the throne he was received with acclamations by the greater part of the population, and even when the situation began to be critical he would have been able, by following a fairly reasonable and straightforward policy, to hold his own. The majority in Parliament was invariably on the side of the monarchy, though opposed to absolutism, and even with the lower classes the Royalists always commanded more sympathy than the Independents. But Charles began at once to try to govern in opposition to, and even without, Parliament. He took for his adviser the Earl of Strafford, who — true to his device: "Thorough" — tried by every method of law-twisting and compulsion to create an effectively absolute despotism. And his principal ecclesiastical adviser was Archbishop Laud, whose ambition it was to bring the English Church as near to identity with the Roman as possible — a prospect regarded with horror by most of the population. The revolt broke out, however, not in England, but amongst the Scots. The bitter hostility aroused by the ill-considered attempt to introduce Laud's liturgy into that country led them to sign a Covenant for the protection of their religious and political liberties. Charles thereupon sent an army against them, and since a mistrustful Parliament would grant him no money for troops, the funds were raised by voluntary contributions among the Royalist sympathizers. The latter, who became known as the Cavaliers, were opposed everywhere and at once by the democratic Roundheads, who, though they did not at first go beyond the idea of a monarchy limited and controlled by Parliament, presently inclined more and more to a republic. And the Civil War became inevitable.

Cromwell And now there arose out of the darkness the brazen figure of Cromwell, who swept the country like a steam plough at the head of his "Ironsides," overthrowing everything: King and people, High Church and Covenant, Upper and Lower Houses, Irishmen and Scotsmen. It cannot be said that any one party served him unconditionally during his ten years' government. The Royalists hated him as a regicide, the republicans as an oppressor of Parliament, the Episcopalians as a brutal fanatic, the Independents as a lukewarm compromiser, the landowners as a social revolutionary, the Levellers as a protector of capital, and one and all as a dictator and tyrant. He stood completely alone, because, like the brilliant politician he was, he never had any definite preconceived standpoint, but always a policy to suit the given situation and the given business. Unlike the small, narrow-minded people around him, he did not adapt things to suit himself, but adapted himself to them. In a word, he always, whether as diplomat, organizer, or strategist, knew what the real point was. And that was just what people so intensely disliked about him.

As a matter of fact, he was in the happy position of not having to trouble much about what people thought of him. For by means of this gift, as simple as it is rare, of seizing the heart of every case with an unbiased mind, he beat them all. And although the Cromwellian party, strictly speaking, consisted of himself alone, he ruled all three kingdoms with an unlimited power which not a Plantagenet of the Middle Ages had possessed. Great Britain has only once obeyed an absolute king, and that king was the Lord Protector Oliver Cromwell. For this there was in the first place an external reason: he was the only ruler who owned a standing army. But his true inward title rested not in his power, but in his right to power: the right unwritten and " unlawful," vouched neither by solemn Parliamentary Act nor by conveyance of the people, and yet the best-founded, the legitimate, the only right to kingship. He was, in plain words, the strongest, the wisest, and — if we look at things from a higher standpoint than that of the morals of philistine democracy — the most moral man of his country. He said himself that he proposed to serve the nation " not as a king, but as a constable." But is not a constable the best king, and indeed more than a king? This plain country squire did more for his country than the most rabid Lancasters and Yorks, the slyest Tudors, or the proudest Stuarts. He brought order into the whole internal administration, pacified Ireland, broke the commercial tyranny of the greedy rival over the water, won a new Calais, conquered one of the loveliest and richest islands in the West Indies, and laid a firm foundation for England's illustrious future as the world's leading sea-power. Perhaps we come nearest to doing justice to Cromwell's importance if we read the word "constable" in its modern sense, and see in Cromwell no more and no less than the faithful, tireless, energetic, and common-sense "*Schutzmann*" of his country.

It is an old historical tradition to regard Cromwell as one of the greatest hypocrites and intriguers who ever lived; in fact, as the "prince of liars." To set against this, Carlyle, his chief apologist, declares that he never lied in his life. At bottom both conceptions are right. Cromwell had in his make-up a tendency truly British, a habit of confused thinking, double reasoning, reserve, of ambiguous, much-qualified, and deliberately obscure utterance, and to that extent he was tortuous, curved, and complicated. But a confirmed liar he certainly was not. The Englishman's attitude to truth is, as was pointed out in our first volume when discussing *cant*, not at all plain or uncomplicated, and the solutions of problems to which it leads are never net. And indeed, in general, the relation of the individual nations to "reality" varies very considerably. The Frenchman behaves towards it like an impassioned lover, though one who in his blindness is easily deceived; the German treats it in the manner of a thoroughly honest but somewhat boring and pedantic fiancée, and the Englishman adopts towards it the rôle of the brutal husband, the house-tyrant. The pleasure-loving Frenchman wants pleasantness, whether true or false; the worthy German wants the truth at all costs whether it is agreeable or not; and the practical Englishman decrees that the acceptable is true and the unacceptable false.

The Puritans In the Puritans, who at that time ruled England, English cant reached its peak. They constituted the army, the government, and even the newly-created Upper House. Everyone hurriedly made himself scarce when these ludicrous but dangerous new saints went about snuffling and rolling their eyes, with cropped hair and black clothes, walking slowly and moving deliberately, nosing out dissoluteness, godlessness, and scandals wherever they went. It was, of course, a sin to drink, play, or be noisy; but it was also a sin to dance or go to the theatre, to write love-letters, wear starched collars, or enjoy food; and on Sundays anything and everything was sinful. For on this holy day it was forbidden to water a flower-bed, be shaved, pay a call, or even laugh; and even on Saturdays and Mondays, its near neighbours, it was, to say the least of it, unwise to do these things. This exaggerated sanctification of the Sabbath betrays the spirit of Jewry, and, to be candid, it is difficult to regard the Puritans as a Christian sect at all. They based themselves in almost every respect on the Old Testament. They called themselves after the Israelite heroes, prophets, and patriarchs; their conversation bristled with Hebrew idioms, proverbs, and parables; and they thought of themselves as Jehovah's militant servants, called by him to wipe out idolaters, heretics, and stubborn Canaanites with fire and sword. For had not Jehovah himself forced his people into the true faith by means of plagues and punishments, and spread terror and destruction among the backsliders? They were God's fighters, the chosen people, the rightminded Puritans, and every method of cunning, force, and cruelty was permitted to them in their good cause of overthrowing the heathen and establishing theocracy. Their God was the God of Moses, a god of revenge, of wrath, of merciless justice and tireless casting-down of sinners. So yet again did the unhappy union of the Gospels with the book of the Jews, of which we have spoken already, take its revenge on a section of Christianity.

Only one branch of Puritanism can really be included among *The Quakers* the Christians, the Society of Friends of the Light, nicknamed " Quakers," who settled in Pennsylvania along the Delaware. These people took not only the theory but the practice of the New Testament doctrines seriously — as seriously as the Independents had taken the Commandments of the Old Testament. They refused to do military service, to take an oath, to countenance slavery or even the sale of war material, and extended their colonies in a peaceful way without fighting or even exploiting the Indians. They scorned the regulation sermon, which they had learnt to know in the mother country as an offspring of unspiritual routine and self-satisfied dishonesty. In place of it they permitted everyone to speak, but only when moved to do so by the inward light. They rejected liturgy and sacraments and also all the ceremonial of everyday life, addressed everyone as " thou," and took off their hats to none. And although, as a result of their exaggerations and fads, they retain a certain quaintness of type, they are one of the most lovable and pleasing phenomena in the history of Christian confessions.

The poet of Puritanism is the great John Milton, who was at *Milton*

39

the same time one of the most prominent publicists of his country. In his famous *Defensio pro populo Anglicano* he gave a scientific defence of the King's murder. The grandiose rhetoric of the Miltonian Satan served the younger Pitt as a school for oratory, and it is anything but an accident that in the whole gallery of his figures it was precisely the Prince of Hell himself who — almost against the will of the poet — grew into such an overwhelming figure. The reason is that in Milton the Puritan spirit became form — a spirit which is of the Devil, because it avenges and judges. In Milton's titanic epic the whole of world-history is arraigned, tried, and judged from the standpoint of Puritanism, which alone is truth and righteousness — judged strictly and mercilessly, with partisan bias and without the least will to understand, let alone love, the enemy. Against the hosts of the rebellious angels God sends his Son, who flings ten thousand lightnings on them; they flee and plunge into the depths like a herd of goats overtaken by the storm — Christ as the god of thunder! This is blasphemy as monumental as Michelangelo's Christ enthroned in the clouds as Apollo or Hercules. A God who conquers with bow and quiver, lightning and war-chariots, with battalions of fighting saints: this is quite obviously not God's Son of the Gospels, the Christ in whom Christians believe, but the legitimate Son of Jehovah.

Hobbes   Milton's opponent was Thomas Hobbes, keen and powerful thinker, advocate of monarchy, Restoration, and legitimism. His philosophy is not mean or evil, as it used to be thought, but merely pessimistic. Looking about him, he sees on the one hand a world of wild and strong, hard and calculating master-natures, and on the other a mass of dull, slavish herd-humanity, kept in motion only by the law of inertia; and both he sees as merely the puppets of their more or less gross instincts to devour and to snatch. From this material he draws his inductive conclusions, from these premisses his laws. On these hypotheses he sees the State as Leviathan, an all-powerful monster which ruthlessly devours all who set themselves in opposition to it. The State is a mortal god, and the existing order is at all times the right one — because it is order. Liberty is that which the laws do not forbid, conscience is private opinion, but law is the public conscience, to which alone the citizen owes obedience. A religion not legitimized by the State is a superstition. This does not mean that he regards kings as appointed by God; but he holds that the people have invested the head of the State with supreme powers, and that, having done so, they have themselves no further rights. Monarchy is the best form of constitution, simply because it is the most centralized; and its absolutism follows necessarily from the thesis that the direction of the State, to whomsoever it be entrusted — even if to a corporation — must possess absolute powers.

If we take these doctrines literally, they appear to have been made to justify the Stuarts — the megalomania of James I, the intransigence of Charles I, who even on the scaffold was still the supreme autocrat, and the Restoration plans of Charles II, whose teacher was Hobbes. If on the other hand we interpret them according to their spirit, it appears that their shrewdest disciple, their most triumphant embodiment, was none other than the plebeian rebel and usurper Oliver Cromwell.

The foundations of this political philosophy, which goes considerably further than Machiavelli's in its hard, clear unsentimentality and its pure scientific evaluation of political phenomena, are just what they necessarily must be with so logical a thinker as Hobbes. A nihilistic ethic: nothing is good or bad in itself, a definite standard of moral can only be set when there is a state to set it. A materialistic ontology: all being is body, all happening is movement, and even sensations are called forth by bodily movements. A sensualistic psychology: there are only sensations, everything else is abstracted from them, and conceptions of genera and so forth are nothing but faded reminiscences of earlier perceptions. A mechanistic epistemology: words are notes or marks for ideas, arguments and conclusions are the addition and subtraction of these signs, and all thinking is calculation.

But Baruch Spinoza, perhaps the most remarkable thinker *Spinoza* who ever lived, went much further still. In a history of philosophy he would have to be dealt with after Descartes, on whom he builds; but in the present connexion it is not the system but the world-outlook that matters, and even this only in so far as it has been effective as the formative principle of representative personalities or the great currents of an age: it does not, therefore, seem essential here to adopt a lecture-room arrangement conforming to the conceptual development. In his private life Spinoza was neither a saint, as the sentimental eighteenth century asserted, nor a reprobate, as the fanatical seventeenth saw him. He neither put up a fight against the persecutions to which he was exposed, nor endured them like a martyr: he simply evaded them in a cool and collected fashion. His father was a Portuguese Jew who, while quite young, had fled during the Inquisition to Amsterdam, where numerous fellow-believers had found asylum. But hardly had the Jewish communities found their liberty in the " New Jerusalem," as they called it, before they began to develop with renewed energy that destestable intolerance which has always been characteristic of their religion, and which unhappily the Christian Church inherited in some degree. The spirit of Caiaphas, which determined the whole history of the people of Israel as long as they had national independence, frequently lost its potency in later times owing to external conditions, but it always came to life again when the Jews attained to power. And so it was on this occasion. The case of Uriel da Costa, who, for his free religious views, was sent to his death by the venomous persecution of the Amsterdam Synagogue, is a tragic instance. Spinoza was then eight years old. Half a generation later he was engaged in a similar conflict himself. His philosophical interests and activities became known, and attempts were made, first to convert him, then to bring him back to orthodoxy by threats. When both methods failed, bribery was tried: he was offered a salary of a thousand gulden if he would remain true to Judaism. Since he was not to be moved even by this, a member of the community felt that murder was indicated. But the attack failed. And now there was no course left to the Synagogue but to excommunicate him. Before the assembled congregation the solenm ban was pronounced, the concluding words being: " Curse him by day and curse him by night! Curse him sleeping and curse him waking! Curse his comings-in and curse his goings-out! May the Lord never forgive him! He will burn with hardness and wrath against this man who is laden with all the curses that are written in the Book of the Law. He will blot out his name from under the heavens." Thus did Jewry treat a man whose whole offence was that he led a more serious, peace-loving, and unworldly life than his fellow-Jews. But, as it had always been a good old Jewish tradition to stone the prophets, there is nothing extraordinary in this, particularly as Spinoza does not seem to us one of the greatest among those sons of Israel who suffered this fate;

for we can only regard him as a curiosity — though a monumental and unique one.

Spinoza himself, through all the screaming of the Rabbis, never lost his calm. Thenceforward he lived in complete retirement, buried in his studies, entirely disinterested and without pretence, and avoiding all contact with worldly pleasures and honours, diversions and disturbances. He declined the professorship offered him at Heidelberg, flattering as were the terms. His philosophical fame (which, however, only became world-wide a century after his death) rests on his *Theologico-Political Treatise* (*Tractatus theologico-politicus*), the first great attempt at a historical criticism of the Bible, and on his *Ethics,* in which his system is exhaustively set forth. Incidentally, no book ever merited its title less than this.

Spinoza's system was built up in a very unusual and somewhat whimsical style. Because he was convinced that certain knowledge can only be obtained by using the mathematical method, he decided to demonstrate his whole system *geometrico modo.* Every paragraph starts with the necessary specification of ideas (Definitions), leading on to the principles (Axioms) which produce the theorems (Propositions). Then follow proofs (Demonstrations) and consequent propositions (Corollaries), and finally the elucidations (Scholia). Thus the whole work reads like a mathematical text-book, and in its content there is something not only archaistic and dry, but forced and artificial.

Since God, concludes Spinoza, can only be comprehended as an absolutely infinite and, therefore, absolutely indeterminate being, he can possess no self and no personality. And as both reason and will presuppose a self-consciousness, both these attributes must be denied to him. Outside this absolutely infinite substance, nothing can exist. Consequently the whole world is identical with God, and we have the famous formula *deus sive natura.* Out of the God-Nature all things are produced as inevitably as it follows from the nature of a triangle that the sum of its internal angles equals two right angles. Therefore there is no human freedom: a man who believes himself to be free is like a stone which imagines itself to be flying when in the act of being thrown. And as God has no reason, he lacks the power to set himself a mark — ends, too, are therefore a human illusion. Values are

43

equally non-existent, for they define, not the properties of things in themselves, but their effect on us.

In his Psychology Spinoza makes *appetitus,* the striving for self-preservation, the basic force in human nature. That which assists in this striving we call good; that which handicaps it, evil. We do not desire things because they are good, but we call them good because we desire them (thus ignoring the fact that all the higher religions, and particularly Christianity, have invariably seen the principle of Evil in desire and the sense-world that is the object of desire). All emotions may be divided into two basic forms, active and passive; the first of these are accompanied by pleasure or joy, the second by pain or grief. Under this classification sympathy belongs to the harmful emotions, because it causes pain; therefore, although we should help those who suffer, it should be done without personal concern and as the result of reasonable judgment. It is the same with repentance; for to the bad deeds, which are in themselves a misfortune, it adds the pain of contrition. Similar non-moral principles are laid down by Spinoza in respect of politics. He says, for instance: " A treaty between nations exists as long as the cause for it exists: fear of shame or hope of gain." But the soul reaches its highest peak in the *amor Dei intellectualis,* the intellectual love of God, which is nothing else but knowledge of the infinite substance — something remote indeed from the love of God as commonly conceived. And since every man is but a portion of the God-nature, God in this love loves himself.

The equation of two zeros We make bold to declare that the system, of which the foregoing is only an aphoristic sketch, is the work of a diseased mind of marvellous acuteness. Cartesian rationalism was tolerable by reason of its inconsequence; but Spinoza thinks out each idea with such inexorable logic as to annul it: the idea of God ending in naked atheism; the idea of causality in dead automatism; the difference between mind and body in the assertion that there is no relation whatever between them; the desirability of controlling the emotions in the postulate of insensibility; pantheism — the identity of God with Nature — in a hopeless naturalism which completely despiritualizes the world and makes it a ghastly spectral waste. In short, his abnormally consequent thinking abolishes the objects of this thinking, destroys them, disintegrates them,

44

thinks them out of existence. What is left as "ultimate truth" is an empty equation made up of a God who is a nothing and a world which is less than a nothing.

It is usual to class Spinoza's system among the pantheistic systems, but this is misleading. Pantheism is based, it is true, on the equation of God and the world, and in so far the classification is justifiable. But it must be remembered that the *Deus* whom Spinoza identifies with *natura* is no god, but a blind dead nullity, an impotent mathematical figure, such as the sign or the number o. Irremediable confusion has resulted from aligning the Spinozistic pantheism with that of Mysticism, for the latter arrives at its principle of universal Godhead, not by formulation of logical conclusions, but by religious experience; and if likewise it reaches a vision of God as infinite, intangible, indefinable Substance, it does so out of deepest reverence and loftiest faith and not out of nihilism and mathematical obsessions. In other words, the mystic arrives at his conception of God through pious agnosticism; he is so filled with the greatness of God that it vanishes beyond his ken, whereas the Spinozist, on the contrary (if indeed there has ever been a genuine one except Spinoza himself) arrives at a similar result through self-glorified rationalism: he is so absorbed in his own greatness and the infallibility of the operations of his thoughts that the Godhead vanishes from his ken also, dissolved in sheer logical concepts.

The monstrousness of this system (which at the same time *The World* constitutes its incomparable originality) becomes perfectly clear *aimless* if we consider that it is the only one which has been able to get through without a single trace of teleology. It goes without saying that all spiritualistic philosophers have placed the conception of a purpose in the forefront of their systems. But those of the opposite tendency also have been unable to dispense with it. Not the sturdiest materialism, not the airiest scepticism, before or after Spinoza, has dared to maintain that cosmic causality unwinds itself in the same volitionless and intentionless fashion as a sorites. Many have been the attempts to operate with blind forces, unconscious impulses of the will, and unintelligent instincts. But all these powers pursue, whether they know it or not, a definite aim. Even if we imagine the world as built up of nothing but just stupid atoms, they too want something or other, in virtue of a certain dull directionalism which determines their order and movement. Darwinism itself, which is regarded as the most forcible antithesis of all metaphysical attempts to explain the universe, is in fact a superlative teleological system, in that it makes the concept of evolution its cardinal principle. Monism again, its derivative, which boasted of having dethroned the theological view of the universe for ever, is diligently exerting itself to prove a supreme final rightness in all natural phenomena. And the most extravagant of pessimists still believes in *evil* purposes and admits of at least *one* purpose in the world's happenings: namely, its ruin; just as the most complete atheist accepts a world which, though godless, obeys definite intentions, and the most extreme phenomenalist the illusion of such a world. But a world in which one thing follows from another in the same manner as the equality of the radii follows from the nature of a circle; in which, in a word, the sole cause of any object or phenomenon is its *definition* — there is only one man who could have invented it. It may be that the imagining of purposes is really only an unavoidable anthropomorphism; but on that very account one who completely denies these purposes places himself beyond the pale of humanity. Such a creature is less or more than a man — in either case, inhuman.

*The logic of
" Folie
raisonnante "*Spinoza was possessed of an excessive, penetrating, *pathological* logic, which devoured and absorbed everything, and he therefore arrived at entirely pathological results. It is true that anyone who acts with perfect consequence and thinks exclusively " *geometrico modo* " must arrive at these conclusions; but it is not natural, not human, and probably not divine either. For both nature and man and God (at least the God of Christianity and all the higher religions) all fail to act with complete consistency and logic and mathematic — they act paradoxically and superlogically.

The truth is that " *le misérable Spinoza,*" as the excellent Malebranche called him with a mixture of horror and pity, was certainly not mentally normal. It is well known that some insane people are remarkable for impeccable logicality. They go wrong on the major premiss only; after that they proceed with an amazing power of deduction, intelligence, and acuteness. This is the form of mental disease described as *folie raisonnante*. Naturally we do not mean to say that Spinoza was actually mad, but only that in him the understanding was developed to an unnatural degree of exclusiveness, one-sidedness, and autocracy. Chesterton writes: [1] " And if great reasoners are often maniacal, it is equally true that maniacs are commonly great reasoners. . . . If you argue with a madman, it is extremely probable that you will get the worst of it; for in many ways his mind moves all the quicker for not being delayed by the things that go with good judgment. He is not hampered by a sense of humour or by charity, or by the dumb certainties of experience. He is the more logical for losing certain sane affections. Indeed, the common phrase for insanity is in this respect a misleading one. The madman is not the man who has lost his reason. The madman is the man who has lost everything except his reason. The madman's explanation of a thing is always complete, and often in a purely rational sense satisfactory. . . . His mind moves in a perfect but narrow circle. . . . In the same way the insane explanation is quite as complete as the sane one, but it is not so large. . . . Now, speaking quite externally and empirically, we may say that the strongest and most unmistakable *mark* of madness is this combination between a logical completeness and a spiritual contraction. . . . He [the madman of experience] is in the clean and well-lit prison of one idea: he is sharpened to one painful point. . . . Materialism has a sort of insane simplicity. It has just the quality of the madman's argument; we have at once the sense of it covering everything and the sense of it leaving everything out. . . . He [the materialist] understands everything, and everything does not seem worth understanding." This characterization fits Spinoza and his system like a glove.

It is this pure rationality in Spinoza, too, that produces that intolerable chill which emanates from his work: not, as some of his admirers would have us believe, the cold of aerie heights, but the cold of the vacuum. We have the austere and comfortless feeling of being somewhere in the vast interstellar spaces — in a medium which permits of no life, no heat, no breathing, no sound, and lets nothing through but the severe light of a distant unknown sun. We freeze when we read in his *Ethics* that nothing could be or should be different from what it is; that all things are equally

A System in vacuo

[1] In *Orthodoxy* (London: John Lane; New York: The John Lane Company; 1909).

perfect, all actions equally good, because all are equally necessary, even as no mathematical theorem is more perfect than another. In the section " On the origin and nature of the emotions " he writes: " I shall consider human actions and desires exactly as if I were dealing with lines, surfaces, and solids," the idea being — and this is one of his most famous sayings — that we should " neither pity them, nor deride them, nor loathe them, but comprehend them." But that a bridge is more easily built with the souls of fellow-men by sympathy, humour, or even passionate opposition than by sterile intelligence, he knew not.

Spinoza stands unique in his age, and indeed in the whole human race. He was, naturally, no Christian: concerning the Incarnation he wrote to a friend (dragging in one of his terrible mathematical examples as usual) that as regards this dogma he must definitely say that he did not understand it; that it seemed to him indeed as preposterous as to pretend that a circle had assumed the nature of a square. Neither was he a pagan, for the sensual near-to-nature pantheism of the Classical age and the Renaissance was of a very different colour from his. Least of all, however, was he a Jew: the " Chosen People " principle, the regulation piety, and the disguised materialism of the Mosaic religion have never been more thoroughly penetrated and exposed to the light than by him. Nay, he was not even what is currently called an atheist, and for that reason it was a perfectly right instinct that for a long time caused a Spinozist to be regarded as an atheist, only more so. Only in one respect could Spinoza be called a Jew — in his extremism. For the Jews are a race of utter polarities: no nation has so wide a spanning power. They are the stoutest pillars of capitalism and the most furious champions of socialism; the inventors of Church and priesthood, and the most passionate preachers of liberty and tolerance; they were the first to spread the gospel in the European sphere of culture and are the only ones who to this day deny it. Thus they have produced both the creator of monotheism and its most powerful denier — Moses and Spinoza.

Freud says, at the close of his essay, *Die Widerstände gegen die Psychoanalyse:* " It is perhaps no mere accident that the first exponent of psycho-analysis was a Jew. To become a convert to it,

48

there must be a fair amount of readiness to accept the fate of isolation in opposition, and with this the Jew is more familiar than most." Spinoza stood in a similar, though even more desperate, situation. He was completely isolated: without family or community, without a single like-minded or understanding person, without even a listener. He speaks wholly to the void, or to himself. His philosophy is one single heart-breaking monologue, delivered in the quiet of his miserable room, by one who was rejected by the world. And the fact that he was so entirely cut off and shut out undoubtedly intensified the pathological strain in him. Because of this — because of his heroic renunciation of every responsive voice, which he knew from the first to be inevitable, and his dogged soundless struggle against his contemporaries and posterity, against the whole human race indeed — because of this his figure grows to the stature of tragedy and enters into a timelessness where it eludes human understanding and human tests as completely as the deity of his *Ethics*.

The early Baroque was indeed the least receptive *milieu* imaginable for such a philosophy. We attempted to indicate in brief, at the end of our first volume, how in the second half of the sixteenth century an ascetic, spiritualistic tendency laid hold of the Catholic portions of Europe. This return to the severity and spirituality of the Middle Ages was the answer to the seriousness and purism of the Reformation, and it was for this reason that the name of Counter-Reformation that has been given it characterizes it so well. In art the nude and the profane were rejected and persecuted; in poetry the indecent and the merry; in philosophy libertinism and scepticism. Michelangelo's figures were given clothing, and Petrarch's sonnets were "purified." But this clerical reaction remained as much a mere episode as had been the gloomy attempt at reform made by Savonarola at the height of the Renaissance. In proportion as the Papacy recovered its former sway over men's minds, it began to open out to the world again, all the more so as it perceived that it was just its broad-minded, mild comprehension of the sensual half of the human being that gave it so great an advantage over doctrinaire and unimaginative Protestantism. And so, at the opening of the new century, the struggling, suffering Church becomes the dominant, triumphant Church, which celebrates its victory in a whirl of jubilant music and gives free rein to the sensualism of a humanity that was longing for an outlet for its forces. For the new humanity, once it had come into being, could not in the long run be held down. And yet no entirely clean solution offered itself here. The Church's hereditary enemy was rationalism, and, being unable entirely to eradicate this enemy, it sought to drive it out by that other great power of the age, sensualism, a power dangerous indeed, but less so. Sensualism, accordingly, was to take the place of rationalism, to release it, to redeem it, and in this wise there came upon the scene that strange psychosis that we call the Baroque. The Baroque is no natural and normal reversion to irrationalism, but a shrewdly imagined therapy, a vicarious satisfaction, a provocative exorcism. Incapable of finding the way back to genuine naïveté, men produced within themselves a spurious variety by means of various drugs, opiates, elixirs, intoxicating and stupefying poisons. They did not denounce their reason — that was not in their power — but merely tried to mystify and confuse it, to drown it or eliminate it by a process of refined narcosis. And it is precisely this artificiality which explains the overwhelming and perhaps unique triumph of artistry achieved by the Baroque.

The world-theatre   The attitude towards colour adopted by the *tenebrosi*, who kept everything down to dusky tones, and the " cellar-peephole-style," which represented everything as though in a dark cellar lighted from above, were typical, not only of the painting, but of the world-feeling and form of life of the entire generation which came after the Council of Trent. Then, all at once, music and decoration, pomp and incense forced their way into the Catholic Church and thence into art. Architecture took on a spectacular, expansive, eloquent, almost chatty character. Arcades and colonnades, loggias and galleries crowded upon each other; twisted and bent columns, daring ornaments and roof-profiles asserted themselves. The form-language could not be ostentatious and insistent enough. The façades, which even in the Renaissance had the appearance of being stuck on, have now the character of magnificent and self-sufficing coulisses: frequently they rise whole storeys higher than the real building. Interior decoration revelled in mirrors, damask flowers, garlands, gilt mouldings, and stucco. It was obviously an entirely theatrical style, but on that very account it was a real style such as had never been known since the

50

age of Gothic. As in the theatre, so here, everything is subordinate to one great central purpose, which like a tyrant draws all the arts and vital activities into its dominion. Every pore exudes the feverish and passionate determination to create a fantastic illusion stronger than reality; a hypnotic fascination which grips and overwhelms, a magic atmosphere which bathes everything in the scent and glitter of a more colourful, more aromatic world. And, as in the theatre, the tendency was to erase the boundary lines which separated the arts. Domed ceilings were painted to look incredibly like real architecture, and the light and shade effects of the niches designed to hold sculpture in a building became an integral part of the plastic monument itself; fragile stone was called upon to produce results that had hitherto hardly been expected from painting — modelled levin-bolts, light-rays and flames, fluttering beards, swelling robes, clouds of the sky and waves of the sea, the sheen of silk and the warmth of flesh. Pillars and architraves lost their original function of carrying: the pillars were doubled and trebled, and set in places where they had nothing to support, and the wall-arches were broken in the middle. They were not to be an organic part of the building, or even to pretend to be so, but were there solely for rhetorical effect and noisy decoration; and three pillars shout louder and more vigorously than one, just as split arches are more original and striking than closed ones. As to logical or practical scruples, no question could arise, since the whole thing was a theatre. Even nature was staged, made into a dramatic " set " by the aid of artificial rocks, waterfalls, fountains, gorges, and wells. And since in every case (even in that of cold marble and rigid bronze) artists strained to enhance emotional appeal and mysterious stage effect, by suggesting melting formlessness rather than unambiguous and powerful contours, they flung themselves with special passion on waterworks and fireworks, which — built of materials perpetually changing in colour and form — freakishly eluded all attempts at fixation. The gifted producer of this theatre was Cavaliere Bernini. Architect, sculptor, poet, master-mechanic, and scenery-designer all in one, he became, through his inexhaustible wealth of ideas, his grandiose and dauntless imagination, and his insistence (for all his bizarrerie) upon a relentlessly uniform style-will, the art dictator of contemporary Europe.

Visibly, it was all an extreme reaction against the Renaissance. There the ideal had been *gravità riposata,* here it was unrestrained (in many cases artificially decontrolled) passion, movement, and exaltation. In architecture and sculpture, in painting and ornamentation, in creative and in imitative minds, we constantly are met by gusts of this rushing, rustling, snorting, and yet languishing, swimming, and soaring quality. This art had neither the dignified aloofness of the High Renaissance, nor the gentle persuasiveness of the Early Renaissance, nor the reverent self-absorption of the Gothic: it carried on an undisguised propaganda, declaiming, shouting, gesticulating with such passion and even shamelessness that protests could not even be heard. It was always relentlessly bent on giving to the utmost extreme of its power. Whether it represents the adoring, affectedly humble upward gaze of yearning, contrite figures, or renders the visionary spasms of an ecstasy amounting to hysteria, or ruthlessly pictures reality in its most monstrous and terrifying forms, always it is the exaggerated and the exorbitant, shrillness and glare, at which its productions aim. It seizes with ardour on the very material which the cool æstheticism of the Renaissance had disdained: the sick, the defeated, the outcast; the old, the decrepit, the worn-out; the ragged, the weather-beaten, the deformed; death, skeletons, and corruption. It shows humanity howling, grinning, trembling, writhing in contortions and convulsions; it likes extravagant, ugly things because they are stronger and truer. And whereas it was the profound determination and highest aim of the Renaissance to define and make clear, to harmonize and order, the new art takes the most elaborate pains to spread around its creations the perfume of perpetual yearning and unfulfilment, the charm of enigma and confusion and dissonance. The triumph of its artistic achievement is that it pressed into its service even light — that dividing and clarifying power which, from time immemorial, has been the interpreting medium of all the arts — for by the indefiniteness with which it carried out its transitions from shade to light, by the emphasis it laid on the indefinable aura which envelops all objects and thus all contours, it is able to generate opaqueness and vagueness and to raise the mixing of colours to the level of a mystical art — one of the most forceful and revolutionary acts that the history of Sight has to show.

At the same time it imparted to everything a general atmosphere of sultriness and tension — in fact, of latent eroticism. The figures were clothed, but the clothing, by its concealment, was far more suggestive than the nakedness that preceded it. Man, who had been merely anatomically beautiful in the Renaissance, now became endowed with a sexual beauty. Under the decent draperies there breathed much warmer flesh. At times the covering was so arranged as to appear to be ready to fall off; at times again, all the sensuality was concentrated in the face. Cruelty and lust were intermingled. Art revelled in scenes of bloodshed, in martyrdom and wounds. The sweetness of pain was glorified. Finally eroticism, algolagnia, and yearning for the supernatural were combined in that bizarre mixture which found its most powerful expression in Bernini's St. Theresa, a work which, apart from anything else, will always be memorable for the sublime art — comparable only to that of the stage — by which it is made to express the most subtle illusions. There is no doubt that the conception is profoundly religious; yet the impression of secret make-up and footlights is inseparable both from the composition as a whole and from the arrangement of every detail. But why, after all, should the theatre and religion be irreconcilable? Is not the theatre, for all who serve it seriously and devotedly, a sort of religion, and is not religion, on its ritually impressive side, a sort of *theatrum Dei,* a presentation of God's greatness?

There will always be some who place the Renaissance higher than the Baroque. These are predominantly the people who consider that a work of art can only be called noble if it is dull, just as many assume that a philosophical work can only be profound if it is incomprehensible. They forget that here we are dealing with matters of taste, on which an impartial judgment is almost impossible. One thing does, however, seem to us irrefutable, often as the contrary is maintained: namely, that Baroque art is more natural than that of the Renaissance. Only a few decades ago this statement would have sounded like a bad joke, for the nineteenth century had been accustomed to think of the Baroque as the extreme of unnaturalness, perversity, and distortion — just as, for that matter, in the eighteenth century, Gothic was practically synonymous with coarse, inartistic, barbarous. In this change in the connotation of art terms, there lies a whole history of æsthetics, and

Natural unnaturalness

53

it is not impossible that even the word "classical" will one day be transformed by a like process into a term of contempt. Actually the key-word of the Baroque was precisely "*naturalezza*," and, seen as against the Renaissance, it does amount to a release of uncurbed instincts, of welling passion, of vital pleasure in the play of form, colour, and motive. It is a return to nature in form as in content — in form because it makes for elemental expression always, without any feeling of being tied by the one-sided rules of a chilling etiquette of art; and in content because it descends into the depths of spiritual life and takes as its favourite theme the very one rejected by the Renaissance as unlovely — man in his torments, his convulsions, his manias, and his abysses. In its anxiety never to render the normal, the mean, the straight line, it frequently comes near to caricature. To put it paradoxically, it was so natural precisely because it was so unnatural. For normality is not the rule, but the great exception. Out of ten thousand men there may be one who is constructed exactly according to the anatomical canon, and probably not even one whose soul functions in a completely normal way. It is the man of mark, the monstrosity, the pathological case, the man who is nature's blunder and failure that is "normal," and that is why he alone arouses our æsthetic interest and our moral sympathy. Naturally, this standard of beauty is just as subjective as the Classicist's; one thing, however, it does make clear: namely, that "naturalism" is a highly problematical conception. *Every* new tendency considers itself more naturalistic than the foregoing, against which it reacts to obtain victory for truth, liberty, and an enhanced sense of reality.

The hegemony of Opera

In every age some particular art holds the supremacy. For the Renaissance it was the art of sculpture; in the Baroque, music. An over-rich orchestra blares at us from out of all its creations. And for music itself the turn of the sixteenth century is the birth-period of *moderna musica,* of the *stile nuovo.* Almost simultaneously we have a number of innovations of the first importance. The *sonata,* as an instrumental piece, appears in triumphant opposition to the *cantata* or vocal piece, and the *a cappella* style (part-singing without orchestra) is beaten. We know that the principle of polyphony reached its full development in the first half of the fifteenth century. Now it was the turn of monody again, of solo-singing with instrumental accompaniment. That is, as the whole of the other voices had in comparison with the leading voice only the importance of an accompaniment, this function was now assigned to instruments, and it became the practice merely to sketch in the accompaniment in the form of a so-called *basso generale* (figured bass). This substitution of instruments for the human voice is an expression of the light-hearted artistry of the Baroque, of its love of the picturesque and the " mood," its will to refinement of art, to colour and nuance, mass and wealth of expressiveness; and correspondingly of its small need of vernal immediacy and simplicity as media of emotion.

Quickly, too, music annexed to her dominions the most telling of all forms of artistic expression — the dramatic. Emilio de' Cavalieri's *Rappresentazione di anima e di corpo* (Rome, 1600) counts as the first oratorio, and in a short time this art-form — which is to the opera more or less what a cartoon is to a painting — was brought to a high degree of perfection. But historical development did not restrict itself to the proper order, according to which oratorio should have preceded the real music-drama. This first oratorio was more what we should now call a concert-opera (in general, Italian oratorio showed a leaning towards opera during the whole of the seventeenth century, and it was not unusual, even in the eighteenth, to find it performed with operatic scenery), and real opera begins three years earlier with the first performance of *Daphne*, during the Carnival at Florence in 1595, for which Ottavio Rinuccini wrote the text and Jacopo Peri the music. The *dramma per musica*, as it was at first known, arose out of the experiments and discussions of a clever coterie of amateurs which was aiming at the revival of Classical tragedy. This they conceived of as a succession of recitations to a cithara, relieved by choruses. They accordingly chose various simple plots, primarily mythological in character, with situations that lent themselves to singing, and proceeded to set these to music. A work of this description was still far removed from our modern opera. The singing was something more in the order of musical declamation — a kind of psalm-singing in the manner employed for the litanies in mediæval churches — and this was supported by a scanty orchestra which, though behind the scenes and invisible, played its part from the very beginning in the dances and various stage effects.

The name given to this spoken singing — which was a decided improvement on earlier vocal styles in point of naturalness and clearness, since it followed the normal accent of the words — was *stile rappresentativo* or *stile parlante*. By 1607 opera had advanced a stage in Monteverde's *Orfeo*. Here the recitative is more animated and the rôle of the music becomes much more independent, both the interludes and the tone-colour effects being handed over to it as its particular function. The opera of that day also owes to this its finest master the introduction of the duet, the invention of the tremolo for the violin family, and the *leitmotiv*, which appears in the very first of his operas.

In outward splendour the operatic performances of the Baroque outshine those of all their successors. One beheld the goddess of Dissension with her dragon steed and Pallas Athene in her owl-drawn coach floating through the air, Jupiter and Apollo enthroned in the clouds, and the ship of Paris steering through waves and storms; the underworld belched forth spirits and monsters from its red jaws; horses and buffaloes, elephants and camels passed across the stage; bodies of troops (often several hundred strong) filed past, delivered battles, battered fortresses; and the heavens, with sun and moon, stars and coloured comets, played their parts almost without intermission. Bernini, master of all these arts, once staged the Castle of S. Angelo with the rushing Tiber, full of boats and people, in the foreground. Suddenly the dam which divided the river from the stalls burst, and the waves swept towards the audience with such violence as to start a panic. But Bernini had calculated to a nicety that the water would stop short of the front row. Another time he put a brilliant carnival procession on the stage with masked dancers and torches at its head. A part of the wings caught fire and everyone began to rush away. But at a given signal the flames were extinguished, and the stage was transformed into a blooming garden in which a fat donkey placidly grazed. It is by such grotesque and glittering devices as these that we may gauge the jaded taste and excessive demands of theatre audiences in those days.

The opera soon became the queen of the age. In 1637 the first public opera-house was built in Vienna, and by the year 1650 there were already four in that city. In 1627 the first German opera — likewise called *Daphne* — appeared; it was the work of Heinrich

Schütz, the most important forerunner of Bach and Handel, and the text was personally — very personally — adapted from Rinuccini, by that pontiff of German literature, Opitz. Gradually the aria detached itself from the recitative, the chorus withdrew almost completely, its singers becoming mere supers who had only to utter occasional cries such as : " *Viva!* " " *Mori!* " " *All' armi!* " and so on. Innovations, however, as in our own day, did not meet with unmixed approval; we read in the work of the canon Giovanni Maria Artusi, a contrapuntist to the bone (*Delle imperfezioni della moderna musica*) that " the new composers are ignoramuses, who merely make a noise and do not know what it is permitted to write and what not."

The summit of the Early Baroque is seen in Spain. Here again *El Siglo de oro* is a proof that a wave of political and economic prosperity is by no means always the essential preliminary to high artistic development. For, to the Spaniard, the seventeenth century signified the loss of his country's position as a world-power and its complete economic ruin. And yet he called it — and rightly — *el siglo de oro,* the golden century. Philip II, whom we have already studied at close quarters, was succeeded, at the turn of the sixteenth century, by the phlegmatic, flabby Philip III, of whom his father is reputed to have said: " God, who has given me so many kingdoms, has denied to me a son capable of ruling them; I fear it will be they who rule him." The aimless and corrupt domination of favourites under which his government suffered became even worse with his successor, Philip IV, whose interests were the pleasures of love and the chase, though drama and painting were included in them also. This incapable and indolent form of *étatisme* (which took care to suppress every independent movement on the part of both town communes and country population) and the universal corruptibility, lack of enterprise, and protectionism led to a complete decline of the nation's economy. In the end the State was reduced to the desperate measure of promising hereditary nobility to every field-labourer; but even this proved fruitless, for work was a disgrace to the free-born Spaniard. The impolitic and inhuman oppression of the Moriscos has already been mentioned; in the year 1609 it culminated in their complete expulsion, with a literally disastrous effect on the home industries. Similar results followed the enforced emigration of the Jews to Holland, where they played a considerable part in the economic rise of the new power. In the open country and among the proletariat of the towns — which was nowhere more numerous and more demoralized than in Spain — there was famine, and even the lower middle-classes fell into a very depressed condition. It became increasingly difficult to collect taxes, and thus the nobility and the court also were involved in the general bankruptcy. It was no unusual sight to see the royal body-guard begging for the soup distributed to the poor at the monastery gates. Bread, onions, dried grapes, a little sheep's-milk cheese, and an egg or two formed the Spaniard's diet; he could but rarely afford the famous national dish, the *ola podrida* soup, concocted of cabbage, turnips, garlic, mutton, and bacon. There were neither state schools nor compulsory education of any sort. Only the members of the nobility and the higher bourgeoisie were able to read, and even they were only allowed such books as a strict and fanatical censorship permitted. The Court of the Inquisition was as active as ever, and by its ruling that an accused man should not see his witnesses and accusers face to face, the door was opened wide to cowardly revenge and treacherous denunciation. A widespread criminal association, the so-called *germanía*, which was in league with the police, troubled the whole country-side. In spite of the general poverty, gambling was universal among high and low, and the State, as holder of a monopoly for the manufacture of playing-cards, was the beneficiary of this vice. Drunkenness alone was not among Spain's national evils. The word of abuse " *borracho* " (drunkard) was an insult which could only be avenged by blood. In all ranks, indeed, the outward conception of honour was developed to an unwholesome point. This side of the Spanish national character, that in which its hardness, passionateness, and bizarrerie most strikingly express themselves, is familiar to all through the country's literature and has been most movingly described in Calderon's *El Médico de sa honra*. Lope de Vega says: " Honour is something which depends upon others; no one is honoured through himself, for it is from the other that he receives honour." (This curiously coincides with Schopenhauer's definition: " Honour is, objectively, the opinion of others as to our value and, subjectively, our dread of that opinion.") It is very typical of the almost pathological loyalty of the Spaniards that — despite their extreme susceptibility, which made death itself preferable to an unavenged insult — no offence could come from the king. This is illustrated in a number of famous dramas, as, for instance, in Zorilla's *Del Rey abajo ninguno;* here the idea actually gives the work its title, which substantially means that no man below the king may insult another. The king's word had also the power to restore anyone's injured honour.

Not only the villages, but also the towns consisted of mud houses — palaces and public buildings excepted. There were no pavements, and for sole illumination there were the little oil-lamps under the Madonna shrines. Cleanliness was hardly better than in Russia, the dirt of Madrid being indeed proverbial. Post-coaches were unknown, and inns were in such a miserable condition as simply to be undeserving of the name. There was no question of anything like an organized system of information or public safety or suchlike things. And yet life was not without colour, poetry, and gaiety. The numerous religious feast-days brought with them their magnificent processions, in which Church and court displayed the splendour of their power; there were rollicking national festivals, too, imposing bull-fights, and, above all, dramatic performances such as could be seen nowhere else in the world. And even the poverty of everyday life was seasoned by perpetual love-intrigues, jests of both grace and gallows-humour, and the intoxicating perfume of gardens and moonlit nights, which cost nothing.

The crown and summit of this strange world is represented by a race of glossy, melancholy drones — the Grandees — who often lived in great poverty, but even then wore their threadbare *capas* and ever-ready *espadas* with an air and dignity that have remained proverbial to this day. Their pride did not abate even before the king, in whose presence they remained covered. Velasquez has preserved for us the tired, well-bred hauteur of their anæmically pure blood, the devitalizing exclusiveness of their class-consciousness, their mentality become all mask and form, with the same incomparable skill as that shown by Titian in delineating that very different type of self-consciousness which characterized Renaissance man. And woman, at once queen and slave of this Christian-oriental world, petrifies completely into a doll. Every facial emotion is hidden under a thick layer of white of egg and sugar, and the lower part of her body is covered by an

59

enormous barrel of a crinoline, known as a *guardia de vertu*. When Philip IV's bride was travelling through a Spanish city, and the Cortes made a ceremonious presentation of costly silk stockings, the Master of the Ceremonies flung them down indignantly, crying: " I would have you know that the queens of Spain have no legs."

Gracian The world-outlook of that class of society raised a characteristic monument to itself in a work called *Oraculo manual y arte de prudencia,* published by the Jesuit father Balthasar Gracian in 1653 and translated into admirable German by Schopenhauer. In it we find such rules of life as these: " Leave others in uncertainty as to your intention: it is neither useful nor agreeable to show your cards, it should always be allowed to appear that there is something mysterious in the background "; " keep people hoping, but never quite satisfy them "; " do not countenance extravagant expectations "; " think like the few and speak like the many "; " indulge in pardonable faults, for a certain negligence is at times the greatest recommendation "; " beware of triumphing over your superiors "; " do the popular things yourself, the unpopular through others "; " do not wait to become a sinking sun, drop things before they drop you "; " belong neither wholly to yourself nor to another, for both are a degrading tyranny." And at the close these maxims come out at this surprising résumé: " in a word: be a saint — and in saying that we say everything. There are three things beginning with S which bring happiness: *santitad, sanidad, sabiduria* (holiness, health, and wisdom)."

El Greco Yet it was in this curious atmosphere that Calderon's marvellous eloquence blossomed; and the flaming colour-orgies of decorative art, with its ranked lustrous *azulejos,* remind us of that poet's mosaic-like splendour of imagery. The wooden sculptures, unique in the history of art, which, with their glaring paint, naturalistic flesh-colouring, blood-drippings, crystal eyes, crowns of thorns, silver daggers, real silk garments, tears made of glass pearls, and wigs of real hair, achieve both the coarsest waxwork illusionism and at the same time a mysterious, suggestive effect that eludes all artistic criteria. In painting, again, Ribera's massive solemnity and pitiless naturalism, and Zurbarán's simple but most profound monastic piety, accomplished creations of the highest order. Beside them, to mention Murillo — who yet throughout the nineteenth century counted as the greatest Spanish painter — is almost blasphemous. His art, with its artificial perfume and its billowy clouds, has the silky optimism and the cheap *élan* of the popular virtuoso whose success with the larger public is unfailing; and his famous scenes of Spanish peasant life are just pleasing bits of opera and glazed idylls, which flatter the philistine with highly coloured misrepresentations of reality that show only too clearly why this artist became the idol of the middle classes. Murillo is the Spanish Raphael; true, but it is characteristic of seventeenth-century Spain that it regarded as most representative, not the shallowest of its leading artists — as (we have had to admit) Italy did in the case of Raphael, and the Netherlands in that of Rubens — but the most profound: namely, El Greco.

El Greco lived in Toledo — a city which, though its death-agony was setting in precisely at that very time, was still the proud home of the Inquisition and the Councils — and it was the soul of Toledo that he painted: the triumph of the world-church of Rome and the dying pomp of the world-dominion of Spain. But it is not this alone which gives his pictures their incomparable power; it is above all the complete detachment, unreality, and transcendence which breathe from every one of his figures — their blanched air, their strangely contorted and elongated bodies, their eyes of visionaries initiated into the higher mysteries, and the quite unnatural (indeed definitely magical) foreshortening and light-distribution. Gravitation, likeness, perspective — these things and their like seem to us, as we stand before his paintings, immensely secondary and insipid — even false. This " Greek " did not paint the truth — the " suspicious truth," as Calderon's forerunner Alarcón calls it in the title of one of his plays — and for centuries he was regarded as a fool because he realized that reason was foolishness, as the " court jester of humanity " that Calderon represents him to be. But on that very account he stands along with Loyola and Don Quixote as the most powerful expression of the Spanish Baroque.

It is not yet the time to write anything really comprehensive about the Baroque; but certain features stand out clearly even now. The Baroque is, like every self-contained world-outlook, an attempt to get even with reality and to reconcile its conflicting

The three therapies for Rationalism

61

elements. We have recognized rationalism as the leading theme of the Modern Age, the attempt to subject all phenomena to the autocratic rule of Reason. Through rationalism a gigantic hiatus entered into the soul of modern man, a weakly jointed cleft which tore it apart. In the Middle Ages everything was still true, real, divine: the world was a fact of faith. Rationalism undermines faith, and with it reality.

But even in that era of transition and preparation which we have called the " incubation " period, life, although it lost a great deal of reality, was still definite, tangible, ascertainable. We have seen how with the triumph of Nominalism the two-souled man appeared in history, the contrapuntal man who is no more and no less than the corporate form of the *coincidentia oppositorum,* the union of two extreme contrasts and contradictions. Though no longer single, this type of man was still unambiguous; he was as it were a fractional number, yet still a rational one. The type to which we now come is a different one. For the first time we see really complicated people figuring on the stage of European history, people who defy every formula. Something new again makes its appearance.

We have described rationalism as a toxic element which invaded European humanity at the beginning of the Modern Age. We shall now see that the whole history of the next centuries is a conscious or unconscious struggle against this toxin. Such a struggle can naturally assume many forms. One way — held by many to be a particularly happy form of treatment — is simply to deny the fact of the poisoning. Another way is to try to expel the poison from the blood; this can in most cases be achieved only by the agency of antitoxins. Or, finally, resort can be had to accustoming the body to the poison — an exceedingly doubtful method.

All these possibilities were tried in the course of the Modern Age. Renaissance and Reformation each tried the method of denial, the former by maintaining that rationalism was identical with that which for it ranked highest: namely, Art; the latter by declaring that rationalism came from God. And the last phase of the Modern Age (which has by now run its course), a phase beginning with the mid-eighteenth-century " Enlightenment," has adapted itself to the poison, ceased entirely to fight the disease, and let it become a " condition." The Baroque, on the other hand, had recourse to " anti-body," the antidote.

At first it sought to drive out rationalism by sensualism. But since both (as we tried to show in our first volume) are fundamentally the same thing, this did not prove to be a very suitable counter-poison. Very soon, therefore, it turned its attention to another way out that presented itself. As actuality happens to be rational (or, rather, as modern man is incapable of seeing it otherwise) the trick was tried of stultifying it, degrading it into a second-rate reality, either by refusing to take it seriously, playing with it (the artistic form of the solution), or by declaring it to be untrue and illusory, a fallacy (the religious form of the solution). The two forms could easily combine; nay, their manifest tendency was to do so.

Something like half a generation ago, there appeared an extremely important but to this day inadequately appreciated work, which might have been named: " The World as Fiction." In fact it was called something else: namely, " The Philosophy of the ' As if ' system, or an idealistic Positivism," edited by Hans Vaihinger (*Die Philosophie des Als ob. System eines idealistischen Positivismus, herausgegeben von Hans Vaihinger*). But this tale in itself is a fiction, for Professor Vaihinger, the Kantian scholar, was in reality not the editor, but the author. According to his basic definition a fiction is nothing but a deliberate mistake, a conscious error. The verbal expression for this function of thought is the particle " as if," a combination of words found in the language of almost every culture. Now, strangely, these consciously false conceptions often bring us to new and right knowledge. For there are not only harmful truths, but also fruitful errors. It frequently happens that it is only through the medium of such fictions that we arrive at the possibility of orienting ourselves in reality; they have, therefore, in spite of their theoretical incorrectness, an extraordinary practical value. The assumption of free will, for instance, is the indispensable foundation of our social and legal systems; yet our logical conscience tells us that such an assumption is nonsensical. In natural science we operate with " atoms," although we know that this concept is arbitrary and incorrect; but we operate happily and successfully with the wrong concept, and without it we should not attain our end as easily, or even at all. We calculate

63

with "infinitely small" magnitudes, a completely contradictory conception (for that which is infinitesimal can no longer be a magnitude), and yet the whole of higher mathematics and mechanics is still based on this wrong idea. The whole of algebra rests on the fiction that symbolic letters represent real numbers. This occasions furious brain-racking in many pupils; and yet every living being who speaks does something quite similar: he uses symbolic signs — namely, words — for real things: Geometry, from its simplest basic ideas upward, works in fictions, unrepresentable ideas: points without magnitude, lines without breadth, and space without filling matter. It regards the circle as an ellipse whose two foci coincide: an obvious absurdity, for two points which coincide are just *one* point. All the botanical and zoological systems — in fact, all scientific classifications — are arbitrary fictions, yet they are excellent aids, both for closer determinations on individuals and for general surveys of the various domains of nature. In mechanics the centre of gravity of a floating ring is removed outside itself to its centre — that is, completely into the void — which is indisputably false. One of the basic concepts of the Christian religion is the fiction of the "invisible Church." In the more ordinary phrases of social intercourse we see the predominance of the fiction. If, for instance, I say: "Your servant," it does not mean: "I am your servant," but: "look upon me *as if* I were." And indeed no advanced culture is possible without hundreds of these "as ifs" of every description. When a housemaid says her mistress is "not at home" although she actually is at home, we do not consider that she is telling a lie; for this information only means that her mistress wishes to be treated as if she were not at home. Art, philosophy, religion, politics, morality, science — all are for the greater part based on such more or less complicated fictions. Why, this very book only pretends to be a cultural history while in reality it is something quite different!

In the Baroque, then — and possibly only in the Baroque — we have the whole of life in all its forms and activities presented, tyrannically and as a matter of principle, under this "as if" aspect. For Baroque man all happening is dissolved into a pleasant semblance, a fiction. He plays with reality as the supreme actor with his part or a master-fencer with his partner. Reality cannot get at him, for he knows quite well that it is a phantom, a masquerade, a false tale, a living lie; only he conducts himself as if he believed it to be real. From this curious Baroque attitude Hermann Bahr, in his sketch *Wien*, alluded to earlier — which contains the essence of a whole cultural history in its eight pages — seeks to derive even that complete unscrupulousness in sinning and enjoying to which, it must be confessed, not a few men of the Baroque gave way. "Who shall prevent us? A feeling of wrong-doing? And are we really doing wrong? Surely we are only dreaming . . . clear conscience . . . no blame attaches to us, for it is not we who do it . . . right is here as much a delusion as wrong." But, to be fair, this can only be taken as applying to those meaner spirits who, in any age, manage to turn the prevailing world-outlook, whatever it may be, into an excuse for their own greed and selfishness. The optics of the Baroque were, as we have seen, those of the artist and the *homo religiosus*. And the artist, although he regards his work and indeed the whole of existence as a colourful illusion and mirage, excels precisely because his feeling of moral responsibility is so acute, and plays the game with a degree of conscientiousness, devotion, and care which we may seek in vain among the "serious" occupations of the philistines. The religious man, again, although he is aware that the temporal world is a delusion and a snare, a phantom of the Devil, for that very reason regards it as the preparation which will determine his destiny in that true world of which this one is the caricature. The true explanation of Pre-Baroque is not to be found in Jesuitism, but in its most devastating opponent: Blaise Pascal, one of those few who shoot across the ever denser and greyer, ever more godless and egoistic chaos of the Modern Age as heralds and heirs of a purer and loftier and less actual world.

The uniqueness of Pascal lay in this, that he had at once the most modern and the most Christian spirit of his generation. An exceptionally sharp logicality and power of thought conflicted in him with an exceptionally passionate and profound religiousness. He is the most lucid thinker ever produced by the motherland of *clarté,* and the most subtle soul-analyst of his century: beside him Descartes seems a mere artist in arithmetic, a virtuoso in mechanics. But he was at the same time a man almost hysterically religious and God-seeking, a theomaniac. Religiousness as a gigantic devouring passion, welded to an analytical research-intellect of

65

the first order — this was the overwhelming psychosis of Pascal, a picturesque and thrilling drama of the spirit such as has seldom happened. It is not for nothing that Nietzsche in his polemics against Christianity comes back again and again to Pascal. Even where he does not name him, when he is generalizing on the corruption of the European mind by Christian valuations, we perceive that privately he is thinking only of Pascal. A correct instinct told him that in fighting the Christian thought-world it was in Pascal, above all, that it must be attacked — nay, more, we are always left with the impression that he had an inkling that in Pascal it could not be attacked at all.

Pascal's very life-story has its double face: it is half the brilliant career of a modern savant and half the tender legend of a mediæval saint. At twelve years old he discovered, quite by himself, without other aid than that of a bit of chalk and some paper, the greater number of Euclid's axioms. At sixteen he wrote a treatise on conic sections, the like of which, according to his contemporaries, had not been seen since Archimedes. At nineteen he invented a counting machine on which all arithmetical calculations could be correctly carried out without any knowledge of the rules. At twenty-three he astonished the learned world by his epoch-making treatise on the *horror vacui* and the famous experiments in barometric pressure which bear his name. But even at that age he began to recognize that science, with all its advances, was worthless to man in the higher sense, and that the spirit's true task lay in devotion to God. He became associated with the Jansenists, a body of pious and learned men who had accepted the doctrine of Bishop Jansenius of Ypres. The Bishop had proved, in a posthumous work, *Augustinus,* that both the Papacy and Scholasticism had stood, and still stood, nearer to the heretic Pelagius than to Augustine. These views traversed in particular the theory and practice of the Jesuits, and Pascal's *Provinciales,* that masterpiece of satiric prose, of which we have already spoken, was inspired by the same idea. The congregation lived near Port-Royal des Champs, in monastic seclusion, but without actually forming an order. From it there arose the famous school at Port Royal, which had later a branch in Paris also, and became the focus of the whole scientific and religious life of the times.

During the second half of Pascal's short life of thirty-nine years, he was condemned to great physical suffering, which he bore with the noblest patience and composure, almost with serenity. A chronic victim to colic, neuralgia in the head, inflamed gums, and insomnia, he yet denied himself every form of comfort, waited on himself entirely, and even took in an invalid pauper and nursed him. He praised God for his illnesses — for, as he said, to be ill was the only condition worthy of a Christian — and had a positive dread of becoming healthy again. And his sufferings did in fact raise him to heights which are barred to ordinary mortals; endowed, so to say, with weightlessness, he was able to lead a magical, mystical existence in the midst of the profane and greedy world of Mazarinian France and the hard daylight of his rationalistic century. His last years are bathed in an ethereal, astral glow.

Pascal's philosophic method is embodied in the sentence: "One must be three sorts of a man: mathematician, sceptic, and devout Christian." He arrives at belief — and this is the noteworthy and typically contemporary thing about him — not by way of dogma, but of scepsis. He shows too — in direct opposition to Spinoza — that mathematics does not destroy faith, but founds it. It might be said that for him religious truths hold the same position as higher mathematical truths: inferior understanding may consider them nonsensical as long as it fails to grasp them, but from the moment that it does grasp them it is bound to recognize them as essential, proved, and irrefutable. *Pascal's soul-anatomy*

It is this that the *Pensées* — which may fairly be taken as the profoundest book in French literature — set out to expound. They deal with the " study of man." For Pascal the scientist the human soul is one large field of experiment and he approaches it with the most subtle precision-instruments of analysis; exposes its most secret and delicate, its darkest and most contradictory impulses; measures its heights and its depths; illumines and fixes its most fluid nuances. In short, he applied to psychology the theory of probability of which he was the founder, and, just as he was the first to measure air-pressure, so now he was the first to weigh the apparently imponderable and to make it an object of exact examination. The final result is, all the same, a vast " *amas d'incertitude.*" " For what, after all, is man in the midst of nature? A nothing, set against the infinite; a world, set against nothing; a middle thing between nothing and everything. He is infinitely remote from both, and his nature is just as far removed from the nothing from which he emerges as from the infinite into which he is cast. This is our veritable condition. This confines our knowledge within fixed limits which we are unable to transcend, being both incapable of knowing everything and incapable of ignoring everything. We are situated on a wide middle plane, always unsafe, always swaying between ignorance and knowledge. . . . We burn with the desire to found everything and to build a tower that reaches up to infinity. But our whole structure crashes and the deep earth opens its abyss." " We are powerless in proving — no dogmatism can refute that; we carry within us the idea of truth — no scepticism can refute that. We yearn for truth and find only uncertainty. We seek happiness and find only misery. . . . But our misery is the result of our greatness, and our greatness the result of our misery. . . . For man knows that he is wretched. He is wretched because he knows it; but he is great because he knows that he is wretched. What a chimera is this which we call man ! Miracle, confusion, contradiction ! Judge over all things and impotent earthworm, treasure-chamber of truth and dark room of uncertainty, glory and shame of the universe: let him praise himself, I will humiliate him; let him humiliate himself, I will praise him; and so persistently will I contradict him that he shall at last comprehend that he is incomprehensible." (Whereon Voltaire, who commented the *Pensées,* remarked: " Sheer invalid's babble "; and we in turn should retort that while it is understandable enough that the brilliant herald and spokesman of the eighteenth century should hear nothing but " babble " in this passage, it is incomprehensible that Voltaire of all people should make a reproach of illness, for whence did he himself derive his genius if not from his " physiological inferiority," his crooked spine, his abnormally feeble constitution, and his pathological irritability?)

The Pascalian anthropology may be summed up in the sentence: " Man is but a weak reed, but a thinking one." " *Ainsi toute notre dignité consiste dans la pensée. . . . Travaillons donc à bien penser: voilà le principe de la morale.*" But good use of the power of thought must not lead anywhither but to Christ. " All the bodies that are — the firmament, the stars, the earth, the natural kingdoms — do not count for as much as the smallest of minds; for it has knowledge of all these and of itself, and the body has no knowledge of anything. And all bodies and all minds put together with all their works do not count for as much as the least stirring of love; for love belongs to an incomparably higher order. Out of all bodies taken together there could not be formed the smallest thought: that is impossible, because thought is of a different order. All bodies and all minds together are unable to bring forth a single stirring of true love: that is impossible, because true love is of a different and entirely supernatural order."

We have already had occasion to observe, and shall soon see more definitely, that the seventeenth century marks the victory of the scientific mind: in all spheres it makes its triumphant entry, laying hold of nature-research, language-research, politics, economics, war, even morality, poetry, and religion. All the systems of thought produced by this century, in dealing with every vital problem, either begin with the scientific outlook as their foundation or else regard it as their highest and final goal. One only took a different way, the way of the god-illumined genius, in that he not only sought after science like everyone else, not only found it like the few of the elect, but conquered it. This one was Pascal, the greatest mind that the Gallic race has ever borne. *The overcomer*

The greatest, but not the most effective. The most effective was another thinker, equal to him in breadth but not in depth, in brilliance but not in illuminating power. This man created the brilliant age of Louis XIV — the *grand siècle*, to which we are about to turn — and, what is more, the complete modern Frenchman as he remains right up to the Revolution and the World War. This man, although his life was spent in quiet and solitude under the overcast skies of Holland, was in fact the true Sun-King, and Louis was no more than a gilded decorative doll and lay figure invented by him — a most extraordinary process, and one which the more deserves close study in that it contains a very valuable and surprising lesson: namely, that permanently effective results, historical results in the true sense, have ever been achieved by a few individuals who struck their contemporaries as unessential, superfluous, and even harmful pedants and would strike us in the same way if they were alive now; the work of a few fantastic oddities whose sphere of activity lay completely aloof from all that men of their age considered important and central; and on the other hand all the apparently important things which made so *The true roi soleil*

69

much noise and glitter have now sunk into nothingness, under the ban of oblivion, if not of contempt and ridicule. In short, we shall have to take to heart the lesson that all great things are unprofitable, and no profitable things great, and that true world-history consists in the action of a few unworldly dreams, visions, and delusions.

The miracle to which we allude, a sort of second order of creation, was brought about all unconsciously by a poet-weaver in concepts, a shy aristocrat: the *Chevalier René Descartes, seigneur de Perron.*

CHAPTER II

LE GRAND SIÈCLE

" Aimez donc la raison! "
Boileau

The golden age of France begins with Richelieu. This statesman, at once grandiose and unworthy, fertile in ideas and narrow in mind, who united in himself not only all the admirable and detestable qualities of an eminent politician, but also all the shining virtues and ugly vices of his race, is generally regarded as the real founder of Bourbon absolutism; and in fact he did contribute the greater part of the imposing edifice that the gifted and unfortunate Henry IV had begun and which Louis XIV, more fortunate than gifted, had only to complete. When we remember on the other hand that he not only employed every method of craft and violence to oust Marie de Medicis, the Queen-mother, who at first acted as regent for her young son, but also treated Louis XIII himself — a pathological ne'er-do-well with nothing of value in him except his blind submissiveness to the Cardinal's superior mind — as a dummy in king's clothing, we arrive at the conclusion that the impulse which stimulated Richelieu's powerful policy was not royalism, but that typical French will-to-centralize which strives to organize everything — State, Church, economy, art — around one single shining centre. Therein, in this profound knowledge of the national character and the tendency of the age, lay the secret of his success. Aristocratic feudalism lay dying, bourgeois liberalism was not yet in its birth-pangs, and the only effective vehicle of power therefore was the Crown. This was the feeling of the age; and this was what made Richelieu one of the first of modern politicians — in a double sense, alike one of the greatest and one of the earliest. To call him modern is, of course, far from being a compliment according to the spirit of history as conceived in this work, but it is certainly one in terms of ordinary profane history. He understood what mankind in his century wanted before it really knew for itself, and he possessed sufficient sagacity and decision to transform his perception into reality.

This prince — amiable and brutal, noble and vengeful, as only a cavalier of his day could be — had also, over and above these qualities, the discernment to see politics as the art of using forbidden methods and the system of unprincipledness. He accordingly followed totally different principles in his internal and his external diplomacy. Surely a more extraordinary cardinal has seldom been found under the red hat! It is he who is mainly responsible for the fact that the Thirty Years' War did not end with an Imperial victory; it was his doing that the leading Catholic power, Spain, sank to a second and even a third-rate position. He deprived the Huguenots of their fortress, it is true, but he granted them complete religious liberty and access to official posts; he suppressed the centrifugal ambitions of the Catholic clergy with equal severity, in accordance with his principle that the Church is within the State, not the State within the Church. Although the representative of power and the majority, he displayed what was for those days and in those circumstances an almost incredible religious tolerance, whereas the tolerated, strange to say, bore themselves very intolerantly. And he was equally " unprejudiced " in his interventions in the internal affairs of neighbouring states. It was only as a Frenchman that he championed the omnipotence of kings; for the rest he supported the Catalonian and Portuguese insurgents against Spanish rule, German princes against Emperor and Reich, and the Scots against the English throne. He was a thoroughly modern politician, too, in that he strove to play a powerful part in the colonization movements of the day. He founded the *Compagnie de l'Orient* for the purpose of gaining possession of Madagascar, though the venture met with only very partial success. Later Colbert founded the East India Company with the same intention, but it again was able to gain only a few marginal footholds. On the west coast of Africa, Senegambia, the land between Senegal and Gambia, was captured and Fort St. Louis erected. In South America, French Guiana came into existence, with Cayenne as its capital. But what held first place in the public interest was Canada, or *La France Nouvelle,* though it was not until the end of the century that Louisiana came into

French hands. On the whole, the French of those days had but small success as colonizers, for in this domain Richelieu's centralistic system was a failure; no manifestation of vigour could thrive under such a handicap of state tutelage, especially in an age when all European colonization was a superior form of piracy. In other domains also Richelieu was the forerunner of Colbert. He sought to protect home industries (in particular the flourishing cloth-manufacture) by duties, established new branches, encouraged agriculture, and improved communication by constructing magnificent tree-bordered high roads which became models for all Europe.

The Hôtel Rambouillet

We should do very inadequate justice to Richelieu if we estimated him merely as a politician. Like all great masters of statesmanship he made his mark not only on administration and diplomacy, but on the whole intellectual and social life of the day. His principles were the same here as in politics — intense concentration, breadth of outlook, order. To bear splendid witness to his power he built the *Palais Cardinal* (which later, as the *Palais Royal*, played so interesting a part in history). For the guiding of public opinion he founded, and himself contributed to, the *Gazette de France,* and for the purification and perfection of the French language he created the *Académie française,* which from then on remained the supreme arbiter of correct writing and speech, and through which the language first attained its perfect clarity, sublety, and correctness — though at the cost of assuming a certain mechanical regularity and fettered uniformity. Similarly the " three unities " which he succeeded in imposing upon the drama produced a greater precision and transparency of structure at the cost of a sensible loss in colour, naturalness, and poetic life. It was under Richelieu, too, that the first great salon was opened. The house of the beautiful, witty, and amiable Marquise de Rambouillet became the meeting-place of the intellectual cream of the aristocracy, and thus the cradle of that sublime union of nobility and literature which remained typical of French society for the next two centuries. The ideal of this circle was "*le précieux*" — the choice and the tasteful in speech, in thought, and in manners — and out of it arose later, when the effort towards these ideals degenerated into finicking and superior airs, the contemptuous connotation that the word " precious " now possesses.

As a matter of fact, in the beginning the tendency was towards the very opposite: towards simplicity, artistic frugality, tasteful reserve; *ordre, économie, choix,* were the fundamental qualities demanded by good form. In sum, in the age of Richelieu we already sense all about us the cool and bright, thin and pure air of the *grand siècle.*

Mazarin

When Richelieu and the King died, at almost the same time, it was once more a foreigner — Anne of Austria — who acted as regent for her son, a minor, and once more a Cardinal who had the real governance, though this time not as an enemy of the Queen, but as her lover. Apart from that, Mazarin was more or less a weaker double and understudy of Richelieu. But his outward success at any rate was almost greater than his predecessor's. He completely crushed the insurrection of the Fronde, in which the feudal elements made their last stand against the exclusive power of the throne. He secured for France, by the Peace of Westphalia, the long-coveted Rhine frontier; by the Peace of the Pyrenees he on the one hand made good the Pyrenean frontier, and on the other acquired, in the possession of certain very valuable south Belgian fortresses, a strong sallyport into the two Netherlands. He created the Rhenish league, which, completely under French influence, turned west Germany almost into a Bourbon protectorate; and he formed advantageous alliances with Sweden, Poland, Holland, and England. In short, France at that time reached a height of diplomatic power which was never, even under Louis XIV, regained. And yet with it all he seems but a genre figure beside the great Richelieu. His insatiable avarice, for instance, was grotesque enough for Molière; no means of satisfying it was too vile or too adventurous. At the time of the Fronde, when bitter pamphlets against the unpopular minister poured in great numbers from the press and were eagerly bought, he had them all confiscated and then proceeded to sell them in secret himself at high prices. Even on his death-bed he occupied himself with weighing gold pieces with the intention of using the lighter ones at cards.

The Cartesian Age

This was in the year 1661. After Mazarin's death it was thought by many that a third prince of the Church, the talented, intriguing Cardinal de Retz, would be promoted to the position of ruler of France, but to the general surprise the twenty-three-year-old monarch announced that now he himself was going to rule. On that day begins the age of Louis XIV, which we may call the height of the Baroque or, most accurately perhaps, the Cartesian age.

The life of the remarkable man to whom really the spirit of the *grand siècle* owes its form stands apparently in utter contradiction to the tremendous effect that it produced, for outwardly its course ran on very unassuming and almost conventional lines. Descartes went through the normal upbringing of a nobleman of the time: he attended the Jesuit school, became a licentiate of laws, did military service in Germany, Bohemia, and Holland, and made a pilgrimage to Loretto. The last twenty years of his life were spent in complete seclusion in the Netherlands, his only contact with the centre of the world — the Paris of Richelieu and Mazarin — being his comprehensive correspondence. He felt, as he said himself, no desire whatever for fame, rather indeed a positive dread of it. " Savages," he wrote to one of his admirers, " maintain that monkeys could speak if they wished, but deliberately refrain lest they should be forced to work. I have not had the wisdom to give up writing, therefore I have no longer the peace and leisure I might have had if I had kept silence." He wished to have as little as possible to do with the world, which was to him merely a disturbing element, and he therefore avoided every kind of conflict with the ruling powers. His work on the Cosmos, which was based on the heliocentric (though as a matter of fact not on the Galileian) theory, he suppressed when he learnt how Galileo had become involved by his new theory in differences with the Church. Superficial minds have tried to ascribe this to a lack of will-to-truth and personal courage, but they forget that Descartes the man never ceased to be an aristocrat of France and son of the Holy Roman Church, and that in refraining from tilting against the existing order of things he was but following the voices of his blood. And as regards the rest, it was of more importance to him to be able to develop his great thoughts unmolested than to show them to the world amid molestation and controversy; so much so, that he did not even desire a following.

Yet even in his lifetime he could not prevent both opponents and disciples from swarming about him. For his achievements in the mathematical and physical sciences alone were sufficient to

The magic cross of co-ordinates

create for him a world-wide reputation. He discovered the law of refraction of light and the function of the crystalline lens in the human eye; he solved the riddle of the rainbow, and his theory of vortices, by which he sought to explain the movements of astronomical bodies, carried great weight in his day, although now discarded in the light of later research. His greatest work was, however, the founding of analytical geometry, by which it became possible to express the properties of every plane curve in an equation whose main constituents were formed out of two variable quantities, the co-ordinates. This was not only a perfectly new, and in the sequel extraordinarily fruitful discovery; it was also something of far greater importance: namely, nothing more or less than a giant's effort to apply algebra — that is, pure thought — to geometry; which means the use of real existence to discover the attributes and laws of existence of actual things *before these things themselves exist;* the capture of reality in a permanently fixed network of lines with reference to which it must orient itself, and from which it can at any time be defined and foretold — a supreme victory of rationalism over matter, even though it be only a fictitious one. Cartesian man holds up the *magic cross of co-ordinates* before irrational reality, and so turns it into his spellbound servant. The symbolical significance of this is incalculable: it contains the key to the whole of French Baroque.

Deductive man

After mathematics it was the turn of metaphysics to develop its propositions deductively from principles known immediately and self-evidently. Everything is true that I "clearly and distinctly" represent: we can, therefore, draw conclusions only from that which we either are able intuitively to know of ourselves, or can with certainty deduce from such knowledge. It is in a strictly tested and ordered series of such progressive and discovering conclusions that the Cartesian method consists.

The principle at the top of Descartes's structure reads as follows: everything is doubtful, *de omnibus dubitandum.* Those sense impressions from which we construct our world-picture do certainly deceive us sometimes, and perhaps always. All the same, even in case we were justified in doubting everything, one thing would remain quite indubitable: that is, this very doubt of ours. Even though all our conceptions may be false, there is a positive remainder in the fact that they are conceptions; even though everything be an error, the existence of our error itself is no error; even though I deny everything, I am still the I who denies. In this manner Descartes arrives direct from his starting-point *de omnibus dubito* at the conclusion *dubito ergo sum,* or — since all doubt is thought — *cogito ergo sum.* But he immediately proceeds to identify this with a third, *sum cogitans,* by setting up the hypothesis not only that man is a being whose existence is distinguished by its thought, but that the whole existence of his spiritual half consists in thought. The world, for Descartes, is divided into two substances: bodies, whose fundamental quality is extension, and spirits, whose essential attribute is thought. The body is never without extension, the spirit never without thought: *mens semper cogitat.* This leads Descartes to two curious conclusions, strikingly characteristic of himself and his age: first, that man, if he applies the Cartesian method with the necessary caution and only agrees with that which he has "clearly and distinctly" recognized, can never be in error, that error is his own fault into which he falls only when failing to make proper use of the divine gift of knowing; and, secondly, that as thinking substances can never be extended, extended ones never think, the human body is a machine which has nothing in common with the soul, and animals, since they do not think, have no soul of any sort and differ in no wise from complicated automata.

Let us try to gain a closer view of this philosophy, which Descartes expressed in a crystal-clear and at times almost dramatically emotional langauge. The first fundamental trait that we perceive is a strict methodic of all-round application and, with it, a passionate belief in its power to win victories. There *is* a method, a logical master-key: he who owns it owns the world; if I have this method, the "true method," I have the whole thing — such is the cardinal conviction of Cartesianism, and it develops into the dominating life-passion, determines the whole future evolution-process, of the Latin soul from Descartes, by way of Voltaire and Napoleon, to Taine and Zola. This method is the analytical method. It dissects the given reality, or such of its sections as are under examination, first of all into its "elements," and then deductively, following the "right" way, gets back to it. It corrects the world and the observation of it, or rather it corrects the world *through* observation of it. " To find truth methodically, we must bring back its confused and obscure propositions step by step to simpler ones and then, starting from our view of these latter, work on, also step by step, until we arrive at knowledge of the former." First dissect, then construct — both functions are rationalistic and mechanical in the extreme. Mathematics is the universal science because it alone can completely satisfy these demands. It alone possesses the power to analyse its objects down to their ultimate constituents, and it alone is able to ascend, by the aid of a consistent chain of proofs and conclusions, to final knowledge of these. At bottom, then, everything is a mathematical problem: the entire physical world around us, our mind which absorbs it, and even ethics. This last is a most characteristic and extraordinary part of the Cartesian system. In his treatise *Les Passions de l'âme* Descartes presents, brilliantly and acutely, an exhaustive analysis of human passions, which is at the same time a guide as to how they may be controlled and fought. This famous essay of his, which evoked the intense admiration of his contemporaries, was nothing more or less than an attempt to trace the whole of the emotions back to a set of general basic forms, and then to produce a kind of *algebra of the passions*. Everything, in short, is a problem of analysis, of analytical geometry. But what, then, is analytical geometry? We have already said that it is nothing but the art of finding the law and form of a thing without the necessity of clearly seeing it: to find the equation of the circle, the ellipse, the parabola, before they are there, and in virtue of their following self-evidently from the equation — which they *must* follow, to which they *must* show logical mathematical obedience. And Descartes could regulate his own existence, too, according to this algebraic method. He began by sketching for himself, so to say, the equation of his biography and then constructed his life's curve quite accurately by this theoretical formula. In his development process there was nothing accidental, nothing enforced from without — everything was determined by himself in advance. It was with his eyes open that he spent the first half of his existence in the great world in order to " read in its book," and it was with equal deliberation that he shut himself out of it for the remainder of his earthly career in order to philosophize over it. Descartes is the first *deductive man* to appear on the historical stage.

This deductive man's first rooted conviction is that only that which man thinks is real, and only that which man thinks systematically is really thought. That which I " clearly and distinctly " perceive is true: the *clara et distincta perceptio* is the infallible criterion of rightness, and even incidentally in his writings Descartes was fond of using metaphors belonging to this order of ideas, such as day, light, sun. In natural science he devoted himself with particular affection to optical problems, and in his lost work (which was probably meant to have the title *Le Monde*) he dealt with the entire cosmos from the standpoint of his theory of light. The aim of his whole philosophy is "*la recherche de la vérité par les lumières naturelles*" (the title of one of his posthumous works). There is nothing which this natural light of reason cannot illumine: that which does not lie in its sun is not worthy of being shone upon, and indeed does not even exist; but that which it does illumine enjoys the full brilliance of day and is clearly and evenly lighted, without shadows or nuances, darknesses or contradictions. For pure reason, aware of and secure in itself, there is but a single great certainty without qualification: it is a sort of noonday height which the mind of the human being here climbs on one side only, but heroically.

This zenith can, of course, only be reached by a process of neglecting, and indeed denying, everything that does not lie within the beam of clear *Ratio*. In this world-philosophy, therefore, there can be nothing subconscious or even half-conscious, no undefinable soul-stirrings, no dark impulses, no secret inklings; no sensations even, except in so far as they are the expression of clear thought. To covet anything means to regard it as true; to abhor anything is to regard it as false. Good actions are those based on an adequate knowing; evil actions those which ensue from incorrect imaginings. Animals and plants are, as we have heard already, mere automata; their sensations are nothing but bodily movements which obey purely mechanical laws; for everything which happens without thought is a purely physical process. Descartes goes so far as to assert that they neither see nor hear, hunger nor thirst, rejoice nor sorrow. They know, he says, no more about their vital manifestations than does a clock which

79

strikes six or seven. He goes, in his logical course, even further still and declines to place even human sensations among the spiritual processes; for him they are likewise mere phenomena of movement. The passions are only false judgments, confused, incorrect, obscure notions; and there is therefore no justification for their existence, and they can and must be conquered by reason, reason being the faculty of " clear and distinct " conceptions. We recognize here the habit of mind — akin to that of the Greek Stoa, but adjusted to the point of view of the man of the world — which hovered over the seventeenth century as an ethical ideal: that of the man who has tamed and rationalized all his instincts by the clear methodology which has become his *life-form;* who looks down upon everything that is the outcome of elementary instincts and the unregulated sphere of the will as uncivilized and plebeian, tasteless and barbaric, unphilosophical and unæsthetic; who feels everything not subject to reason to be subaltern and in bad form. But already the eighteenth century is heralded in the conviction that everything that conflicts with reason represents an unripe moral formation and an aberration of nature, destined to be overcome in the course of progress.

The soul without brothers   In each individual province the Cartesian system did no more than draw logical conclusions from its supreme principle of *cogito ergo sum.* From thought Descartes extracted the fact of the human ego and of the whole world. It is true that when Gassendi argued that man could draw conclusions as to his existence from any of his other activities, and say, for instance: " *Ambulo ergo sum* (I walk, therefore I am) " Descartes quite rightly replied that man could only be assured of the fact that he was walking by his conception of that fact; that is, by thinking he was walking. But he brought thought and existence not merely into such a relation of major and minor premiss, but also into that of identity, by establishing that the being of the mind consisted solely in thought, and that things thought were therefore the only reality. If, for instance, Gassendi had challenged him with the maxim: " *Volo ergo sum* (I will, therefore I am)," on which Schopenhauer's philosophy takes its stand, Descartes would not have been able to produce the same rejoinder; for even if I become conscious of my will only through my imagining it, the question still remains, may not this will nevertheless be the origin of my existence? Through the fact of my thought my ego is merely *proved* to me. Thus in reality Descartes turns a logical basis into a metaphysical one. He was nevertheless fully justified in this fallacy. For the task of the great philosophers is not to draw correct conclusions, but to be the voice of their time and to reduce the world-feeling of their epoch to a system. And the man of that day was profoundly convinced that only the activity of which he had knowledge was *his* activity: "*Quod nescis, quomodo fiat, id non facis,*" says the Cartesian Geulinx. Only he who thinks has a soul, and he who has a soul must think: "*L'âme pense toujours,*" says the Cartesian Malebranche.

This mind, which is always thinking, has no brothers. Cartesianism presents, in a remarkable degree, that rigid isolation into which any consistent rationalism shuts the human being. It is out of the heroic void and autonomous solitude of pure thought that Descartes formulates his terrible *cogito ergo sum.* Man, as he conceives him, stands alone in the wide world with his *cogito,* his noble power of thinking, ordering, and clarifying, which builds up the whole Cosmos for him: God, man, and nature; world-risings and world-settings; sociologies, astronomies, physics; atoms, vortices, planets; states, passions, virtues. Yet at bottom (although it will not admit it and is perhaps unaware of it) this *Monas Cartesius,* which thinks and thinks and thinks, is alone real. Sense-perceptions are not true, but only the thought of these perceptions. Similarly in geometry what is real (or at any rate what is essential) is not the actual curve, but the general formula of it that reason discovers. Sensual conceptions have less reality because they are "unclear." And what guarantee have we that the whole world of the senses is not a dream? "When I consider the matter carefully, I find not a single characteristic which would serve definitely to distinguish the waking conditions from a dream. So similar are the two that I am completely at a loss to know whether I myself am dreaming at this moment." Here Descartes unmasks himself suddenly as a true Baroque philosopher, by degrading the world of the senses to a reality of the second order, conceiving of it — even though only in hypothesis — as a dream, and in any case showing the profoundest distrust of the whole. He shows himself a child of the Baroque, too, in combining with his fundamental scepticism and extreme revolutionary rationalism an unconditional recognition of actuality so far as its property of power is concerned. In his human capacity he was, as has been pointed out, strictly conservative, almost reactionary, and in his heart an anti-reformer. For the Reformation was individualistic, democratic, " progressive," libertarian in *practice* — and to this Descartes was ever opposed. Bossuet said of him that his prudence before the Church went to extremes, and he himself recommends his readers to observe under all circumstances the laws and customs of the country in which they live, hold fast to the religion in which they were bred, obey the most moderate and widely accepted rules in society, and avoid altogether the discussion of ethical matters, since it is the business of those invested with power, and those only, to set up moral standards for others. He was an aristocrat and a Catholic, and never in any connexion a " protestant," but in spite of this (or more probably because of this) he created a philosophy more unprejudiced than anything that any bourgeois or reformer of his country ever achieved. In it there breathes the air of a mind so free that it despises freedom itself.

Transition from Pre-Baroque to full Baroque

And, in fact, the first opponents of his philosophy appeared in the ranks of the Protestant republic of the liberated Netherlands. Thirteen years after his death, however, the Jesuits also came out against him and succeeded in having his books put on the Index; and soon afterwards his teachings were condemned by the French universities. But, for all that, nothing could check the spread of his school — and by his school we mean not merely the " occasionalists," as his immediate disciples and followers in the history of philosophy are called, not merely the famous *l'art de penser* of the Port Royal logic, or the fashionable *art poétique* of Boileau, but the whole of France, with the Sun-King, who banned his works, at its head. State, economics, drama, architecture, social intercourse, strategy, the art of gardening — all these became Cartesian. In tragedy, where concepts of the passions fought among themselves; in comedy, where the algebraic formulæ of the human character were developed; in the avenues of Versailles, which are abstract equations of gardens; in the analytical method of conducting war and economics; in the (so to say) deductive ceremonial of gestures and manners, dancing and conversation — everywhere Descartes reigned as absolute ruler. It may even be asserted that to this very day almost every Frenchman is a born Cartesian. The French Revolution crushed the absolutism of the Bourbons as completely as is possible to imagine, but so far from dethroning Descartes, it confirmed and even extravagantly heightened his power.

With Louis XIV the transition from Pre-Baroque to full Baroque is completed. His autocratic government covers about five and a half decades. At his death the late Baroque, known as Rococo, set in. We have previously remarked that the epoch of his becoming absolute monarch is marked by a number of other dates of decisive significance; and so it is with the end of his reign likewise. His death took place in 1715, and in the same year Malebranche, the most important of the Cartesians, died. In 1713 Frederick William I came to the throne of Prussia, in 1714 the house of Hanover began its rule in England — two significant turning-points in politics. And in 1716 Leibniz died — in whom, as we shall see, the Baroque spirit found its highest concentration. The death of the Sun-King signifies therefore, in more ways than one, the end of a historical epoch.

The extreme absolutism that Louis XIV set up followed self-evidently from the supremacy of Cartesian Reason, which requires a centre from which everything may be uniformly and methodically ruled and directed. The motto: "*l'État c'est moi*" had for the men of the time a meaning very far removed from that which frivolous critics have since attached to it. The king was the centre, selected by God and Reason, of the earthly system of co-ordinates. Everything had to orient itself on him, and if anyone had been rash enough to think otherwise, he would have appeared to the feeling of the age not only as a traitor to the State and to majesty, but as something far worse, a person unable to think systematically. The king is, to begin with, and then the State — developed from him just as the cross of co-ordinates precedes the actual points, lines, and surfaces. The king does not rule the State, he makes the State. From this a radically absolutist theory naturally and necessarily follows, and its clearest and most impressive exposition is to be found in the writings of Bossuet, the "eagle of Meaux," who was both one of the most moving pulpit-orators and one of the most brilliant historians of his time. In his *Politique tirée de l'Écriture Sainte,* he asserts

The King as origin of the earthly co-ordinate system

83

that the king is the viceroy and image of God upon earth, his majesty the reflection of the divine majesty; the whole State, the will of the people, reposes in him, and only those who serve him serve the State. In Bossuet this was not flunkey-theology, nor flunkey-politics, but profoundest conviction. And when we observe how the finest and boldest minds of the day were imbued with the same feelings in this regard as the mass of the people, we are forced to the view that Louis XIV was no megalomaniac autocrat, but merely accepted what public opinion offered and even forced upon him. He ruled, not merely by means of outward power, but as the legitimate mandatory of the spirit of the age. He was actually what to Hobbes the State was theoretically — a " mortal god." His favour conferred bliss, his disfavour death. There was nothing unique or preposterous about the case of " the great Vatel " (surely a genius among cooks, for does not Madame de Sévigné say that his head would have been equal to absorbing all the cares of state government?), who flung himself on his carving-knife because a feast given by Condé for the King was not a complete success. The great Colbert, too, fell into a fatal nervous fever when his protests against the all-too-costly building at Versailles brought down on him the King's angry retort that there must have been embezzlements. Vauban, again, published a most penetrating study of taxation reform; this, however, excited the royal displeasure and was accordingly seized and destroyed, and eleven days later Vauban was dead. Then a fourth, as great in *haute tragédie* as Vatel in the culinary art, Colbert in finance, and Vauban in fortification, was overtaken by the same fate: this fourth was Racine, who, from absent-mindedness, committed a gross error in tact. One evening at Madame de Maintenon's he was conversing with Louis (who often sought and enjoyed his company) on the subject of the Paris stage. The King inquired how it was that comedy had fallen so low from its one-time high level. Racine replied that in his opinion the chief reason was that too many of Scarron's pieces were played. This assertion made Madame de Maintenon (Scarron's widow) blush, and there was a painful silence. The King broke off the conversation and never afterwards spoke a word to Racine, who fell into melancholy and died. In a word, the feelings with which the King was regarded are expressed with no undue exaggeration in the words of Madame de Maintenon's brother, who, when his sister said she could not endure her dull life by the side of Louis, exclaimed: "Are you thinking of marrying God the Father, then?"

Louis XIV's home administration

The external instruments by which Louis XIV wielded and sustained his unshakable authority were bureaucracy, police, and standing army — the three outstanding and characteristic elements of the modern state — which were brought to their highest development in his reign. Over the whole land was drawn the net of a carefully graded and organized official hierarchy. There was prompt and relentless enforcement of taxation, an ever open source (which, however, eventually ran dry) for the immense expenditure on the business of state. The capitation-tax (*la taille*) was very high and at the same time inequitably distributed, since the nobility and clergy were exempt. In addition there were heavy indirect charges on a number of the most essential domestic articles, above all the notorious salt-tax (*la gabelle*). Equally detested and feared were the *lettres de cachet*, by means of which the King could intern whom he pleased without trial for an indefinite period.

The nobility, deprived of its proud feudal independence, was transformed by Louis XIV into a court aristocracy which had no other purpose but that of enhancing the splendour of royalty. He did, it is true, fill the public offices and, above all, the higher military posts, with nobles for preference, but, even so, from being minor sovereigns they had become crown officials, distinguishable from ordinary subjects only by outward honours and decorations. And apart from them the King, as a matter of fact, drew into his service large numbers of the bourgeoisie, wherever he found talent and enterprise, and not infrequently he put them into the highest posts, especially on the administrative side — hence the nickname that Saint-Simon gives him in the *Mémoires,* "*le roi des commis.*" In this wise there arose a new and very influential caste, the *nouveaux riches*, which by the purchase of land and consequent ennoblement, by lucky speculations, and by securing aristocratic connexions by marriage climbed rapidly.

The King's closest attention was given to the army. He was not himself what is called a "militarist," but he realized that constant wars, which flattered patriotic pride and at the same time directed abroad the craving for action, were the surest means of retaining the permanent respect of so fame-coveting, restless, and domineering a nation as his own. (It is the system which has since been adopted by all French governments, whether Bourbon, Jacobin, or Napoleonic.) Within a short time he succeeded in making his army the strongest and the best drilled, equipped, and led in Europe. Turenne, Condé, Luxembourg, and Catinat were the unrivalled masters of strategy. Vauban, greatest military engineer of the century, encircled France with a wonderful ring of fortresses, raised the art of siegecraft to a hitherto unknown level, and perfected the artillery arm by the introduction of bomb-throwing mortars and ricochet fire, the first attempt at indirect fire. The minister of war, Louvois, the infamous devastator of the Palatinate, reformed the whole army system. He replaced the clumsy matchlock gun by the handy flintlock, and the pike by the bayonet — thus creating a weapon equally suited to distant and to close fighting — and made infantry once more the arm of major importance. Even the dragoons were in a sense only mounted infantry who, armed with carbine and sword, dismounted to fight, the horse in their case playing the part of a means of transport, much as the railway does in the case of bodies of troops today. He was also the first to introduce a general uniform: up till then soldiers had provided their own dress according to their choice. This was another feature in which the new spirit of rational organization, visible in every sphere of life, was displayed. The army became for the first time a system. The soldier was no longer a living and distinct individuality, but one of the values taken by an algebraic symbol — namely, his uniform. Instead of a particular soldier, there is only the concept of a soldier, for use in any desired operation; just as in the avenues of Versailles there are no single trees, but only a number of identical specimens of the *genus* tree, a dressed line consisting of uniformly trimmed examples, subsumed under a common type.

The same mania for unity swayed Louis XIV even in his religion. The severity which he displayed towards the Jansenists (to whom largely the literary splendour of the time was due) proceeded solely from his desire for uniformity and correctness. His resistance to the Pope had the same motives as his attack on the heretics. He summoned an assembly of the Church in Paris, which declared that Peter and his successors had power from God only in spiritual and not in secular matters, and that even such power was limited by the higher authority of the General Councils and the rules and customs of the Gallican Church. This Gallican Church is a French national Church, which allows the pope no say in the bestowal of benefices, and as a *political* body it is, therefore, not very far removed from the Anglican Church. Unfortunately the King, in his struggle against any and every centrifugal tendency, let himself be persuaded into revoking the Edict of Nantes, with the result that all the Huguenots were outlawed and subjected to the most abominable persecution. By this act, as unwise as it was inhuman, he injured himself and his country exceedingly, besides stirring up against himself the opposition of all the fair-minded people in Europe. And from that point his decline set in. During the second half of his reign his " sun " revealed its ugly spots with increasing distinctness, became slowly paler, and finally went down in mournful grey twilight. The Huguenots had been forbidden to leave the country, but the strictest regulation was unable to prevent the emigration of a large section of them — about half a million. This loss meant far more to France than a diminution of the population figures; for the Huguenots were among the most skilled and hardworking of the Sun-King's subjects: brocade, silk, and velvet weaving; the making of elegant hats, boots, and gloves; the manufacture of braid, ribbons, and wall-paper; clock-making and lace-making; tobacco manufacture, and glass-cutting — all these were almost exclusively in their hands. Not only did they remove these industries from their motherland — where they revived only gradually, and nevermore with the same perfection — but carried them into other countries, which thus became more considerable as rivals. They succeeded abroad, too, as seamen and engineers, and they organized wherever possible — notably in Holland — a free press, which by informing the whole world of its egoistical and brutal character, brought Louis XIV's much-admired government into the gravest disrepute.

Daily life was subordinated to the same principle as religious and political life: everything had to be " noble," grand, pompous, and telling, yet at the same time " simple," correct, systematic, and overseeable. Under Louis XIV the *Place Royale* and its ancillary streets were built with the most completely geometrical regularity.

The theatre of Versailles

87

Lenôtre is the creator of French garden-construction, which lays out its parks in the form of mathematical figures, and plants them with the aid of compass and ruler. Fountains and pools were laid out with the same symmetry, as for instance the *Bassin de Latone* at Versailles, where frogs are set round at regular intervals, all sending out their jets in the same faultlessly equal curves. The same spirit breathes from the minuet, perhaps the most remarkable dance ever invented, in that it achieves the feat of wedding the most chilling affectation, deliberation, and marionettism to the most bewitching grace, vivacity, and airiness. And indeed at bottom the whole salon-life of the period was a minuet. Were there not strict regulations as to how many steps one took before it was permitted to bow, the particular line of the bow, and the depth of it in each particular case? There was nothing in this society which did not conform to a minute and considered regulation, nothing that was left to chance. Life was one great drawing-board squared in standard units, a chess-board on which certain uniform figures made their moves to order.

Even the great King could not escape from this strict moral etiquette. It was the one power stronger than he. His day was strictly ordered: every hour had its prescribed occupation, dress, and company. The absolute monarch was at bottom no more than a great doll which certain persons chosen to that end dressed, undressed, fed, took out, and put to bed. No one might hand him a handkerchief but the head of the handkerchief section; the inspection of his night-stool was a separate court office; to pass him a glass of water was the work of four people. His whole life was one tiresome, boring reception of the same faces and the same expressions. When the ceremonial of the French Court was described to Frederick the Great, he remarked that if he were king of France his first governmental act would be to appoint a viceroy to hold his court for him.

The life of the court was one long repertory piece, always the same, which began at eight in the morning and ended at ten at night, only to begin all over again next day. But, what is more, the life of all France was a similar comedy. It took an amazing amount of self-control and self-denial to carry out the ticklish, exhausting title-rôle of the hero in this comedy, but Louis XIV solved this difficult problem with such consummate mastery that we do not even see the effort behind it. For fifty-four years he performed for the benefit of Europe: it was a very tasteful, very pompous, very intelligent performance — and a very superficial, very brutal, very mendacious one too.

Louis XIV was determined to impress, but to do it gracefully. For his portraits he posed for choice as *Imperator*. Bernini's magnificent equestrian statue shows perhaps most clearly how he wished to be presented to the world. It depicts him on an untamed horse which is in the act of climbing the hill of fame. The French sculptor Girardon carved marble flames on the hill, as an indication that Louis XIV had sacrificed himself like a modern Curtius for his fatherland — a shameless lickspittle touch which naturally ruins the work from the artistic standpoint as well. In his actual manner, however, the King never paraded the autocrat. He was always tactful, always self-possessed, amiable even in bad temper, and angry only in the deliberately assumed rôle of a *Jupiter Tonans*. With women, particularly, he observed the most chivalrous courtesy, and he would take off his hat with a sweep to the lowest kitchen-maid. He understood the art of giving without humiliation and of refusing without wounding. The extent of his delicacy is seen in his attitude towards James II of England, who sought asylum with him after his dethronement. He not only treated him as a sovereign of equal standing, but even permitted him to style himself King of France and retain the lilies on his shield, according to the ancient tradition of the kings of England. On one occasion he threw his stick out of the window to be saved from the temptation of striking the haughty marshal Lauzun, who had insulted him. When a senior officer, who had lost an arm in battle, once said to him: " I wish I had lost the other too; then I should no longer need to serve Your Majesty," he merely replied: " I should be sorry for that, both on your account and my own," and made him a handsome present.

His excellent constitution alone enabled him to endure the fatigues of his position for so many years. His midday meal consisted usually of four plates of different soups, a whole pheasant, a partridge, a large dish of salad, mutton with garlic and sauce, ham, a plate of cakes, fruit, and conserves. In the sexual domain he developed an equal vitality. " Anything was good enough for the King so long as it wore a petticoat," wrote Liselotte. His household included, besides the acknowledged mistress of the moment, the *maîtresse en titre,* a number of *dames du lit royal,* also officially recognized, who were ranged according to rank. He possessed almost all the women around him, in fact, and was father to a legion of legitimate, half-legitimate, and illegitimate children: by the Queen, Madame Lavallière, and Madame de Montespan alone he had all together sixteen.

The policy of Louis XIV has been severely condemned, both by his contemporaries and by his later critics. It stands as the pattern of ruthlessness and brutality, injustice and perfidy. The attack on Holland, the seizure of Strassburg, the *chambres de réunion* which traced France's claim upon German lands back to Pippin the Short and King Dagobert and on this justification annexed numerous cities for the King; the reduction to ashes of Heidelberg and Mannheim — this and much else roused the indignation of the age and of posterity. Nevertheless, as long as politics is regarded as being nothing more than the art of deceiving and outwitting one's enemies and the insolence to abuse one's power until a stronger power calls a halt, so long will it remain ludicrous to arraign the arts of statesmen before a judicial or even an ethical tribunal. We will not, therefore, deal too severely with the misdeeds of the Sun-King, but regard them merely as the expression of their age and of the general crudeness and blindness of humanity.

His political program was no less grandiose than that of Philip II, and it fell as far short of fulfilment. He aimed in the first place at acquiring Belgium, Holland, and the command of the North Sea — a constant dream of the French nation right into the days of Napoleon III, but one which was only temporarily realized under Napoleon I. In addition to this he coveted Spain with all its dependencies, the West Indies, Milan, Sardinia, Naples, Franche-Comté, and — to round it all off — Savoy. In Germany he wanted to possess himself of the whole of the west, either by direct incorporation or by the establishment of dependent principalities. He mobilized the Turks, with whom he had an alliance, against the Habsburgs, in the hope that they would conquer Vienna and Austria, so that he could at the last moment intervene as saviour and mediator between hard-pressed Germany and the Porte, and so earn for himself the Imperial crown. All this might have led to the revival of Charlemagne's empire, which, as is well known, the French no less than the Germans claim as their own. But the day for universal monarchies was as irrevocably past as the day of universal churches. In the end Louis had to be content with the Franche-Comté, portions of Alsace, and a few Belgian frontier fortresses.

The last part of his reign is taken up by a thirty years' world-war, that of the Spanish Succession, in which almost all Europe took sides. Louis's chief opponent was the Emperor Leopold I, a true Habsburg, with lack-lustre eye and hanging under-lip, whose nature was an unhappy blend of slovenliness and obstinacy. Both monarchs laid claim to the Spanish throne, for which each had set up a pretender from his own family. On the side of France were Bavaria, Cologne, and Savoy, though the last-named eventually went over to the Emperor. Leopold's allies were Portugal, Prussia, Hanover, and, above all, William of Orange, who at that time ruled in personal union both Holland and England and was all his life the most dangerous and obstinate of the Sun-King's enemies. The main theatres of war were South Germany, the Netherlands, Italy, and Spain. This time Louis was unfortunate from the first. At the head of the coalition against him stood the most distinguished generals of the age: Marlborough and Prince Eugene, who were victorious in almost all the battles of the war. In addition, France was completely exhausted by decades of heavy taxation, bad harvests, and famine. The King resolved to negotiate for peace and declared himself willing to make enormous sacrifices. He was willing to revert to the state of things fixed in the Treaty of Westphalia, to hand over the Netherlands fortresses, and to acquiesce in the bestowal of the Spanish crown on Charles, second son of Leopold I. But the Allies were narrow and cock-sure enough to insist on stiffer, and in fact unacceptable, conditions. Had they made peace at that point, Leopold's son Charles, as possessor of all the Spanish and Austrian lands and the German Imperial dignity, would have raised Habsburg to be a European world-power, for it was not long before he succeeded his brother Charles VI. And indeed this very fact brought about a complete revulsion, for such overwhelming power in the hands of one ruler was not at all desired by the states allied with that House. To all this was added the fall of the Whig ministry in

England, which meant a political change of front and the recall of Marlborough. And thus France was, after all, able to make a tolerably advantageous peace, in which the Spanish possessions were divided so that Louis XIV's grandson was confirmed on the throne of Spain and in the possession of the colonies, while Charles VI received Belgium, Milan, Naples, and Sardinia, England the extremely important position of Gibraltar, and Savoy Sicily. But it was nevertheless a profound defeat of the French bid for hegemony, and an unmistakable sign that Louis XIV's day was over.

Already throughout the second part of his reign the evil effects of levelling Reason had made themselves felt. Beneath the sun of the régime of unity everything gradually became a shrivelled waste. The court, and with it the world around, became sanctimonious, senile, morose, and — most unpardonable of all from the French point of view — boring. The golden glitter of Versailles became duller, the bright lacquer peeled off; everyone fell to praying — and yawning. Even the people began to realize that it had all been a monstrous swindle, a bubble splendour with nothing but blind greed and selfishness behind it. When the great King was dead, there was jubilation not only among his enemies, but also among his subjects. The walls of Paris were covered with lampoons, the crowd which followed his funeral procession abused him and threw stones, and in the provinces thanksgiving services were held. And even a whole generation earlier Colbert had had to be buried under military escort.

Colbertism   Yet Colbert was one of the greatest organizers of the century; and indeed his only fault was that, in his big way, he really translated the errors of his time into fact. His restless activity embraced nearly every department of government: he reformed justice and taxation, raised the mercantile marine and the navy to a commanding position, founded the Academies of Science and of Architecture, set up an observatory and a botanical garden, and constructed the *Canal du Midi,* which connects the Atlantic with the Mediterranean. But his most important achievement was his economic system, which under the name of Mercantilism, dominated the whole period, and of which the principles were so much the product of this one man's intellect that it was often known simply as " Colbertism." Mercantilism starts from the basis that the wealth of a country lies in its store of precious metal, and that as much of this as possible should be brought into the country and as little as possible allowed to pass out. This is the theory of the active balance of trade. Raw materials should, to the limit of what is practicable, remain in the country, because they represent capital; industrial products, on the contrary, require to be exported because they serve to bring in money. Conversely the intrusion of foreign industrial products should be prevented or rendered difficult: hence high export duties on raw materials and high import duties on finished articles. In pursuance of these principles the colonies were reduced to mere consumers; they were forbidden to trade, or even to manufacture, for themselves and were forced to accept in exchange for their raw materials (which they were forbidden to deliver elsewhere) the mother country's manufactured articles. At home, on the other hand, manufactures were supported in every imaginable way: by export premiums, monopolies, exemptions from taxation, state loans free of interest, free building-sites, the bestowal of titles of nobility on energetic contractors, and similar favours. Thus there arose in France, under state aid and control, a number of flourishing industries which supplied the half of Europe, the chief of these being silk goods, lace, tapestries, and every description of luxury and fashion articles, such as fine furniture, clothes, wigs, and scent. Diligent efforts were also made to learn from other nations: stockings were woven after the English manner, hardware manufactured after the German, mirrors after the Venetian, and cloth after the Dutch pattern. The logical correlative to the veto put on foreign goods was the removal of internal taxation, and this also Colbert to a great extent succeeded in bringing about, which in itself would have sufficed to give France an economic lead over Germany. With a view to maintaining the high pitch of industrial activity he then turned his attention to lengthening the hours of labour, fighting unemployment by police measures against beggars and vagabonds, raising the birth-rate by means of premiums to large families and special taxes on the unmarried, and ensuring the supply of skilled labourers for the country by forbidding their emigration and encouraging them to enter. Later, when the system of state tutelage became more and more rigidly and one-sidedly established, mercantilism led to some very peculiar practices: it was responsible for organized smuggling with the object of dumping more goods in foreign countries; it sought to keep wages artificially low, and in general became a burdensome and frequently ludicrous tyranny. Frederick William I forbade the wearing of wooden shoes in the interests of the leather-manufacturers, Frederick the Great appointed his own " coffee-smellers," whose duty it was to sniff round and find out whether anyone was defying the state monopoly, and under Frederick I there was even a hogs' bristles monopoly, by which everyone who owned pigs was bound to make a regular delivery of bristles to the authorities at midsummer.

It was not long before the principle of such a welfare-state was questioned. John Locke opposed it as an infringement of the liberty of the individual; in reality, he held, men entered into a contract with the State for the greater security of the inalienable rights which were theirs by nature. It should, however, be remembered that at that time nearly all European states were preponderantly agrarian, providing almost their entire corn-supply themselves and producing the most important raw materials, such as wool, silk, flax, in sufficient quantities within their own boundaries. It must be remembered also that Colbert himself said that his measures were to be regarded as crutches by the aid of which people might the more rapidly find their feet. Unfortunately, the crutches did not even remain crutches: they became intolerable stilts, and, after a short spell of apparent prosperity, the final outcome of Colbertism was indebtedness and poverty. This " active balance of trade " offered a most satisfactory theory, while in practice the people starved. The State of Louis XIV had become literally a Leviathan; the wars, even when victorious, contributed nothing to the people's good, and the large-scale export trade only enriched a small upper stratum of society. The deductive method which set out to construct a world-system out of a few maxims of its own, to overpower reality with an abstract formula, revealed its brilliance and its impotence in the economic spheres as in others.

Dramatic crystal- lography

In one respect at any rate the fame of Louis XIV is solidly founded. He was not content with conducting wars and holding his court, but cherished the higher ambition of making his reign a golden age of art. He was on that account compared with Augustus, a comparison that was just in some ways, but by no means so flattering a compliment as his contemporaries imagined.

For that which arose under his auspices was in fact nothing more than a magnificently arranged, tastefully gilded court-art and ultra-refined artiness, in which etiquette choked imagination. The grand master of the ceremonies in this particular connexion was Nicolas Boileau, *législateur du goût*, who dictated what was to be written, and how, as rigidly as the Académie française had fixed the limits and use of words. The point of departure of his æsthetic was once more the Cartesian *clara et distincta perceptio*. That which is not clear and distinct is not beautiful either; illuminating, regulating Reason is poetry's lawgiver also: "*Tout doit tendre au bon sens.*" The aim of art for Boileau is the same as that of philosophy for Descartes: namely, truth. The leading maxim of his art of poetry was: "*Rien n'est vrai que le beau.*" Nicole, too, a notable member of the Port Royal group, gives as the three fundamental principles: *ratio, natura, veritas.* Now this, though it sounds quite naturalistic, was really the precise opposite; and so once more we are brought up sharply to recognize how problematical the concept of naturalism is. The artists of the *grand siècle* regarded their creations as a triumph of nature, whereas in fact these creations violated nature in a manner as sublime as it was ridiculous. The riddle is easily solved, however, if we remind ourselves that these people were simply Cartesians. They equated nature with reason. And, given these premises, we shall see that their works were really the most natural ever seen, for they were the most reasonable. Truth was, for them, not conformity with experience, but conformity with logic. It was logic that laid down the laws for the conduct of life, for the general outlook, for the creative activity: and whoever followed these laws acted naturally.

Out of this attitude of mind there arose the ideal of the *grand facile,* the grandly simple, as set up by Fénelon — the " swan of Cambrai" and author of the *aventures de Télémaque.* It was significant that this work, although it was expressly a didactic poem for the education of the Duke of Burgundy in the duties and tasks of a ruler, was considered the greatest epic of the age and even of the world. Moreover, the requirement of easy oversight led naturally to the rule of the three unities, erroneously attributed to Aristotle. We might in fact describe unity of place as the ordinate, unity of time as the abscissa, and unity of action as the ideal curve. Further, with reason ruling everywhere, it becomes necessary to subdue and civilize the passions, to avoid any manifestations whatever of unrestrained elemental vitality, and to command the most extreme situations with reasonableness and decency: so that even in their death-scenes the heroes of tragedy remember what they owe to themselves, the court, and Descartes. Things happen, not in wild eruptions and sudden jumps as in Shakspere (who is a barbarian), but like the elements of a continued argument or the columns of an equation. These writers were — excellent crystallographers, but never mineralogists. We are given a most exhaustive, enlightened, broad, and accurate account of the general form-language of things, but learn nothing about their hardness, their colour, their glitter, their density, their occurrence, their deviation from type: in short, their individuality.

"*Le grand Corneille*" was a poet of the *Fronde* still, heroic, daring, at times almost fiery; yet even in him we can see the stamp of the academician and the reasoner. His ethic is a superior Stoicism, which finds its greatest satisfaction in man's victory over himself and the sacrifice of the individual to an idea — usually the good of the State. Descartes in his treatment of the passions declares the highest virtue to be great-heartedness, *la magnanimité* or *générosité*, "which is as it were the key of all the virtues and the principal remedy against the riot of our passions." It is this same quality which takes the rôle of hero in Corneille's tragedies. If we compare the three great dramatists of that day with the great tragedians of Greece — drawing, of course, no parallel on the ground of poetic quality, but only in respect of their relation to each other — we shall find that in some ways Corneille, with his streaks of archaism, corresponds to Æschylus; Racine, more feminine and differentiated, to Sophocles; and especially Molière, full of problems and psychology, to Euripides, who also was not far from being a comic poet, and whose campaign against the dramatic art-form imposed upon him was as obstinate and as ineffectual. For the democratic and sceptical Greeks about Pericles were, in matters of outward form, as relentlessly conservative as the aristocratic and dynamic Frenchmen of Louis XIV's *entourage*. Euripides, the rich tired heir to a culture that in worldly wisdom, technique of expression, and art of seeing and hearing had reached almost the extreme limits, saw himself obliged to present an exercise in the psychological calculus to the public under conditions that were just good enough for a wild Indian dance or a village circus; and Molière's struggling liveliness, misanthropic tormentedness, and opalescent nuances of mood were confined in a tiresome gilded salon full of people whose highest ambition it was to achieve the appearance, and to attain to the emotional life, of a puppet on strings. And that is why Molière, apparently the most amusing of the three, is in reality the tragic figure among them. That he was also the greatest, certain of his most enlightened contemporaries had already realized. When Boileau was asked by Louis XIV who was the most important writer of the age, he replied: "Monsieur Molière, Your Majesty." "I should never have thought it," said the King, "but of course you know best."

In the epilogue to *Fräulein Julie* Strindberg says: "The desire to see people simply is still in evidence in the great Molière. Harpagon is only miserly, although Harpagon, besides being a miser, might have been a prominent financier, a model father, a solid member of the community." In principle this criticism is completely justified, but it is unjust to Molière in so far as it overlooks the fact that he was *not allowed* to present anything but the equations of the miser, the hypochondriac, the hypocrite, the parvenu, the pert lady's-maid, the faithful lover. He had to work to given patterns because his clientele would have it so, and it does him double credit that with this lumpy and spiritless technique he was able to produce such varied, piquant, original, and life-like models. He was forced to impersonate his chaotic inward discontents and unrest in figures which seem to us to have the artistic crudity of spectres, for he was clown to a great master, a more powerful, self-glorious, and obstinate one than even Louis XIV; he was court jester to the Spirit of the Age! But more than that: he was a moral lawgiver, though secretly and, so to say, anonymously. This at bottom is the mission of every inspired writer of comedy: Shakspere fulfilled it as well as Shaw, Ibsen as well as Nestroy; all are secretly teachers of custom-ethic.

The painters, too, were imbued with Cartesian principles — so much so in Poussin's case that he appeared too severe even to his contemporaries. It is characteristic of him that he learnt drawing from Classical reliefs. His figures have only types of

Painting and decoration

faces, they are mere specimens of a genus like plants in a herbarium. We never have, as in so many of the figures of Renaissance art, the impression of a personal acquaintance with them. Poussin was a learned painter, an accurate connoisseur of the Classical. He did the great service of bringing the landscape into the picture, but he did it as an archæologist: it is invariably a Classical scene that he paints. While on the stage long-dead Romans appeared in hoop-petticoats and wigs, on the canvas living nature wore toga and cothurnus: both are expressions of the fashionable Classicism, only of opposite sign.

Poussin saw everything mathematically: trees, with their exquisitely fine but geometrical silhouettes; rocks, with their magnificently clear and harmonious edges and surfaces modelled according to crystal-structure; circular lakes, clean-angled mountain chains, even cloud-formations, and the lines of human bodies systematically disposed as ornament. Yet with all this he was, strange to say, a mighty master of mood: a true Baroque painter, and the most forceful pioneer for the subtle Claude Lorrain and his virtuosity of light-treatment and foregrounds. With him Nature is genuine nature, but he paints her only in her domesticated, well-behaved, drawing-room moments. She is never wild and uncouth, never forgets herself so far as to be more than life-size, never seethes or bellows. It is that particular degree of Nature which can still be combined with Reason and good court-manners. Then there is Rigaud, chamberlain and master-of-the-robes-in-chief, as it were, of the age. He paints his men with the " correct " facial expressions and posture, coiffure and costume. They must stand, lean, and sit just so; stretch out their hands, carry their swords, clutch their cloaks with exactly the right effect and sense of proportion, with majesty and self-respect, masters of themselves as of others: every one a miniature Louis XIV.

The palace buildings also had exactly this physiognomy. The exteriors only aimed at being imposing in virtue of the same aloofness as characterized the King's pose, and their proud simplicity had almost the effect of shabbiness. The façade was kept unadorned, because this was the front that showed itself to the common people; but the halls within were of extravagant splendour. Floors were artistically parquetted, ceilings covered with choice paintings; from the walls there came a glow of costly coloured marble, rich stucco, velvet and brocade, silver, bronze, and, above all, gold — the symbol of the sun. Immense mirrors multiplied the effect. André Charles Boulle, *ébéniste du roi*, filled the rooms with console-tables, *guéridons* for candelabra, and ebony furniture decorated with marquetry in metal, tortoise-shell, mother of pearl, and ivory. The *Manufacture royale des meubles de la couronne* in Paris developed, under the court painter Lebrun, into a model factory for artistic cabinet-making. In 1680 Jacquin invented a method of producing artificial pearls, which came into very general use. Marble Herms, Tritons, Naiads, Atlases, and globes lent a stately air to the extensive grounds of the parks; rushing cascades precipitated themselves over wide stone steps; trees and hedges were given the shapes of vases, prisms, pyramids, and animal silhouettes, and sometimes positively formed rooms. It is interesting to hear of the *ascenseurs* of the time, which corresponded more or less to our lifts, but were used only in the larger palaces. An acute difference between their civilization and ours is evident here: theirs was in its essence unsocial; it would have occurred to no one that a new and practical invention could be utilized otherwise than to contribute to the comfort of the highest class of society.

Music was devoted chiefly to the service of drama. Jean Baptiste Lully (a Florentine, whose name was really Lulli) was the creator of grand opera, the *tragédie lyrique*. His librettist was Philippe Quinault, whose art ranked him above the great tragic dramatists in the public mind. Lully contrived to create a positive monopoly of opera for himself by obtaining a royal warrant forbidding any theatres except his own to employ more than two singers and six stringed instruments. He was not merely composer, but director, conductor, producer, and stage-manager into the bargain. His work, indeed, possessed him to such an extent that he is reported to have died of his passion for the theatre, the story being that in beating time furiously with his cane at a performance one day, he dealt himself a fatal wound on the foot. The chorus, which had sunk to being a mere accessory, was restored by him to its full significance. He gave the rhythmic element precedence over the melodic and used music solely to strengthen the effect of the word and to lend it emotional richness and depth. His art is declamation and rhetoric in the finest and most correct form, the very counterpart to that of Corneille and Racine, with which indeed it entered into deliberate and successful competition. It was fundamentally designed for recitation, without coloratura or true arias, but on the other hand with a magnificent equipment of scenery, ballet, costumes, women's and men's choruses in many parts (even behind the scenes), musical descriptions of storms at sea, battles, thunder-storms, volcanic eruptions, and the torments of hell. The *tragédie classique* was already music in a sense, responding as it did to the rhythmic currents which bore it along and moulded it; but in opera the will-to-style of the period reached its summit: there everything was ordered and clear, sonorous and pure, brightly and pleasantly cadenced. In such conditions the most successful music was bound to be that which most fully mathematized itself and absorbed the Cartesian spirit of symmetry.

La Rouche-foucauld If the age of Louis XIV were to be judged by its operas and tragedies, its buildings and paintings, its dissertations and sermons, the impression gained would be that of a race of heroes striding across the earth, grandiose but very dull heroes, bigger than life, but lacking souls. To find out what these people were really like we must go to the second category of their art and literature, their caricatures, lampoons, and satires, memoirs, anecdotes, and aphorisms. This was merely the natural result of the prevailing attitude towards life. For since, according to Descartes, the exclusive activity of the human mind consisted in thinking (whereas on the contrary real life exhibits just those stirrings that either have nothing to do with, or are directly opposed to, the activity of pure reason), this age was incapable of developing a psychology by way of its more important representative creations. Such a psychology was, one might say, officially forbidden and could, therefore, only be smuggled in as contraband under the harmless outer packing of disconnected occasional observations and irresponsible private collecting. And so it became the field of action of certain distinguished amateur writers whose works still live — everyone knows the portraits of La Bruyère, the memoirs of Saint-Simon, the letters of Madame de Sévigné. Out of the mass of these expressions of real life we will single out the one which speaks for all: the *Maxims* of the Duc de La Rochefoucauld.

La Rochefoucauld is the first real aphorist of modern times. His short sentences are compressed moral and psychological treatises. In them too there lives the *esprit géométrique*, which is seen in their razor-sharp antithesis, their crystallographic phrasing. He is none the less the man of the world and of the salon, even in point of style. His sketches are not merely witty, but also pleasing and graceful, elegant as drops of a choice perfume, the strong extract of the fragance left by many thousands of minor experiences. The author's philosophical system is very simple. Just as psycho-analysis explains everything on sexual grounds, so he derives all human actions from a single motive: namely, *l'orgueil, la vanité, l'amour-propre* (pride, vanity, self-love) : " many as are the discoveries that have been made in the realm of self-love, it still holds many an unexplored country "; " selfishness speaks all languages and plays all rôles, even that of unselfishness "; and " even virtue would not get so far did not vanity keep her company." And, because he is ever on the alert for the secret under-layer of vanity, he succeeds in rooting it out of its last hiding-place and catching and holding its most delicate nuances: " we should rather hear evil spoken of us than nothing at all "; " to decline praise is to ask for it twice over "; " we often pardon those whom we find tedious, but never those who find us tedious "; " whether philosophers regard life with affection or indifference is merely a matter of the direction taken by their vanity." Virtue, too, is only a form of vice: " the virtues lose themselves in selfishness as rivers in a sea "; " we are often only prevented from giving ourselves up to a particular vice because we possess several varieties "; " when the vices desert us, we flatter ourselves that we have shaken them off "; " old people give good advice by way of consoling themselves for no longer being able to give bad examples "; " the vices are an ingredient of the virtues just as poisons are an ingredient of remedies: prudence mixes and mitigates them and uses them with good effect to combat the ills of life "; " if love be judged by the majority of its works, it more resembles hatred than friendship," for " true love is like supernatural apparitions, which everyone speaks of, but only the very few have seen." Yet La Rochefoucauld is no cynic, but a sceptic full of secret aspirations. He is convinced that intellect cannot for long play the part of soul, and that the real *politesse de l'esprit* rests in "thinking nobly and delicately," that cunning and treachery arise solely from ineptitude, and that the surest way of being deceived is to believe oneself more artful than other people. A large number of his *bons mots* are distinguished by extreme delicacy, as, for instance: "It is a greater disgrace to mistrust our friends than to be deceived by them"; "To be in too great a hurry to clear off a debt is a sort of ingratitude"; "We are easily consoled for a friend's misfortunes when they give us an opportunity to show our love for him." This blending of frivolity and nobleness, harsh materialism and sensitive tactfulness, makes La Rochefoucauld the finest bloom of all the intellectual flora which sprang to life around Louis XIV. His saying: "Ridicule is more shaming than shame," mirrors the whole world of Versailles with all its light and shade, and he once summed up the whole of this culture in the words: "Every member of every class of society adopts a particular look and posture which shall make him appear what he wishes to be regarded as; we may say, therefore, that the world is made up of nothing but attitudes." And in fact we scan this race in vain for faces and spontaneous movements; wherever we look there is nothing but pose and gesture.

The Allonge The costume of the period illustrates this very clearly. It is exclusively for salon wear, designed for parade occasions, for persons perpetually "on show." The doublet disappears under the *justaucorps*, a richly embroidered gala coat, reaching to the knees, with wide sleeves, long cuffs, and enormous buttons. Ladies wore the full robe with tight bodice, a train — whose length might be six to forty feet according to the wearer's rank — and the *cul de Paris*, a padded bustle suggesting abnormal development behind. Boots gave way to buckled shoes, and gloves of fine white leather were indispensable for both sexes. The chief article of external apparel was, however, the *allonge* or large state wig, which was introduced in 1625 and universally worn by 1655. As the chancellor von Ludwig said, "it made men like lions," and that is why light brown or blond was the favourite colour. At about the same time there vanished the last indication of a beard, the "fly"; and all the world went clean-shaven. The feminine counterpart to the *allonge* was the *fontange*, a towering head-dress made of lace, ribbons, ruchings, and false hair, which not infrequently rose to a height of nearly five feet.

It was commonly held that the wig owed its origin to Louis XIII's baldness, and that the ladies, not to be left behind, seized upon the *fontange,* and that after that all Europe followed suit out of servility. Now, nothing could well be more feeble and incorrect than this. First of all, as we have just seen, it was not France that led the fashion in Europe at that time, but Holland; and, above all, a nonentity like Louis XIII was the last man likely to impose a costume on his generation. The cultural beginning of France set in only with Louis XIV, and he personally fought against the wig for many years — having fine long hair of his own — and first mounted one in 1673. Indeed, no monarch can ever create a fashion; he can but experiment with it and make himself ludicrous by so doing. The beard of the cut known as " *es ist erreicht,*" and the Austrian " imperial," only labelled their wearers as travelling wine-merchants and members of veterans' societies. The " Emperor Frederick " beard, on the other hand, which was no whit more ornamental, did not degrade, because it really happened to be the fashion that the spirit of the age demanded. It should also be remembered that the wig was at no time designed for the concealment of a lack of natural hair, like the present-day toupet, but was from the first an *article of dress,* adorning and completing the outward appearance in the manner of a plumed hat or scarf. Finally and emphatically, it would be idiotic to try to trace the cause of such a universal phenomenon as the wig to the bald head of an individual contemporary.

For the wig is the deepest symbol of seventeenth-century humanity. It enhances and it isolates (we shall see presently that these were the two underlying tendencies of the age) ; moreover, it imparts style, and that by its very unnaturalness. It was, for that matter, no novelty in history. The peoples of Hither Asia were familiar with it, and so above all were the Egyptians — they also a people whose culture was based on a supreme style-instinct, and who even used artificial beards. The same spirit of abstraction which created their pyramids and sphinxes insisted upon erections of elaborately plaited hair and square-cut beards made to hang on. The shallow nineteenth century regarded Egyptian art as primitive; nowadays we begin slowly to realize that in comparison with the inconceivable grandeur and depth of its creations it is the whole of Western art that appears primitive. By the same token we are bound to admit that that nation's customs as well were anything but " barbaric " and " childish," but rather the precipitate of a world-sense which, though certainly foreign to our own, may very well be superior to it. Both the Egyptian and the Cartesian wig are undeniably " paradoxical," but, then, every costume is a paradox, because it is the expression — developed to the point of caricature — of the ideal picture which humanity in every age makes of its own physical appearance. Every culture, for that matter, is a paradox, for it is the opposite of Nature, even when (as usually happens) it believes itself to be in agreement with her. All cultural creations, from the artist's visions and the philosopher's mind-figments to the most everyday forms, are paradoxical or, in other words, unpractical. A system of life in which everything superfluous and aimless, everything contrary to nature and logic, was rejected would no longer be a culture, but " pure civilization." But so pure a civilization is an almost unimaginable monstrosity. Never, in the history of humanity as we know it, has it been seen, and there exists the definite hope that in the future also it will never make its appearance in the world.

Coffee   The characteristic beverage of the mature Baroque was coffee, introduced into Europe about the middle of the century by the Arabs and Turks, who had long been acquainted with it. The first European coffee-house was the " Virginia," which was opened in London in 1652, and this gradually found imitators everywhere. It was in London too that the fashion arose for political parties, classes, and professions to have their own special coffee-houses: there were Papist and Puritan, Whig and Royalist coffee-houses, houses for dandies, for doctors, for prostitutes, and for artisans. Wills's famous coffee-house was the house of the littérateurs; there Dryden and his circle forgathered; and a poet whose verses won applause there was a made man for the coming season. Not until twenty years later were the first coffee-houses opened in France, and not until the beginning of the eighties did Germany follow suit. Once installed, however, they immediately became very popular. A particularly famous one was the first Vienna café, founded just after the siege by the Serbian envoy Kolschitzky with the captured stores of Turkish coffee. By about 1720 Paris had as many as three hundred coffee-houses, and already special rooms were reserved for play, billiards and ombre being the favourite games. On the other hand smoking was allowed only in the less polite establishments. It may even be said that coffee then played an even bigger part as a universal tonic than it does today. It is indeed very typical of that naturalist age, for it represents a stimulant that produces what may be called a *sober intoxication*. Voltaire, for instance, was a confirmed coffee-drinker. He may or may not have put away fifty cups a day, or rather a night, as he is said to have done, but he was certainly incapable of living and working without the beverage, and the effect of it is clearly seen in his nervous, transparent, overwrought, and, as it were, over-exposed manner of writing. Besides coffee there were other new foods and drinks. Fruit ices; sparkling wine (not yet, for a century, called " champagne "), the production of which only became possible with the introduction of corking; and chocolate, the favourite Mexican drink, to which Europe only began to accustom itself after someone had conceived the idea of sweetening it — poverty-stricken Spain in particular found in this a popular form of nourishment, and often enough the people's meal would consist of it alone. Yet this tea, coffee, and chocolate did not drive out alcohol. The Germans were still famous or infamous for their reckless drinking, and French and English did not lag far behind, whereas the southerners remained (as ever) relatively moderate. Finally, the fork, whose appearance, or non-appearance, has been noted from time to time, became recognized as a useful implement. From being mocked at as " affected " by the satirists of the first half of the century, it established itself at the French Court about 1650, and thenceforward it was generally accepted. Up till then meat had been conveyed to the mouth either by hand or — as was thought more elegant — by the knife. Another new custom was the taking off of hats. Previously the head-covering had been either not touched at all in greeting or had been merely pushed back on to the neck. On the score of cleanliness much was lacking even in the highest circles, and in this respect one perceives a definite set-back. The public baths, which existed everywhere in the declining Middle Ages and even at the Reformation, now disappear completely, and there was an almost entire lack even of private bathing-facilities. The toilet consisted normally of dipping the hands in water and dabbing the face with a little eau-de-Cologne. Underclothing was only changed at appallingly long intervals, and even the Sun-King's bed had its bugs. Under these circumstances it is only too easy to account for the extravagant use of every description of scent, hair-salve, and perfumed cosmetics.

The Post   Means of transport were still decidedly primitive. Only towards the end of the century was the carriage promoted to equality with the riding-horse, after its introduction had been violently opposed by the many who considered it a concession to effeminacy and a menace to horse-breeding. Big towns already had their cabs, known in Paris as *fiacres,* but the middle classes for the most part used the sedan-chair, although this again was at first widely disliked, from a sentiment that it was ignoble to employ men as beasts of burden. The upper classes kept magnificent coaches, which were accompanied by runners and drawn by at least four horses (in consequence not merely of the general tendency to self-importance and pomposity, but also of the bad condition of the roads). During that period, too, the posting system gradually developed, a regular service organized by the State or by large-scale proprietors, concessionaires such as the Taxis family, and providing for relays of horses at certain points. These posting stations usually also provided accommodation for the weary travellers, and so there arose the type of the " *Hôtel de la Poste,*" embryo of the modern hotel. The first comfortable travelling-coach, the light two-seater "berline," was built in Berlin in 1660 and copied all over Europe. The rate of travelling was very slow. A journey from London to Oxford, now covered in an hour by rail, lasted two days; and when it was found that a coach on a newly-organized route could cover the distance in thirteen hours, its extravagant speed earned for it the nickname of the " flying coach." It was quite usual for coaches to overturn, or to be held up by highwaymen. Communication by water was even more complicated and uncertain. A sea voyage of any length counted as an adventure, for shipwrecks and fights with pirates were looked upon almost as a matter of course and provided the main theme for nearly all the travel tales of the time. The accommodation in the close cabins was most unhygienic and the food (consisting exclusively of salt meat, flour, and dried vegetables) produced much sickness.

It was the merest chance whether one caught a connexion anywhere. But in the beginning of the eighteenth century a service
of packet-boats was organized, plying regularly between England
and the Continent, carrying at first only parcels and letters, but
later passengers also.

The establishment of a post was followed by the advent of
newspapers. At first these took the form of mere hand-written
communications, which the high-placed personages who received
them from special correspondents passed into circulation as
" gazettes." The first printed newspapers were handed out by the
postmasters, who were the foci of all the news. They usually
appeared weekly, and contained mere factual material without
comment or criticism, for they were strictly censored. All the
freer, therefore, the expression of sentiments in the secretly
distributed pamphlet literature which, from the Reformation
onward, constituted so powerful a political weapon. Dutch lam-
pooners in particular were the terror of every European government. The first weekly paper appeared in 1605 at Strassburg; the
first daily (the *Daily Courant*) nearly a century later in London.
Great importance attaches also to the learned periodicals: the
Parisian *Journal des savans*, the London *Philosophical Transactions*, the Roman *Giornale dei Letterati*, and the Leipzig *Acta
Eruditorum*.

The scientific life of the time shows an extraordinary development. Pascal's wonderful achievement we have seen already,
Spinoza's researches in biblical criticism were carried on by the
Parisian oratorian Richard Simon, who, though he took his outward stand definitely on the basis of tradition, displayed the
utmost boldness in his historical explanation of individual texts,
thereby bringing upon himself the violent animosity of Catholic,
and even more perhaps of Protestant, theologians. Mézeray
showed equal independence and critical eminence in his *Histoire
de France;* his program is the Boileau combination of the true
and the beautiful. Jean Mabillon became the founder of " diplomatic," or the scientific inquiry into historical sources, and Pierre
Bayle produced his learned and sagacious *Dictionnaire historique
et critique*, which is probably the most witty and amusing dictionary ever written. In it all the phenomena of State, Church, morals,
art, and science are " anatomized," as Bayle likes to phrase it,

thereby showing that the Cartesian analytical method ruled even in this hardened sceptic, to whom almost the entire French Enlightment can be traced. At the same time, this work did once more attempt — the last effort of the kind for a long period — to find a way back to the *credo quia absurdum* position. Bayle begins by exposing all the contradictions that exist between philosophy and religion, reason and revelation — the figures of the Old Testament were not always holy persons, while on the other hand men of stainless grandeur were found among the heathen and even among atheists; the fact of man's fall, again, is an insoluble paradox to our understanding, for either man is not free (in which case his action is no sin) or he is free (and God willed the sin, which is in contradiction with his goodness), or if he did not will it, but was merely unable to prevent it, then he is not omnipotent (which again is contrary to our conception of him). But out of all this Bayle draws the conclusion, not that faith is nothingness, but that reason is nothingness. Reason has to subject itself to religion, to believe without criticizing, and to realize, from the very fact that it cannot unite itself with revelation, to perceive at last its own impotence. So that, although Bayle is undoubtedly a sceptic, his scepticism is directed not towards religion, but towards philosophy. Nevertheless, in his effort to prop up blind faith, he had collected such a mass of reasoned objections to a positive Christianity that a result contrary to his expectations could not fail to ensue. The keen weapons of the well-stocked armoury were still there, even if the front was changed. And in fact this change of front was accomplished in the eighteenth century. Voltaire said of Bayle, very aptly, that not a line of his contained an attack on Christianity, but that there was not one that did not lead to doubt; so that, although not himself an unbeliever, he made unbelievers of others.

The
microscope The real glory of the seventeenth century was the building-up of the exact disciplines: it is the heroic age of natural science, not so much in the practical fields as in the conception of brilliant and comprehensive theories. Medicine was relatively the least advanced. The Paris school, ridiculed by Molière, recognized in essence but two universal remedies: blood-letting and " irrigation," the frequent use of which was not altogether unjustified, since the upper classes suffered almost without exception from

hyperæmia, owing to lack of exercise and lavish eating and drinking. The Dutch school pinned its faith to " polypharmacy," the use
of large quantities of the most varied medicaments, which often
had a directly opposite effect to that desired, but were in general
just harmless herbs. Even in such things as these we observe
the Baroque excess, the tendency to overloading, to flourishes,
and overwhelming quantity-effects. Descriptive natural philosophy made better progress: John Ray was the author of a comprehensive zoological system; he classified animals as vertebrate
and invertebrate — dividing the former into viviparous lung-
breathers, oviparous lung-breathers, and gill-breathers, and the
latter again into molluscs, crustaceans, shell-fish, and insects.
An advance of the first importance was the perfecting of the
microscope, which, although invented before the telescope, only
now came into extensive use. Through its aid Nehemiah Grew
discovered the ducts of the epidermis; Leeuwenhoek the Infusoria,
the papillæ of the inner skin, the faceted eyes of the insects,
and the striæ of the voluntary muscles; and Malpighi, besides the
red corpuscles of the blood, a whole series of anatomical details
that bear his name to this day (the "Malpighian network," a
mucous stratum under the epidermis; the "Malpighian corpuscles," peculiar branchings of the blood-vessels in the kidney of
mammals; the "Malpighian bodies," tiny lymph-glands in the
spleen; and the "Malpighian vessels," intestinal appendices
which in insects take the place, functionally, of the kidneys).
Nicolaus Stenonis established that the heart is the centre of the
blood-circulation, which had hitherto been supposed to lie in the
liver, and discovered the Stenonian duct of the ear. Time, too,
was subjected to a sort of microscopical investigation by Olaf
Römer, who was the first to measure the velocity of light.
Christian Huygens explained the double refraction of light in
Iceland spar, discovered Saturn's ring (which had already been
investigated by Galileo, but with contradictory results that had led
him to give up the task), invented the powder machine and the
pendulum clock, and made a conclusive inquiry into centrifugal
force, for which he obtained the formula MV^2/z (M being the
mass of a body in circular movement, V its velocity, and z the
radius of the circle). But above all he is the creator of the undulatory theory, which only achieved its victory over the Newtonian

corpuscular theory in the early nineteenth century. His assumption was that light is propagated by the vibrations of a special material, which is not the same as that by which sound is propagated (for the latter is nothing but air, and experiment shows that empty space does not convey sound-movement, whereas light passes through it without hindrance). This material different from air, " the æther," fills the whole universe, the infinite vault of heaven and the tiny interspaces between ponderable particles alike; it behaves perfectly elastically, possesses no weight, and is, therefore, not subject to the law of gravitation. (Newton on the contrary regarded light as a subtle material shot out by luminous bodies.) Huygens also declared against Newton's " forces acting at a distance," which he proposed to reinterpret by pressure- and impact-effects.

Newton   In Newton himself the age made a present to humanity of one of the greatest speculative geniuses that ever saw the light. As a mathematician, no less than as a physicist and astronomer, he constituted a revolution. In his *Optics* he demonstrated that white sunlight results from a combination of all the colours of the spectrum, and that the properties of the colours depend upon the differences of the light-rays. With the reflecting telescope that he himself built he made a series of astronomical discoveries that were big with consequences, and in his method of fluxions he became the discoverer of the infinitesimal calculus, by which infinitely small magnitudes and their imperceptible variations were made susceptible to exact calculation. The sum of his researches emerged in his all-embracing theory of gravitation. A falling apple directed his attention to the general force of attraction exerted by the earth's centre, and the assumption that the same force was the cause of the moon's movements, of the earth's revolving round the sun, and indeed of all the mechanical processes in the universe, gradually developed in the course of long years of study to a certainty. The law of gravitation, as set forth in his principal work: *Philosophiæ naturalis principia mathematica* is as follows: the force of attraction is directly proportional to the square of the distance. As all moons gravitate towards their planets, and all planets towards their suns, this law is valid for the entire universe. By the aid of this theory, too, it became possible to elucidate a whole series of cosmic movements that had hitherto been enigmatic

—— the perturbations of the elliptical paths of the planets, the inequality of the moon's motion, the ebb and flow of the tides. But Newton was too profound a thinker to draw materialistic conclusions from the results of his researches. It was precisely this admirable ordering of the universe that confirmed him in his belief in a divine founder and controller. He even tried his hand at theology and wrote a treatise on the prophet Daniel and the Apocalypse. In his last years he gave himself up almost exclusively to religious problems. Neither the almost superhuman achievements of his speculative powers, nor the extraordinary number of honours bestowed upon him in recognition of these during a long life, could rob him of his modesty. "*Evangelij simplicitatem moribus expressit,*" runs the inscription on his tomb in Westminster Abbey.

England at this time held the leading place in scientific development. Cromwell's system had crumbled at his death. The son of Charles I returned from banishment and ascended the throne as Charles II, amidst general rejoicing. He displayed a great interest in science, was a member of the Royal Society (to which the most prominent national scientists of the age belonged), busied himself with astronomy, and founded the famous observatory at Greenwich. He was tactful, good-natured, sociable, and extremely intelligent; his urbanity went so far as to lead him, after the night of his last battle with death, to make his excuses to those around him for being such an unconscionable time in dying. He danced, played ball, or told anecdotes, brilliantly; was a great patron of the arts, particularly the drama; but with all his amiable (and in some respects dazzling) qualities he remained internally a cold and soulless being, idle, frivolous, and entirely unprincipled, intent on nothing but the satisfaction of his ever-present unslakable thirst for pleasure. He even visited Parliament solely for amusement, and was wont to say that a political debate was as entertaining as a comedy. The licentiousness of his court was a byword in London, and it was not without an undertone of contempt that his people nicknamed him the Merry Monarch. One day, when the Earl of Shaftesbury waited on him, he remarked, smiling, that here was the most dissolute of all his subjects. "True, Your Majesty; of your subjects," replied Shaftesbury.

Though anything but a revengeful fanatic, Charles was equally far from possessing noble and passionate convictions. He had nothing of the senseless despotism-mania of the Stuarts, but neither had he any of their lively ambition. He regarded himself neither as absolute monarch by divine right, nor even as the responsible director of the nation's destiny. At bottom he was nothing. He was a man of peace, but purely from indolence; tolerant, but from superficiality. He had but one passion, and that the most harmless — and the lowest — namely, love of money. For money anything could be obtained of him: alliances, changes of faith, concessions to party despotism, concessions to the people's liberty, edicts of toleration, deeds of terror, declarations of war, or peace-treaties. He sold Dunkirk, his neutrality, his allies, his royal privileges, whatever was demanded of him. His extravagance only applied to his loose and vulgar amusements; when it was a question of reasonable sums for the upkeep of the State he was stingy. His officials followed his example and were of a corruptness hitherto unknown in England: the ministers in particular made vast fortunes in their official capacities. In other respects, too, his reign was unfortunate: there occurred, for instance, the unheard-of thing that an enemy fleet — the Dutch under Admiral de Ruyter — swept up the Thames and threatened England with invasion. Then a new and terrible outbreak of plague devoured the country, and a monstrous fire laid the whole city of London in ashes. It was precisely at that time that the doctrine of "passive obedience," advocated earlier by Filmer, won general acceptance — that the king has the power of a father over his children, he was responsible only to God and not to his subjects, who would not be justified in offering resistance to any manner of treatment the monarch chose to adopt. Yet never has such absolute subservience been rendered to a prince who desired it less, wanted it less, and knew less what to do with it.

The "Glorious Revolution" Charles II was succeeded by his brother James II, a zealous partisan of the Romanism to which Charles only confessed his adherence on his death-bed, and of the autocracy which he had shown no inclination to assume. The new King possessed all the bad, but none of the good, qualities of his predecessor, for he was malicious, stupid, and obstinate. Men of other faiths and political opponents he treated with cruel severity. He was supported by Judge Jeffreys, a grotesque monstrosity of a brutal, bloodthirsty drunkard, who is still execrated in England today, after over two hundred years, for his misdeeds; it was his boast that he had had more traitors executed than all his predecessors since the reign of William the Conqueror. James II was apparently a sadist like Henry VIII and also sexually perverse in other respects: he took only mistresses of exceptional ugliness. One of them, Catharine Sedley — who was witty into the bargain — once remarked that she did not know what he found in her to attract him: it could not be that he saw any beauty in her — since she had none — or any intelligence — since *he* had none. His method of argument was to meet all objections by repeating his own statement in the same words, believing that he had thereby won the debate. His daughter (later Queen Anne) did precisely the same, and Marlborough said she inherited it from her father. Here, however, as she was a woman, it is perhaps hardly necessary to bring in heredity as an explanation.

After he had for three years done everything possible to embitter even the most devoted and patient of his subjects, there came the "Glorious Revolution": his son-in-law William of Orange was unanimously summoned by Whig and Tory alike to take the throne. To reconcile the right to revolt with the duty of passive obedience was a simple matter for English "cant." The theologians explained that, although religion forbade any opposition to the king, the Commandments were not valid for every occasion: in certain cases it was permissible to put them aside. It was forbidden to kill, yet this general law allowed of exceptions in war; similarly, it was forbidden to swear, yet witnesses were bound to take the oath in court in the interests of truth. In the same way it was lawful in certain instances to resist godless princes: examples of this were to be found in the Old Testament itself. Others pointed out that it was not the people who had risen against James, but James who had risen against God, whose laws he had broken; that it was he who had failed to render unto Cæsar that which was Cæsar's. In spite of all this, however, William of Orange would not have reached his goal had he not had a most effective ally in James's own incredible narrow-mindedness and tactlessness. The new King's foreignness and sober reserve were not calculated to make him much more popular with the English than his forerunner; all the same, the complete devotion of his wife who as

James's daughter was in the nation's eyes the really legitimate ruler of England, made his precarious position easier, and in addition he was one of the greatest diplomats and generals of his time. As a Dutchman — and such he remained all his life — he recognized in Louis XIV the hereditary enemy. He therefore effected a complete change in English policy — which, on account of Charles's perpetual need of money and James's absolutist and Catholic tendencies, had till then stood under French influence — and brought into being that great coalition against France of which we have already spoken.

In the externals of civilization England was at that time little more advanced than the other countries of Europe. We have seen something already of the deplorable condition of the communications. Travelling by coach was slow and dangerous on account of the swamps, and costly on account of the strong teams required. The only way to make speed was to ride. In the towns streets were almost too narrow for carriages to pass, and goods were accordingly carried chiefly on go-carts, drawn by dogs. On the other hand, the inns were famed all over the world for their excellence, and letters were safely conveyed with a degree of punctuality and speed that was very striking in those times. The nobility still lived for the most part as country gentry in quite peasant-like conditions. Some idea of the lighting arrangements outside the capital may be gleaned from the fact that, as late as 1685, a private contractor named Edward Heming undertook for an annual sum to keep a light before every tenth house in London up till midnight. Most houses in the country were still built of wood, and the rooms had neither wall- nor floor-coverings and were painted with a mixture of lamp-black and beer. Strong beer formed the usual drink of the country gentleman. How customary it was to take on board quantities of liquor is vividly illustrated by the fact that an order of the time forbade courts martial to pronounce a death sentence except between the hours of 6 a.m. and 1 p.m. Obviously, the theory was that after dinner the gentlemen would be in no condition to assume the responsibility of so grave a decision. The men had few intellectual pursuits, their principal occupation being hunting, gambling, and politics. Women's education was on a still lower plane and showed a great falling-off in comparison with that of the ladies of Elizabethan times; for, whereas many of the latter had a knowledge of music, mathematics, and classics, the former could hardly spell and were capable at best only of doing needle-work and reading novels.

London was, however, by this time already a real capital, con- taining half a million people — the tenth part of the population of all England — while the two next biggest cities, Bristol and Nor-wich, had not quite thirty thousand inhabitants apiece. After the Great Fire the city was rebuilt by Sir Christopher Wren in an original and softened Renaissance style, which made it both far more imposing and far more comfortable than of old. Artistically, no less than politically, England was at this period more or less a vassal state of France. William Davenant, dramatist and the-atrical manager, reformed the stage by creating a pompous illu-sionist theatre in the Classical taste of Louis XIV, with a con-siderable use of musical aids. (He even arranged Shakspere's plays as " dramatic operas " with numerous musical interpola-tions.) John Dryden, the poet laureate of the day, emulated Boileau, Corneille, and Racine in a cold but brilliant art of verse, cleverly calculated to please the public taste of the moment. Dr. Johnson said of him that, like Augustus, he found a city of bricks and left a city of marble. But in the course of time Shak-spere's coarse bricks have proved more beautiful and lasting than the empty and unsolid marble splendour of Dryden. Nevertheless Rymer, William's historiographer, asserted at the time that a monkey knew more about nature and a baboon possessed more taste than Shakspere, and that in the neighing of a horse or the growling of a dog there was more living expression than in all Shakspere's tragic pathos.

The Puritans had always looked askance at the theatre, and eventually they had put a ban on it. On the return of the Stuarts a reaction naturally set in. Not only did the people throng to all the public amusements that had so recently been scorned; they also insisted on their being as riotous and licentious as possible. Not only were the old prudery and bigotry shaken off; but hon-ourable conduct and piety were looked on as a sheer disgrace and the surest sign of hypocrisy. In consequence of this, English comedy took on some extraordinary forms. Women, who even in the gay Elizabethan age had not been allowed to appear as ac-tresses, now took over the female parts, and it became a great game to put the coarsest ribaldries into their mouths. A whole generation of comedy-writers flooded the stage with the most daring obscenities. The hero, in nearly all these pieces, is the profligate who dashes from one seduction to another. In Wycherley's *Country Wife,* for instance, the leading figure is a man who passes himself off as a eunuch in order to win the confidence of husbands, a theme which provided for endless scenes in which young women, introduced to the hero, were delighted to find themselves mistaken. Yet literary history, which as we know is written exclusively by philistines, has been very unjust to Restoration comedy: it catches real moods and is full of clever intrigue and brilliant conversation, and actually it forms the basis of the English society comedy which, throughout its development through Sheridan and Goldsmith to Wilde and Shaw, forms one of England's greatest international claims to fame.

Locke The philosopher of the " Glorious Revolution " was John Locke, who represented in theology the standpoint of the liberal " latitudinarian " and in politics the case for parliamentary constitutionalism. In his *Letters on Toleration* he declares religion to be a private matter; in his *Treatises on Government* he demanded that the power of the State should be divided between the people and the king, in the precise manner actually adopted in the Bill of Rights of William III. In *Some Thoughts concerning Education* he argued in favour of a more natural form of education which should provide a practical preparation for a life devoted to the good of society. In his famous *Essay concerning Human Understanding* he formulated a system of empiricism and worked it out to its logical conclusions. His answer to the question: Whence comes all the stuff of reason and knowledge? is the one word " experience." He argued that no " innate " ideas existed, as is demonstrated in the slow development of the child, which only gradually attains to abstract conceptions through individual experiences; that the human mind was nothing but the faculty of receiving impressions, a piece of wax, an unwritten page, a dark room, able to take in pictures from outside through certain openings and to fix them. Perception may be outward or inward, according to whether it is concerned with our objects or our conditions; in the one case he calls it " sensation," in the other " reflection." All perceptions, internal and external, are merely ideas; therefore we can perceive only the qualities and not the substance of things, their phenomena, but not their being. He considered, however, that even this relative knowledge sufficed for the needs of life and the ordering of our actions. The existence of God is demonstrated directly from the existence and nature of the world; the maxims of morality can be demonstrated with the same precision as the rules of arithmetic. In Locke we have the first genuinely English philosophy, which embraced all the decisive national characteristics: it is deistic and moralist, democratic and practical, a triumph of sound human understanding, of the golden mean and the truth of facts; we shall often meet it again in its varied forms.

England was the sole European great power that emancipated herself from the contemporary absolutism; Germany, on the contrary, may almost be said to have swallowed it whole. The reverence of the Germans for even their smallest potentates was boundless. A publicist wrote to the duodecimo prince Ernst Ludwig of Hesse: " If God were not God, who would have more right to be God than Your Princely Serenity? " And even before officials — of whom Christian Wolff said that as the monarch's assistants they should be regarded as " princes in miniature " — people almost died of awe. In consequence of the theory of state omnipotence, sovereigns felt themselves privileged, and indeed obliged, to interfere in everything, surpervising and correcting the entire private life of citizens like tyrannical fathers of families or form-masters. Even the *Acta Eruditorum,* Germany's only scientific publication of those days, announced that nothing that concerns the rights and the actions of princes would be criticized in its columns. The king's subjects bent the knee not only to his person, but even to his empty carriage when they met it in the street. It was at this time, too, that the army of court offices was established — chamberlain, chaplain, medicus, master of the stables, master of the hunt, master of the ceremonies. Tradesmen regarded it as the highest honour to be appointed court baker, tailor, shoemaker, or gardener. The untitled, the bourgeoisie and the common people, were despised as *roturiers,* existing merely for the purpose of supplying money, soldiers, and hands to the court. It was not that they were treated with cruelty: they were merely considered as creatures of a different order with correspondingly different duties and different rights — or, rather, no rights at all. Macaulay says, very aptly, that Louis XIV had no scruples about sacrificing his subjects, because he regarded them at best with the feeling one has for an overworked post-horse or a hungry robin. It was a result of the gallicizing of Germany that this outlook came to prevail in that country also. " French clothes," says Christian Thomasius, " French dishes, French furniture, French talk, French manners, French sins, French diseases even, are all the rage." This same Thomasius is one of the few credit entries in the account of German intellectual life at that period. He was one of the earliest and most passionate opponents of the torture-chamber and of witch trials, the first eminent man of learning to write and lecture in German, and editor of the first popular German periodical — " Free-spoken, grave and gay, yet reasonable and lawful Thoughts, or Monthly Confessions upon everything, especially upon new books." In this organ, for nearly half a century, he fought against the evils of his people and his age. His style was still in the bombastic and heavy mode and interlarded with French phrases, but his wit and insight and his amazing boldness enabled him to battle successfully against the pedantry and self-satisfaction of the professors, the intolerance of the clergy, the charlatanism of the doctors, the pettifogging of the lawyers, the coarse morals of the students, the dishonesty of tradesmen, the laziness of artisans, the loose living of the nobility, and much besides. His chief exhortation is that men should strive after *honnêteté*, learning, *beauté d'esprit, un bon goût,* and gallantry ; his exclusive criterion of values is : " their use and availability for life." Thus he is the father of the German Enlightenment — and that at a time when courage and originality were still very necessary if such principles were to be championed — and the father of German journalism in that he first undertook to treat intellectual problems in a form that should be comprehensible and inspiring to all. Beside him there is very little worth mentioning, unless it be the Pietists, whose efforts conquered the zealotism and hair-splitting of the theological mind and gave the nation a practical Christianity of brotherliness and simplicity ; and the splendid sermons of Abraham a Sancta Clara, that *cabaretier* of the pulpit. In Thomasius we find the whole of the Thirty Years' War with its plunderings, its killing, its violation of women, its primitive mother-wit of brutal men here today and gone tomorrow. He followed the customs of the day in his dealings with the German language: laying it mercilessly under contribution for his imagery, ravishing it in his parables, and using it as a pole-axe in his moral lectures.

In this period also occurred the first rise of the state of Brandenburg-Prussia, which the Great Elector elevated to a European power. By pursuing a policy both shrewd and perfidious he freed the duchy of Prussia from the overlordship of Poland, and by overthrowing the Estates — a process attended by great brutalities and illegalities — he established unlimited monarchy in his lands. For the external security of his government, and for protection against the ever-present threat of Sweden — then a great power — he created the standing army, the *miles perpetuus*. He constructed the Friedrich Wilhelm Canal, which connected the Elbe with the Oder; organized his own posting system, which was far quicker than that of the Taxis business; improved the fiscal and educational system; established the university of Duisburg; promoted agriculture, cattle-breeding, and the reclamation of marshland; enlarged and beautified his capital (amongst other things by the Schlossbibliothek and the avenues of trees in front of the Schlossbrücke, which received the name: " Unter den Linden "); ran a small navy (which, however, went to pieces under his successor); and even founded a trading colony with a fort on the Gold Coast of Guinea. In his religious policy he was guided by the greatest tolerance. Himself a member of the Reformed Church, he extended complete freedom, not only to Lutherans and Catholics, but also to Socinians and Mennonites, and his Edict of Potsdam invited all who were persecuted to come under his protection. As a consequence of this the Huguenots in particular came into the country in great numbers, and rendered highly valuable services as engineers and architects, merchants and financiers.

Frederick William was doubtless one of the strongest political personalities of his age. But the whole age was very fruitful in outstanding personalities. One of these — and the chief — was Prince Eugene, who, though originally destined for the Church on account of his insignificant figure and shy manner, became one of the most brilliant generals of his century. His victories at Zenta and Peterwardein, Blenheim and Turin, Oudenarde and Malplaquet roused the astonishment of all Europe and had the result of securing to the Habsburg monarchy Italy and the Netherlands,

Hungary and Siebenbürgen, Serbia and Wallachia. At the same time he was the most supple and far-seeing of diplomats. Had his counsels of moderation been followed, the Spanish Succession War would have been concluded earlier, and on terms more advantageous to the Emperor, than was possible after the great political revulsion had set in. He was, moreover, the only Austrian statesman to recognize that the Habsburg empire could only maintain itself permanently as a great power if it possessed colonies and an adequate fleet; it was his idea, therefore, to build a considerable fleet, with Ostend and Trieste as bases. With all this, he was a true friend of the arts and sciences, not from the empty desire to shine which inspired most of the rulers of his time, but out of a genuine desire and profound appreciation. His collections of precious coins and gems, paintings and engravings, showed the ripest expert knowledge and the finest taste. Leibniz's chief work, the *Monadologie*, is not only dedicated to him, but was actually inspired by him; the two most brilliant architects of Austrian Baroque were employed to build for him, Fischer von Erlach being responsible for the noble, smiling Stadtpalais, and Lukas von Hildebrand for the summer residence of Belvedere, coquettish and original, set in wonderful harmony with its park and lake. The Prince was a true product of the Baroque: he had that sublime sobriety which is ever the stamp of great leaders of destiny, and he was full of secret yearning for those gay, confusing, narcotic things which alone make life desirable and interesting. He had a strong, enlightened mind that knew its course, and yet scented the fascination of enigmatic nature.

Another highly original figure was Queen Christina of Sweden, one of the most widely discussed personalities of her century. In appearance she was not beautiful, but interesting. The forced masculinity of her manner and tastes made her notorious everywhere, and even led to the assumption that she was a hermaphrodite. Knowing what was rumoured of her, she once deliberately overturned her carriage when driving and lay on the ground with her skirts up, crying to the lackeys who came hurrying to the spot: "Don't be shy. Come closer and convince yourselves that I am no hermaphrodite." She wore her hair cut short, was a passionate horsewoman, fencer, and hunter, and liked to compare herself with the Queen of Sheba. She took the greatest interest in the sciences, particularly in mathematics and astronomy; she knew eight languages, corresponded with Pascal, summoned Descartes to her court to assist her in founding an academy, and herself wrote numerous *Pensées*. She was the first sovereign to suppress trials for witchcraft. Tiring of her throne, she abdicated and went to Rome, where she embraced the Catholic religion. Her own sense of her position assumed such preposterous proportions as to amaze her own contemporaries. She dedicated her book *Histoire de la Reine Christine* to God, because no one on earth was worthy of the honour. In her letters she repeatedly declared herself to be greater than any other mortal and that she felt every other earthly being far beneath her. One of the medals which she had struck bore her head on the front and a sun on the back, with the inscription: " *Non sit tamen inde minor,*" the meaning being that she, by leaving her kingdom, forfeited as little of her greatness as the sun by leaving the earth. This self-consciousness, which verged on the pathological, reappeared with fantastic results in Charles XII — most unhappily for Sweden.

One of the outstanding events of the age was Russia's entry into world-history, and this again is traceable to a single personality. Up to the time of Peter the Great, Russia had been a Christian-oriental state; indeed, it is said that at the moment of abandoning paganism it was mainly the fact that Mohammedanism banned alcohol that turned the scale for Christianity. After the conquest of Constantinople by the Turks, the Greek Church transferred its centre to Moscow, and Russia took over the inheritance of Eastern Rome. But it was already essentially a Byzantine empire in respect of its adoration of the sovereign, its rigorous and absurd court etiquette, its perpetual palace revolutions and tumultuous dethronements, its despotic priesthood, and its bizarre and magnificent architecture. At the same time the Mongol domination, which lasted a quarter of a millennium, had bred in the people that spirit of submission and slavery which has determined its history through all the later phases down to the present day — for the Soviet régime is itself nothing but a Tsarism of the left. As a matter of fact, the seed of the Bolshevistic tendency had been in the Russian peasantry from time immemorial, since the arable land had for many centuries been common ground. In the monotony and uniformity of the Russian plains we see the symbol and foundation both of the patient passivity and of the communistic potentialities of this nation. Towards the end of the fifteenth century the great political expansion set in. In 1480 Ivan the Great succeeded in throwing off the Tatar yoke. Some two generations after, Ivan the Terrible occupied Kazan and Astrakhan; within the same century the conquest of Siberia had begun; by about 1650 the invader had reached the Pacific Ocean, and in 1667 the greater part of the Ukraine passed from Poland to Russia.

This, then, was the nation whose face Peter the Great forcibly turned towards the West: a nation fitted, as it seemed, in every way to spread itself slowly but insistently southward and eastward, and gradually to swallow up Turkey, Persia, India — nay, even China itself. A " window into Europe " was Peter's lifelong ambition. In the course of the long and eventful Northern War, when Russia, Sweden, Denmark, and Saxony-Poland fought for the possession of the Baltic, he succeeded in annexing Livonia, Estonia, Ingermanland, and Karelia. He was thus able to penetrate to the Baltic and beat down Sweden into the position of a second-rate sea-power. While the war was still in progress he founded St. Petersburg, the city he designed to be his capital, and provided it with factories, hospitals, barracks, libraries, theatres, and other Western features. With the bloody suppression of the Strelitz, who had raised themselves under his predecessors to the position of a powerful Prætorian Guard, and of the conspiracies of his own family and the discontented nobility, he became the real founder of Tsarism. The same violent tactics were employed to plant Western culture throughout the land. He brought in foreign officers, merchants, professors, and artists; forbade the wearing of beards and oriental dress, introduced the Julian calendar (dates having previously been reckoned from the Creation of the World), built the Ladoga Canal, limited the number of monasteries, dragged women out of their harem-like existence, ordered his nobles abroad for the purpose of study, and forced the people to attend the new schools. Yet, for all his greatness, farsightedness, and terribleness, he remains to a great extent a grotesque figure, with his frequent paroxysms of rage and epileptic fits, his dress that was never quite that of the finished European, but had always the look of a stage costume, and his three constant companions: the monkey on his shoulder, the grinning court-jester, and the flask of spirits that he distilled himself.

Peter's over-hurried reforms were, on a broad view, anything but a blessing to the Russians. As a nation they had only just arrived at their Middle Ages, and they were flung forcibly and without preparation into the cultured condition of a highly developed Baroque world. At bottom what Petrinism achieved was one more victory for the Cartesian spirit; for within one generation, by the aid of a preconceived formula, it conjured up a European capital with a stamp of the foot, transformed a theocratic peasant state into bureaucratic sea state, and civilized and Westernized a race of barbaric Orientals. Catherine the Great and most of the later Russian autocrats carried on this perverse program of inorganic Europeanization. And its final phase is Bolshevism. Lenin admitted this himself when he described Peter the Great as his political ancestor and the first revolutionary to sit on a throne, and for the same reason he opposed the renaming of the city of Petrograd by his own name. Petrinism and Leninism represent the opening and finale of a single great act of violence perpetrated on the Russian soul. The effect of it has been to make a deep and probably irremediable rupture in the development of this nation. One does not jump over a thousand years with impunity. Even now the Russian is mediæval man in a European family of nations. Accordingly it is only in Russia that we find genuine expressionism, genuine collectivism, prophets such as Tolstoi, and saints such as Dostoievski. But as, from Peter the Great on, Russia has also consistently adopted every modernism of the day, the life of the Russian soul has been one great psychosis. In a dull consciousness of this overwhelming fact the Bolshevists had recourse to the extraordinary measure of getting rid of the soul altogether: again a truly Russian solution, but signifying, of course, but the beginning of new and more terrible tragedy.

Looking back once more, we see, broadly outlined, this picture: for about half a century all Europe lies in the shade of the Sun-King; but on the borders — in Russia, Prussia, and England — new forces are secretly growing, and by the time Louis has finished his task, the world has a totally different aspect.

It must be remembered, however, that even during the period when France's cultural hegemony was absolute, there was a difference between the Baroque of France and that of the rest of Europe. As was pointed out in the first volume, France was the sole European country to take over and permanently to adopt in their entirety the style-principles of the Italian (which may equally well be called the Latin or the Classicist) Renaissance. In Cartesianism, which was destined from that time on to remain — with such changes as the times necessitated — the legitimate French form of intellect, this measured, clear, and well-proportioned attitude towards life found its most finished expression. Yet the Baroque is, as we said in the last chapter, anything but an unbroken rationalism: it is inspired by a general and indefinite will to intoxication and haze, twilight, and darkness, a secret yearning for the underworlds of the soul into which the sun of Reason never shines. French Baroque is therefore not pure Baroque, and non-French Cartesianism is not pure Cartesianism. France has remained fundamentally Classicist for four centuries from the High Renaissance: whether in Calvinism or Jesuitism, Baroque or Rococo, Revolution or Romanticism — it is always *clarté* which wins the day. Hence Cartesianism is on French soil the true local colour of intellectual life, in other countries it is only a fine transparent glaze. Or in other words: in France, throughout all the changing times (including therefore the Baroque), Cartesianism forms the common denominator, and the tendency of the age the numerator; whereas for the rest of Europe it was, on the other hand, the spirit of Baroque which stood for the common denominator, while the prevailing Cartesianism was only put up as a fashionable numerator. In France the world-feeling is a Baroque-tinted Classicism; in other countries, an irrationalism impregnated with Cartesianism — or, one might say, Berninianism. The position, however, was far more complicated than this formula implies: for, on the one hand, the French of that day were also true Baroque men in one corner of their soul, and, on the other, rationalism was stamped on all their contemporaries not merely by the cultural hegemony of France, but also as an inborn ingredient (and one of the strongest) of Modern Age man.

World-fictions   The various races and ages may, in fact, be classified according to the extent to which they conceive of the world as a reality or as a delusion. All unsophisticated races do the former: the world is for them something to be partly overcome, partly endured; and we find the same reaction in the Romans, though they were, among all the civilized nations, perhaps the only complete realists. In the second group there are many varieties. Men conceived of the world as a work of art, a *beautiful* delusion; as a world transfigured and purified of all that is ugly and gross; this was what the Greeks did. Or as a *logical* delusion: as a simplified, schematized, linearized world; this possibly the Egyptians did. Or a mere hallucination, a *pathological* delusion: this was the case with the Indians. Or as a *magical* delusion: as the scene of supernatural and transcendent forces; this, as we have seen, was the world-outlook of the Middle Ages.

All these variants are found combined to a certain degree in Baroque. We have laid stress on the fact that it æstheticized the whole of existence by living as if life were a game; it attempted to subject reality to the power of pure logic, it dissolved the world in a dream and experienced it as a *theatrum Dei;* and, heterogeneous as these varying aspects may seem, it welded them into one cultural phase and one that possessed a uniformity which few others could boast.

One of the strongest of the rivets that at first held this culture firmly together in all its vital manifestations was its extreme cult of form, in which both its geometrical mind and its will-to-illusion found expression. It is at this point that Cartesian rationalism and Berninian irrationalism intersect: in both there is the passionate determination to achieve the triumph of form over matter, and indeed to reduce matter to mere form. The Baroque age stands out in world-history not only as one of those which most delighted in form and possessed most power over it, but as one of those most distinguished for their formality and obedience to form. Even in externals we see its striving towards stiff detachment, the ideal of which the wig was the insistent symbol; quick movements and impulsive actions are rendered simply impossible by the costume: everything — walk, gestures, expression of feeling, carriage — is captured in a grid of invisible co-ordinates. Improvised talk and writing are equally impossible: not only the permissible topics, but even the words in which they are to be discussed are laid down. If any other words were used it would be ascribed, not to originality, but to lack of taste and artistic tact. On the other hand, those who fulfilled the conditions most successfully were

The ideal of corpulence

125

considered the most intelligent; for to be intelligent means to help towards the triumph of form. The high-heeled shoe, the long waist-coat, the enormous sleeves and buttons: these and similar details of dress were designed to heighten the outward impression of dignity and gravity. Corpulence came into fashion at that time for the same reason. If we examine the typical appearance of the corpulent man — his big flushed face with pouched cheeks and double chin, his barrel-shaped figure, his slow arm-movements, his circumspect gait with head erect and the upper part of the body thrown backward, his weary and passionless expression — we have the exact bodily *habitus* cherished as an ideal by Baroque man. The manner of fat people often strikes us as affected when no such affectation is intended, but these people *wished* to look affected — or, rather, the point which for us is the beginning of mannerism was to them but the beginning of politeness. Besides wig, dress-coat, and the straddling attitude, the walking-stick also played its part; crowned with an immense knob, it served no useful purpose save as a part of the costume, and as such it was retained even in the salon.

The isolated individual

Since form can, up to a point, be learnt, it came to be accepted that everything could be attained through perseverance and study, or at least that thoroughly self-conscious virtuosity founded on strict science was the tool to be applied to all cases. It was the high tide of poeticalness and of correct works of art, of painting, gardens, dramas, treatises, all laid out with compass and ruler. The strongest, most essential function of reason is, however, its power to analyse; that is, to solve, divide, differentiate, isolate. And in truth we see that in those days there were really only isolated individuals. Men formed among themselves mere aggregates, no real unions. Guilds were honeycombs of detail-regulation, and rigidly exclusive. The bread-baker might not bake cakes, the smith could manufacture no nails, the tailor sell no furs; saddlery and harness-making, shoe-making and slipper-making, hat-making and feather-dressing were all separate trades. The hierarchy of the Estates was meticulously insisted upon. The court was completely cut off from the rest of mankind, and above the court stood the sovereign, he again completely isolated — *absolute*. These same conditions gave birth to the " social contract " theory, according to which the State was formed by the voluntary coming together of perfectly independent persons. The atomic theory of Nature too, under which all physical phenomena resolve themselves into a movement of minute isolated particles, became generally accepted; and even that mightiest achievement of the age, the theory of gravitation, was also in the highest degree representative of this prevailing attitude to life. The Newtonian bodies do not touch one another, but are steered by mysterious distant forces singly through empty space — for if Newton did not explicitly posit the *actio in distans*, belief in it dominated his whole school; for them, at any rate, the idea was a logical consequence of his system, and, indeed, it is not impossible that Newton himself thought of atoms as separated by infinitely small but unbridgable spaces.

As to the painting, one might readily believe that it expressed a world-feeling entirely opposed to this; but this is only so in appearance. We have said in the foregoing chapter that Baroque smudges the contours, making them indefinite and unclear; but it does not yet go so far as to dissolve them. Though it has become impossible to take a knife and cut the figures out of the picture, yet the aura of light in which their outlines float acts as an isolating agent, as a bounding zone if not as a bounding line. With Baroque painters light is still bound up with the objects around which it plays; it is not yet a fully dissolved, independent free light, not yet *Freilicht*. Each object lives like a monad in its mysterious cone of light, undefined, infinite, and infinitesimal, a little universe, but one for itself. The harmony which it achieves with other objects is still a matter of external pre-adjustment by the artist, precisely as in the Renaissance; but more wavering, hovering, problematical, mystical, " religious."

One discipline there was which rose in this period to the height of a science: namely, mechanics. And this is very characteristic; for to explain a thing absolutely according to reason means to explain it mechanically. Now, the ideal which haunted that age consisted in the extension of the mechanical principle to life and the entire system of the universe; to the end that it might be taken to pieces like a machine, its parts explained, and all its movements calculated. To that same ideal we may trace the fact that the men of that age modelled their behaviour and bearing on wire-pulled puppets. Let us take this for the moment quite literally. Crinolines, coat-skirts, waistcoats, cuffs, and wigs were all stiffened with wire.

127

And so we come up against a fact which, possibly, contains the very key to the Baroque soul — its Platonic Idea is the *Marionette*. The rigid garments which sought to reduce the impression of the three-dimensional human body to effects of line: the deep circular bowings, deliberately angular movements, geometrical postures in standing and sitting that always tended to achieve effects of angle, the monstrous *dead* wig, which gave the head a grimacing effect; all these things lead up involuntarily to the suggestion of a puppet-show. Descartes had set up the theory that the human body was a machine. And Molière had dramatized the mechanistic psychology — his figures are spectral automata which he sets in motion from outside. This holds good even for his treatment of the dialogue, which delights in short sentences and counter-sentences, merciless staccato and sharply rapped-out delivery; highly effective speech-duels, but reminding one of the familiar tin clowns hanging on to a pump: when you pull the one, up goes the other and vice versa. The action also is controlled by a perfectly mechanical causality, which is fantastic and grotesque precisely because it functions so promptly and punctually, as it never does in real life: it is an arithmetical, plotted, chess-men's causality.

The case of Molière, however, suffices to warn us that it would be a huge error to jump to the conclusion that this idealization of the marionette went with insipidity and soullessness. Kleist writes very illuminatingly on the problem of the marionette theatre in his uncommonly clever little treatise entitled: *Über das Marionettentheater* (1810). The marionette, he says, is superior to most human beings as regards equilibrium, mobility, and lightness because its soul is always in the centre of gravity of its motion: " since the mechanic through his wires has no power over any other point than this, the other limbs are — as they should be — dead, mere pendulums obeying the law of gravity." He maintains that more grace can exist in a mechanical jointed man than in the structure of the human body; that in this regard it is simply impossible for a man to attain equality with the puppet. And he concludes thus: " We see that in proportion as in the organic world the reflection becomes darker and dimmer, the grace inherent in it becomes more and more brilliant and commanding. And just as when . . . the picture in a concave mirror, after retreating into infinity, suddenly reappears close before our eyes, so, when knowledge has as it were passed through an infinite, grace again makes an appearance; it therefore appears at its purest at once in that bodily structure which has either no consciousness at all or an infinite consciousness: that is, in a puppet or, equally, in a god." Such were the gods that Baroque man aspired to become. Out of his "infinite consciousness," out of his almost painful sharpness and superclarity of thought he created the ideal of the marionette, in which, as Worringer somewhere points out, are combined "abstraction on the one hand and strongest expression on the other." The marionette is at once the most abstract and the most passionate of images: and in this paradox the riddle of Baroque man is propounded and solved.

But just because every person in those days led an entirely solitary existence, he made of his own life a thing of hitherto unheard-of refinement and complication. Everyone was a world only to himself, it is true, but it *was* a world, a microcosm. It is anything but an accident that just at that time the microscope came greatly into prominence. A new realm of the infinitely little was opened up, a wealth of astonishing perspectives, all gained by a loving concentration upon infinite detail. The Infinitesimal Calculus, too, belongs with all this, and (what is more significant still) man began to develop a scent for differentials even in the domain of psychology. As the sphere began to be conceived as the sum of innumerable cones, so the human soul began to be thought of as the aggregate of innumerable small conceptions. There arose in consequence a sort of microscopy of the soul, which, it must be admitted, not infrequently degenerated into intellectual myopia. Baroque man had it in his blood, this subtlety and complexity, this overdone preference for miniatures and trifles. Together with an unparalleled enthusiasm for sculpture — which, though the most rigid and monumental of the arts, was chosen as a means to express passionate ecstasies and tenderest, subtlest emotions — we find an almost pathological craze for trifles: wherever we look, we see a mishmash of pillars, bosses, scrolls, garlands, conchs, and fruit-festoons. The curling, twisting process was applied to Nature herself: gardens were filled with cascades, terraces, grottoes, urns, glass balls, and freak fountains. Dresses bristled with passementerie, lace, galloon, and brocade; and everyday speech was carried on all in quibbles and ingenious antitheses. Even the face had to have its ornament, the indispensable beauty-patch. The whole world-picture of the period is a mosaic of *perceptions petites,* of infinitely small imaginings, and every individual is a monad, self-contained, without windows, alone in his isolated plane within an elaborately graded cosmos — which is to him the best of worlds, in that its course is in every respect pre-established and pre-determined and it runs as smoothly and mechanically as clock-work. For with that age it was a profound inner conviction that the most marvellous and beautiful, the most artistic and ingenious of all things was a clock that went well.

Leibniz   It may have been remarked that we have already made use of some expressions taken from the philosophy of Leibniz. And, in truth, no one has expressed the meaning of the Baroque more profoundly or more completely than Leibniz in his doctrine of Monads. In it Baroque man stands before us, grasped in his inmost essence, detached from all external accident. For Leibniz is Baroque through and through: in his literary style, which is that of a philosophic *pointilliste* who carried on, as it were, the trade of an intellectual lace-maker; in his character, which was bizarre, crotchety, particular — in fact, "baroque," as we use the word today — and even in his outward appearance, for his enormous bald head was crowned with a growth the size of a pigeon's egg. Truly Baroque, too, was his multitude of occupations, arising out of a curious form of many-sidedness which never left him time to collect his forces in one *magnum opus.* Diderot said of him that he brought as much fame to Germany as Plato, Aristotle, and Archimedes all together to Greece; and Frederick the Great declared him to have been a whole academy in his own person — thereby differing, as on so many other points, from his father, who described him as a good-for-nothing fellow not even fit for sentry-go.

Leibniz discovered, for the second time, and independently of Newton, the Differential Calculus; improved it considerably in its application, and by means of it arrived at the formula $\frac{1}{2}mv^2$ for kinetic energy; while as to this kinetic energy itself he recognized, even thus early, that its quantity in the universe remains always the same. He busied himself with mining and geology, wrote a history of the earth, took part in the preparation of phosphorus, worked at the improvement of watches and the invention of ships which could sail against the wind and under water, began a critical history of the Welfs, and edited large collections of mediæval historical sources and documents on international law. In addition he wrote a series of striking political memoirs, among them one addressed to Louis XIV, in which, with marvellous historical vision, he propounded the very scheme for the conquest of Egypt that was carried out by Napoleon a century and a quarter later. He also wrote long letters and drew up schemes for the union of the Latin and the Greek, the Catholic and the Protestant, the Lutheran and the Reformed Churches, and for the founding of learned societies in Berlin, Dresden, Vienna, and Petersburg, hoping thus to bring to fulfilment his grand dream of a European republic of learning. It can be said that there was literally nothing which did not arouse in him a fruitful interest. He once said of himself: " It may sound strange, but I approve of everything I read, for I know well in how many different ways things can be grasped." This generous, humane, and fundamentally artistic approval of everything that is lies at the root of his matchless universality and his whole philosophy. He was in correspondence with numerous outstanding contemporaries, among them Arnauld, Bossuet, Malebranche, Bayle, Guericke, and Hobbes; and it was chiefly in these letters — which he wrote with the utmost care, sometimes three times over — and in the essays which he contributed to the leading scientific journals (particularly the *Acta Eruditorum* and the *Journal des savans*) that he expounded his philosophy. In his lifetime only one book of his appeared: the *Essais de théodicée sur la bonté de Dieu, la liberté de l'homme et l'origine du mal.*

Frederick the Great, in his witty extravagant way, called Leibniz's system a philosophical novel. It is a spacious, well-developed construction in many parts, albeit over-decorated with flourishes and ornaments; a profound irrationalism, but one born of Reason. The Leibniz system might well bear as its motto the Faustian phrase: " In the beginning was force." Force is the basic substance of all minds and bodies. It lies in the nature of force, however, that it is active, perpetually active, and that it expresses itself and its individual quality through that activity. Force, therefore, is individuality, it is life, and hence there is nothing in the world that is unfruitful and dead. Every bit of matter can be regarded as " a garden full of plants or a pond full of fish," and "every branch of the plant, every limb of the animal, every drop of moisture is again such a garden and such a pond." Each of these world-units, which Leibniz calls "monads," is "a world in little," "a living mirror of the universe," "a concentrated universe": it has no windows through which anything shines into it; rather is it a mirror which represents the picture of the universe by its own force, "actively." These monads form a graded world. There are as many monads as there are differences of "clear and distinct" perceptions, degrees of consciousness. In this progressive series of infinitely small differences there is never a leap and never a repetition. "As one and the same city, viewed from different sides, varies in its aspect, and thus is as it were perspectively multiplied, so the endless number of monads can give rise to the appearance of innumerable different worlds; these are, however, but perspectives of a single world seen from the different points of view of the monads." And, correspondingly, it was Baroque painting that first put on canvas such "*points de vue*," by means of its new technique of shading-off, perspective, and chiaroscuro.

But the grandest and most fertile of Leibniz's conceptions is his theory of unconscious perceptions. He distinguishes between "perception" and "apperception," explaining this distinction by the analogy of the sound of waves. The roar of the sea is composed of the beating of individual waves. Each of these individual sounds is in itself too small for us to hear; we receive it without taking note of it; we perceive, but do not apperceive it. The sensation aroused by the motion of the individual waves is a weak, indistinct, infinitely small perception, "*une perception petite, insensible, imperceptible.*" Similarly there are in our soul-life innumerable shrouded, dark, and, as it were, sleeping perceptions, which are too small to enter the light-circle of waking consciousness; they play the same rôle as the tiny elementary bodies of which visible nature is built, they are more or less the atoms of our soul's existence. It is precisely these "*perceptions petites,*" however, which give to each individual the stamp of his individuality; it is by means of these that a man is able to distinguish himself from all other men. Each one of them leaves some small trace in our soul, and thus, in motionless silence, unnoticed by us, effect is added to effect until the character is there, unique and individual. The advance that this Leibnizian psychology makes beyond the Cartesian is immense.

In a world which proceeds thus stepwise from the least to the greatest, from the lowest to the highest, there can be nothing superfluous, nothing harmful, nothing unjustified; therefore we live in the "best of worlds." God, whose essence is truth and goodness, chose it from among all possible worlds on that very account. As the world is composed of monads — that is, of individuals — but on the other hand the essence of the individual consists in limitedness, it follows not only that evil exists, but that it is necessary, evil being nothing but a physical or moral limitedness or incompleteness. If incompleteness were not, the world would not be complete, but would simply not exist. The evil in the world may be compared to shadow in a painting, or dissonances in a piece of music. That which appears confused and discordant as an individual detail, affects us as beautiful and melodious when seen or heard as part of the whole — an argument which (as may be remembered from our first volume) we find in St. Augustine. Since God could not create perfect beings, he created such as could become more and more perfect by degrees: not perfect, but perfectible. Even the greatest artist is limited by his material: instead of an absolutely good world (which is merely impossible) God created the best — that is, the best possible — world. In this world everything is pre-ordained by the divine wisdom and made to harmonize by the divine creative power: and it is this pre-established harmony, presiding over all, which reveals the world as a work of art. But Leibniz gives a truly Baroque turn to this train of thought in equating the art-work to clock-work. For this is how he tries to explain one of the main problems of the philosophy of his day, the correspondence between body and soul: they behave like two clocks, so perfectly constructed that they always keep exactly the same time.

At first sight it might seem that the Baroque, which culminated in Leibniz, was merely going to carry on the tendencies of the Renaissance, in that its effort was ever to render existence more and more logical. And indeed it does take one important step further, in the fact that it mechanizes. But the Baroque is a far more limited, fissured, and enigmatical problem than the Renaissance: its soul-life is incomparably more labyrinthine, more hidden, composed of many more planes both horizontal and vertical — one could almost say, more underhand. It flutters, restless and unsatisfied, between the two poles: on the one hand the mechanical, and on the other the infinite — which it invents as the correlative of a purely mechanical world in which it cannot bear to live. The Baroque felt, and was the first to feel, infinitesimally.

" It is as if the Baroque had shrunk from ever saying the first word," says Wölfflin in his authoritative inquiry into " basic conceptions of cultural history." The Baroque never did trust itself, it was afraid of committing itself in some way, any way. This fear of definitive conclusions is a product as much of its urge to freedom as of its piety, for just as the Jew dared not speak the name of God, so did Baroque man shrink from reducing the deepest riddles of nature, life, and art to an unequivocal formula. Behind his apparently so clear and sharply defined formulations there stands ever something unindicated and never to be indicated. The universe is a mechanism, moving in accordance with strict mathematical laws — but controlled by mysterious distant forces. The human soul is a piece of clock-work; but it is built up of the irrational " *perceptions petites* " which evade our waking observations. The human form appears on canvas with such truth to life as never was before, but playing around it is an astral shimmer which makes it again incomprehensible and subject to a thousand interpretations. Men's outward manner attained the precision of a puppet-theatre, but therewith also its magic unreality. And so Baroque humanity passes us by like a well-arranged and brilliantly lighted procession of masks. Its real face it hides, both from us and from itself. This is the secret of that high æsthetic charm which breathes around it and causes it to stand out from the early and the later periods of the Modern Age. For, for all its high tension of intellect, it knew that life is a mystery.

CHAPTER III

THE DEATH-STRUGGLE OF THE BAROQUE

" The present is loaded with the past and pregnant with the future."

Leibniz

Antoine Watteau, who was born in 1684 and died of consumption in 1721, has preserved for us, in nearly eight hundred paintings, the perfume of that knowing but infantile, serene but weary world which we call Rococo; and he has done it with such power and delicacy, such innocence and virtuosity, that we cannot think of this period without being reminded of him. We have indeed come to regard Rococo and Watteau as almost interchangeable notions. There is perhaps no other artist who has been so completely successful in translating the fleeting life of his particular world, with all its sparkle and splendour, into non-living terms. Here they sleep, these people, who are even more remote from us in feeling than in time — caught and held fast in colour, charmed into magic and immortal slumber, abiding with us as contemporaries and intimates.

In the attempt to account psychologically for this singular fact it has occasionally been remarked that Watteau was a foreigner and a proletarian. It is true that an immigrant does on occasion embody in his art the essence of his second home more penetratingly and brilliantly than a native. To take only one example: it would be hard to find two more genuine depictors of Viennese life than Nestroy and Girardi; yet both names indicate foreign origins. The fact that he was a poor thatcher's son from the country no doubt sharpened Watteau's sense of the shimmering charm and narcotic beauty of the Paris of this day. After all, the most savorous and intimate descriptions of nature do not usually come from peasants and farmers, but from city-dwellers and café habitués, and Don Juans are rare among the writers of passionate and tender love-lyrics. Watteau, too, loved — and all the more

Watteau

135

deeply for loving without hope — the world of care-free grace and charm, wherein enjoyment was a matter of course, and the cool and delicate, aromatic and sun-warmed mountain air in which these privileged creatures played their divine comedy. He knew that he was not and could not be a proper member of the company, but only act as its observer and chronicler, and on this basis he became the incomparable painter of *fêtes galantes*.

There was a third point. Watteau was physically and emotionally a disinherited outcast. He was ailing and ugly, awkward and melancholy. We have already, in the beginning of the first volume of this work, tried to show by a whole series of examples that bodily and mental defects may occasionally be the origin of extraordinary achievements: that military heroes like Attila and Charlemagne, Napoleon and Frederick the Great were of small stature; that Byron limped, Demosthenes stuttered, Kant was deformed, Homer blind, and Beethoven deaf. It was out of another such physiological inferiority that Watteau rose to create his marvels of colour. As he could not possess the Graces, there was nothing left for him but to give them artistic form. In his works of art he compensated, and more than compensated, his natural defects. As a hopeless consumptive he preached gay light-heartedness, as one staggering gravewards the dancing affirmation of life, as a worn-out victim of disease the drunken enjoyment of existence. His is the art of a phthisical subject who in the midst of the greyest sickness develops the rosiest optimism.

And this brings us to the real solution of the problem. Watteau was so perfect a mirror of his time because, in his destiny and his personality, he was its most speaking symbol. He was a dying man, and his whole life and creative work the euphoria of the consumptive. And Rococo also was a dying age, and its joy in life nothing but a sort of tubercular sensuality, a last craving for illusion to carry one over the gateway of death: the cheerful red on its cheeks is either rouge or a hectic spot. Rococo is the agony and euthanasia of the Baroque, its sunset — that hour of the day which Watteau most loved to paint. Loving and dying: that is the formula for Watteau and the whole of Rococo.

The small house It was, in contrast to the Baroque, a *disintegrating* style, purely picturesque and decorative, playful and ornamental, smothering everything in festoons of garlands, shells, and twining plants —

swamp motives, these, that now obtain the mastery, while the fine
earlier forms begin to dissolve in an aristocratic decay. Over all
there is the soft cool breeze of evening, the fading blue and tender
rose which herald the close of the day. A grey autumnal mood is
settling upon humanity and is reflected in the faded tints of its
external covering, which, for choice, was of honey-yellow and
tea-green, dark grey and pale red, violet and brown. This
decadence-style *par excellence* is weary, toned down, anæmic, and,
above all, feminine: affectedly infantine and naïvely obscene, as
a woman is; veiled and boudoirish; perfumed and painted; satiny
and sweet-toothed; without masculine depth and worthiness, but
equally without virile heaviness and pedantry; lightly poised as
if dancing, and so achieving the miracle of an architecture that
almost defies the laws of gravitation; for ever ambiguously smiling, but seldom with a whole-hearted laugh; amusing, piquant,
capricious, epicurean, witty, coquettish; full of anecdote, short
story, and point; chattering and open-minded, sceptical and popular, with the atmosphere of comedy, theatrical and yet domestic:
even the caryatids of the age, such as Frederick the Great,
Bach, and Voltaire, were in a sense genre figures of more than
life-size.

This late Baroque has indeed an intimate character which the
High Baroque never possessed. It is in the best sense a tapestry
style, which sets out purely to please, to decorate and refine, and
regards violence of expression as not only vulgar, but incon-
venient. The characteristic building to which invention and care
were devoted was no longer the pompous palace, but the *petite
maison*, the small pleasure-house, furnished with all the charms of
a luxury of intimacy rather than display, and, as compared with
the preceding architecture, having something discreet, reserved,
and personal about it. Under Louis XIV men lived only in public:
that is, for and by reason of the court; they counted only when
they appeared before the King and as long as they continued so to
appear. For that reason every vital manifestation, from a profound thought to a graceful bow, was designed for parade and
calculated for the effect it would make at Versailles. Now, however, fifty years of gala performances had left them weary, and
they began to appreciate the joys of retirement, of letting themselves go, of belonging to themselves, of the *petit comité*. The very

names of these villas — *Érémitage, Monrepos, Solitude, Sans-souci* — are an index to the change in taste. Gone are Jove-like aloofness and heaviness of line; their aspect is now gracious, unconstrained, hospitable. In the rooms within there are no longer the stiff ceremonial chairs with high, hard backs, or the imposing decorative pieces of heavy material, but comfortable upholstered chairs, sofas with silken cushions, and small white lacquered tables with fine gold lining. Even such quiet effects as these were further toned down by replacing the gold with silver, or shading it to mat; here as in all else the positive was avoided and preference given to broken, fading, mixed colours and delicate materials such as rosewood, violet-wood, tulip-wood. The items of the inventory begin to wear the subjective stamp of their owners and to serve their personal aims. A host of new articles of furniture, expressive of the new mood, came into fashion about this time. There was the *boîte à surprises,* a secretaire with cunningly contrived secret drawers and surprise mechanisms, and the lady's writing-table prettily called " *bonheur du jour.*" All the objects in daily use were impregnated with scent, and enamelled perfume-pans filled the apartments with exquisite odours. The leading artists took an interest in every one of these details and were able, by bringing them all into harmony, to create a finely graded atmosphere of artistic satisfaction and comfort. Watteau painted fashion-plates and shop signs, and Boucher designed headings for note-paper, menus, and business papers.

Pastel and porcelain   A special note of these Rococo interiors was the predominance of pastel and porcelain. Indeed, no kind of painting could have expressed so well the intellectual attitude of this whole period — its delicate, fleeting, pale, expiring character, so well attuned to a soft velvet background — as the pastel, even apart from the fact that it is a medium particularly suited to the intimate portrait. European porcelain was first manufactured in 1709 by the Saxon Johann Friedrich Böttcher, whom Augustus the Strong kept in captivity for himself as his alchemist; and, as it turned out, this discovery of his did in fact develop into a sort of gold-making, for the new material made a conquest of the whole continent. The Meissen factory, which was founded shortly after, supplied everyone with cheap, handsome, and practical eating-utensils and drove not only earthenware and pewter, but even silver from the table.

The classic maker of German porcelain was, however, Joachim Kändler, whose enamoured shepherds and shepherdesses and life-size birds, monkeys, and dogs were the delight of the elegant world. As for Augustus the Strong, he was so obsessed by his new craze that he sacrificed half his fortune to it and filled a whole castle with porcelain. In Vienna, too, a fine porcelain-factory was opened in 1718, but the German manufactures had a powerful rival later in the Sèvres factory, built on the initiative of the Pompadour. In England Josiah Wedgwood invented the material named after him, using it chiefly for masterly reproductions of Classical vases. Finally all Europe was seized by a veritable mania for china. Not only candlesticks and lustres, clocks and stones, flower-pieces and inlays for furniture were made of it, but whole rooms and coaches and more than life-size monuments were formed out of it. All this sort of thing was of course merely the diversion into inappropriate paths of a very subtle art that, so long as it respected the nature of its material, was a vital and pregnant expression of the soul of the times; the reason why it found the eager response that it did in the Rococo soul was precisely that it was so extraordinarily and exclusively suited to the polished, coquettish, select, fragile, and demure art of miniature.

Before Böttcher's discovery porcelain had been imported from China, and even after it Meissen goods were for a long time exhibited for sale as Chinese. And this was not merely a business trick, but a prompting of the instinct of the age. China was, to the Rococo mind, the pattern country of wisdom and art. In the beginning of the century " Chinoiseries " — Eastern pictures, vases, sculptures, wall-papers, lacquers, and silks — came into vogue. Novels transported the reader into that fairy realm in which a happy, serene people enjoyed a blissful existence under learned governors; historians, with Voltaire at their head, extolled China as an El Dorado, pre-eminent in morals, religion, and administration; pagodas and tea-houses, bell-pavilions and hanging bamboo bridges appeared in the gardens; and even the pigtail is traced back to Chinese influence. The peacock, too, which just then enjoyed great popularity, has something Chinese about him, as well as being a thorough Rococo bird — decorative, bizarre, self-satisfied, and theatrical, Sunday-afternoonish, and domestic as well.

Chinoiserie

In 1765 — when a new spirit was already stirring — Diderot remarked about Boucher that he "went in too much for petty play of feature." We can well apply this remark to the whole Rococo. Voltaire, already, had called his age the *siècle des petitesses*. In every sphere its only genuine products were charming trifles. Baroque shouted and placarded, Rococo whispered and hushed. Both were fond of flourishes, but in Baroque the flourish was a passionate exclamation-mark, which Rococo changed into a discrete and elegant mark of interrogation.

In the height of French Baroque rule the tyrant and abnormality were regarded as sins against the Holy Ghost. Now, on the contrary, the two ideas swung right round into a bizarre and ingenious union. In the Cartesian age the sovereign measure for all values was correctness and symmetry: for the *genre rocaille,* on the contrary, a fondness, not to say a caprice, for the unexpected, the arbitrary, the paradoxical set the current and determined the form. These people were possibly only half-atheists in their philosophy, but they were complete atheists in their art. What attracts them is invariably the variant, the discontinuity, the diversion. An aristocratic Italian lady once said as she was eating a delectable fruit-ice: "What a pity it is not a sin!" This passion for the illegitimate and abnormal not infrequently reached the level of perversity. In no age, perhaps, was flagellantism, both active and passive, so widespread as in this; it had degenerated literally into a mass-psychosis. Yet we should remember in considering this and similar phenomena that all high and late cultures invariably tend towards perversity, that indeed an element of the perverse lies buried in every culture. Culture — as we have tried to show in the last chapter, in connexion with the wig — is and remains the opposite of Nature; and an ageing Culture of course displays this opposition in an enhanced degree, for the cycle of "normal" possibilities is complete and imagination soars over and beyond it. Neither the Egyptians of the New Empire, nor the Greeks of the Alexandrine era, nor the Romans of the Empire liked "healthy" conditions. The "immorality" of ancient Rome in particular recalls the Rococo period. "For a long time I have been trying all over the city," says Martial, "to find a woman who says no: not one says no. Is not one of them chaste, then? Thousands are chaste. But what do the chaste do, then? They do not say yes, but neither do they say no." Juvenal declared that some women had themselves divorced before the green boughs which welcomed them to their homes as brides had faded. And Voltaire wrote to the same effect in his article *Divorce* : " Divorce probably arose in the same period as marriage. I believe nevertheless that marriage is the older by a few weeks." Even the sadistic circus-enjoyments of the Romans find their pendant in the fact that in Paris members of the highest circles liked to go to an execution by way of a society sensation, and that, as witnesses assure us, many women became on these occasions sheer orgiasts.

Esprit

Boredom had to be avoided at all costs. Accordingly in the eighteenth century French culture received a new fillip. *Esprit* was born, the spirit of champagne, which is froth and wine in one. But with this almost morbid straining to be, under all circumstances, stimulating and brilliant, aromatic and effervescent, the old monumental air, the dignity, seriousness, and depth disappeared. Great tracts of the soul wholly withered, were contemptuously avoided or flippantly ignored. The glitter which streams from the departing Baroque is the phosphorescence of corruption.

Men thought, no longer in laboriously built-up and compartmented systems or heavy drugging syllogistic chains, but in close piquant polemics, faceted epigrams, time-killing satires, peppered pamphlets, and razor-edged aphorisms; or, again, in *poésies fugitives*, lyric-epigrammatic *niaiseries* that had only a shimmering streak of any train of thought in them. Dialogue, novel, short story, all became vessels for philosophy. Even the conscientious and profound Montesquieu draws the coloured ribbon of a scandalous harem adventure through his *Lettres persanes*. It was essential to be understood by everyone, even the half-educated, the society man, the public, and, above all, the ladies.

This speaks out of the portraits too. Scholars are no longer painted with book, pen, and spectacles, but as smiling, nonchalant men of the world. Nothing is allowed to disillusion us by suggesting the technical aids to their work; nor indeed must this work itself smell of oil, ink, and work-room, for it would have you believe that it is nothing more than a light, tasteful, and pleasant article of luxury, one of the many indispensable superfluities of the self-indulgent life of society. The gardens of science, guarded from the eyes of the profane as holy ground in the Middle Ages, hedged in by the barbed wire fence of Latin learning in the Renaissance, were thrown open for general use in the eighteenth century and publicly set out for the entertainment, refreshment, and instruction of all: of nobility and bourgeoisie, of man and wife, of clergy and laity. The People are still not admitted; not because they are despised, but from a still more curious reason — namely, that the fact of their existence has not yet been noticed. But there will come a day when this stratum of society also makes use of these gardens, and a strange use it will be: it will neither cultivate them to the greater glory of God like the Church, nor extend, enrich, or carefully divide them into lots like strict science, nor transform them into a general place of amusement as the philosophers did for society, but will plunder and demolish them. It will use the material collected there, first as a wooden sword with which to threaten its opponents, and finally as a mass of combustible material with which to set the world in flames.

Love as amateur theatricals Seeing that this age knew how to turn even science and philosophy into highly select stimulants, to be swallowed like a gum-tickling *apéritif*, it goes without saying that it was equally well able to deal with all the other aspects of life. There was but one desire, to make life an uninterrupted round of pleasure. " For safety," as Madame de la Verrue said, " we get in our paradise on earth." Moreover, one insisted on having one's fun without paying for it: the fruits of riches without the trouble of working, the glitter of an influential social position without its duties, the joys of love without its pains. Therefore the grand passion was avoided, and even branded as not *chic*, and only the sweet frothy cream of love was tasted: one was always amorous, never seriously in love. "We take each other," wrote Crébillon *fils*, "without loving; we leave each other without hating." Love and hate were passions, and passions were uncomfortable things, besides indicating a lack of *esprit*. Love was to be enjoyed without much fuss, like a tasty bonbon which soon melts on the tongue and is only there to be followed by a second of a different flavour.

Eroticism became a graceful society game, which imitated love in an amusing way and was subject to definite rules. Love was turned into an *amateur stage,* a mapped-out comedy with everything foreseen and prearranged — the casting, in which the lady always receives the part of the capricious mistress, the man that of the chivalrous adorer; the speeches and gestures with which the several stages are to be marked — wooing, hesitation, granting, happiness, surfeit, parting. It is a complete scenario, created by long tradition and art, in which everything has its conventional place and everything is permitted, excepting only " scenes "; for to have seriously upset one's partner would have been to betray a deplorable lack of tact and good manners. Even jealousy was only allowed to be of a playful character: " *la gelosia è passione ordinaria e troppo antica,*" said Goldoni.

But even this hothouse love could only thrive in the close atmosphere of illegitimacy. Everything which suggested family life was considered bad form. Pregnancy infallibly made women comic and was therefore to be avoided as far as possible; if it occurred, it was hidden as long as might be. Love in marriage was precultural, ridiculous, or — what was worse — in bad taste. In good society married couples addressed each other, even at home, as " Monsieur " and " Madame." Conjugal fidelity on the part of husband or wife was considered positively improper. Four-cornered marriages, in which the couples changed about, were on the other hand just tolerated. A woman without lovers was not regarded as virtuous, but as unattractive, and a married man without mistresses as impotent or ruined. It was so completely a matter of good form for a society woman to have her forbidden pleasures that she was obliged, from time to time, to show traces in public of her nights of love. She therefore painted dark rings round her eyes, put on a tired expression, and spent a whole day in bed, while on the other side of the picture it was *de rigueur* for the man of the world not to omit to comment with ironic surprise on her exhausted condition. The husband's rôle on such occasions was to take a reasonable and courteous view of the situation, and the more wit, amiability, and ease he displayed in so doing, the more sympathy did he receive. Voltaire, as is well known, lived for half a generation with the Marquise du Châtelet at her castle of Cirey in Lorraine, but never a word do we hear of any unpleasantness on the side of the Marquis. His tolerance went much further than that. The day came when Voltaire too was betrayed by Émilie, who had conceived a violent passion for the young author Saint-Lambert; but this did not prevent Voltaire from remaining with her, or from becoming a fatherly friend to his rival. The affair had its consequences, however, and there developed out of it a delightful Rococo farce which might well have served for one of Maupassant's best stories. Voltaire announced: "*Pater est, quem nuptiæ declarant.* Let us include the child in Madame du Châtelet's miscellaneous works." Monsieur du Châtelet was then invited to Cirey. He came at once and spent some very agreeable days there. Madame was unusually kind to him, and shortly after his departure he was able to announce to his friends that he expected a child. The piquancy of the whole incident lies in the probability that everyone concerned was playing a part before the others. This kind of vaudeville in real life occurred almost daily. It would be difficult to find a more brilliantly comic "curtain" than the remark of the gentleman of France who, finding his wife *in flagrante delicto*, said: "But how careless of you, madame! Think if it had been anyone else but me!"

The Cicisbeo   Every woman had to have at least one lover, otherwise she was more or less compromised socially. In Italy many ladies stipulated for a particular *cicisbeo*, or even two, in the marriage contract. The bridegroom, having himself long since figured as a *cicisbeo* in some other similar contract, raised no objection. In her famous letters from Vienna, Lady Montagu reported that it was considered a serious insult there to invite a lady to dinner without her two men, the husband and the official lover. Her astonishment at this shows that the custom had not spread beyond the Continent; the hegemony of the middle-class element came so much earlier in England than elsewhere (as we shall presently see) that there is no question of an English Rococo in the proper sense of the word.

The declared lover — called in France *petit maître*, in Italy *cavaliere servente* — who was not infrequently an abbé, attended his mistress like a shadow: on her visits and her walks, to the theatre and to church, to balls and to gaming-tables; he sat beside her in the carriage and walked beside her litter, carried her sunshade and petted her lap-dog, which was his most dangerous rival in the lady's affections. In the morning he woke her, pulled up the blinds, and brought her chocolate; later on he made himself useful over her toilet and escorted the visitors to her bedside. For ladies preferred to receive even slight acquaintances at the hour of the toilet and even, at a later period, when in their morning bath. This custom is all the more curious in that bath-tubs were hardly used in the Rococo. At Versailles there was no provision made for a bath anywhere; and even in Goethe's youth swimming was considered a crazy form of exercise. The numerous pictures of women and girls bathing which belong to this period are no proof to the contrary, since they merely served the purpose of stimulating erotic imagination. If we consider the absurdly small dimensions of the wash-basins of the day — roughly those of a soup-plate — we might almost assume that there was no water in those piquant and intriguing covered tubs.

There is another requisite article which appears much more often than the bath-tub in the pictures of the time: that is, the swing, which was set up everywhere and with the utmost nonchalance. Coming into fashion about this time, it expressed many typical Rococo elements, such as: playfulness, the pretence of infantile innocence, the dawning feeling for fresh air, the gallantry of man and the coquetry of woman; and the agreeable giddiness which it produced acted more or less as an aphrodisiac. There were, of course, other far less harmless stimulants, such as " love pills " and " Spanish fly," which all the world took without scruple. But it is incomprehensible that these and similar phenomena should lead to the conclusion that the Rococo age was really strongly erotic. It was, on the contrary, unerotic, being merely anxious on no account to forgo any of the delights of love. The fact that all the thoughts and endeavours of Rococo man were devoted to the problem of love and the enriching, refining, and intensifying of its technique makes it clear beyond all doubt that in this domain as in others he had come to an end of his creative power. The moment when form and not content, method and not subject, is made the principal problem signifies always and everywhere the beginning of decadence. It was only when the Middle Ages had exhausted the fullness of its feeling for God that Scholasticism developed its highest subtlety and keenness. It was only when Greek philosophy had hazarded its grand throws of the dice that the Classical systematizers appeared. Æschylus and Shakspere were not playwrights — it was left for the Alexandrines and the Romantics to fill that rôle. On the other hand, we must in justice admit that it is precisely in the period of their decline that art, science, and social life develop the refinement, complexity, and psychological flair which are in fact their special quality. Thus in the age of Rococo,

145

although there were no erotic geniuses, there were great " amorists," incomparable virtuosi in the art of love, which developed at that time into a veritable science. At the head of these virtuosi of both sexes stand Madame de Pompadour, whose name became a legend, and Casanova, whose name was promoted to the level of a generic label, while a figure like the Duc de Richelieu may be taken as the representative of the whole species; for although he lived to be ninety-two, he received daily, right up to his death, a fat bundle of love-letters, many of which he did not open. An experience at Château Tournay, when he was sixty-six, was the first and probably the only defeat of his life: he wooed the beautiful Madame Cramer in vain, and his failure so amused him as a curiosity that he himself told the story everywhere. Another time he was even the cause of a duel with pistols fought over him by two ladies of the highest aristocracy.

The ugliness patch Neither is the fact that Rococo was an age of gynæcocracy to be accounted for by any specially strong development of eroticism. The source of this is to be sought in two other places. First, in the feminization of man, which increased decade by decade. " Men," said Archenholz, " are more like women now than in any other period of time." For another thing social life in the Latin countries had gradually taken on the most grandiose forms, and wherever a complicated social standard reigns, there also reigns woman. The social primacy of the femal sex in the Renaissance originated in the same way. Only the Renaissance was a definitely virile age, and its feminine ideal was the virago; in Rococo, on the contrary, a woman could not look feminine and childish enough, and the prevailing ideal was one of fragility, in conscious imitation of the china doll. Health was considered uninteresting, strength plebeian. The aristocratic ideal, which in the days of Corneille and Condé still corresponded to a sort of *Kalokagathia*, was now transformed into an ideal of refinement, hypersensibility, and elegant languor, an emphasis on unfitness for life, and morbidity. The beauty-patch — which had already come up in Louis XIV's time, but only now became the dominating element in the physiognomy of the woman of the world and ought really to be called the ugliness patch — was meant to serve as a piquant interruption in the regularity of a face and thereby emphasized the tendency to asymmetry, innate in Rococo; while at the same time it suggested a beauty-defect, a

146

wart, thus making of every woman a *belle-vilaine* and endowing her with a new and perverse charm — it was, in fact, one more trait of morbidity. Later on, the stage of sheer bad taste was reached, in giving the *mouche* the form of various stars, crosses, and animals, and edging it with diamonds. The majestic *fontange* had dropped out as early as 1714; by about 1730 the *crapaud* or hair-bag had supplanted the wig, which had been growing steadily smaller since the beginning of the century: men's locks were now tucked away in a little bag which was tied up with a coquettish silk bow. By the middle of the century (earlier in the case of the army) the pigtail (*la queue*) had become universal. Powdering, which was indispensable for well-groomed people, whether they wore real or false hair, was an extremely laborious performance. Usually the powder was flung up towards the ceiling and allowed to float down on to the head, the face being protected by a cloth. Prince Kaunitz used to walk through a double row of lackeys whose duty it was to powder him as evenly as possible. Count Brühl owned five hundred wigs, which were all kept permanently powdered — " a lot for a man without a head," was Frederick the Great's comment. Faces, too, had to be kept under a heavy layer of powder.

The Rococo powder, like the Baroque *allonge,* was no freak of fashion, but the most eloquent symbol of the age. In the Rococo a man past forty had done with life, and a woman far sooner. Marriages were earlier than at the present day. Girls often married at fourteen or fifteen, youths at twenty. In his letters Voltaire calls himself an old man from his forty-fifth year on. His friend the Marquise du Châtelet felt that she cut an impossible figure when at forty she found herself expecting a child. Standards such as of this kind may and do undergo great transformations, but all the time the spirit of the age, whatever it may be, is their foundation. As late as the end of the nineteenth century a woman of thirty acted as chaperon at a ball; now she takes dancing-lessons at fifty. In the French dramas of morals of the eighties the philosopher who looked on at life and love with the eyes of a resigned observer was seldom over forty; the modern films like to make the unprincipled seducer a man of fifty. The Rococo felt itself to be old, while at the same time it was filled with the desperate longing of life for the youth that is vanishing, and that is why it eliminated

147

differences in age by ordering grey hair for all. Rococo felt sick and anæmic, and therefore powder had to give it, as it were, a uniform of pallor and anæmia. The young or young-painted face with its white hair is a moving symbol of the Rococo soul, the *tragic mask* of the time: for every age wears its appointed character-mask, in which all its *velléités* are consciously or unconsciously summed.

The men's dress was the costume of a spoilt boy, with its delicate silk coats, knee-breeches and beribboned shoes, rich jabots and lace cuffs, glittering gold braid and silver embroideries, and the gala sword that was purely a toy. The toning of these garments was delicate, discreet, and feminine, favourite colours being pistachio, mignonette, apricot, sea-green, lilac, and dun. Some of the shades reached unheard-of refinements: a new yellow-green was called " goose dung (*merde d'oie*) "; a brownish yellow "*caca Dauphin,*" in honour of the new-born heir to the throne; in *puce,* or flea-colour, there were many grades, such as flea-head, flea-shank, flea-belly, and even flea-with-milk-fever. Beards were so completely out of fashion during the whole of the eighteenth century that actors were distinguished, not by their beardlessness — as was the case until recently in our own day — but by their moustaches, and even this is true chiefly of those who specialized in brigand parts.

The most important feature in a woman's exterior was her thin girlish waist. This was produced by means of a whalebone corset, which finished off in a long, acute angle. These unfortunate ladies began their lacing early in the morning and tightened the strings every quarter of an hour until the desired wasp's waist had been achieved. The massive crinoline, too, which was called a pannier (that is, hen-coop) on account of its vast dimensions, had no other purpose but to emphasize by contrast the slenderness of the upper part of the body. It also was stiffened with whalebone, and the enormous demand for this material was a novel windfall for the Dutch, the whalers for all Europe. It will be remembered that in Spain the crinoline had been called the " guard of virtue," but by this time it certainly was not that; it left the feet free and was merely a coquettish covering which not infrequently exposed, as if by accident, the naked body beneath (for ladies wore no drawers in the Rococo). Over the crinoline was worn the silk robe, richly trimmed with garlands, passementerie, lace and ribbon, real or artificial flowers, and occasionally with hand-paintings. On the dress of the Queen of Portugal, for instance, could be seen the whole story of the Fall, complete with Adam, Eve, apple-tree, and serpent. Gradually the crinoline, which by 1720 had taken possession of Europe and was worn by peasant women and servants as well as by society ladies, grew to so colossal a size that its wearers could only enter a door sideways. Equally uncomfortable was the preposterously high-heeled shoe, which made walking almost impossible. At home and in intimate circles the crinoline was replaced by the " Adrienne," a loose, voluminous garment, but this also was worn with a tightly laced bodice. At the beginning of the century it became the custom for ladies to carry gracefully beribboned walking-sticks. Another indispensable item in the coquette's battery was the fan, which only now came into its own with the introduction of the folding variety. Another new discovery was the umbrella that could be folded up (this was the *parapluie;* the fixed sunshade or *parasol* was somewhat older). The whole costume was copied exactly for the children, who not only wore hair-bags and panniers, patches and fancy swords, fans and three-cornered hats, but painted and powdered, curtsied and kissed hands, like the little ladies and gentlemen that they were.

We find it delightfully comic that the figure on a monument is made to hold some object suggestive of the late lamented's sphere of activity, such as the scroll of the poet, the wheel of the inventor, or the telescope of the nautical hero. By analogy we might regard some particular utensil as peculiarly representative of each culture-period: the man of the dawning Modern Age might be represented with a compass, Baroque man with a microscope, nineteenth-century man with a newspaper, the man of today with a telephone. For Rococo man this symbol would be a mirror. This article accompanied him through his whole life. The reception-rooms of the period were filled with full-length Venetian panels which confronted the visitor with his own complete image. Small pocket-mirrors were introduced into all kinds of articles of daily use, and the glittering light of chandeliers and lustres was reflected in the looking-glasses of every shape and size which hung on the walls. There were even rooms — the extremely popular " mirror cabinets " — that were completely lined with glass, in which the likeness of the beholder was multiplied to infinity. This

The passion for mirrors

mirror craze is expressive of many things — not only of the most obvious, such as vanity, self-love, narcissism; but also of pleasure in regarding oneself, of self-analysis and absorption in the ego-problem, which, indeed, frequently amounted to a veritable mania for introspection. Rococo saw the dawn, amongst other things, of the classic letter and memoir literature, of self-descriptions and great confessions, of psychology. This new science was an achievement of the eighteenth century, and we shall see how the craving for self-dissection and soul-fathoming rose with each succeeding generation until, towards the end of the century, it had almost attained to its modern levels. And there is a second thing which the mirror of Rococo man reflects; the love of appearances, of illusions, of the variegated outer shell of things. And what this signifies is not so much superficiality as an extreme, sophisticated artistry. We have life in its reflection as we have a torrent in its rainbow, said Faust, and a similar *leitmotiv* Nietzsche would have us believe of the Greek culture: " Oh, these Greeks! They understood the art of *living:* it consists essentially in keeping valiantly to the surface, the fold, the skin; in worshipping the semblance . . . these Greeks were superficial from a sense of *depth!* "

Theatrocracy   There was one profession to which the mirror was as indispensable as the retort to the chemist, or the blackboard to the schoolmaster; namely, that of the actor. And here we get to the very core of Rococo: it was a world of the theatre. Never, before or since, has there been such a passion for witty masquerading, beautiful illusions, scintillating comedies, as in the Rococo. Not only was existence itself an everlasting carnival of masking, intrigue, and a thousand fleeting jests and secrecies, but the stage was the dominating factor in daily life, comparable to the orator's tribune in Classical antiquity or the sports-ground of today. Amateur theatricals were everywhere: at court and in the villages, in castles and in middle-class houses, in universities and in nurseries. And almost everyone played the game well. In this mania for the theatre we have the strongest, clearest indication of the most profound will of the age: a yearning for the final uncovering of one's own soul. The art of the stage has often been called a sort of " prostitution," and rightly. Men have a deep-rooted instinct to prostitute themselves, uncover themselves, show themselves naked. This was at the root of the immemorially old Dionysus-cult, in which men and women in their intoxication tore their clothes from their bodies. The Greeks did not call this a shameless orgy, however, but a " sacred raving." And if we try to put it all in terms of psychology, we stumble against the strangely suggestive *haut gout* which is inherent in all cynicism. In everyday life it is exacted by State and society that we shall skilfully avoid being ourselves, but always wear coverings, draperies, veils. The curtain is always down, except in the one case where it is up — the theatre. It is, therefore, in the very place which the mistaken layman regards as the supreme domain of masks, disguises, and transformations that the human being appears more undisguised, more genuine and unpainted, than anywhere else. This is the real meaning of that " prostitution " which forms the essence of acting. The soul's vizor falls, the inner substance becomes manifest: the secret must out whether the bearer will it or no. The theatre stands, in fact, for more than most people think: it is no garish superficiality, no mere playing, but something that unseals and releases, something literally magical in our existence.

Gynæcocracy and theatrocracy determine the course of the Rococo throughout. As to the division of the age into periods, however, no clear definition or unanimity of opinion has been reached. For the Regency, which lasted from 1715 to 1723, we generally speak of the *style Régence;* from that time up to the middle of the century and later, of the *style Louis XV,* and finally of the *style Louis XVI,* which is substantially identical with the " pigtail " style. The first section of the Rococo was marked by a reckless unrestraint and laxity which in its quality of violence retained something of the triumphant Baroque vitality. Then its vital manifestations become steadily more weary, anæmic, and filigree-like until, on reaching the Classicizing " pigtail " stage, they lapse into numb, stiff-jointed old age. It used to be the custom to make the notions of pigtail and Rococo synonymous, but for this there is no justification whatever; rather it is doubtful whether what the pigtail belongs to is the Rococo at all.

We have already remarked the undisguised rejoicing with which the death of Louis XIV was received. All the world — court and nobility as well as commonalty and canaille — breathed more freely when the double pressure of despotism and bigotry was removed from the land. " God alone is great, my brethren," were the

151

opening words of Massillon's funeral oration on the great Louis, " and great particularly in these final moments when he inflicts the penalty of death on the kings of earth." As after the fall of Puritanism in England, so now in France men sought to indemnify themselves for the long repressions and tutelage of the old régime by elevating pleasure to be supreme lord of life and declaring all virtue to be hypocrisy and all morality prudery. In his family affairs as in other things Louis XIV had been very unhappy during his later years. All the direct heirs to the throne died one after another down to a great-grandson who was a minor, and the regency fell to his nephew, Duke Philip of Orleans, the son of the " Liselotte " who had played the part of the ingénue in the theatre of Versailles and still enjoys posthumous celebrity on account of her letters. Popular wit was justified in recommending for her gravestone the epitaph: " Here lies the mother of all the vices," for the Duke was the very type of the " waster " as it figures to this day in the serial shockers; brilliantly clever, seductively amiable, but sceptical and frivolous to the last degree. His sole standard in all his actions was his own enjoyment. Louis XIV used very aptly to call him " *fanfaron de vice* "; and in fact he made his sins into a sort of bizarre cult. This was not only in the true Rococo style, but truly French, for the Frenchman delights in underlining his good points and his bad ones alike, going all out, so to say, for success in two rôles at once. And because of this the nation forgave the Regent everything and did not even revile his memory. It was he who originated the term " *roué* " to describe the companions of his orgies, " gallows-birds, broken on the wheel of all the vices." The ingenuity with which this company thought out ever new excesses provided admiring town-talk for Paris, and it was the ambition of all the women to be admitted to the " *fêtes d'Adam* " organized at Saint-Cloud. Even the Regent's relation with his daughter, the beautiful and temperamental Duchesse de Berri, roused no particular repulsion, for incest was anything but rare just then in the highest circles. The Duc de Choiseul, for instance, who played a great part as premier in the Seven Years' War, was known by all the world to have an affair with his sister the Duchesse de Gramont. In other respects, too, the normal limits of sexual intercourse were but little observed and it is in keeping with the " elderly " character of the age that the violation of children was perhaps never so widespread as in the Rococo period.

On the occasion of one of these orgies a document was brought to the Regent to sign. He was already so drunk that he could not do so, and he therefore handed the paper to Madame de Parabère with the words: " Sign, whore." The lady replied that it would not be fitting for her to do so, whereupon he said to the Archbishop of Cambrai: " Sign, bully." As he also refused, the Regent then turned to Law with the command: " Sign, crook," but neither would he do it. " Here's a well-governed realm," said the Regent finally, " run by a whore, a bully, a crook, and a drunkard." But it looks as if there was a little of fanfaronade in this case too, for his government was in more than one respect better than that of either his predecessor or his successor. He expelled the Jesuits from his court and favoured the Jansenists, paid off a fifth of the two thousand million livres of state debts left by Louis XIV, effected a rapprochement with the sea-powers, and, with the help of his tutor, the lascivious and adroit Cardinal Dubois, was able to carry out a pacific policy. Oppressions of the censorship and arbitrary imprisonments came almost entirely to an end under him, particularly as he, like all genuinely dignified persons and most genuinely witty ones, was impervious to personal attack. When Voltaire, in his first drama, *Œdipus,* had the incredible audacity to make an allusion to the Duke and his daughter in describing the incestuous relation between the King and Jocasta, the Duke sat unmoved in his box, although he naturally understood it all, clapped applause, and granted the young author a considerable annual allowance.

One of the greatest public catastrophes of France prior to the Revolution was undoubtedly that associated with John Law, to whom allusion has just been made. This wealthy Scotsman — handsome, clever, fashionable, and undeniably a financial genius — had conceived the fruitful (and in itself correct) idea that the capital of the state and the great private banks was not something expressed merely by their stock of gold and silver, but should include the natural values and man-power available for their transactions. He claimed, in consequence, that it was justifiable to call for credit from the public and to issue bank-notes which could not be fully covered by the cash in hand. His private bank,

The Law crash

153

which later became royal, was founded on these principles in 1716, and already in its third year was able to pay a dividend of forty per cent. The *Compagnie des Indes,* which he floated for the exploitation of Canada and Louisiana, attracted to itself the savings of all France, and when its Mississippi shares rose to twenty and forty times their nominal value, the frenzy of speculation knew no bounds. It was then that the typical *" chevalier d'industrie "* was born, the adventurous knight cf industry whose fortune consisted wholly of paper. In 1719 Law volunteered to reorganize the finances of the State at one blow by taking up the *fermage* of the whole of the taxes. He was made finance minister in the following year, and the notes which he put into circulation amounted finally to eighty times the value of all the money in France. But the colonies brought in nothing, the public became suspicious, and a general run on the state bank brought down its notes to a tenth, its Indies bonds to a twenty-fifth, of their original value. In 1721 the State went bankrupt, Law fled to Venice (where he died later in great poverty), a terrible scarcity set in, and the whole of France was ruined. The Law crash, as is well known, figures in the Second Part of *Faust,* where it is represented as a Mephistophelian transaction; it is not Faust, but Mephistopheles who is the originator of the paper swindle by which the Emperor sets his affairs in order; and the credulous crowd, which is put off with paper for good money, is personified in the *Fool.*

> To all whom it concerneth, and so forth —
> This note of hand that purports to be worth
> A thousand crowns, subject to such demand
> The boundless treasure buried in the land.
> And furthermore, said treasure underground
> To pay said sum is, whensoever found
> And wheresoever, firmly pledged and bound.
>
> (Anster's translation)

In fact, however, Law's schemes were anything but fraudulent or diabolical, for his notes were covered, not by invented fairy-tale hoards, but by very real values in land and materials. But they were in the hands of men incapable of handling them productively, and the credit principle, though sound in itself, was applied with the utmost recklessness by a frivolous and greedy administration. In addition, the whole system was beyond the economic grasp of the people of the day, who, being not yet ripe for it, lost their heads and behaved foolishly.

Louis XV, too, was a thorough Rococo prince in his own way: bored with, and yet hungry for, life, light-hearted and melancholy, and senile from his youth up. His autocracy lasted almost as long as Louis XIV's, but with this difference: that he left the conduct of affairs almost entirely to his councillors of state and his mistresses, and for the two first decades to Cardinal Fleury — the third prince of the Church to be all-powerful in France. The vigour that had inspired the orgies of the Regency faded in Louis XV to a feebler sort of infamy. He was intelligent, but infinitely less witty than the Duke, and libertinage and bigotry were strangely blended in his soul. Being entirely without conscience, he nevertheless went in perpetual fear of hell, and the Jesuits, trading upon this, regained their position at court. The five sisters Mailly were the first to be installed, one after the other, as chief " favourites." In 1745 he made the acquaintance of the Pompadour, who was then in the full bloom of her youth and beauty. Although, as a bourgeoise of the *haute finance,* she had the whole of the court camarilla against her, she successfully saved the King from boredom for twenty years. She rode and danced, drew and etched, sang and recited to perfection; read and criticized with the keenest understanding all the new publications, whether dramas, philosophies, novels, or theories of state. Above all she understood the art of renewing herself day by day and of giving some surprising and fascinating new turn to all the amusements into which she plunged her companions. With the Queen — who, though mild and amiable, was rather a bore — she was on the best of footings, even to the extent of giving her lessons in love. Later on she introduced young beauties to the King in the famous Parc aux Cerfs. Her successor was Jeanne du Barry, a stupid and vulgar person, who must have been endowed with an indescribable sexual attraction, due perhaps to the *haut goût* of her vulgarity. She had in particular a lustful way of blinking her eyes which is said to have been irresistible.

While the court amused itself in this wise and the bourgeois became yearly better educated and wealthier, the country-folk lived in rags and mud huts, and (as an English economist has shown) their agricultural standpoint was that of the tenth century. It is difficult to form any idea today of the high level of the taxes or of the severity with which they were collected. So senseless were they that the peasant often chose to leave his land untilled or to destroy his harvest. The nobility still lived like a higher race with its own rights and habits of life in the midst of the rest of the population of France: inactive, untaxed, with no real duties, and obeying no law but the King's whim. All the wealth, all the honour, all the women belonged to it by right. When, for instance, Marshal Maurice de Saxe, the son of Augustus the Strong and the beautiful Aurora von Königsmark, failed to win the affections of the actress Chantilly (who had elected to marry the librettist Favart), he obtained a royal decree ordering her to become his mistress. This brilliant cavalier, who in general was not at all unsuccessful with women, was mixed up in a second scandal, equally characteristic of the time. The focus of it was again an actress, the great Adrienne Lecouvreur. After having had a liaison with him for many years, she was, according to all the indications, poisoned by the Duchess of Bouillon, who was also in love with the future great captain; at any rate the director of police received orders to make any inquiry into the manner of the actress's death impossible and had the body thrown into a pit uncoffined and then covered with lime. Yet already there were signs of the approaching dissolution of absolutism. Since Francis I, Paris had been steadily acquiring a more and more central position as the residence of the kings, until at last *la cour et la ville* had come to be identical with France as a whole. This was still the case even in the reigns of the two last Louis. But with the beginning of the century these two elements of power, court and city, had themselves begun to fall apart and they were now engaged in an increasingly hostile rivalry. Under Louis XIV the city served the court with all its intellectual resources, its art and eloquence, its drama and philosophy, its theories of state and of economics. Racine and Molière, Boileau and Bossuet, were in a sense crown officials. But under Louis XV the city becomes the home of emancipation, of free-thinking, and of recalcitrance. Its seat of opposition was in the Parliament of Paris, the assembly of judges, whose posts — owing to the chronic indigence of the French kings — were salable and hereditary and eventually became entirely independent of the court. This "*noblesse de la robe*" formed a powerful clique, hostile to the court and the Jesuits, which (by reason of the numerous marriages of its members to rich merchants' daughters) formed at the same time a plutocracy of bourgeois colour. After Fleury's death the court no longer commanded respect in either home or foreign politics. Frederick the Great characterized the French system of government in an apt and witty remark one day at the opera, when the curtain did not come right down and the feet of the dancers were left visible. " Absolutely the Paris ministry," he exclaimed, " legs without heads." It says much for the long-suffering royalism of the French that this King, the most unlovable and useless that they had ever had, nevertheless was named *le Bien-Aimé* from the popular joy at his recovery from a dangerous illness in 1744 and ruled happily for thirty years thereafter.

During this epoch France's rôle in European history was no more than that of a lustful and impotent intriguer. After the War of the Spanish Succession the notions of a " European balance of power" and a "Concert of the Powers " began to come into fashion, the idea being that the existing system of states formed, as it were, a well-appointed orchestra in which no one leading part was allowed to domineer. But as these catchwords were obviously dictated, not by any genuine love of peace and justice, but by pure envy and a jealous fear of allowing others to rise too high, they did not prevent wars; they merely extended the theatre of war, in that the coalition type of war became even more typical than it had been before. It was rarely that individual states went to war; we see nothing but alliances, which are promptly dissolved when one of the members scores a decisive victory. The great France-Habsburg opposition remained a fixture; Spain and Sweden dropped out of the array of great powers, their places being taken by Russia and Poland, while England was even thus early the arbiter of Europe in virtue of her long diplomatic training and riper political experience.

The territorial changes during the first two-thirds of the century are — apart from the change of ownership in Silesia — casual and uninteresting, consisting in an unintelligent and arbitrary exchange of provinces and scraps of provinces. At the Peace of

Passarowitz, Austria gained New Serbia with Belgrade and Lesser Wallachia, but in twenty years' time she had to give everything back again, and at this time also she handed over Naples and Sicily, which she had exchanged with the Duke of Savoy for Sardinia, to an independent line of the house of Bourbon, receiving Parma and Piacenza in return. These places again she soon afterwards lost to a newly-founded third Bourbon dynasty. Duke Francis of Lorraine, husband of Maria Theresa, the heiress to the throne of Austria, became Grand Duke of Tuscany, while his own duchy fell to the titular King of Poland, Stanislaus Leszczinski, with reversion upon his death to France. An attempt made by Philip V of Spain to recover the Netherlands (lost by the Peace of Utrecht) was wrecked upon the quadruple alliance of England, France, Austria, and Holland.

Now, the Emperor Charles VI had spent the greater part of his reign in gaining recognition for the Pragmatic Sanction, by which he hoped to secure the unchallenged succession of his daughter to the sovereignty of all the hereditary lands. He negotiated with all the European powers, and he obtained in every case promises — which, on his death, were promptly broken. Out of the situation thus created there arose the eight years' War of the Austrian Succession, which was to plunge the Habsburg state into one of the most dangerous crises that it ever had to face. It involved nothing less than the break-up of the Empire. By the secret " partition treaty " agreed upon by the opposing powers, Bohemia and Upper Austria were allotted to Bavaria, the Margraviate of Moravia and Lower Austria to Saxony, Belgium to France, the Italian territories to Spain; the Habsburg possessions were to be reduced to little more than the eastern half of the Empire, with Ofen as a capital. At the conclusion of the peace, however, it was only Prussia — the least considered of all — which really gained anything. At first the course of the war was catastrophic for Austria. The allies occupied Linz and Prague, the Elector of Bavaria was acclaimed by the Bohemian Estates and was elected German emperor as Charles VII. But a change then set in: the Austrians and Hungarians expelled him not only from the conquered provinces, but from his own country as well; and so it came to be said of him that he was *et Cæsar et nihil*. After his death his son relinquished all claim to inherit Austria, and it was again a Habsburger, the husband of Maria Theresa, who received the Imperial crown.

In all these political happenings the feelings and wishes of the people played not the smallest part. It was all a matter, so to say, of private understandings among the individual potentates turning upon marriage connexions, territorial desires, contracts and breakings of contracts, personal ambitions and leanings. We have drawn attention to the imitation of French absolutism by rulers and subjects all over the continent. Germany in particular developed a limitless servility, which was the more grotesque, being practised chiefly by the smaller states. A Württemberger parson informed his Duke that his grace's " most high swine " had eaten his own " most humble potatoes." Every duodecimo princeling cherished the ludicrous ambition of copying Versailles and had to have his Italian opera, his French pleasure-seat, his pheasant preserve, and his parade troops. It was equally indispensable that he should keep expensive favourites : so definitely was this demanded of him by custom that in some cases — for instance, that of Frederick I of Prussia — the prince felt obliged to maintain a merely titular concubine. Said a citizen of a minor capital with emotion, as he watched his ruler drive past with his newly-wed young bride: " Now there is nothing wanting to our prince but a handsome mistress." Augustus the Strong — whose nickname was no mere flattery — had over three hundred illegitimate children, one of whom, the Countess Orszelska, became his mistress. Duke Leopold Eberhard of Württemberg was even less scrupulous, for he allowed the thirteen children whom he had by his five mistresses to intermarry. No one dared to criticize such behaviour; everything which took place at the courts of these little god-kings was justified, and the subjects celebrated the name-day of the illegitimate sovereign lady of the moment as if it had been a national festival, feeling themselves highly honoured when the prince stooped to a townsman's daughter. Other encroachments on their liberty were suffered in the same unresisting way. The innumerable hunts did indescribable damage to the fields and often ruined a whole harvest. Preparations for court diversions would sometimes absorb the services of half the population, and the cost of all the disturbance as often as not be met by recruiting and selling the people. Withal, nothing whatever was done to raise

Duodecimo absolutism

the working power of the country. In eighteenth-century Germany there was an accepted standard of one cleric and five beggars to every twenty of the population.

Athens-on-the-Pleisse
The most intellectual capital in the Germany of that day was Leipzig, which, as the seat of the great fairs and the most distinguished German university, as the metropolis of the artistically minded Polish-Saxon kings and the book trade, and as a centre of fashion and frivolity, had achieved the proud position of an Athens-on-the-Pleisse. For all that, everything that Saxony produced in the way of literature was of the purest repetitive kind: well-informed and methodical, thrashed-out and finicking, pedantic, furiously revised, and equally tireless and tiresome with its wearisome repetition of the same elementary commonplaces. A pleasing figure is Christian Fürchtegott Gellert, clergyman's son and professor, who, though weak alike in physique and creative power, was spotlessly pure in style and in character. He was a really effective influence, not only through his novels and comedies, lyrics and works of edification, but also through his well-attended " moral lectures " and through an extensive correspondence in which he played the part of wise and sympathetic father-confessor to all and sundry. Frederick the Great said of him: " He is a very different fellow from Gottsched " and " There's something so *couplant* in his verses." This was an excellent characterization: he owed his extraordinary popularity to the soft, ingratiating form in which he expressed his harmless wisdom. The tenderness with which he approached his readers made him an ideal women's writer. His humour leaves us somewhat cold, suggesting, as it does, grandpapa in the nursery; his fables — which are all that survives of his work — give the impression of having been written definitely for a class-book, as pieces for the lower school. The fundamental trait in his nature was a touching, albeit rather tiresome, old-maidishness, just as Gleim, for all his love-songs, was typical of old bachelordom. The " Anacreontics " who sat at the feet of " Father Gleim " were anything rather than amorous, being far too gauche and well-behaved for that. They were not even straightforwardly in love, but merely in love with a perfectly nebulous and schoolboy notion of the state of being in love which had taken possession of their childlike souls. Neither were they ever really intoxicated, but again only drunk with the

bare notion and possibility of intoxication which the sight of rose-garlanded winebottles had the power to arouse in them. So that Kant was possibly not so far wrong when he said that Anacreontic poems commonly came very near to flabbiness.

From about 1730 onward the position of absolute literary dictator was filled by Gottsched. This was after the appearance of his main theoretical work: *Versuch einer critischen Dichtkunst vor die Deutschen,* in which he preached the Aristotelian doctrine of the imitation of nature and the Horatian demand for *delectare et prodesse,* expressing both with all possible commonplaceness and narrowness. But already after one decade he was overthrown by the two Swiss, Bodmer and Breitinger, who held that the main object of poetry is the extraordinary and the marvellous, but that these " must ever be kept within the bounds of possibility." This ideal they found to be most completely incorporated in the fables of Æsop. At bottom the standpoints of the two parties were not so different as their embittered polemics suggested. The opponents were more like quarrelling brothers, disagreeing in particular judgments and details, but completely indistinguishable from one another as regards their ignorance of art, their attitude of knowing better, and their sterile philistinism. All the same, the two Swiss undoubtedly did a great service in bringing about the fall of that complacent, narrow-minded, intriguing art-tyrant Gottsched. By 1765 the young Goethe was able to say that " all Leipzig despised him."

For a time Gottsched stood also for the literary conscience of the actress Friedericke Karoline Neuber, who played a not unimportant part in the history of German dramatic art. Eventually, however, she quarrelled with him, and even parodied him in a stage figure that searched for errors with a bull's-eye lantern in his hand and a gilt paper sun on his head. Madame Neuber was pretty, clever, temperamental, and not uneducated; but, like all stars who are managers into the bargain, she was domineering and dogmatic, and her preference for masculine rôles was not confined to the stage. As founder of the so-called Leipzig school, she insisted on assiduous and punctual rehearsing, on the respectability of her company, on scrupulously correct declamation, and on consciously curving, well-studied, and graceful poses. Her symbolic burning of Harlequin on the stage was a famous episode. Besides

Gottsched's numerous copies and adaptations of French pieces, she produced Gellert's and Holberg's works and the early dramas of Lessing. But with time the company became less and less in demand; the manager fell out with the best " pullers " among its members, her own playing began to be old-fashioned, and it was only thanks to the help of friends that she did not end her days in poverty. Meanwhile the improvised farce of the Baroque reached its high-water mark in Vienna under the "buffoon" dynasty of Stranitzsky, Prehauser, and Kurz. This great tradition — more artistic, more human, more respectable even, than the empty, pretentious Gottsched-Neuber presentations — has maintained itself to this day on the Viennese stage, surviving everything because it was capable of absorbing everything: Classicism, Romanticism, Naturalism; and faithfully carried on by such figures as Raimund and Nestroy, Girardi and Pallenberg.

Klopstock   This period also saw the rise of Klopstock, whose verses roused the " Seraphics " to such frenzied ecstasy. The cult of sentimental adorations and friendships was just coming into vogue; " holy " soul-affinities, pledged in kisses and tears, heralded the dawn of " sensibility." And in truth no more ideal poet could have been found to give expression to the still half-unconscious urge of the slowly changing age. His poems are heroic landscapes before which a cloud-curtain is stretched. The outlines are only dimly visible; occasionally a streak of lightning flashes in the sulphurous atmosphere, but for the rest everything is wrapped in an inhospitable mist. The effect was confusing, irritating, and in the long run paralysing; but it *was* absolutely new, for here was a poet who, for the first time for so long, moved in an atmosphere of unreality and inarticulateness, indefiniteness and irrationality. Those who came after him were no longer sensitive to his strange novelty and mysterious suggestiveness, but felt only the grey monotony and vagueness of these aspects, which often degenerated into incomprehensibleness and oftener still into dullness. " I confess," says Schiller in his work on naïve and sentimental poetry, " that I tremble for the brain of the man who is truly and unaffectedly able to adopt this poet as his favourite reading. . . . It is only in certain ecstatic moods that one can take him up and find him sympathetic." The only way, indeed, to explain the universal Klopstock mania — to which Schiller in his youth also succumbed — is by the law of contrast: by the reaction, that is, against the intolerably bald and doctrinaire outlook of German literature in the first half of the eighteenth century.

That which Gottsched had done for poetry and poetics Christian Wolff did for all sections of learning and philosophy. He put into palatable form for the general public the ideas (though not the most profound and original ideas) of Leibniz, broadening them and watering them down to a thin, fluid, saltless porridge, but at the same time bringing them into a definite and self-contained system that, incidentally, was most unsuited to the restless genius of Leibniz. No one could accuse Wolff of being either restless or a genius, however. His self-assured phlegm, his habit of saying everything and explaining everything, his spinsterish tidiness, and his middle-class love of golden middle-truths made him the lauded and dreaded leader of his class for all Germany. For a generation — roughly from 1715 to 1735 — practically all lecturers were Wolffites; but doctors and lawyers, too, preachers and diplomats, fine ladies and society folk all found it advisable to " Wolffize." Societies arose for the " spreading of truth " according to Wolff's principles, and a contemporary satire on the fashionable Wolffian philosophy bore the title: *The Cobbler's Apprentice truly instructed according to Mathematical Methods, as being the very best, newest, and most natural.* Wolff wrote numerous stout volumes — more than thirty in all — on logic, metaphysics, teleology and moral, physics and physiology, the laws of nature and of nations, and empirical and rational psychology (the former describing the mind as it appears to external experience, the latter showing it for what it really is). He wrote his textbooks at first in German, and later in Latin as well, with a view to securing for them an international circulation as *præceptor universi generis humani.* His services in purifying the German language and constructing a philosophical terminology were by no means negligible: he coined, for instance, such expressions as " *Verhältnis* " (relation), " *Vorstellung* " (conception), " *Bewusstsein* " (consciousness). There are, in England and to some extent on the Continent, so-called general outfitters, who equip their clients to perfection from head to foot in the latest fashion. It was something of the kind that Wolff achieved in the realm of intellect for the German citizen of his generation — without, however, turning him out very elegantly: the equipment was complete, but extremely modest, dull and unprofitable, and not even really up to date, being more in the style of those suburban businesses that at a small cost rig out their customers in such a way that they are just fit to be seen in the street.

The leading ideas of the Wolffian philosophy are incredibly stale and insipid. The ultimate aim of all things lies in men: through man God achieves the main intention which inspired him at the Creation: namely, that he shall be recognized and worshipped as God. Correspondingly, all phenomena are estimated — in a positively grotesque fashion — solely from the point of view of their usefulness, and the degree of their usefulness, to mankind. The sun is praised because by its aid men can find the meridian, make sun-dials, and determine the latitude of a place; daylight affords us the advantage of "being able to undertake in comfort those daily tasks which can be done either not at all by night or at least not so easily nor without some expense." The stars are useful in that they enable us to see to some extent in the streets at night. "The alternation of day and night is advantageous in that it enables men and animals to refresh themselves at night by sleep; the night is favourable also to various undertakings which cannot well be carried out in the day, such as bird-catching and fishing." And the whole trend of ideas is summed up in the profound sentence: "The sun is there in order that changes may take place on the earth; the earth is there in order that the sun may not exist in vain." All the same, Wolff's enemies succeeded in representing this childish philosophy to the even more naïve Prussian King as dangerous to the State, persuading him that it was a doctrine of Fate and, consequently, that his "long-legs" might desert with impunity if Fate so willed it. Whereupon Wolff, who was at the time a professor at Halle, received an order from Frederick William to quit the royal provinces within forty-eight hours on pain of being hanged. Immediately after the accession of Frederick the Great he returned in triumph, but in the end — as Steinhausen pithily said — "everyone became so Wolffian that there was no one left to go to his lectures."

Pietism Wolff's expulsion was due in part to Pietism, which also had its centre in Halle. This movement formed a half-irrational side- and under-current during the whole of this period and was to swell

164

to vast proportions in the second half of the century. Within the domineering and bone-dry Protestantism of the day it took up much the same position as Mysticism had taken within the rusty creed-bound Church of the fifteenth century; and it bore a further resemblance to this Mysticism in that it was to a great extent a women's movement and produced a religious literature of diaries, " awakenings," confessions of the soul, and edifying " correspondences." But in point of depth it does not bear any comparison with the older movement. Its strongest champions on German soil were the Herrnhut sect, called the " Moravian Brethren " (after a group of pious Hussites who had gone into banishment centuries before), which made itself a settlement at Hutberg in the Lausitz on the estate of Count Zinzendorf. In the " Cross and Blood " theology of this nobleman religious experience centred exclusively on the Redeemer's bloody death on the Cross. This theme was treated with a fervid and rich sentimentality which not infrequently lapsed into extremes of bad taste, going so far even as to produce imagery taken from conjugal relations. The English section of Pietism was represented by the Methodists, who aimed at the methodical practice and teaching of piety, and whose religion was spread by the brothers John and Charles Wesley from Oxford to America, where with their imaginative, fervid, and even wild manner of preaching they have made a very deep impression, on the lower masses above all.

The Austrian states remained practically untouched by all these spiritual movements. Charles VI was peacefully inclined and good-tempered, but in mind and temperament he was dull, cold, and heavy. In political matters he was vacillating and unreliable, always on two sides at once; as an administrator he was diligent, but so mentally inert that it was his habit to reply to awkward questions by unintelligible mutterings. He clung obstinately to the old traditions of manners, religion, and government. At his court the black Spanish dress and the reverent Spanish ceremonial still held sway, and even the highest dignitaries fell on their knees to salute him and served him kneeling at table. To the Pragmatic Sanction, the *idée fixe* of his life, he devoted all his powers, while he allowed finance and the army to fall into the most desperate condition. In vain did old Prince Eugene warn him that he had better equip a hundred thousand men than be for ever

The bel canto

165

negotiating with everyone. He was a great theatre-lover, and the plays he had performed were perhaps more gorgeously mounted than any Europe had seen. He both played and composed and would often take part in his own private concerts and operatic performances. It was, of course, the all-prevailing Italian music that predominated at his court in Vienna (where Italian was customary even in ordinary conversation), and for many years there lived there the greatest musical theorist and the greatest librettist of the day — Johann Josef Fux, author of the famous *Gradus ad Parnassum,* a treatise on strict counterpoint and fugue, and Pietro Metastasio, who supplied texts to three generations of composers. This librettist was extraordinarily musical; his poetry was already melodrama in itself and dominated the accompanying orchestra. Words and music, consequently, were neither in rivalry nor coordinated in parallel; they were two sides of the same thing, an ideal unity. This was the basis of his pre-eminence, which was uncontested even in an age in which every branch of art " felt " musically and life as a whole was regarded as a sort of fantastic opera. Everything he wrote was coated uniformly with shimmering drawing-room varnish, smoothly rounded and planed, softly shining, sweet, and intentionally blurred. It is in his operas that the three-part construction first occurs: the *recitativo secco,* a declamation accompanied only by detached chords on the harpsichord; the sung *recitativo accompagnato,* strengthened by the orchestra, to which the music rises at dramatic moments; and the closing lyrical *aria,* which, according to the taste of the period, had often a " philosophic " tendency. This solo was by far the most important element with him, the ensemble movement parts playing a very definitely minor part. The action, consisting mainly of amorous intrigues and state plots, is highly complicated in its artificial subdivisions and ramifications, but at the same time extremely primitive in the violence of its progress and denouement.

The Italian fashion was so powerful that many musicians found it advisable to Italianize their names. For example, Rosetti's real name was Rösler and he was a plain native of Leitmeritz; the celebrated virtuoso Venturini answered originally to the name of Mislivecek. Everywhere the ear-tickling *bel canto* ruled supreme, the bravura aria imported from Italy, together with the Italian leaders, prima donnas, and *castrati* to express it; while in another field the violin-makers Amati, Guarneri, and Stradivari achieved such a mastery in their art as has never since been equalled. In 1711 the Florentine Bartolomeo Cristofori invented the *piano e forte* or hammer-piano, which gradually pushed all other stringed instruments into the background. Along with the *opera seria* the *opera buffa* appeared, Pergolesi's *Serva padrona* being the most famous example; and it was under the influence of the " buffoonists " that Rousseau wrote the first comic opera: *Le Devin du village*, which brought him a brilliant success. He and the Neapolitan Duni, who also lived in Paris, were the founders of this new type, in which the frozen passion of the *dramma per musica* dissolves in playful grace, and the stiff pompous aria is replaced by the coquettish chanson. In serious opera, too, Jean Philippe Rameau with his orchestral colouring went a certain way to meet the Rococo taste for brightness and glitter, though the Lully tradition was too unbreakable in France, and there was no real departure from program music, but only its expansion and enrichment with imagination and charm.

Even Handel, as we know, only broke away from Italian influences in his old age. He carried the art-form of the fugue to its greatest height in vocal as Bach had done in instrumental music. In his full choruses, particularly in *Israel in Egypt* (which is almost entirely made up of them), we have for the first time, as the object of an art-creation, something — namely, the mass, the people — of which the dramatists were still unaware, for it was not until *Tell*, or even, more accurately, not until *The Weavers* that a playwright attempted to bring the collective soul on the stage as his hero. Bach, on the other hand, put the awakening power of the German bourgeoisie, the Pietists' inner fervour and sturdy love of God, into music and gave it immortality. In his monumental chamber-music the rhythm and weight of Baroque were wedded to the intimacy and introspection of Rococo. Of the two, Handel is the less problematical, but the more *cantabile;* he is the psychologist, Bach the metaphysicist. In fact, one might perhaps place them in parallel with Leibniz and Kant, and not only for this reason, but also in the sense that Handel, as a sought-after and revered master, set up the macrocosm of his creation in sight of all, while Bach, living in the constricted atmosphere of lower social conditions, built his still mightier and more universal realm within himself;

Leibniz and Handel forced their own world upon the world at large, Kant and Bach encircled the whole world in their own. Bach and Handel, however, were alike in the intense Germanic ethos which fills all their works. This gigantic double sun forms one of the two undying titles to fame won by the Germany of that time in the realm of the spirit. The other is Frederick the Great.

The King   " Find in any country the Ablest Man that exists there," says Carlyle; " raise *him* to the supreme place, and loyally reverence him: you have a perfect government for that country." A recipe as admirable as it is simple, but, like almost all good and simple recipes, very seldom followed. Obviously it would be the most natural thing if the best were always at the head of things, the cleverest and wisest, the strongest and best-armed, the eye that sees furthest with past and present, the gleaming focus in which all the world's rays unite: if, in a word, the brain were in command as is the case with the simplest human individual! Yet this self-evidently normal case has happened at most a dozen times in the better-known sections of the history of humanity: a dozen times in three thousand years. One of these few cases was Frederick the Great.

The Father   The year 1740 was a year of change of government, not only in Prussia and Austria, but also in Russia, where the Tsaritsa Anna was succeeded by her grand-nephew Ivan VI, a minor; and in Rome, where Clemens XII was followed by Benedict XIV, " *il papa Lambertini* " — the most popular pope of the eighteenth century, a deeply honest man and a scholar, even-tempered, modest, passionately interested in contemporary literature, and so unprejudiced that Voltaire could risk dedicating his *Mahomet* to him. Frederick, it has sometimes been argued, owed his success in great part to his extraordinary predecessor, and the relation has been likened to that of Philip and Alexander. This grotesque opinion is represented by two parties who are in other respects entirely opposed to one another: the official Prussian historians who would make out every Hohenzollern to be a genius, and the equally biased Socialist history-writers who will have no king a genius at any price. Actually Frederick William I handed down to his son only the instrument of policy — that is, the army — and not a single political or even philosophical idea. Philip, on the contrary, who was probably a greater man than his successor, planned out the whole scheme of what the latter accomplished. He was in a sense the author of Alexander's conquests, and the " King of Asia " but the splendid actor of the heroic part.

But even among those who give Frederick William his proper place in Prussian history, we find the most contradictory judgments. The same critics will, without rhyme or reason, call him considerate and brutal, clear-sighted and narrow, malicious and self-sacrificing. It is fairest perhaps to regard him as a cranky, paradoxical genre figure. Certainly it is characteristic that he should have introduced the pigtail into his army a generation before its general adoption in Europe, and he undoubtedly carried the idea of patriarchal absolutism to the point of caricature. He concerned himself not only with the taxation and military service, the economic situation and the hygiene of his subjects, but with their clothes and lodging, reading and conversation, choice of wives and of callings, culinary arrangements and church attendance. He was in fact the well-meaning and severe, faithful and tiresome, father of his country, and he made liberal use of the paternal right to misunderstand and ill-treat the children. Small wonder that the said children developed a formidable " father-hatred."

He possessed neither many bad nor many good qualities, and what he did possess he possessed in only a moderate degree. But his minor faults — his coarseness, his stinginess, and his detestation of all intellectual and artistic aspirations — were of the sort which humanity finds it harder to forgive than the major sins; and his unpretentious virtues — his love of order, his diligence, his modest personal needs — did no one any good. Nor did his people thank him for raising the army to an imposing strength; for this also was one of his freaks. The army was not a means, but an end in itself. He regarded it as an entirely personal property, as a sort of gigantic toy, and he collected tall fellows as Augustus the Strong collected china, or Pope Lambertini fine prints. Prussian recruiting methods became a byword for baseness. In this respect this otherwise worthy prince knew no restraint. Every conceivable means was employed to entice more Grenadiers into his ranks: women, cards, alcohol, false promises — and, if none of these served, brute force. The troop movements were models of precision, the Prussian cadenced step went like clock-work. The introduction of the iron ramrod, combined with this iron discipline, made it possible to develop an exceedingly rapid fire. And without these achievements the virtuoso strategy and wide-ranging policy of his son would have been impossible.

Frederick was the opposite of his father in almost every respect, even in his attitude to militarism. From several of his intimate and therefore unquestionably genuine utterances we know that he loathed war. This did not, however, prevent him from making it when he considered it necessary, and making it more vigorously and aggressively than anyone else. He called war a " scourge of Heaven " and regretted that he could not live to see the day when humanity would be rid of it. For another thing, he was not even a monarchist. This may sound a strange and almost incredible thing to say of an eighteenth-century king (and the strongest and most victorious of them into the bargain), but there is not the least doubt that it was so. All his life he treated his crowned colleagues with a truly extravagant contempt, and he was full of bitter mockery for everything connected with court ceremonial, holding his own crown without the slightest sense of doing so by higher investiture, or even merely by juridical title. He knew, of course, that he was something more than most other mortals, but it was for that reason, and not as happening to be a king, that he wanted to be honoured.

Frederick William had all his life been a pious man in the matter of orthodox church beliefs, a scorner of the subtleties of diplomacy and the refinements of literature, gnarled, robust, primitively healthy and primitively honest, simple to the extreme in his daily needs, and single-minded to the point of half-wittedness. Frederick, on the contrary, had a sovereign scorn and distrust of all positive religions that was but a degree removed from atheism. He placed a far higher value on works of art and philosophy than on any achievement of practical life, was a past master in diplomatic juggling, and a supreme gourmet in all the higher pleasures ; at the same time he was anything but " healthy " in the sense of a normal person, having an extraordinarily irritable, complicated, and contradictory nature, highly labile in his inner equilibrium, and physically also delicate and sensitive. Like every genius he was " physiologically inferior " and psychopathic, and like every genius he became master of his psychosis by developing a hypertrophy of strength in his moral and intellectual capabilities.

It is often said that he inherited his delight in work and sense of duty from his father; but the diligence of genius is something of quite a different order from that of the average man: the latter arises out of a mechanical sense of orderliness and the instinct to be active (which is a primitive bee-like vital instinct), but the former from an almost maniacal devotion to an exalted mission, a sublime sense of responsibility towards one's own magic destiny.

The fact that Frederick the Great was dominated all his life by a great leading idea not only made him the invincible hero of his time, but endowed all his individual actions — unlike those of his crowned rivals — with imagination and genius and meaning. This basic idea of his was no more and no less than the Platonic demand that kings should be philosophers, and philosophers kings. In his book on Plato, Walter Pater says of Marcus Aurelius that it was precisely because the philosophic outlook was so essential a part of him, because he was the passionate devotee of philosophy and in particular of Platonism, that he was so excellent a servant of the Roman people in peace and war. Just such a ruler was Frederick the Great. In this alone lay the true meaning of " enlightened absolutism," the slogan of the day, of which only he could grasp the deeper meaning and which only he could transform into a living reality. Absolutism means unlimited control, and enlightenment spreading of light; this formula, therefore, asserts nothing more or less than that light shall reign, the strongest soul rule, the clearest head organize. There is no need to discuss the outward forms by which such an ideal may be realized; this is a matter of complete indifference, a mere question of costume. Whether such a ruler be styled Cæsar or High Priest, President of the Reich or People's Commissar, he will always be the legitimate king because he is the philosophical king. *The Philosopher*

His tolerance alone suffices to show Frederick as a true philosopher. We mean tolerance, and neither free-thinking nor liberalism. It is possible to be " liberally " minded and yet have a very illiberal mind, in which (as is the case with most free-thinkers) an understanding for differently constituted points of view has no place. This type of the " enlightened " is as much the prisoner of his narrow one-sided doctrine as the reactionary whom he scorns. The same is true of liberalism as usually practised. It is liberal towards liberals only; the rest of the world are obstinate heretics and blind *The Genius* fools on whom the better world-outlook must be imposed in spite of themselves. And this, after all, was the typical behaviour of the Enlightened in Frederick the Great's time. In the eighteenth century we see everywhere in the high places these dictators of progress, who held it to be their mission to force happiness upon a lagging humanity. Peter the Great and Charles XII, Catherine II and Joseph II, Cardinal Fleury and Robespierre and many others were guided by this fixed idea, which penetrated even as far as Portugal, where the Marquis of Pombal built up a positive reign of terror of Enlightenment. Thus in reality these rulers were nothing but converted children of darkness, and they furnish yet one more proof of the psychological fact that tolerance is essentially obnoxious to average humanity. But Frederick the Great was tolerant, not in his capacity of free-thinker, but as a genius. Genius tolerates everything because it contains latent within itself every imaginable specimen of mankind, every impulse of the soul, and knows how to conform to everything because it possesses creative imagination. Frederick practised that genuine tolerance which consists simply in recognizing every alien individuality and its laws. For this reason he could even tolerate reaction. He, as the head of the chief Protestant power of Germany, was far more lenient to the Jesuits than was the Roman Emperor. The latter abolished monasteries while the former restored burnt-down Catholic churches. Not that Frederick was by any means without personal prejudices, but, sharply marked as were these very subjective and one-sided convictions of his, clear-cut, strong, and luminous as was the profile of his personality, he had yet a sufficiency of understanding for all other opinions, and, what is more, he actually took them into account in practice. Certainly he was in a way a spiritualist and ideologue, for he always argued from certain abstract principles, direct soul-experiences. But this was counterbalanced by his highly developed mental elasticity, his capacity for accommodating himself at any time to the special " conditions of the problem " which reality imposed upon him in his experiments. He was unusually tenacious and conservative in matters of theory, and correspondingly supple and progressive in his application of theory to life ; and it is this double quality which in fact forms the basis of all productive thought and action.

Another eminent mark of genius was his boundless sincerity, a quality which, rare enough in any case, seems almost an impossibility on the throne. Even his attitude to truth shows the contradictoriness, and yet in a higher sense the unity, of his nature. As a politician he had no qualms about giving the whole world a false impression, and he prided himself on beating all his enemies at sleight-of-hand and double-dealing. Yet, living though he did in that age of hollow lying and empty masks, he was one of the least mendacious men that ever lived. Untruthfulness was to him a sort of technical language of which he made use in masterly fashion in the transaction of his business; but in all things which he thought really serious and important he was actuated by incorruptible probity and merciless self-criticism. This is why, in spite of being raised so high above his fellow-men by birth and position, talents and deeds, he figures to posterity largely as a private individual free from any historical nimbus. A number of endearing minor traits also help to bring him nearer to us. There is, for instance, something impish yet touching in the remark made by this great monarch and controller of battles that the only fame worth having was that of an author. He would polish away at his verses in the midst of his campaigns, and in the presence of literary men of note he felt himself a pupil desirous of profiting by their art. Everything he did or left undone secures for him our personal attachment. How charmingly unkinglike, for example, is his detestation of hunting! The marked and even consciously ambitious wit which, like a fine essence, pervades all his doings, from big affairs of government to the most everyday conversations, also affects us as a " private " attribute. Even his decrees were glittering *bons mots* worthy of a Swift or Voltaire. One day, when he confirmed the acquittal of a thief convicted of sacrilege, whose defence " that the Blessed Virgin had herself given him the silver " was admitted as not incredible by Catholic authorities, he added that he forbade him in future, on pain of heavy punishment, to accept any presents whatever from the Holy Virgin. Another time, in reviewing the case of a soldier convicted of having had unnatural connexion with his horse, he settled it with the words: " The swine is to be transferred to the infantry." Very attractive too is his lively feeling for escapades of every sort, which clung to him until well into middle age. Macaulay thus describes this side of him, not, of course, without implying a black mark for bad conduct: " If a courtier was fond of dress, oil was flung over his richest suit. If he was fond of money, some prank was invented to make him disburse more than he could spare. If he was hypochondriachal, he was made to believe that he had the dropsy. If he had particularly set his heart on visiting a place, a letter was forged to frighten him from going thither." With such things did Frederick the Unique occupy himself while engaged in making his army the most powerful striking force, his administration the most capable, and his State the most feared in all Europe. The respectable Macaulay deduces from all this the wickedness of his nature. We are inclined to think that it is only through such traits that human greatness becomes human and bearable. They are rarely absent from the nature of true genius and, far from indicating an evil disposition, they express an indestructible childlikeness and a supreme artistic playfulness which takes everything and nothing seriously. In this, as in so many other respects, Frederick the Great resembled Voltaire. The old friendship between these two men, as registered in their correspondence, forms one of the wittiest chapters in the history of the eighteenth century. There we have French pepper and Prussian salt thrown together and so intimately blended that the mixture became too sharp and biting for any philistine to sample without tears of vexation.

The Hero from curiosity   So complicated and paradoxical, yet so clear and transparent is the character of this king that it leaves the democratic historian nothing to " debunk." He went so far in self-criticism as to make himself out at times worse than he was. He admits frankly that the mainspring of his policy was ambition. He tells us how, when as Crown Prince he heard of the Turkish War, his heart thumped as if he had been an actor waiting for his cue. Yet when it came, he advanced from the wings without hesitation, and it was clear from the earliest scenes that he was determined not to play the little episodic rôle assigned to him by the European management, but to improvise an entire new text as protagonist and filler of the title-rôle of the age. In 1740 he wrote to his friend Jordan: " My youth, the fire of my passions, the craving for fame, even — to conceal nothing from you — my curiosity, in a word, a secret instinct tore me from the sweetness of repose I had been tasting; it was the satisfaction of reading my name in the papers and eventually in history that tempted me." And long afterwards in his

Historical Memoirs he repeats that his decisions in 1740 were influenced by the desire to make himself a name. These, again, are quite the trains of thought of an actor. This king who goes to war out of psychological curiosity, a species of theatre-mania, and from the ardent desire to appear in the paper, and not only so, but frankly admits such impulses — this detached independence, this bizarre coquetry, this sophisticated and yet naïve craving for the limelight, is Rococo of the most genuine kind.

Strange as it may sound, Frederick the Great was not an earnest person. By an " earnest " person we can only understand one who is caught by reality, the " practical " man, the materialist; and by a non-earnest person we mean the intellectual man who is capable of looking down on life from above, taking it now humorously, now tragically, but never earnestly. Both the humorous and the tragic aspects have one and the same root; they are two polar and therefore complementary expressions of the same worldfeeling. Not to take existence seriously is something that belongs no less to the tragic than to the humorous focus. Both are based on the profound conviction of the worthlessness and vanity of the world. And so it comes about that Frederick the Great is one of the few figures of his age that are truly tragic and are yet at the same time enveloped by the breath of a sublime irony.

But at the close of his life, as " Old Fritz," he — like all other really great men: Goethe and Kant, Ibsen and Tolstoi, Michelangelo and Rembrandt — becomes completely unreal and ghostly, transcendent and transparent, already half an inhabitant of the other world. An immense solitude spreads itself about him, he is weary of " ruling over slaves " and wants to be buried beside his greyhounds.

Doubtless he had great faults; but then, the favourites of mankind are not the proper ones. The whole age did him joyous homage because he was the strongest and most human, wisest and most foolish of all: Cæsar and Don Quixote, Hamlet and Fortinbras in one person. In Switzerland there were people who fell ill with mortification when he lost a battle; in England, which even as an ally has never liked to see a development of power on the Continent, his victories were celebrated like national festivals; in Paris one became socially impossible if one took sides against him; in Russia he had an enthusiastic following at court, headed by Peter, the heir to the throne; even at Naples and in Spain his portraits were on sale.

The Danish minister Bernsdorff called pre-Frederician Prussia a young lean body with all the appetite that belongs to this stage of physical development, and Voltaire mocked at it as a "border state." A glance at the historical map will show that such a state, consisting in the main of two disconnected coastal areas with a few oddments of territory in the west, was incapable of existence in such a form. One cannot reproach Frederick the Great for his aspirations towards Silesia, unless one is prepared in principle to deny to a political organism the right of forcible expansion. Through this addition, which enlarged the extent of the state by a third and the population by a half, Prussia first obtained that stability and solidity of territorial basis without which a great power is unthinkable. It is only too comprehensible that Frederick succumbed to this temptation. But from the moment when he incorporated Silesia with hungry Prussia, he looked upon the latter as sufficiently provided for. In 1745 he declared, at Dresden, that from that time on he would not attack a single cat, unless indeed he were forced; that he regarded his military career as closed. And beyond a doubt he honestly meant it. No one but an imbecile would maintain that he embarked on the Seven Years' War otherwise than against his will; only, as he himself was anything but an imbecile, he naturally began it at the moment which appeared to him relatively the most favourable.

Endless rubbish has been written and printed about the "brutal surprise attack" and "perfidious breach of treaty" in 1740. It is an Austrian lie that Frederick was bound by the Pragmatic Sanction. The fact is that the Emperor had guaranteed the succession of the Rhenish dukedom of Berg to Frederick William in return for his assent to the treaty and yet ten years later took diplomatic action against him in collusion with France, England, and Holland with the object of forcing him to relinquish these claims. That Frederick did not wait until Austria was fully equipped, but occupied Silesia in mid winter — an unheard-of proceeding according to the strategic practice of the day — is merely a proof of his courage and originality in not thinking on traditional lines, and of Austria's heaviness and mental apathy. His simple and therefore crushing logic was: first to obtain possession of the country and then to negotiate on the question of its cession. " I will put a problem to you," he wrote to his minister Podewils; " when one has the advantage, should one take advantage of it or not? I am prepared with my troops and with everything. If I do not exploit my opportunity, I shall have in my hands an asset that I do not know how to use; but if I do exploit it, they will say that I am clever enough to turn to good account the advantage I possess over my neighbours." And in 1743, he says, looking back in the preface to the first draft of his *Memoirs:* " I do not claim to defend the policy which the established custom of the nations has handed down to us as legitimate. I merely expound in simple fashion the reasons which, it seems to me, bind every prince to follow the practice authorizing deceit and misuse of force; and if he did not, I say frankly that his neighbours would only take advantage of his integrity, and that the wrong assumption and the fallacious conclusion would ascribe to weakness what had been only virtuousness on his part. These reflections and many others, well weighed, have made me decide to conform to the custom of princes. . . . One finds oneself confronted, at bottom, with choosing between the dreadful necessity of sacrificing one's subjects or one's word. . . . And so the sovereign sacrifices himself for the welfare of his subjects." What other prince would have been able to discuss with such deep and clear, such honourable and plainly worded objectivity, this immense moral dilemma, which, unfortunately, is an undeniable reality! Who else indeed would have been even conscious of this tragic conflict? The sense of an overwhelming life-tragedy breathes to us out of these and countless similar confessions made in widely dissimilar periods of his life. They are the words of a genius predestined by its intellectual form for a world of pure reflection, but flung, a martyr, into the troubled sphere of action, to which — humbly accepting its fate — it sacrifices itself. This, in all nudity, was the real soul of that intriguer and unscrupulous *Realpolitiker*. But men are very odd: when one man rises up in their midst, sharing their guilt, indeed, but knowing it and suffering under it, they do not call him greater and better than themselves, but throw it in his face that he is no saint.

For that matter, not only the inner life of Frederick the Great, but his system of foreign policy is very often entirely misjudged. He was in no sense Austria's " hereditary enemy." We have seen the terrible crisis in which the Habsburg monarchy was involved at the beginning of the War of the Austrian Succession; it was Frederick who saved it then by making a separate peace. The Convention of Klein-Schnellendorf released the only strong army which Austria was able to put in the field for use against the Bavarians and the French. In any case he did not and could not seriously intend the complete break-up of Austria, for this would merely have given France an intolerable superiority. All he wanted, and always wanted, was just Silesia; but to this Maria Theresa clung obstinately. That he was in the right over this annexation — not perhaps in the light of an ambiguous *Völkerrecht* (to which, as a rule, only the vanquished appeal), but certainly before the higher tribunal of cultural history — becomes entirely clear when we compare the later intellectual and moral condition of Prussian Silesia with that of the part that remained Austrian. One of the greatest achievements in his foreign policy (and one worthy to rank with his holding of Silesia through three wars after the conquest, but seldom adequately appreciated) was the bloodless incorporation of West Prussia, by which he first made his kingdom a really effective Northern power. This was one of the most important " rounding-off " achievements in modern European history.

The Administrator His administration of these provinces was a model. His energetic but moderate reforming activity extended over every domain. He was the creator of the general national law of Prussia, he encouraged education by establishing a general schools system, and he improved the land by draining great stretches of marsh and waste and facilitating trade by the construction of important canals. On the other hand, he would have no new roads made, for he wished to force the traffic to stay longer on the country-side and consume more of its produce. In this he was sacrificing to the spirit of the age. In our last chapter we noted some of the exaggerations which mercantilism allowed itself in Prussia and elsewhere. Frederick William I forbade prolonged mourning, lest the market for bright woollen stuffs should be damaged thereby, and threatened to put into the pillory any woman who wore the English prints then in fashion. And Frederick the Great writes in his *Political Testament* of 1752: " For trade and manufacture it is fundamental that money should be prevented from leaving the country, by producing at home everything that till now has been imported." In the same spirit he forbade his officials to visit foreign watering-places for cures, and limited his subjects, when they went abroad, to a certain sum for travelling. Every household was bound under official supervision to use a fixed minimum quantity of salt, and permissions to marry were only obtainable in return for the purchase of goods from the royal porcelain-factories. Nevertheless, this tyranny had its good points: enormous mulberry plantations were laid out for the home production of silk, and hop- and potato-growing made excellent progress under state fosterage.

Napoleon once said: " Genius is diligence." And this definition of it, like others, will fit Frederick the Great remarkably. It sounds incredible, but is nevertheless true, that in this country literally everything, from the greatest and roughest tasks to the smallest and most subtle, was done by the brain and working-power of one man. It must have been instructive, paradoxical, intriguing, and alarming for the contemporaries to see this thousand-eyed manager running the whole state-system down to the last thread. Here the King showed not only the diligence, but the all-roundness of genius. It is not too much to compare him with Julius Cæsar in this respect. The man of genius can do everything, knows everything, understands everything. He is never a specialist. He is there, ready, and able to do exactly what circumstances may require. Frederick refused to let himself down at any particular standpoint, he was a polyhistor of life. Whatever he took in hand became transfused with his vigour, which, ever the same, one and indivisible, needed only to be given a sphere, any sphere, of action to expand instantly and triumphantly.

For this reason Frederick the Great's strategic achievements, recognized as extraordinary by even his bitterest enemies, cannot be considered apart from his personality as a whole. We have grown used to thinking of generalship as the expression of a specific professional knowledge and a definable professional talent for which it is sufficient to graduate in a few military courses. But just as it is not enough for a great doctor merely to have studied medicine, or for a great artist to know how to use his colours, so is a great commander unthinkable without some deeper knowledge of the human soul, the way of the world, and in general all things worth knowing. He must be a sort of artist and, above all,

The Strategist

a philosopher. That Prince Eugene possessed these attributes we have seen: it was for him that the greatest thinker of the age wrote his principal work, not simply " dedicating " it to him (which would signify nothing at all), but literally composing it for him. Julius Cæsar, again, was not only the friend of Cicero (who was his political opponent), but his superior in literary and philosophic talent. As for Moltke, a look at his skull suffices to show that we are dealing with a first-class thinker. And who is able to say how much Alexander owed to his father's grandiose act in giving him Aristotle, the most spacious and the best-filled brain in all Greece, for a teacher? To draw any distinction of principle between the activity of a Napoleon and that of a Shakspere is nonsensical.

And yet who would not rather be a sort of Shakspere than a sort of Napoleon? Who would choose to command dull, boring armies of grenadiers when he might have the entire world-history in all its vividness and abundance for his army of operation? Who would care to translate his inward strivings into ugly, obstinate, and at best disillusioning realities when he has power to summon radiant idealities that never fail him? Who would desire to drive men's bodies when he can lead their souls, direct the march of thought instead of the march of feet?

The tragedy of great men of action is the tragedy of poets who are stuck fast in life. Only so can we account for that loathing for life which so filled and so drove Julius Cæsar in his last years that he went almost knowingly to his death; or for the great Alexander's jealousy of the little Achilles: for in truth it was not Achilles, but Homer, who was the object of that jealousy. And Frederick the Great would joyfully have given his throne and his army and all his conquests and victories for the power to become, not indeed a Voltaire, but just a modest Maupertuis.

He did not approve of war. He bore it with sorrow as the field chosen by destiny for his creative activity. And nobody, at the bottom of his heart, really approves of it. But history up till now — which is after all no more than a sort of prehistory of real humanity — has taught that war is manifestly one of the biological functions of our species. And, admitting frankly that it has to happen anyhow, it is at least desirable that it should be in the hands of men of genius.

The strategy of that period, like its theology, its medicine, and its poetry, had gradually degenerated into uninspired automatism and rigid routine. As late as 1753 the service regulations of Electoral Saxony laid it down that battles should be avoided and the object of the war attained by " cunning manœuvring." Of course it came to battles all the same, sooner or later, but they happened more or less by chance and in a mechanical way, just as a long-exposed head of inflammable material will in the end almost explode of itself. Frederick the Great, too, regarded the battle as an " emetic " to be resorted to only in extreme necessity ; but he made the application of this remedy the subject of deep and daring speculation. Similarly, he retained in principle the linear tactics of the period, in which the entire body of infantry advanced in close columns and in cadenced step as if on the parade ground, and the individual fighting-man was denied any personal initiative. A battle consisted purely in the meeting of the two hostile bodies. The conception of a reserve in the sense of modern warfare was still unknown. Frederick the Great now arrived at the idea of forming a sort of reserve by holding back a wing temporarily (" refusing " it) in order to bring about a decision with it at the suitable moment. In his time this method was of the highest originality, though it was not entirely new to history : it was a link — skipping two thousand years — with Epaminondas. Before the Theban general arrived, the Greek tactics, of which the Spartans were unrivalled masters, consisted in opening the battle along the whole line simultaneously. Epaminondas, however, arrayed his troops in varying degrees of depths, reinforcing them in a sort of wedge towards the right or left side. By this means he defeated the Spartans at Leuctra in one of the greatest and most decisive battles ever fought between Hellenes. This " oblique order " secures for the general the initiative, in that it allows him to choose the point of attack ; but it is only fully effective when supported by the ingredient of surprise. Consequently, only a swift thinker of clear head and strong mind like Frederick the Great could handle it, and even with him it did not always succeed. He was supported in the execution of this method by his cavalry attacks, which he managed with the completest mastery, and by his concentration of artillery fire at the decisive points. The essential, and indeed revolutionary, point about these innovations was, however, the fierce offensive spirit which was expressed in them. War was no longer waged in order to carry out all manner of clumsy and complicated operations, but in order to win. This simple and obvious train of thought had been lost to that generation, and it is hardly an exaggeration to say that it is only since Frederick the Great that we have had offensive battles in modern history. Further, there was the amazing speed of his troop movements, which made him the miracle of his century and, at its close, the model admired by Napoleon. "Those are my three points," he said to the Marquis Valory: "emphatically, rapidly, and from all sides at once"; and these words contain practically the whole essence of his generalship. This *élan*, combined with his cool consideration and his sovereign command over circumstances, enabled him to defeat his opponents, who all more or less resembled the ever-hesitating Daun. He had the art of infusing this dash and vigour into his regiments, which, although not actually patriotic and, at the most, "Fritzian," moved from the first moment with a compelling rhythm. With them he was able, at Rossbach and Leuthen, to defeat enemies of more than twice his own strength, which is almost a unique feat in the history of modern wars. Already in the fifth year of his reign, after Hohenfriedberg, he was known as "the Great."

Phlogiston, irritability, and the primary nebula

In Frederick the Great, Baroque and Enlightenment appear intermingled, queerly and yet naturally, for this, in fact, is the hall-mark of the whole age, and it, precisely, is the condition of soul that we call Rococo. In the sphere of the exact sciences, too, there still reigned in principle the great Baroque tradition of a half-playful delight in theoretically directed experiments and discoveries. To mention only a few of the most important achievements, selected purely as characteristic examples: at Lisbon in 1709 Father Lorenz Gusman sent up the first balloon, which, however, struck a corner of the King's palace and came to grief; in 1716 Johann Baptist Homann edited his famous *Great Atlas*, the maps which already covered the whole of Europe, Asia, Africa, and South America, and about half of Australia and North America. At the same time Fahrenheit constructed the first mercury thermometer, which was followed ten years later by Réaumur's alcohol thermometer. In 1727 Stephen Hales published his *Vegetable Staticks*, a basic work on the physiology of plants, in which the phenomena of root-pressure and the movement of sap are clearly recognized, and the mass of fluid taken from the soil by the plant and given off again is determined by accurate measurement. In 1744 Trembley made a great sensation by his experiments with fresh-water polyps, by which he proved that these creatures, hitherto regarded as plants, not only were to be counted as animals, but possessed a strange and almost incredible facility of reproduction. He cut them up into three or four pieces, divided them in half lengthwise, even turned them inside out like gloves; yet all these procedures did not hinder their complete regeneration as living specimens. A year later Lieberkühn described the structure and function of the connivent valves of the intestine. In 1752 Benjamin Franklin, the printer and newspaper-editor, invented the lightning-conductor in the course of his experiments on the electric spark, so that later d'Alembert could say of him: "*Eripuit cœlo fulmen sceptrumque tyrannis;* he tore the lightning from heaven and the sceptre from the tyrants." In the course of his voyage of discovery in Arctic lands, Maupertuis discovered the polar flattening of the globe. Lambert founded photometry, defined the cometary paths, and reformed cartography. The engraver Rösel von Rosenhof discovered and described the peculiar movements of the amœbæ (which he called "water-insects") and illustrated them by magnificently coloured copperplates. Borelli defined bones as levers to which the muscles are attached; Baglioni compared the circulation of the blood to the action of a hydraulic machine, the respiratory organs to bellows, the entrails to sieves. Friedrich Hoffmann, who established admirable dieting cures and is still famous for the stomachic drops named after him, regarded the human body as a machine, while Georg Ernst Stahl took the opposite point of view of "animism." The latter is also the author of the Phlogiston Theory, which rested on the hypothesis that in combustion, putrefaction, and fermentation a "combustible principle," *phlogiston,* escaped from bodies and made them lighter. Boyle, it will be remembered, had already produced proof that, during the process known later as oxidization, weight was added, but he did not discover the cause of this phenomenon — it was not till 1771 that oxygen was first discovered, by Priestley and Scheele — and for this reason its importance was not realized, the principles of pyrochemistry ruling unchallenged for almost the whole of the century. The leading physiologist of the age,

Albrecht von Haller, based the whole of medicine on the theory of irritability, his doctrine being that all illnesses can be explained by the increase or lowering of the normal capacity for irritation and are to be treated by lowering or stimulating remedies accordingly. Physics continued, and long, under the influence of Newton. A Newtonian, too, was the young professor of philosophy Dr. Immanuel Kant, who in 1755 published an explanation of the origin of the solar system which afterwards found universal acceptance as the Kant-Laplace theory. According to this the world was originally composed of a cosmic nebula; gradually, as a result of differences of density, there were formed certain clumps which, owing to their greater mass, exercised an attraction over the lighter elements and thereby constantly enlarged themselves. Friction produced perpetual fire, and so the sun was formed. The bodies which happened to be within the sun's circle of influence either added to it by falling into it or, if their tangential force held its own against the force of attraction, revolved round it. The relation of the moons to the planets was completely analogous; they also by their tangential force transformed the falling movement into an orbital one. The first state of all heavenly bodies is the fiery liquid, which, owing to the continual radiation of heat, pass to the particulate-liquid and finally to the solid state. Our own central body is only a part of a higher stellar system which arose in the same way. World development is everlasting, but the span of life of individual bodies is limited. One day the moving stars will fall into the sun, and one day even the sun will fade out. But in this mechanical cosmogony Kant by no means saw any grounds for atheism, but rather the most strong argument against it: it was precisely this strict obedience to laws that afforded the most illuminating proof of the existence of God.

Immoral plants The most productive naturalist of this period was the Swede Carl von Linné, who worked out a complete *systema naturæ*. His principal merit consisted in his rigorous application of a "binary nomenclature": that is, he gave all plants and animals two Latin names each, the first being that of the genus, and the second that of the species. Thus dog, wolf, and fox became *canis familiaris, canis lupus,* and *canis vulpes;* cucumber and melon, *cucumis sativus* and *cucumis melo.* To each name, moreover, he attached an excellently clear and brief diagnosis. Minerals also he described according to their outward form and inner structure, their hardness and their optical behaviour. The flora (the expression originated with him) he divided into: hermaphrodite plants, the number, length, and order of whose stamens served him for further classification; separate-sexed plants, among which he distinguished those with male and female flowers on the same plant, or on different plants, or mixed with hermaphrodite flowers; and cryptogams or secret-flowering plants, by which he meant those whose flowers and fruits were too small to be accurately detected. This method of classification brought him much abuse on the score of its indecency. It was considered positively revolting that there should be talk of plants on which several anthers lived with one seed capsule in a state of concubinage. The assumption of such scandalous conditions was held to be a slander not only against the plants, but against God, who would never countenance such horrible lewdness. A system so unchaste, wrote a Petersburg botanist, must not be communicated to young students. Linnæus also roused much antagonism by grouping men with monkeys among the Primates. But this by no means implies a Darwinian outlook — on the contrary he stated his adherence to the scriptural story of the Creation by saying: " *Tot numeramus species, quot creavit ab initio infinitum ens.*"

The chief centre of " enlightened " and " practical " thought, founded on natural science and liberal in tendency, was even at that time England. It was there that the highly significant institution of the Order of Freemasons originated. The first Grand Lodge was formed in 1717. The name Freemason is a reminder of the fact that the order rose out of workers' combinations. The ideal which it set itself to achieve was the erection of a Solomon's temple of universal tolerance and active human kindness. England was also — and this is far more important — the country of origin of the modern nature-sense. In 1728 Langley sketched out the first program for the " English Garden," in his *New Principles of the Art of Gardening*. In this he protests energetically against the geometrical park tradition of Versailles, which cripples and devitalizes nature. He will have no more straight rows of trees, but only irregular avenues, free-growing shrubs, small patches of woodland, hop-gardens, grazing-meadows, rocks, and precipices. But all this — and here the true Rococo spirit comes to the surface

The feeling for Nature awakes

185

again — must be artificially created. Stags and deer in enclosures are designed to give the *illusion* of living nature, and ruins were specially built, and even mountains painted on canvas, to suggest a romantic wildness. The Baroque principle of staging nature still ruled, though with the opposite sign. These ideas were to some extent realized by William Kent in his *fermes ornées*. Montesquieu, the first great Anglomaniac in France, on his return from England transformed the park of his ancestral château into an English garden. Typical of the awakening nature-sense, too, are the popular *bals champêtres* of the day and the " inns," so called, where fine ladies and gentlemen dressed up as barmen, peasants, huntsmen, and fishermen and played at the simple life. Sleighing was a favourite amusement, and Klopstock sang the praises of skating. In summer fashionable ladies formed the habit of wearing wide straw shepherdess hats. At first it was merely a coquetting with Nature, and this Nature was not yet that of Romanticism — notwithstanding its mountain backgrounds and its cult of ruins — but the idyllic, inviting, touching, lamb-brook-and-meadow Nature lying caressingly at their feet. The highest praise for any scenery at that period was to call it " pleasant." Moreover, Wolffian rationalism and utilitarianism strongly pervaded everything still. The country was lovable above all as the donor of tasty vegetables, nourishing milk, and fresh eggs. The high mountains were held in abhorrence. As late as 1755, in the *Dictionary* which the English contemplated with astonishment as a world-wonder, Dr. Johnson described mountains as diseased growths and unnatural swellings on the earth's surface, and complained, after his journey in the Scottish Highlands, that an eye accustomed to flowery pictures and waving corn was appalled by this wide domain of hopeless barrenness. The only comfortable landscapes to look at were evidently the bread-and-butter-producing regions. The high tracts were barren and therefore could not be beautiful. Haller's poem *The Alps*, again, which made an immense sensation, contemplates only the human accessories of the Swiss landscape and has a moralizing, political tendency even at that.

Bible and ledger

By this period the modern Englishman was already complete and ready-made: a mixture of spleen, cant, and business, with his shrewdness and sobriety occasionally seasoned with fixed ideas, with thoroughness in place of depth, and plainness instead of significance; didactic, idiosyncratic, and pharisaical, and no less pious than business-like. On Sundays he believes in God and eternity, on week-days in physics and the Stock Exchange, and with equal fervour in both cases. On Sunday the Bible is his ledger, and on week-days the ledger is his Bible.

After the death of Queen Anne the crown had fallen to the Elector of Hanover, which circumstance brought about once more a personal union between England and a Continental power: George I, intellectually as much of a nonentity as his three name-sakes who succeeded him, had not even mastered the language of the country, and conversed with his officials in dog-Latin, so that it was useless for him to attend a Cabinet meeting. His prime minister was Robert Walpole, who had been active in promoting the Hanoverian succession and secured a permanent majority for its support in the Commons by means of an elaborate system of bribes. The corruptness of the age is satirized in Gay's *Beggar's Opera* (which was, incidentally, a parody of the fashionable Italian opera of the day). But when, at the first performance, a couplet on these bribes was encored after wild applause, Walpole had the wit to call for a second encore, and so brought down the house in his own favour. In Parliament, into whose hands the direction of the whole of foreign policy had fallen, he relied upon the Whigs, and he still kept his position under George II.

During this reign an extraordinary event took place which was perhaps more fraught with consequences than anything in English history: Robert Clive established the British supremacy in East India. An inexhaustible stream of rice, sugar, spices, and vege-table oils poured over England. Until Clive's time, Macaulay tells us, the English had been mere home-keepers. But now the race for money set in, and the little self-sufficing, exclusive island-people became at one blow a nation of international dealers, mer-chant traders, and colossal speculators. The " nabobs," as they were called, returned from India, with the parvenu's display of their newly-acquired riches, and formed a new social class — the despised but envied " self-made man." The commercialization of the whole of public life made rapid progress. *Trading on the basis of samples* set in, and there developed also the warehouse type of business, in which financiers merely dispose of manufactured articles, secured at a low price by advance payments. (These are

Comfort

in fact the two typical forms of modern economy.) Simultaneously the abundant influx of ready money introduced "comfort," a thing until then unknown to modern times. This English word had a curious origin. It meant at first "consolation" or "encouragement," and only now acquired the sense of "ease," "well-being," or "convenience," under which meaning it has been adopted in German. To an Englishman it is actually the supreme consolation and encouragement, and the final legitimation of his existence in his sense of well-being in it. The Calvinistic divine Richard Baxter, living in England in the times of the Restoration and the Glorious Revolution, tells his followers in his *Reasons for the Christian Religion* that they may work for God in order to become rich. Success in business counted as a proof of election; such was his — and in general the English — idea of Predestination. In place of Christian justification there appears the bourgeois, practical prosperity-justification: the well-to-do on earth are the righteous; the unblessed and the damned are the poor — an inversion of the gospel teaching unparalleled in its impudence and shallowness.

Franklin and Robinson Crusoe — Writing in his incomparable plastic way on the England of that time, Taine says: "A preacher here is nothing but an economist in priest's clothing who treats conscience like flour, and fights vices as if they were prohibitions on imports." In real life this type is most closely embodied in the story-book hero Benjamin Franklin, author of the phrase: "Time is money"; in literature we have the most complete representation of it in Defoe's *Life and Strange Surprising Adventures of Robinson Crusoe of York, Mariner*. Robinson Crusoe is the very able man who is equal to any emergency: a practical economist, politician, and technician; a deist who believes in God because he has discovered that this also is a practical sort of thing to do. It is significant that, besides writing his books (more than two hundred of them), Defoe established the first hail- and fire-insurance societies and savings-banks. The extract of his philosophy is found in the words with which the father Crusoe sends forth his son on the journey. He tells him that "the middle station of life was calculated for all kind of virtues and all kinds of enjoyments; that peace and plenty were the handmaids of a middle fortune; that temperance, moderation, quietness, health, society, all agreeable diversions, and all desirable pleasures, were the blessings attending the middle station of life; that this way men went silently and smoothly thro' the World, and comfortably out of it, not embarrassed with the labours of the hands or of the head . . . or harass'd with perplex'd circumstances which rob the soul of peace, and the body of rest. . . ."

After Franklin and Defoe came Richardson, creator of the English domestic novel, and likewise primarily a shopkeeper. His most successful work (of over four thousand pages) is called: "*Clarissa, or the History of a Young Lady;* comprehending the most important concerns of private life, and particularly showing the distresses that may attend the misconduct both of parents and children in relation to marriage." Another equally famous novel is so well characterized in its title that there is nothing to add: " *Pamela:* or, Virtue Rewarded. In a series of Familiar Letters from a Beautiful Young Damsel to her Parents. Now first published. In order to cultivate the Principles of *Virtue* and *Religion* in the minds of the YOUTH of BOTH SEXES. A Narrative which has its Foundations in TRUTH and NATURE; and at the same time that it agreeably entertains, by a variety of *curious* and *affecting* INCIDENTS, is intirely divested of all those Images, which, in too many Pieces calculated for Amusement only, tend to *inflame* the minds they should *instruct*." The father of the middle-class bourgeois drama — a pendant to the family novel that is even more sickly sweet and more false — was George Lillo, a jeweller. This was a type which quickly became popular in France as the *comédie larmoyante* and was considered " touching " by its admirers and " blubbering " by its enemies. Nivelle de la Chaussée was the first author to take it up, having been advised to do so by the actress Quinault, who pointed out that sentimental scenes went down better with the public than tragic ones. Voltaire, too, ever on the alert for others' successes, soon began to produce plays of this *genre*. The first German attempt was Gellert's *Zärtliche Schwestern*. Only Holberg — the " Danish Molière," as he has been (a little extravagantly) called — succeeded in giving his countrymen a national comedy, a national theatre, and, above all, a national looking-glass in which they could see and observe themselves, not unduly flattered, but quite kindly caricatured. He was a rapid versifier (like all true comedy-temperaments) and also a hard-working journalist, historian, and popular philosopher. He began as a wandering fiddler and penniless student, and for long years was in constant conflict with fanatical preachers, ignorant philistines, and learned owls; he ended, however, as a landed proprietor and a baron, which was an unheard-of success for a despised playwright and poverty-stricken professor. But the full appreciation due to his merits only came after his death, when people began to realize the value of his work — vigorous to the point of coarseness, vital to the point of banality. Up to the days of Andersen and Ibsen Scandinavia produced no man of such keen and exact observation, such independence of spirit, and such powerful irony.

The Weeklies

The most important literary event for the awakening middle classes was the rise of the English weekly magazines. In 1709 Steele, with his chief collaborator, Addison, founded the *Tatler*. This was followed by the *Spectator* in 1711 and the *Guardian* in 1713. In laying down the program of these reviews Addison said that, whereas Socrates was said to have fetched down philosophy from heaven to dwell among men, his own ambition was to have it said of him that he brought her from the academies and schools so that she might take her place in clubs and in society, at tea-tables and in the coffee-houses, in the home, the counting-house, and the workshop. Imitators were not slow in following him. The great Dr. Johnson edited the *Idler* and the *Rambler*, the graceful comedy-writer Marivaux the *Spectateur français*, and the magazine *Le Pour et le Contre* was for seven years edited by the Abbé Prévost — author of the *Aventures du chevalier des Grieux et de Manon Lescaut*, a continuation of the English novel minus its wearisome moralizing and full of genuine passion. In Italy the elder Gozzi founded the *Observatore*. The first German publication of this description was the *Discourse der Mahlern*, edited by Bodmer and Breitinger and published in Switzerland. Three years later the *Patriot* appeared in Hamburg, Gottsched wrote the *Vernünftigen Tadlerinnen* and the *Biedermann*, and one of these innumerable periodicals even bore the odd and easily misunderstandable title: *The Bride, displayed weekly* (*Die Braut, wöchentlich an das Licht gestellt*). Of Addison, who remains the real classic of this style, Steele said that he never idealized life or customs, but was ever true to nature and reality, copying so faithfully that he may be said to have discovered. He was in fact no more and no less than the adroit, assiduous, banal, and ingenious drawing-room photographer of his day; and his imposing and well-assorted portrait-album is worth just as much and as little as any other work of the kind in any age.

William Hogarth the painter told his story, satirically but without genuine humour, by means of descriptive picture-series such as *The Harlot's Progress, Marriage à la mode, The Rake's Progress,* and *Industry and Idleness.* Engravings of his paintings were widely bought, and thus his art was, not merely in content, but even in form, a sort of artistic journalism. But although these pictures may seem to be the counterpart of the weekly periodicals and moral novels, actually the two phenomena cannot be compared. For it is only secondarily that Hogarth is edifying and didactic. Primarily he is an artist: a delineator intoxicated with reality, and full of weight and perspicuity, a colour-poet of the highest standard of taste and intellect. He was merely serving his times in sermonizing, and without his philosophy he would have been all the greater. Richardson and Addison, on the contrary, draw their greatest inspiration from the moral emotions of the middle class; their whole work depended on this, and without it they would have been neither greater nor smaller men, but would not have existed at all. They wanted to be painters and barely arrived at being writers; Hogarth — strangely misconceiving his mission — wanted to be a writer and remained nevertheless a great painter.

Hogarth

Yet with all this matter-of-fact-ness there was not lacking the element of spleen which is a permanent ingredient of the Englishman's soul. Its embodiment is the grave- and ghost-poetry. In 1743 Robert Blair produced his poem *The Grave,* which, in suggestive blank verse, rings the changes on death, coffins, midnight, horror of the grave, and ghostly terrors! From the same period come Young's *Night Thoughts on Life, Death, and Immortality,* and Gray's *Elegy written in a Country Churchyard,* full of gloomy oppressions and sights and yet suffused with the first gentle murmur of Sensibility. The genius of spleen is, however, Jonathan Swift, dean of St. Patrick's, who stands alone in his pathological dæmonism, a grimacing giant.

The poets of spleen

Every age has some one catchword and largely lives on it. For the age with which we are dealing this was " Free Thought." The

The Free-thinkers

forerunners of the free-thinkers were the " Latitudinarians " of the seventeenth century, who declared all confessional differences of Christian sects to be immaterial, and regarded only the fundamental truths laid down in the Scriptures as binding. John Toland, who in his book *Christianity Not Mysterious,* published in 1696, sought to prove that nothing in the Gospels was contrary to Nature or indeed to Reason, was the first to speak of " freethinkers "; Anthony Collins then discussed them more in detail in his *Discourse of Freethinking* in 1713. Woolston explained the miracles of the New Testament allegorically. Matthew Tindal in his work *Christianity as Old as the Creation* took his stand on the theory that Christ only restored the natural religion which had existed from all time and had been perfect from the beginning. In Germany, too, from 1735 onward, Johann Christian Edelmann began to write anti-clerical pamphlets, in which he described the positive religions as " priests' inventions "; his writings roused less attention, however, than his long beard. The first to attempt a scientific analysis of the beautiful, and a defence of art against theology, was Hutcheson. According to him both the good and the beautiful are to be determined by the dictate of an infallible inward sense. At the beginning of the century the Earl of Shaftesbury had started from a similar standpoint in creating, as it were, an æsthetic of morals. For him the good and the beautiful were identical, their common measure being their quality of pleasing. " Seek ye first the beautiful, and the good shall be added unto you," was his motto. Morality, too, is based on a sort of special sense, a moral tact, which can be and should be developed as taste is. It is man's task to achieve a sort of virtuosity of moral, and the " wicked " man is according to this theory merely a bungler and dilettante. The essence, as well as the art, of ethics lies in the harmony and reconciliation of egoistic and social impressions. In the same sense Pope in his *Essay on Man* very effectively compares selfish and altruistic spiritual impulses with the rotation of our planet on its own axis and round the sun. What Shaftesbury teaches is the philosophy of a fine-nerved aristocrat and artist of life: he is one of the first æsthetes in history, and there is a direct line leading from him to Oscar Wilde, who declared that vice and virtue are merely materials for the artist. On the other hand, an almost grotesque effort to make ethics logical is seen in Wollaston, who regards every unmoral action purely as an error in judgment: in a murder, for instance, there is a mistaken idea that one can restore the dead to life; in torturing animals, the erroneous notion that they do not feel pain; in disobedience towards God, the false belief that one is stronger than he. Similarly, Mandeville in his *Fable of the Bees, or Private Vices made Public Benefits*, as the very title indicates, puts forward the cynical view of the modern statesman that selfish and unscrupulous competition among individuals supplies the motive power for the well-being of the community.

But the most characteristic figure in English philosophy at that time is David Hume. His sensational achievement was his explanation of the notion of causality, which he accounts for by habit, the frequent repetition of the same experience. Our empiric entitles us only to the opinion: first A, then B, the *post hoc*. But our mind is not satisfied with that, and, on the basis of having observed this constantly recurring sequence, says: first A, therefore B, thus making a *propter hoc* out of the *post hoc*. The idea of substance, too, arises solely from our habit of always combining the same ideas with certain groups of characteristic features. In the same way is to be explained the consciousness of one's ego: for by regularly relating our impressions to the same subject we get the idea of an unchanging carrier of these impressions, whereas it is really nothing but a " bundle of ideas." Arguing on the same lines, Hume declared himself opposed to the theory of the Social Contract: long before men were able to sign any state contract, compulsion had already united them, and the obedience which had become a habit through that compulsion brought about the existence of governments and subjects without any such contract. All this is truly English: the prudent and short-sighted insistence of the sole authority of empiricism, the distrust of all metaphysics and ideas, the deep-rooted conservatism which puts down everything to habit, and the relentless superficiality which in its wonderful keenness and vigour becomes almost profundity.

In Weininger's *Geschlecht und Charakter* we find the subtle remark: " The difference between Hume and Kant can also be drawn characterologically, much as I can distinguish between two men of whom the one finds the highest art in Makart and Gounod and the other in Rembrandt and Beethoven." Elsewhere he says that Hume was in general over-estimated — that, when you come to think of it, it does not take much to be the greatest English philosopher, but that Hume could not make even that claim. In our own view, this honour should preferably go to Hume's "forerunner" Bishop Berkeley, an Englishman by origin, but born and educated in Ireland, who is to be regarded as one of the most brilliant representatives of the Irish mind — so far removed from the English. He produced a philosophy that is truly free, intensely original, and creatively paradoxical. From his starting-point he might be taken for the typical English empiricist philosopher, for he taught the strictest Nominalism. Abstract ideas are for him merely the inventions of the Schoolmen, dust-clouds which are raised by the schools and by which things are obscured; they do not even exist in imagination, and are therefore not merely unreal, but impossible. Things such as colour or a triangle do not exist, there are only red and blue colours, right-angled and obtuse-angled triangles of a definite appearance. When a tree is spoken of in a general sense, everyone secretly thinks of some concrete individual tree. There are only the individual ideas which form themselves out of the various sense-perceptions. Take a cherry; you feel it and taste it and are convinced that a nothing could be neither felt nor tasted; therefore this cherry is real. But after the perceptions of softness, moistness, redness, bitter-sweetness are abstracted, there is no longer any cherry, for it does not differ in essence from any of these perceptions. Colour is the being seen; tone the being heard; an object the being perceived; *esse est percipi*. That which we call impenetrability is nothing but the sense of resistance; extension, size, movement are not even perceptions, but relations which we think on to our impressions; the bodily substances are not only unknown, they do not exist. But the uniqueness and supreme cleverness of this philosophy lies in the fact that these propositions bring it, not like all other nominalisms, to sensualism and materialism, but to an exclusive spiritualism and idealism. All phenomena are, according to Berkeley, simply conceptions of God, which he creates within himself and imparts to individual minds as perceptions. The coherent whole of all the ideas produced by God we call Nature; causality is the ordered succession of these conceptions as marshalled by him. As the Godhead is absolute and almighty, it is able at any time to alter the order and break the law of Nature. In such cases we speak of miracles. The result is, there is nothing real in the world but God, souls, and ideas.

It was not Berkeley's system, however, but Empiricism that conquered England and, through England, Europe. The first great representative of English philosophy on the Continent was Montesquieu. In his *Lettres persanes,* published in 1721, he began as a critic, exposing with a fine wit that veiled a deep seriousness the public institutions and conditions of contemporary France: the Papal Church and the monastic system, confession and celibacy, heresy-courts and sectarian disputes, extravagance and iniquitous taxation, corrupt finance and the privileges of the nobility, the decay of the Academy, the Law crash, and in general the régime of absolutism, even though it should claim to be " enlightened." Seven years later there followed his *Considérations sur les causes de la grandeur des Romains et de leur décadence,* an extremely clever and searching piece of history-writing in which he showed — with an obvious reference to democratic England and absolutist France — how the Roman Empire owed its greatness to liberty, and its downfall to despotism. His third work too, *De l'esprit des lois,* is completely imbued with the English spirit, representing law and State as the product of soil, climate, custom, culture, and religion, and praising constitutional monarchy as the best form of government. Contemporary with him was the Marquis Vauvenargues — who became a military officer in defiance of a delicate constitution and died at thirty-two. Vauvenargues's merits were not fully appreciated at the time, but Voltaire was one of the few who at once recognized his high quality, and he wrote to this obscure colleague, twenty years younger than himself: " Had you come into the world a few years earlier, my own works would have been better." For Vauvenargues the highest qualities of a writer were *clarté* and simplicity. This limpidity was the adornment of profoundity, the " philosopher's letter of credit," the " gala dress of master-minds "; obscurity is the realm of error, and a thought which is too feeble to bear simple expression announces itself as only fit to be discarded. In his incorruptible art of soul-testing he sometimes reminds us of La Rochefoucauld: he says, for instance, that love is not so sensitive and fastidious as self-love, as we scorn many things to avoid being forced to scorn ourselves; that most men love fame without virtue, but only a very few virtue without fame; he describes the art of pleasing as the art of deceiving, and thinks it strange that modesty should be demanded of woman, considering that what they value most in men is impudence. But with all this there lived in Vauvenargues the soldier-spirit of the seventeenth century, a heroic enthusiasm for fame, courage, and noble spiritual passion; his favourite word is "*l'action.*" And at the same time he looks into the future and the realm of Sensibility. No one, he says, is so likely to make innumerable mistakes as the man who acts according to reason. "*Les grandes pensées viennent du cœur*," was one of his immortal sayings. He was the first prophet of the heart, but a manly, unsentimental prophet, belonging to an older, stronger, and less complicated race.

The general representative of the century But the lesser lights paled before the star of Voltaire — the hero of the century, even though in an eighteenth-century sense of the word "heroism."

In a much-quoted passage from his notes to Diderot, Goethe says: "When families spread over a long period it may be observed that nature at last brings forth an individual member of it who comprises in himself the characteristics of all his ancestors and unites and gives full expression to all the talents which have up till then made only spasmodic and tentative appearances. It is the same with nations, whose collective virtues are sure, with good luck, to be summed up one day in an individual. So for instance there arose in Louis XIV a French king in the highest sense, and so in Voltaire we have the greatest writer that it is possible to imagine among Frenchmen, and the one most harmonious with his nation." It was pointed out in the Introduction to this work that genius is nothing but the extract of the innumerable small desires and labours of the great mass of the people. One can find such a general representative for every race and every age; and even for the smaller sections, for every family or clan, every town, every season. The circle represented by Voltaire had the widest imaginable radius: for Voltaire is the essence of all France and of all the eighteenth century. And consequently he was a compendium of all the faults and errors, vices and contradictions, of his nation and his generation. If, as Goethe in his fine allegory indicates, he really embraced all the scattered family features in his physiognomy, it is entirely senseless to make it a reproach to him that among his traits some are unbeautiful. Elsewhere, in *Dichtung und Wahrheit*, Goethe writes: "Voltaire will always be regarded as the greatest name in the literature of the modern age and perhaps of all centuries; as the most marvellous of nature's creations." This was felt by his contemporaries in an almost higher degree than by posterity — an unusual case in the history of thought — and the reason was that they could not but see in him their own matchless interpreter. He was a "sight" of the first magnitude. People travelled from great distances to his country-house at Ferney as if to see a mountain peak or a sphinx. When he tried to shake off an Englishman who refused to be sent away, by a jocular message that a sight of him cost six pounds, the intruder promptly replied: "Here is twelve pounds and I am coming again tomorrow." When he travelled, young adorers would disguise themselves as hotel waiters in order to gain access to him. Shortly before his death, when returning home from the performance of his *Irène* in Paris, the people kissed his horses.

And although five generations have passed, few figures in the history of literature are so intimately known to us as he. His biography is a story of our own day, of everyone's day. At no point does he seem remote from us, because in his greatness and his weakness he was always a warm-blooded, intensely vital human being. He was a singular mixture of epicure and work-ascetic. Even as a boy he was very fond of fashionable clothes and good food, and all his life he strove to surround himself with the luxury of a *grand seigneur*, though it was rather his passion for beauty of form and large-scale conditions than actual love of pleasure that attracted him to these things. When he appeared on the scene, the man of letters was a socially impossible person — a desperado, a rascal and outlaw, a toady, a starveling, a drunkard. Voltaire was the first author by profession to break with this deeply rooted tradition. From the very first he lived in the higher style, and in the second half of his life his fortune was that of a prince. He possessed twenty estates with twelve hundred subjects and a yearly yield of a hundred and sixty thousand francs; beautiful villas and châteaux with fields and vineyards, picture-galleries and libraries, costly knick-knacks and rare plants, a staff of lackeys, postilions, secretaries, a park of carriages, a French chef, a fireworks expert, a private theatre, at which famous Paris artists appeared, and even

The Life-Martyr

197

his own church, with the inscription "*Deo erexit Voltaire.*" This wealth he owed in part to pensions and the proceeds from books (the *Henriade* alone brought him in a hundred and fifty thousand francs, and he regularly presented his fees for theatre performances to the actors), but the larger part of it came from dubious money-transactions of all sorts, which he carried out with great skill — stock-exchange speculations, middleman's negotiations, deals in corn, speculation in real estate, army contracts, loans at high interest. One such shady deal in Berlin involved him in a scandalous quarrel with Abraham Hirschel, the Jewish banker, and brought down on him the displeasure of Frederick the Great. It may be regarded as proved that in this business he altered certain words in the agreements he had made with Hirschel, and Lessing gave his view of this incident epigrammatically thus:

> The long and short of this affair
> About the failure of the scheming Jew
> Was simply that Monsieur Voltaire
> Turned out the bigger rascal of the two.

He was not too particular about the truth in private life either. When he wished to be elected to the Academy in Cardinal Fleury's place, he wrote letters to different people assuring them that he was a good Catholic and did not know what those *Lettres philosophiques* were which people attributed to him; he had never had them in his hands. On the second occasion when he aspired (this time successfully) to the honour — which, incidentally, added nothing to his fame — he compared Louis XV to Trajan. When *Candide* appeared, he wrote to a pastor in Geneva: " I have at last been able to read *Candide,* and, just as was the case with *Jeanne d'Arc,* I declare to you that people must have taken leave of their reason and their senses to ascribe such filthy stuff to me." In the *Pucelle,* he deliberately put in rubbish so that it might not be imputed to him. In an open letter to the *Mercure de France* on the subject of his *Histoire du parlement de Paris,* he said: " To have published a work like this, one would have had to burrow in the archives for at least a year, and once one descends into that abyss it is still a very difficult matter to bring up a readable book out of it. It is more likely to turn out a fat protocol than a history. Should any bookseller proclaim me as the author, I can assure him he will gain nothing by so doing. Far from selling a single copy more, he would on the contrary damage the credit of the book. To maintain that I, who have been away from France over twenty years, could have so lived myself into French law would be perfectly absurd." About the dictionary he wrote to d'Alembert: "As far as there is any danger of it, I beg you will inform me, so that I may disavow the work in all the public papers with my accustomed honesty and innocence." And in a letter to the Jesuit Father de la Tour he went so far as to assert that if anyone had ever printed over his name anything that could offend even a village sexton, he was prepared to tear it up; he wished to live and die in peace without attacking anyone, without harming anyone, without taking up a standpoint that could offend anyone. The statement may be hazarded that this intention of causing no offence anywhere was only very imperfectly realized.

We must, of course, take into account that it was extremely dangerous to acknowledge the authorship of works which might incur the displeasure of Church or government, and that almost all Voltaire's colleagues practised the same tactics of denial and anonymity. "I am," he said to d'Alembert, "an ardent friend of truth, but in no sense a friend of martyrdom." Anyhow, in Voltaire we have to recognize a new form of heroism. In the place of the death-martyrs there appeared life-martyrs; purification through asceticism is now not sought within the walls of monasteries, but in the turmoil of the world; death no longer appears as the glorification of life, and the hero is no longer the one who renounces life, but the one who fights on in it with resignation.

To Voltaire's over-stimulated and hyperactive militancy we may also ascribe his many small meannesses, of which his attitude to Frederick the Great is particularly characteristic. The unavoidable friction between these two geniuses produced incessant sparks of hatred, love, and wit. The very manner of their coming together was strange enough. In order to compromise Voltaire in France and thus to get him to his own court, Frederick had a very insulting letter of the poet's circulated among a number of influential persons who were attacked in it. Voltaire, on his side, tried to raise as much money as possible out of the King's weakness for him. Frederick the Great, finding out one day that

Voltaire's character

he had overpaid Voltaire, limited him in the use of light and sugar; Voltaire proceeded to pocket the candles in the salons. Lamettrie informed Voltaire that the King had said of him: " One squeezes an orange and throws it away"; while Maupertuis informed the King that Voltaire had said of him: " I am obliged to look through his verses, he sends me his dirty linen to wash." Voltaire made an anonymous and offensive attack on Maupertuis; Frederick composed a reply, also anonymous and equally offensive. Frederick had Voltaire imprisoned in Frankfurt on his return from France and searched for compromising documents; Voltaire in turn, on his release, wrote compromising revelations in France.

We have deliberately emphasized the most dubious points in Voltaire's life-story, because for a long time, and occasionally even today, these and similar small traits have been combined to form the picture of an ambiguous, treacherous, even squalid character. Of the bad qualities of which Voltaire is accused, vanity is the only one which he possessed in a really full measure, and herein he contrasts most unfavourably with Frederick the Great. But it is a quality that he shared with the great majority of artists, and indeed with the great majority of mankind, besides which it had in him a kindly, childlike, and at times childish note which disarms us. To call him malicious and mendacious, for instance, is only half true; he was malicious only when in a state of defence, mendacious in small things when under the influence of his vanity or timidity (both of which were rooted in an almost pathological sensitiveness); in all major matters he was of the most complete uprightness. And to call him supremely egotistical is completely and unreservedly wrong. He was avaricious only during the time when he was amassing riches; from the moment that he possessed them he used them in the most unselfish and liberal way for others; and as for the incorrect methods by which he obtained them, let us not forget that we are in the age of Rococo, which displayed its decadence by, amongst other things, the loss of moral standards. To the question, then, which so often arises: why did this great mind lack integrity? the reply is: because the Rococo mind lacked integrity. For Voltaire neither belongs to nor wished to be one of those supernatural heroes of morality who, as opposite numbers to the great criminals, stand outside the moral laws of the time and live in an ethical world of their own, constructed from the timeless depths of their souls.

For the ambitious young writer he had always advice and money to spare (in spite of the almost invariable ingratitude of the recipient), actuated, probably, by a sort of tender and rueful piety towards his own youth. He had Corneille's niece educated at his own expense, obtained a rich dowry for her by arranging for the publication of a new edition of Corneille, annotated by himself, and, on the birth of her first child, gave her twelve thousand livres. "It is right," he said, "for an old soldier to make himself useful to his general's daughter." As a landlord he practised charity on a grand scale. He fought against serfdom, drained marshes, laid vast stretches of heathland under cultivation, and set on foot flourishing silk and clock industries by placing houses on his estate and working capital at the disposal of the workers. His advocacy of the causes of the Huguenots Jean Calas and Peter Paul Sirven — each falsely accused of having murdered one of his children who wished to become a Catholic — has immortalized them; here we see him feverishly active in the cause of justice, writing pamphlets and essays, publishing documents and witnesses' statements, and appealing to everyone in authority to whom he had access. The root passion of his life was, indeed, a flaming desire for justice, a burning, consuming, almost drunken hatred of every kind of public despotism, stupidity, malice, or partisanship. And if our world of today consists of no more than two-fifths villains and three-eighths idiots, we have largely Voltaire to thank for it.

He says somewhere that it is just as much in the composition of man to work as it is in the nature of fire to rise, and it is precisely as such a fiery pillar of work and intellect that he rose above the heads of the astonished world, soaring ever higher and illuminating with his unearthly glow all that was gloomy and shunned the light. He often worked from eighteen to twenty hours a day, and dictated so fast that his secretary could hardly keep up with him. At sixty-four he said to himself: "I am as supple as an eel, as lively as a lizard, and as tireless as a squirrel," and he continued to be all this for another twenty years. Frederick the Great wrote to him: "I doubt whether a Voltaire exists, and am in possession of a system by the aid of which I am able to prove his non-

Voltaire's work

existence. It is impossible that one man should achieve the enormous output that is ascribed to M. Voltaire. Obviously there is an academy at Cirey composed of the world's élite: philosophers who translate and edit Newton, writers of heroic epics, Corneilles, Catulluses, and Thucydideses; and the works of this academy are sent out under the name Voltaire as one attributes the deeds of an army to the commander." Shortly before he died, an author came to pay his respects, saying: " Today I have only called to see Homer, next time I will salute Sophocles and Euripides, then Tacitus, then Lucian." " My dear sir," replied Voltaire, " I am, as you see, a fairly aged man. Can you not fit in all these visits at once? " He was not creative in every direction like Leibniz, but his keenness penetrated everything; and after all, as regards most things, it was his artistry in the rounding, outlining, and luminous presentation of them that first gave them classical form, and we can hardly refuse to call this one of the kinds of creative activity. His cardinal literary quality was not (as is so often said) his wit, but his lucidity and perfection of form, his sparkling colourfulness and elasticity. Like the torpedo-fish, which at the least contact sends out a rain of paralysing blows, he was full of stored-up electricity, which only waited to be released to test its triumphant effect in a stream of dangerous force-discharges. His literary work did not stop short at his books, though these form a library in themselves; it included also innumerable letters, which, in the fashion of the day, contained interesting news for circulation and were to a great extent of the nature of " open letters." At Ferney in 1760 he showed Casanova a collection of some fifty thousand letters addressed to himself; and as he had the habit of replying to anything of interest, this gives some indication of the extent of his correspondence. There was his conversation, too, which according to the testimony of all who were privileged to be with him must have been most magically effective; " he is, and always will be, the best edition of his books," said the Chevalier de Boufflers.

Voltaire as poet   Voltaire's first great success was the epic *La Ligue, ou Henri le Grand*, half of which he wrote in the Bastille in pencil between the lines of a book. Five years later he published it, in enlarged and revised form, as *Henriade*. This took the world by storm. Accustomed as he was to base his artistic plans on rational considerations, he had argued that the French were in need of an epic, and that he was therefore bound to give them one. And his countrymen accepted the gift. The effect of this work can only be understood if we recall the intellectual condition of France and Europe at the time. It is the cold pale product of a brilliant craftsman and witty cultural philosopher, a work depending on the empty trappings of allegorical personifications such as Love, Peace, Discord, Fanaticism; and inspired, not by Homer, say, or Dante, or Milton, but by Virgil. At that time, however, it would have been considered ludicrous to place Homer above Virgil, so this was all to the good. Frederick the Great declared that every man of taste must prefer the *Henriade* to the Iliad.

Voltaire's second epic poem, *La Pucelle d'Orléans,* a parody on Joan of Arc, is a private indiscretion which he never intended for publication; but the idea that any work of Voltaire's should remain unknown would have been intolerable to the educated world of the day, and a way was found of obtaining secret copies from his secretary. The poem did in fact possess all the qualities that made it ideal reading for a Rococo public: it was witty, obscene, and anti-clerical.

As a dramatist Voltaire deserves credit above all for breaking with the pseudo-antique tradition. He brought American, African, and Asiatic material on to the stage. He was not so entirely uninfluenced by Shakspere as Lessing's too rigorous criticism would have us believe. He owes to him the wit, the colour, and (in a higher sense of the word) the actuality of his drama. In his *Letters on England* he praises him as a vigorous, fertile, natural, and upstanding genius, full of rare and gigantic ideas — though in his old age it must be confessed that he called him a village clown, a Gothic Colossus, and a drunken savage. In delineation of character and in composition he stands so far below Shakspere that he cannot even be called his pupil. Even in his dramas his strength lay in the finish of his form. The Alexandrine, in its capacity of two-forked antithetical and rhyme-sharpened metre, has the effect of transforming everything expressed by it into a point, an epigram, a dialectical cross-fire a melodic plea. Here Voltaire was in his very element, and it is no wonder that the past master of this tirade-poetry became the favourite dramatist of a nation of rhetoricians and a century of philosophy.

In the *Henriade* the aim and principal theme is the struggle against fanaticism and intolerance, in the *Pucelle* derision is poured on miracle-gaping and superstition, and all Voltaire's dramas are similarly dominated by some such purpose. *Alzire* describes the cruelty and intolerance of the Christians in the conquest of Peru. *Le Fanatisme, ou Mahomet le prophète* betrays its polemic intention in its title, and the hero is, as Voltaire himself says, a mere "Tartuffe with a sword in his hand," having as his confessed aim *tromper l'univers*. Even in *Zaïre*, one of the few among Voltaire's works in which love is in the centre of the picture, it is again the curse of religious prejudices which turns out after all to be the main interest. He himself once described the stage as the rival of the pulpit. It was purely the megaphone for his ideas: rostrum, tribunal, professorial chair, philosophical debating club, or pedagogic Punch-and-Judy show; but never did he create men and their destinies simply from the elemental urge to create. That is why this most powerful satiric genius of the century failed to succeed in comedy. He never experienced that secret process through which the abstractions of an expounding poet mysteriously come alive and the labelled specimens suddenly break away from the strings of tendentiousness and become independent. This coffee-drinker was too wide-awake, too lucid, too self-controlled to let his creatures gain the upper hand of him.

Voltaire as historian

"I should like to assert something which will astonish you," wrote Voltaire to d'Argenson in 1740; "it is only a man who can write a tragedy who can impart interest to our dry and barbarous history. Like a play it must have its exposition, development, and solution." His dual talent of observing and creating, which on the stage only permitted him to achieve creations that conformed to the times, enabled him as a historian to advance far beyond his age. His tragedies might dribble away in a mixture of history and philosophy, but his historical pictures composed themselves into real dramas. His *Siècle de Louis XIV* and the *Essai sur les mœurs et l'esprit des nations* were the first of modern historical works. In place of the customary long and boring descriptions of campaigns, diplomatic negotiations, and court intrigues, he described for the first time culture and manners — in place of the history of kings, the destinies of nations. The stupendous mobility and vigour of his mind, which was interested in everything and could make everything interesting, aided him quite specially in this domain. He was able, too, to indulge in polemics against his arch-enemy the Church, but this tendentiousness was, from the very nature of things, far less objectionable in his historical than in his dramatic and heroic work, and was also, strange to say, far less aggressively in evidence.

To this branch of his literary activity, which brought him such fame, he only devoted himself with full intensity in the second half of his life. In his younger years his main scientific interest was absorbed in the exact disciplines. He wrote a classical description of the Newtonian philosophy which for the first time popularized Newton on the Continent, and he had at Cirey a large laboratory, where he experimented diligently along with Madame du Châtelet, who had a more than ordinary gift for mathematical and physical subjects. Lord Brougham said of him that he would have been on the list of the great discoverers had he worked longer at experimental physics.

In the consciousness of the eighteenth century he figured also as a great philosopher, although he produced no independent ideas and (in this respect as in others) can only claim the credit of his brilliant formulation. If we seek for the greatest common measure of his many-sided philosophical utterances, we should probably find its profound and general principle in an insistent demand for the utmost degree of liberty in all the activities of life. He fought against despotism wherever he found or thought he found it, and defended the unlimited self-determination of the individual in everything, mental or physical, even to the point of justifying homosexuality and suicide. The Revolutionaries accordingly claimed him as their own and in 1791 celebrated his birthday by transferring his body with great pomp to the Panthéon. Yet if he had lived to see the Jacobins in power, he would presumably have been guillotined in honour of his centenary. In truth, when he talked of liberty, he was thinking only of the upper ten thousand. Speaking of the people, he said: " They will always remain stupid and barbarous; they are oxen who need a yoke, a whip, and hay." He expected the reform to come from above, through an enlightened government. In 1764 he wrote: " All that I see happening around me is sowing the seed of a revolution which will infallibly occur, though I shall hardly live to see

205

it. The French are nearly always too late in achieving their aim, but still they do it in the end. Happy they who are young, they will see some fine days." If, wrongly, an emphasis were laid on these last words, they could undoubtedly be considered as a prophecy of the Revolution.

Representing as he did the essence of his age in all that he said or wrote, he naturally reproduced its platitudes in his religious philosophy. Jesus was a "rural Socrates," in whom he admired, above all, the war which he waged against the hierarchy. In the miracles ascribed to him he saw in part later inventions, in part deceptions practised in order to convert the superstitious common people to his doctrine. "The more closely we examine his behaviour, the more do we become convinced that he was an honest enthusiast and a good man whose only weakness was the desire to make himself talked about." Gospel criticism is one of the few spheres in which Voltaire becomes as banal as his worthy biographer David Friedrich Strauss — who had about as much idea of his subject as a schoolmaster might have of a Black Mass — would make him out. The briefest summary of Voltaire's point of view is probably contained in his *Profession de foi des théistes:* "We damn atheism, we loathe superstition, we love God and the human race." At first he inclined towards the optimism of Leibniz; but after the earthquake at Lisbon, which destroyed two-thirds of the city and killed thirty thousand people, he changed his mind. In his poem *Le Désastre de Lisbonne* he violently attacked Pope's assertion that "whatever is, is right," and held out only the faintest hope that one day all might be well, saying that anyone who supposed that all was well at the present time was the victim of an illusion. Free will, also, he accepted at first, but denied later. He frequently expressed his views on immortality, but they were of a wavering and contradictory order. At no point in his writings did he ever question the existence of God, though he did discuss his knowableness. "Philosophy shows us, indeed, that there is a God," he says in his *Newton* and in many similar works, "but it is unable to tell us what he is, why he acts, and whether he exists in time and space. One would have to be God himself to know." His famous saying: "If God did not exist, one would have to invent him," appears to have a sceptical sting because it is always wrongly quoted — that is, only half quoted. The second half of the sentence runs: "but all Nature cries aloud that he does exist."

It is, however, very difficult to say what his true opinion on these matters was, so susceptible and desultory was his mind, and so subject to the personal impression of the moment. And, besides, everything that he openly expressed was only exoteric doctrine; in the secret chambers of his brain there may well have been quite other and more radical ideas. Possibly his true confession of faith is contained in the words he wrote to Madame du Deffand, six years before he died: "I knew a man who was firmly convinced that the buzz of a bee did not continue after its death. He said, with Epicurus and Lucretius, that it was absurd to presume an unextended being; an extended being ruled, and pretty badly at that. . . . He said Nature had so arranged matters that we think with our heads just as we walk with our feet. He compared us with a musical instrument which does not give forth another note when it is broken. He maintained that man — like every other animal and every plant, and perhaps every being in the world — was manifestly made so that he might be and then not be. This man, too, when he had grown as old as Democritus, used to do as Democritus did and laugh at everything." And nine years further back, on the threshold of his eighth decade, Voltaire gave expression to his profound resignation of spirit in a letter to d'Argenson: "*J'en reviens toujours à Candide: il faut finir par cultiver son jardin; tout le reste, excepté l'amitié, est bien peu de chose; et encore cultiver son jardin n'est pas grande chose.*"

Cultiver son jardin: to cultivate this garden which Voltaire had planted, to make it yield more and more profusely, was the task which the age of Enlightenment set itself and solved. Voltaire held it to be a small thing, but to the Enlightenment it was a very great thing.

BOOK III: ENLIGHTENMENT AND REVOLUTION

From the Seven Years' War to the Congress of Vienna

COMMON SENSE AND THE RETURN TO NATURE

*" It is useless for reason to complain that
the world is ruled by prejudice. If reason
wants to rule, it must itself first turn itself
into a prejudice."*

Taine

So far we have made use of the method of breaking up the *Cultural*
course of cultural development into certain large divisions, which *periods and*
geological
succeeded each other like scenes of a play or chapters of a novel: *periods*
first Late Scholasticism, then Renaissance, then the Reformation,
followed by the Baroque and finally the Rococo. This arrangement admittedly involves some inexactness, much that is faulty,
arbitrary, or even distorted; but such simplification or adaptation
of reality is the essence of all science, all art, and indeed of all
human intellectual activity. Yet, necessary as it may be to make
use of such subjective schemes, it is very important not to suc-
cumb to any delusions about their illegitimate character, nor to
let the sense of their factual inaccuracy disappear from our consciousness, or at least from our subconsciousness. It would be a
wholly one-sided notion that the Reformation merely replaced the
Renaissance; for in *both* Humanism was one of the main driving
forces, and the Italian High Renaissance coincides with the periods
of Luther's intensest activity. The case most favourable to the
method was the age of the Baroque, which permitted without excessive violence a subdivision into Pre-Baroque or Counter-
Reformation, pure Baroque or Grand Siècle, and late Baroque or
Rococo; and it was even possible to take definite years as the lines
of demarcation. If we wanted some comparison which would make
clear the true relationship of the separate cultural periods among
themselves, the best parallel would probably be the geological
periods of the earth's development: the three great ages, Primary
or Palæozoic, Secondary or Mesozoic, and Tertiary or Cainozoic.
In the first there were only fish and the lower forms of life; in the

second, reptiles appeared; and in the third, birds and mammals. Of course fish still lived in the second period, and fish and reptiles in the third, just as they survive to the present day, but these forms do not, as it were, set the tone any longer; in each of the three periods one animal type dominates in numbers and variety, in " Antiquity " the fish, in the " Middle Ages " the reptiles, in the " Modern Age " the mammals. In similar fashion the individual periods are marked by a dominating type, even though the earlier ones live on by their side: thus in the country-side today there are countless numbers who are living in the Carolingian stage; the citizens of German provincial towns exemplify more or less the cultural condition of the Reformation, and many members of the teaching professions belong, in the scope and content of their intellectual field, to the age of Enlightenment. There are many species that have vanished entirely: for example, the Classical type has vanished as completely as the Saurians and, like them, now only yields information about itself through imprints and fossil remains of various sorts.

The three aggregate ideas The period with which we are now to deal, from the Seven Years' War to the Congress of Vienna, does not admit even this limited comparison with the geological periods. There are three main streams which pervade the age, labelled Enlightenment, Revolution, and Classicism. By the first, in accordance with ordinary use, we mean the extreme rationalistic tendency of which we have already noted the preliminary stages, and of which the most important representatives were Locke in England, Voltaire in France, and Wolff in Germany. The term " Classicism," too, hardly admits of misunderstanding. " Revolution," however, needs perhaps a little elucidation; under this common denominator we include all the movements which are directed against what has hitherto been dominant and traditional, whether in the sphere of politics, of art, or of standards of life. Their aims are the remodelling of the State and society, the banning of all æsthetic canons, the dethronement of reason by feeling, and all this is in the name of the " Return to Nature." But for the possibility of ambiguities, the whole tendency might be called naturalistic or activist.

To clear up the relationship of these three main currents we must have recourse to another geological parallel. Geology distinguishes " stratified " and " mass " formations: in the former we find various rocks arranged in superimposed layers like the storeys of a house, the second is a block in which all kinds of rocks are mingled together. In our period the three main ideas were *not* arranged one on top of the other like sedimentary rocks, with the stratum of the Enlightenment coming first, then that of Revolution, and last that of Classicism, in the same way as sandstone, slate, and lime succeed one another on a mountain. Rather we have what the petrographer would call "sills" and "dikes," for the whole age was permeated with all *three* tendencies. At most we might say that the strongest and widest-spreading phase of the Enlightenment was from the middle of the century till about 1770; that in the next quarter-century, from 1770 to 1795, it gave place to the Revolutionary current; and that in the last two decades, down to 1815, Classicism finally prevailed. Or, to keep to the metaphor: one type of rock predominates in each part of the mountain range, but all three are found in all parts of it. Right at the beginning of the period each one of the three movements appears with decisive and definitive activity. The *Encyclopédie,* the pioneer of the French Enlightenment, began to appear soon after the middle of the century; Rousseau's *Contrat social,* the code of the French Revolution, was published one year before the end of the Seven Years' War, Winckelmann's art-history, the Bible of Classicism, a year after the Peace; and all three movements only reached their climax towards the end of the period, Enlightenment in Kant, Revolution in Napoleon, Classicism in Goethe.

In political history the epochal event of the French Revolution marks a clear gulf which more or less cuts the period into two discrete sections. For the moment we shall not pass beyond this boundary, except in our account of scientific studies, in which, to avoid later repetition, we shall extend our account to the end of the century.

The Seven Years' War had a double significance for Europe: first, by giving Frederick the Great the opportunity to display his genius in its most brilliant form, it gave the world a spectacle such as it had not seen for centuries; secondly, it was the first world-war in the modern sense, being fought simultaneously in the four quarters of the world and having colonies as its true war-aim. The quarrel appeared to hinge on a few strips of Prussian territory; actually the stakes were immeasurably rich and extensive

The first world-war

213

areas in the East and in America. Canada was conquered at Rossbach, though none but British statesmen finally realized the
interconnexion.

The mind that devised the Seven Years' War was that of the
Austrian minister Count Kaunitz, who pursued against Prussia
an encircling policy similar to that of Edward VII against Germany a hundred and fifty years later. At first he had recommended
the definite renunciation of Silesia, but later he felt his life-work
to be the "*abaissement*" of Prussia and diplomatic preparation
therefor; his scheme, which he called the "great idea" and prose-
cuted with unrelaxing vigour, was the union of Austria, Russia,
and France against Frederick the Great. Several years spent as
ambassador at the Court of Versailles had made such a Gallo-
maniac of him that he pretended to be capable only of a halting
German. To withstand this threatened encircling by the great
powers Frederick concluded the Westminster Convention with
England, in which both powers bound themselves to prevent, with
their united forces, the invasion of German territory by foreign
troops. This purely defensive alliance then led to the Franco-
Austrian Treaty of Alliance, which for France, who could only lose
by it, was an unprecedented piece of folly, explicable only by the
chaotic condition of the government.

In the non-European theatre the chief rivals were England
and France, the latter of whom was joined by Spain in virtue of
the Bourbon Family Compact. England was almost everywhere
victorious. By the Treaty of Paris, France ceded to Britain Canada
and the eastern half of Louisiana and (since the western half fell
to Spain) was completely driven out of America. She also lost the
Senegal region, though she recovered it twenty years later under
the Treaty of Versailles. In East India the *status quo* was restored, but, since France surrendered all right to establish military
settlements, this virtually implied the sole supremacy of Britain.
Broadly speaking, Britain proved a selfish, unreliable, even a
treacherous ally to Prussia, and both George II and George III
were personally hostile to Frederick. William Pitt, the great im-
perialist statesman, to whom Britain owed all her successes in the
war, was the only whole-hearted supporter of Prussia, and that
out of an enlightened self-interest; later he was overthrown by the
anti-Prussian Lord Bute. Russia's attitude throughout the war

was decided by the personal feelings of her rulers: Elizabeth hated Frederick, who had called her a " crowned harlot," whereupon she incontinently plunged into the war; Peter III on the contrary was a fervid admirer of his and became his ally; Catherine II neither hated nor respected him and thus remained neutral. Sweden, too, in hopes of regaining lost ground, joined the coalition, but remained inactive. The states of the Empire also declared against Frederick, but gathered so feeble an army that they did the coalition more harm than good; Saxony, with hypocritical assurances of neutrality, watched for the moment to spring, but was conquered by Frederick immediately on the outbreak of hostilities and thereafter, during the whole war, treated as Prussian territory. Maria Theresa (in this war at least) pursued only anti-German aims: if the encircling powers had been victorious, East Prussia would have become Russian, Pomerania Swedish. Belgium, which the Empress would gladly have bartered, would have become French, simply in order that Silesia might again become Austrian: that is, half-Slav.

Frederick's plan, simple as it was brilliant, was the "blow at the heart" of Austria before Russia and France were prepared or even decided. With this object he moved into Saxony, defeating the Austrian army which had been hurried thither for its defence, at Lobositz; as a result this land was lost to Austria and became for Frederick a permanent base of enormous value. In the spring of the next year he advanced against the Austrians up to the environs of Prague, where, after the Prussian infantry had already begun to waver, the vigour of the cavalry and the heroic death of Schwerin brought about a decisive victory. The summer involved Frederick in three disasters. He was imprudent enough to attack Daun in an almost impregnable position near Kolin and, retreating with fearful loss, had to evacuate Bohemia, so that the entire initial plan was checkmated, with exceedingly serious consequences. The English were defeated at Hastenbeck by the French, who thereupon occupied Hanover and joined forces with the Imperial army. And, lastly, the Russians were victorious at Grossjägersdorf. Thus the concentric crushing of Frederick, which was the aim of the coalition, was on the point of realization, and the war was at its first crisis. But Frederick did not despair; he threw himself with extraordinary energy, caution, and rapidity against each one of his

The three crises of the Seven Years' War

enemies separately, the French at Rossbach, the Austrians at Leuthen, and the Russians at Zorndorf. These magnificent successes, it is true, were followed by his defeat at Hochkirch by Laudon and Daun, but he quickly recovered. In the fourth year of the war came the second crisis, as a result of the complete exhaustion which threatened him: the battle of Kunersdorf against the Russians and the Austrians, which at first seemed almost won, ended in defeat, and at Maxen General Finck surrendered with thirteen thousand men. A second time Frederick succeeded in recovering his position by his startling success over Laudon at Liegnitz and over Daun at Torgau. In 1761, however, owing to the resignation of Pitt, he was flung into the third and most perilous crisis, from which he was rescued by the death of the Tsaritsa Elizabeth. A further defeat of Austria at Burkersdorf, the conclusion of peace between England and France, and the threatening attitude of Turkey finally drove Maria Theresa to the Peace of Hubertusburg, in which her only gain was the acquisition of the Prussian electoral vote in favour of her son.

The Frederician power Frederick's success in maintaining his position through all this defensive struggle cannot be adequately explained by his amazing strategic and organizing abilities; the only explanation is a mystical one, and lies in the profound fear of all mediocrity in the presence of genius, with the consequent shirking of final risks, and in the power of genius to force reality to its own will and to mould it after its own image. What we call achievements are fundamentally, and especially in the case of the creative genius, nothing more than a projection of personality realized in the external world, individual qualities transformed into actualities. Genius strides through the world like some mysterious fate, the emanation of a superhuman anonymous force — of which it itself not seldom stands in awe, for such was the feeling of Goethe and Nietzsche, of Michelangelo and Beethoven, at one and another climax of their lives. That, too, is always the attitude of a people to its heroes; the last of these legendary figures that Europe has experienced was Bismarck. What we call power — power over men and things, peoples and continents — has its source here: the eighteenth century never knew Prussia, always Frederick, as a great power, just as at the turn of the century there was no French, but only a Napoleonic, supremacy. In the same way a true instinct of history has called the Roman Empire Cæsarian and the Greek world-culture Alexandrian.

Like almost all great historical personages, Frederick stands on the bridge between two ages, marking the conclusion of the one, the rise of the other; he joins the absolutism and the artistic impulse of the Rococo with the liberalism and naturalism of the Enlightenment. His direct influence in this way, however, was only on the French Enlightenment; the German, of which Berlin became the centre, benefited only indirectly through the all-pervading intellectual awakening which had streamed from his personality. The qualities of French culture which particularly attracted him were just those that were least German, its playful humour, void of profundity, but also of heaviness; its cool and bright scepticism, with faith in nothing but itself, its penetrating wit, for which it had to pay the penalty in the loss of real creative ability. We can well believe that the choice was not hard between Voltaire and Nicolai, between Diderot and Ramler, and that he had no understanding in his old age for such wholly new phenomena as *Götz* or *Die Räuber,* or even the *Critique of Pure Reason;* but it is curious that he never felt any contact with Lessing, with whom he had so much in common. At bottom Lessing's achievement, in his own field, was similar to Frederick's. He fought on different fronts with vigour and originality, won for himself a victorious position, and in the end raised the realm in which he ruled to be one of the great powers of Europe.

It would be a great mistake to think that during the French Enlightenment there was any conscious struggle against the aristocracy and the monarchy; on the contrary, the almost universal object of attack was the Church. Possibly a well-trained and politically experienced mind could have caught a glimpse of a general revolution even in this form of the opposition, but the French nobility of the time had no conception of national life and the motive forces of history. Above all they had no notion of money: the strongest power of modern civilization was unknown to them. In an age when religious and political disputes were soon to be replaced by economic, they were not only incompetent on all such questions, but literally uneducated. All they knew was that money was necessary; otherwise how could one spend it? Money was necessary, but to them the necessary was the obvious; money was like

*Philanthropy
of words*

217

air, just as essential for life, but just as easy to acquire and hence just as valueless.

Until the last decades before the Revolution there was, superficially, the most beautiful harmony between government and people. On the accession of Louis XVI the cheers for the King lasted uninterruptedly from six in the morning until sunset; at the birth of the Dauphin strangers embraced each other in the streets. When aristocratic virtues were treated on the stage, the people applauded; when those of the people, the nobility applauded. It was a comedy of sentimental brotherhood, with warm words and muzzy emotion, but no one thought to draw from this fine feeling even the most trivial practical result. In a word it was *philanthropy*.

The bureaux
d'esprit The whole movement of the Enlightenment was regarded by the French aristocracy merely as a sort of amateur theatricals which were to give to society a new and piquant interest; but none marked the danger of the play. The French have always been fascinated by the bizarre, and what could be more paradoxical, more original, than a cleric who doubted God or a noble who masqueraded as a democrat? The germs of the great Revolutionary literature, which is usually called Encyclopædist, are to be sought in the intellectual circles, which — at first ironically, but later in all earnestness — were called "*bureaux d'esprit*." The first of these salons was that of Madame de Tencin, a lady with a hectic past which had made her the mother of a number of illegitimate children, among whom was d'Alembert; she had farmed him out immediately after birth and only tried to approach him again when he had become famous; he rejected her proposal contemptuously and continued to live with his foster-mother, a simple woman of the people who had most touchingly protected his childhood. One of her lovers was Law, who helped her to win a great fortune by selling her Mississippi shares before the crash came. At the time of her first salon she was already forty-five years of age and inclined to fatness; she was not yet one of the free-thinkers, but was on excellent terms with the Jesuits and the Pope Lambertini, of whom we have already spoken. Her successors were Madame Geoffrin, a lady of charming and delightful social genius, and Madame du Deffand, who united an exceptional intelligence with a vast egoism. The latter had as her companion a poor girl, Mlle de l'Espinasse, who, though she lacked beauty, exerted a great intellectual fascination on the guests. As a result her mistress, becoming jealous, dismissed her; whereupon she started an " At Home " of her own in a modest house, and with the help of d'Alembert, who retained a delicate friendship for her all his life, won over to her salon all the famous people. Among other well-patronized salons were those of Madame d'Épinay, the patron of Rousseau, Madame Necker, the finance minister's wife, and the famous actress Quinault.

The " En-cyclopédie "

The monumental work which bore the title *Encyclopédie ou Dictionnaire raisonné des sciences, des arts et des métiers* began to appear in 1752; in 1772 it reached twenty-eight volumes, discussing in the most fascinating and fundamental way, in alphabetical order and with magnificent type, all questions of philosophy and religion, literature and æsthetics, politics and political economy, science theoretical and technical. No nation but the French has had the ability to handle a dictionary — which is by nature the driest and deadest of all intellectual undertakings — not merely with lucidity and clarity, but entertainingly, convincingly, fascinatingly. The main object of the work was, however, very different: it was nothing less than a vast arsenal of the subversive ideas which had seen the light during the last generations. The method pursued by the editors was skilful, if deceptive; in articles which might be suspected of containing offensive material — for instance, " Soul," " Freedom of the Will," " Immortality," " Christianity " — they expounded orthodox views, while in quite different places, where such discussions would never be looked for, they presented the opposite views, supported by a mass of arguments; and hidden references (which the initiated reader would soon understand) elucidated the connexion between the two.

Diderot

The soul of the whole undertaking was Denis Diderot, who as a scientist united elegance with soundness, and as author displayed an amazing and iridescent many-sidedness. He was a master unexcelled in philosophical dialogue, but he was also dramatist, story-teller, art-critic, mathematician, economist, technologist; above all he was a fine and unselfish character, enthusiastically devoted to his task. His " *Weltanschauung*," though it underwent considerable changes in the course of development, was in essence a sort of monism, according to which everything is made up of matter, but matter is animated: *"la pierre sent."* His two dramas *Le Fils naturel, ou les épreuves de la vertu* and *Le Père de famille* made him one of the chief French representatives of the middle-class sentimental drama, which began in England, but found its most fertile soil later on in Germany (Iffland, Schröder, and Kotzebue). It is clear that the cult of this new *genre,* which Diderot championed in programmatic writings also, was due more to political than to æsthetic motives. Men discovered or thought they discovered that the " people " and the middle classes possessed more virtue and capacity, more generosity and humanity, than the privileged classes : only they failed to remember that in any case all this is, for the dramatic author, irrelevant. Men at the top of society are almost always dramatically a more *fruitful* type, more interesting on the stage, than ordinary citizens or even peasants, for the very simple reason that they experience more. And in fact the poetical revolution of the time, in turning away from kings and men of high estate, ended in nothing more than cold and artificial melodrama. It can hardly be a matter of chance that dramatic poetry has always reached its highest levels beyond the sphere of the ordinary citizen. Classical tragedy is concerned with the heroes and kings and gods, and never with the people, who are relegated to the chorus. Shaksperian tragedy moves among lords and nobles ; and the same is true of German Classical drama, even of middle-class tragedies like *Kabale und Liebe* and *Emilia Galotti,* which are really court dramas. The true home of bourgeois art is in the novel and the comedy. Aristophanes, Molière, and Shakspere in his comedies used this *milieu* with the same deliberate intention as Sophocles, Racine, and Shakspere in his tragedies avoided it. Ibsen, perhaps the greatest comic genius of all time, is also the creator of a great middle-class drama, by the side of which all earlier efforts appear like imperfect preliminaries ; his few trage-dies, *The Pretenders, Emperor and Galilean, Lady Inger of Ostraat,* deal with royal subject-matter, as the real title of *The Pretenders* indicates. Next to Ibsen the two most brilliant stars in the theatrical firmament of the nineteenth century are Richard Wagner and Heinrich von Kleist : both wrote only one play which deals with bourgeois circles, and each is the author's only comedy — Kleist's *Der zerbrochener Krug* and Wagner's *Meistersinger.*

This interconnexion escaped the notice of Batteux, Diderot,

and their pupils all the more readily since they adopted the stand-point of extreme naturalism, which disregards all differences of height and depth of artistic content. Their theories were a reaction against the exaggerated artificiality of the Rococo. Henceforth art was suddenly to become once more pure imitation, a dry, empty, barren repetition of nature, which, if it were successful, would mean the end of all art. Such programs, in any case, do not as a rule determine the value of the product, or even of the criticism that issues from them. It is possible to hold the finest and rightest views of the meaning of art and yet, when occasion arises to apply them to an individual case, to disclose oneself an insensitive philis-tine, just as one can pay lip-service to the most banausic principles and yet be a man of deep taste, imagination, and fine sensibility, like Diderot. His insistence on the natural, pedantic and anti-artistic though it was, did not in the least hinder him from mani-festing the most brilliant gifts in the judgment and detail valua-tion in any work of art; and his remarks about pictures, about acting, and about the technique of the theatre are bull's-eye hits, maxima of imaginative criticism.

The co-editor of the *Encyclopédie* was d'Alembert, who wrote the mathematical articles, together with a magnificent preface; later he resigned his share in the work, because the radical mate-rialism of Diderot and most of his assistants did not suit his con-ciliatory and somewhat nervous spirit nor his exact scientific mode of thought. Himself he professed a kind of phenomenalism which sounds almost like a presage of Kant and was certainly higher than the naïve dogmatism of the Encyclopædists; he felt himself forced, he declared, to the assumption that " all we see is sense-phenome-nal " and there is nothing outside of us to correspond to that which we think we see.

The work which was the foundation-stone of French material-ism, the notorious *Homme machine* of Lamettrie, had been pub-lished three years before the *Encyclopédie*. Starting with the Car-tesian doctrine that animals are automata — which he says would have been sufficient in itself to cause Descartes to rank as a first-rate philosopher — he tries, by rhetorical rather than scientific means, to prove that man also is nothing but a highly com-plicated machine as compared with animals, what an astronomical clock of Huygens would be, compared with an ordinary clock. The book had an enormous vogue, though no one ventured frankly to support these doctrines. Lamettrie was everywhere persecuted and only found refuge with Frederick the Great, who called him to Berlin to act as physician and reader; a few years later he died there after consuming a whole truffle pasty — to the satisfaction of the reactionaries, who straightway set up his death as a warning against his doctrines, as if the devouring of huge pasties were a normal and natural consequence of materialism!

Condillac, in his book *Traité des sensations,* which appeared in 1754, maintained an extreme sensationalism. According to him all our feelings, judgments, actions, in fact every psychological phenomenon, even up to the highest ideas, are simply after-effects of sense-impressions; all psychological activity is transformed perception, all that is in the mind has been in the senses, and all impulses, even the most moral, rise from self-love. Four years later Helvétius, a mediocre conceited individual, but otherwise of irreproachable and even altruistic character, wrote his *De l'esprit,* which developed these ideas more convincingly, especially so far as they affected the domain of morality: as motion in the physical world, so self-interest in the moral is the ruling element. The book made an immense hit, for it touched the secret nerve of the period; and Madame du Deffand cried: " *C'est un homme qui a dit le secret de tout le monde."* Condillac was the starting-point of the whole scientific materialism of the nineteenth century, the connecting link being his pupil Cabanis, whose doctrine culminates in the sentence " *Les nerfs, voilà tout l'homme."* His statement that the brain served for thought as the stomach for digestion and the liver for gall-secretion, and that as food activates the stomach, so impressions activate the brain, was doubtless a witty remark, but produced in Germany, some decades later, a whole series of treatises which, while just as superficial, were the reverse of humorous or witty. Near Condillac, but not so radical, was Robinet, who like Diderot taught the universal animatedness of matter, of plants and minerals, atoms and planets.

For many years the Encyclopædists had their meeting-place at the famous dinners of Holbach, a wealthy baron of the Palatinate; at these dinners, which began at two o'clock, all the native and foreign celebrities resident in Paris were gathered, and Holbach was called, after a remark of the Abbé Galiani, the *maître d'hôtel* of philosophy. He was the author of the catechism of the materialist movement, the *Système de la nature ou des lois du monde physique et du monde moral,* wherein he displayed a truly German thoroughness in the setting-forth and marshalling of all the arguments and dogmas of his circle. The book, appearing in 1770 anonymously, was for some time regarded as a collective work. Nothing exists, it says, except eternal self-subsisting matter, from which everything takes its birth and to which everything returns. At a certain stage of its development it assumes life and consciousness, and man is but matter organized to the point of sensation and thought. It is only ignorance of nature and lack of experience that induced men to make themselves gods to stir their fears and hopes; nature — working according to inviolable laws, creating and destroying, doling out good and evil — knows neither love nor hate, but only the infinite unbroken chain of cause and effect. Order and chaos do not exist in nature, but are purely human concepts which we read into nature: the universe has no other goal but itself. At the same time man should be virtuous, and from prudence, for other people only forward my good fortune if I do not diminish theirs, and even misunderstood virtue makes its possessor happy in the knowledge of having served righteousness. We see, then, that, even though denying to the cosmic process any moral goal or object, Holbach maintains that the life of humanity must display morality, a humdrum morality indeed, dictated only by common sense, but still sincere. The same is true of almost all the Encyclopædists.

It would have been natural to subject the organisms of State and society to the same radical criticism, both from the moral and from the scientific standpoint, as had been applied to the prevailing theological and philosophical doctrines. But for the time being, only isolated attempts were made in this direction. In 1755 the Abbé Morelly attempted in his *Code de la nature* to prove that private property, which is the offspring of selfishness, is the source of all strife and unhappiness, and on this basis he formulated a regular communistic program: the State is to be divided into provinces, cities, families; land and property and all the means of industry are to be the common property of all; the State is to assign to each of its members a task according to the measure of his ability, and wages in proportion to his needs. In 1772 Mirabeau wrote his

Essai sur le despotisme, in which he declared that the king was nothing but the first minister, "*le premier salarié*," the head but not the master of the people, who is appointed and paid for definite tasks and can at any time be removed if he fails to fulfil them or even misuses his position.

Closely related to the extension of the materialistic ideas was the development of natural science — indeed, it is difficult to say which of the two was cause and which effect. The flourishing of exact research does not lead necessarily to a rejection of spirituality, as is shown by the seventeenth century, which was dominated by Descartes and Leibniz. But in the next century there was a decisive change, for whereas previously the front place had been occupied by mathematics and theoretical physics — which are at bottom idealist sciences — now it was purely empirical disciplines that began to claim man's chief attention.

First, as to the theories themselves, the earlier ones still held their ground for a very long time, and it was only gradually that they gave place to the more modern conceptions. Albrecht von Haller used the whole weight of his authority to support Harvey's "preformation" theory, according to which the whole organism with all future generations was already present in "involution" in the egg. Against it Kaspar Friedrich Wolff set up his doctrine of "epigenesis," propounded in his *Theoria generationis* in 1759: the origin of the organism is a process of growth whose course is decided partly by heredity, partly by latent dispositions, partly by external and mechanical causes. The experiments he made to crystallize this hypothesis make him the founder of scientific embryology. Although his assumption was more plausible and easier by far to grasp, it met at first with little credence, but eventually it proved victorious, and inevitably so, because it contained one of the guiding ideas of the time: namely, the idea of evolution; it gave expression to the same feeling which twenty years later caused Lessing to regard the history of religion as a gradual evolution to an ever purer and more adequate idea of God, and gave to Kant his wonderful conception of the whole world as developing out of the conditions of our reason.

Geology too became the object of increased attention. Here ruled the "Neptunistic" doctrine taught by Abraham Gottlob Werner, who, from 1775 on, worked as a revered teacher in the

224

School of Mines at Freiberg, and who explained all (or almost all) changes of the earth's crust as the result of the action of water. Werner was also one of the first to attempt the subdivision of the minerals wholly by their chemical composition, while not neglecting their external peculiarities. Novalis, who was his pupil, said about him: "The impressions of his senses crowded together in vast many-coloured pictures; he heard, saw, touched, and thought simultaneously . . . he played with forces and phenomena and knew where and how he could find this or that." There was also an opposition to this Neptunism in the "Plutonism" of James Hutton, a contrary theory which likewise only won through to acceptance much later: he saw the main cause of geological change in fire, in the volcanic reactions of the glowing interior of the earth against the already hardened earth surface. There was Buffon, too, who employed the splendid rhythms of a fine and nervous style to present the results so far obtained by the descriptive sciences; and, indeed, it was as a writer that he exercised his greatest influence on contemporaries.

But it was in electrical and chemical theory that the most decisive changes occurred. So far, in both subjects, the dogma of imponderabilia had held undisputed sway. Light, like heat, was regarded as a substance, and similar views were held of electricity and magnetism. The failure to discover any increase of weight in all these processes had been explained by the assumption of the "imponderability" of these elements. Now Lavoisier, almost simultaneously with the Englishman Priestley and the Swede Scheele, discovered that the air is made up of two gases, of which the one is the "cause" of fire; because this acted also in the formation of acids, he called it oxygen. In his further researches he succeeded in explaining breathing and fermentation in a similar way. Again, contemporaneously with Cavendish, the discoverer of hydrogen, he arrived at an understanding of the constitution of water, and thus the enormous rôle played by oxygen in the earthly economy was revealed at last in its main lines. The summit of his achievement was the cardinal law that in all chemical processes the sum of the materials remains an unaltered quantity. Yet, though he had clearly laid down the theory of the elements and had established it irrefragably by exact measurement, he still held in practice to the idea of imponderables, and he included heat

The New Chemistry

and light in his list of the chemical elements. We see from this how even the most powerful genius is subject to the greater power of the ideas of its age; in this concept of imponderables survives the relic of supranaturalism which was still alive in the scientific outlook of the eighteenth century throughout its course. Even in the most radical school it was only a few ineffectual outsiders who took the last step to a self-consistent naturalism which admits nothing in observed science that cannot be confined and controlled by the senses. It was the amateurish confusion between philosophic speculation and exact research, and nothing else, that made it possible for so many even of the most intelligent men of the age to accept materialism as a creed. The solution of the problem had to wait for Kant, who showed that in reality it was two wholly disparate spheres of the human reason that were in question, and that this could not be properly grasped unless they were treated apart from each other. And, for that matter, the efforts that are made ever and again, even today, to gloss over or to reject the limits so clearly marked out by Kant, to be metaphysical as a natural scientist or scientific as a metaphysician, indicate, not a necessary attitude of the time as it did with the materialists of the French Enlightenment, but only an antediluvian imbecility.

The theory of the elements was extended very considerably by Dalton's Law of Multiple Proportions, which also was the result of observing the behaviour of oxygen. Oxygen has the faculty of being compounded with almost all other atoms, and with some of them in more than one atomic relation. Dalton's law says that in such cases the varying quantities of an element which can compound with the same quantum of oxygen stand to each other in simple numerical proportions such as $1:2$, $2:3$, $1:4$. Other elements, such as carbon and hydrogen, also possess the same combining properties as oxygen. It was the natural consequence of these discoveries that Dalton became one of the most logical supporters of the atomistic hypothesis, for which indeed he provided the exact foundation. To him every chemical process is nothing but dissociation and combination of atoms; we might as well try to incorporate a new planet in the solar system or remove an existent one as to create or annihilate an atom of hydrogen, and all changes which we can bring about consist in the separation of atoms formerly united, or the combination of atoms formerly separated. All such processes depend on the mysterious problem of elective affinity, which Berthollet made the subject of illuminating researches, and which stimulated Goethe to his famous romance: " In this grasping and letting go, in this avoiding and seeking out, we really believe we see a higher determination; we ascribe to such entities a sort of willing and choosing, and feel the use of the artificial word ' elective-affinity ' to be fully justified. . . . We must first see before our eyes these entities, that seem so dead, but are always ready for inner activity, we must observe them eagerly, how they approach each other, attract, seize upon, destroy, absorb, consume, and straightway appear again by this secret association in renewed, strange, and unexpected forms; then at last we shall credit them with eternal life, even with sense and reason."

As for electricity, it became the fashionable science of the time. The new apparatus was regarded as an original and amusing toy, everyone was experimenting with it and it was to be found even among the rouge-pots and wig-stands of ladies' boudoirs. The most notable event in this sphere was the discovery of galvanic or contact electricity. In 1780 Galvani noticed that a recently prepared frog's limb, which he had hung out on his balcony, began to twitch if a conductor was made to spark in its neighbourhood, and the same thing happened if lightning occurred near by. The excitement which was aroused by this observation was caused in the first place by the mysterious phenomenon of the twitching of the dead body, and the " animists " saw in it the expression of a secret life-force surviving after death. The passion for the miraculous, as we shall see later, was by no means dead in this rationalistic age. But Galvani himself, in the course of his experiments, found evidentially that the frog's leg only twitched if the copper hook on which it was suspended came into contact with the iron balcony: this had accidentally occurred in the first instance as the result of the wind blowing and was deliberately brought about in the later experiments. His conclusion was that " animal magnetism " really existed. But the right explanation was only found by Volta in 1794: namely, that the frog's muscle merely acted as a conductor, while the real electrical phenomenon occurred between the two metals. He proved, moreover, that for this purpose any two metals were suitable, provided they were different, that these and the frog's leg must form a closed circuit, and

Galvanic electricity

that the leg, seeing that the essential part of the process was its dampness, could be replaced by any other liquid. On the basis of these discoveries he constructed the voltaic pile, consisting of a number of such pairs of metals juxtaposed — for instance, copper and tin, or silver and zinc — and by joining the ends or poles with wires, he produced a continuous electrical current. " It may be paradoxical and inexplicable that the electric fluid passes uninterruptedly," he says in his description of the pile (which he called " an artificial electric organ "), " but such is the actual fact, and it can be grasped as it were by the hand."

Astronomy and Mathematics   In astronomy the main work had already been accomplished, and it only remained to fill in some of the major details in the picture of the construction and organization of the universe. In 1781 Herschel with his giant telescope discovered the planet Uranus. Further, he affirmed that the so-called double stars were not associated haphazard, but formed binary systems, whose movements obey the laws of gravitation; and that not only is the Milky Way composed of countless suns, but that the nebulæ are nothing but huge star-masses, many consisting only of radiant masses of gas which represent future worlds. This was a confirmation of the Kantian hypothesis, and it was extended by Laplace, who also put forth a theory of " disturbances ": that is, the variations from pure elliptical motion, to which the heavenly bodies suffer owing to their mutual attraction. In 1794 Chladni proved the cosmic origin of meteorites.

The most important mathematician of the age was Leonhard Euler, who was in great demand at the courts of Frederick the Great and Catherine, and raised algebra to an international sign-language of mathematics; he also founded the Calculus of Variations and (though for the moment without success) championed the undulatory theory of light. In his *Lettres à une princesse d'Allemagne sur quelques sujets de physique et de philosophie* he opposed the emission theory of Newton, pointing out that if light were a subtle substance flowing from the sun and other radiant bodies, the diminution of the sun's mass should have become perceptible in the course of the centuries. He held that, on the contrary, light originates in a similar way to sound; sound arises through the vibrations of the air, which we call music when they follow at regular intervals, but perceive only as noise if they are chaotic; and thus also light is caused by vibration in the ether — a liquid substance somewhat similar to air, but incomparably finer and more elastic. "In actual fact, then, nothing comes to us from the sun, any more than from a bell whose ringing hits our ear." Euler's successor in Berlin was Lagrange; his *Mécanique analytique* and his classical work on the problem of three bodies and on the differential calculus were epoch-making.

Finally there are three scientific successes which we will not leave unnoticed, though they received little attention from the period, because they were in advance of it. In 1787 Saussure ascended Mont Blanc for the purpose of studying earth structure. In 1793 Christian Sprengel published his *Secret of Nature revealed in the structure and fertilization of flowers*. This, as the book describes in detail, is brought about as follows: insects, in searching for the juice of flowers and for that purpose settling on the flowers or crawling into them, of necessity rub off the pollen on the stamens, owing to the hairiness of their bodies, and bear it to the pistil. This is appropriately covered either with fine hair or with a sticky substance. Nature, moreover, "who never does things by halves," has seen to it "that the insects perceive the flowers from a distance, either through their appearance or their smell, or both. All succulent flowers are, therefore, provided with a corolla and many of them diffuse a scent, which for mankind is mostly pleasant, often unpleasant, sometimes intolerable, but for the appropriate insect is always pleasant. . . . Then when some insect, enticed by the beauty of the corolla or the fascinating scent of the flower, has settled upon it, it either notices the honey immediately, or fails to do so because it lies in some hidden part. In the latter case nature helps by a mark which consists of one or more spots, lines, dots, or figures which are of a different colour from the corolla and so offers more or less of a contrast with it. This mark always lies at the point at which the insects have to crawl in if they are to reach the honey. . . . All flowers, that have neither corolla nor, in its place, any noticeable or coloured calix, and are not scented, possess no honey and are not fertilized by insects, but mechanically by the wind." His work was little heeded, and even less attention was at first given to the Englishman Edward Jenner and his inoculation against smallpox, which even to Kant seemed nothing but the "inoculation of bestiality." The

Fertilization of flowers; Vaccination

229

poxes were at the time amongst the most widespread diseases; the majority of mankind was disfigured by pock-marks, and in some countries they caused a tenth of the annual deaths. At bottom Jenner owed his success to the same method as that recommended by Sprengel when he said that we have to catch nature in the act. Jenner noticed that milkmaids practically never succumbed to the smallpox, because they had already been infected by the animal's udder. What had been a matter of chance he made into a system by inoculating his patients with vaccine and thereby immunizing them from smallpox. The first vaccination centre was opened in London in 1799, but on the Continent the new treatment had for some time to cope with all sorts of prejudices.

The prime plant   Among misunderstood scientists of the eighteenth century we must include also Goethe; for the public is so built that it must always refuse to grant its great man supremacy in more than one sphere of thought — applying its own limitations and one-sidedness to genius, though the essence of genius is precisely that it can work creatively and transformingly in any field which it selects. Goethe himself (in an uncompleted paper on granite) described his transition to scientific research in the following splendid words: " I do not fear the reproach that it must be a spirit of contradiction that has led me from the observation and painting of the human heart, the innermost, most varied, mobile, changeable, and fragile thing in creation, to commenting on the oldest, firmest, deepest, and most unbreakable offspring of nature. For it will readily be admitted that everything in nature stands in definite relationship, and that the researching spirit will not willingly shut itself off from anything accessible. It may even be granted to me, who through the change of human feelings and their movements have suffered and still suffer much within myself and in others, to enjoy the sublime calm which is offered by the solitary still nearness of vast and whispering nature; and let anyone who has an inkling of it follow me." His *Metamorphose der Pflanzen* appeared in 1790; its basic idea is that all parts of the plant should be regarded as transformed leaves; the development takes place with alternating expansion and contraction in six stages of increasing perfection: (1) the seed-lobe or cotyledons, generally underground, whitish, coarse, undifferentiated; (2) the leaves, longer and broader, notched and green; (3) the calix leaves, close-packed and little differentiated; (4) the corolla, greater and delicate and glowing with colour; (5) the stamens, shaped almost like a thread and containing an extremely fine juice; (6) the leaves of the fruit, again extensive and enfolding the seeds. This abstraction, which never actually appears, but exists only as the plan, the scheme or idea at the basis of all formations (though Goethe would not admit this himself at first and only learnt to see it under Schiller's influence), is the Goethean "prime plant." A similar standpoint is to be found in his treatise on the intermaxillary bone (1784), in which he followed the various forms in which this bone, which he had discovered, appeared throughout the whole series of the vertebrates. In the next years, as a result of careful osteological observations, he came to the conclusion that the human skull consists of metamorphosed vertebræ: thus these vertebræ play the same part in anatomical investigations as the leaf does in his botanical, and as a pendant to the "*Urpflanze*" he sees floating before him an ideal model (which he calls an archetype) of mammal skeleton. In all his physical studies he started with the conviction that everywhere he must search for the prime phenomenon, the "*Urphänomen*," to which all the manifold varieties of appearances may be traced.

Manifestly, we are in the "*siècle philosophique*." Everywhere men searched for the idea of things, but for the idea that *appears*. There is a very definite relationship, as well as difference, between Goethe's "*Urpflanze*" and the primitive man postulated by the French Revolution for its political and social metamorphoses. Both are abstractions, but they are not abstractions opposed to reality, like the ideals which, though inaccessible, point the way, or the hypotheses which, purely artificial, yet help us on the path. They are abstractions which ask to be dug out of actuality as its true life-core, and therefore they are regarded as concretely existent. At the same time there is a sharp difference. Goethe conceived the idea of the "*Urpflanze*" in order to make the familiar reality which he observes ever and again, more intelligible, clearer, more uniform, more imaginable, and thus in a sense more real; but the Revolution constructs the phantom of primitive man blindly, arbitrarily, unreally, in order to twist, to distort, to cripple reality, and thus to make it more intractable, incomprehensible, chaotic, and unreal. The "*Urpflanze*" is won from life, the

"*Urmensch*" is forced upon it; the Goethean idea is simplified nature, the Revolutionary idea is unnatural simplicity.

The Enlightenment, from which the later Revolutionary dogmatic sprang, was an English invention and goes back to Locke, or more precisely to Bacon; and in the first half of the century it produced a number of outstanding representatives, culminating in the so-called Scottish school, whose leader, Thomas Reid, founded the philosophy of the healthy human reason in his book (published in 1764) entitled *Enquiry into the Human Mind on the Principles of Common Sense*. He taught that the soul has certain original judgments, natural instincts of thought, "self-evident truths," which form the basic facts of our consciousness and the legitimate content of our knowledge; everything in previous systems that appears clear and congruous, without further ado, to ordinary understanding, is true, and everything which contradicts it or appears unclear is false. Descended from this was the German "popular philosophy," whose ideal was a "philosophy for the world," as one of its most famous representatives, J. J. Engel, used to call his collected essays. By its side there was a whole guild of makers of books, edifying, educative, reasonable, and intelligible. But the centre of the whole of this German Enlightenment lay in a group of influential Berlin journals. First came the *Library of Pure Science and Art* (founded 1757), written almost entirely by Nicolai and Mendelssohn and containing chiefly pedantic art-criticism of all sorts. In 1759 appeared the *Letters concerning the Newest Literature*, which was on a much higher level, for its author was, at first, the young Lessing, and it was here — in keen controversy with Wieland, Gottsched, and the French, and in warm championship of Shakspere — that he outlined the bases of his æsthetic world-view. The *Allgemeine deutsche Bibliothek* saw the light in 1765 and survived for a full forty years, during which period it determined the literary judgments of the educated middle-classes in a reactionary spirit that was usually disastrous. Its editor was again Nicolai, who was a sound and learned man, with good sense and some skill in writing; as the descendant of a respectable bookseller family, he was a sort of cross between tradesman and littérateur and had acquired a wonderful facility in the window-display and exploitation of intellectual tendencies; on the other hand, the dull doctrinairism that was so offensively displayed in his arbitrary revision of contributions sent in to him, and the narrow rationalism which made him persecute and despise anything he failed to understand (and that meant a good deal), have made him a notorious and even a classical example of conceited and insipid Beckmesserism. Even in his own lifetime "Nicolaite" was a pretty stinging term of abuse. Still, considering the incessant demand for themes for the D. Litt. and the comparatively small stock of dead scribes who have not yet been completely worked over, he is worth recommending to ambitious young students as a subject for whitewash. Nicolai was the typical Berliner, logical, factual (or at any rate well-disposed towards fact), highly suspicious of all wordiness, all fantasy or charlatanry; sound, diligent, interested in everything, always on the alert to scoff, yet, being a Berliner, with almost always a basis of good sense. It is true that he possessed in a high degree the defects of these admirable qualities, but they have been so often and so intensively made the subject of bitter criticism that they are not a sufficiently original theme even for a thesis.

As for Moses Mendelssohn, it would be a great mistake to *Mendelssohn* assume that his Jewishness involved any disadvantage. Cultured society of the time made it a point of decency to treat all foreign peoples and creeds as of equal value with their own. Besides, it was a welcome confirmation of their own ideas that they had among their adherents a member of a race that, far more than is the case today, represented a world segregated from the rest of the culture around it; and they were generally inclined to exaggerate the importance of the fact that a Jew was counted among the German writers — confusing rarity-value with intrinsic value. For it must not be forgotten that Mendelssohn — in point of character a figure of thoroughgoing honesty and almost touching excellence — expressed the most superficial Enlightenment philosophy in his writings and at the same time clung to his Judaism. "The religion of my fathers," he said, "knows nothing (in its main principles) of any secrets which we have to believe, but may not understand. Our reason can pass easily from fixed first principles of human knowledge and can be assured of ultimately attaining to religion by that very path. There is no dispute here between religion and reason, no surging of our natural knowledge against the oppressive power of belief." He makes it quite clear, in this and other places, that he takes Judaism to be the true religion of reason, which he secretly opposes to Christianity; and yet, though he scorned Christian ceremonies with smiling superiority, he held with the most scrupulous care to the absurdest ritual demands of his own creed. In him there comes out, in an ultra-modern guise, the bitterness of the Jew against the Saviour, combined with the fanatical worship of the twice-times-table and of interest rates, the Jewish hatred of idealism, of the mysterious, of God. The native spirit of Judaism, even when it loses itself in the most lofty heights (and Mendelssohn was emphatically not one of the lone walkers on high places), ever retains the character of a materialism that has overshot itself. And always it remains rationalistic. The assumption that reality consists of the things that can be proved, or, better, be touched, is a Jewish discovery, though the most appalling nonsense. The Jews have shown the most supreme heroism and the most selfless contempt of death in countless wars, but always for highly realistic motives. All great Jewish reformers have been *Realpolitiker;* Jewish ritual is for the most a matter of sanitary regulation, and the highest conception of Judaism, the Messianic idea, tries inaccessible heights indeed, but is certainly not *other*-worldly: it is a concrete fantasy. *That* was why Jesus was persecuted by the whole of contemporary Judaism with such measureless bitterness; not because he was a reformer, for the fickle people was quite used to reformers, nor because he opposed the hierarchy, which was widely unpopular, nor yet because he championed the lower classes, for the atmosphere was not unfavourable to such, but because he was a dangerous revolutionary who dared to proclaim: "My kingdom is not of this world." It was this which offended the deepest and innermost instinct, the fundamental life-feeling of Judaism, since it was in fact the complete reversal and abolition of the specifically Jewish world-conception. When Jesus introduced the transcendent into religion and ethics and taught mankind that in it alone dwells reality, he began a colossal revolution that Judaism instantly saw in its right light.

If we keep this in mind, it will be quite intelligible that the Jew Mendelssohn should be one of the chief spokesmen of Religion as purified by Enlightenment; for if from the Christian's *credo* we abstract the *absurdum,* as the rational faith of the time did, nothing remains but a Mosaic religion which has one prophet added to its Old Testament quota. Even philosophy, in Mendelssohn's eyes, has only the task of " making clear and certain, by means of the reason, what ordinary common sense has recognized as right." With such primitive weapons he tries to prove immortality in his *Phædo* and the existence of God in his *Morgenstunden.* His aim in the first book is made clear in the preface: " My task was to elucidate, not the grounds which the Greek world of the time had for believing in the immortality of the soul, but those which today a man like Socrates, who would have his beliefs based on reason and has the efforts of so many great minds to build upon, would find for thinking his soul immortal." That means, Plato revised by Mendelssohn and enlarged by " great minds " like Garve, Engel, and Nicolai. If we approve the purpose, we must admit its success, for Socrates does talk about last things just like the worthy tradesman and popular writer Mendelssohn, who sees in him nothing but the founder of a popular ethic and apprehends nothing in him but a rationalistic equation " Virtue = Knowledge "; who perceives nothing at all of the splendid irony which culminated in his voluntary death.

In the *Morgenstunden* he taught the prevailing deism, which, whether openly or tacitly, was the creed of the cultured, and left little of the idea of God except that of a wise being, who fulfils the natural laws decreed by the philosophers. In the matter of revelation they saved their faces for the time being by all sorts of compromises, which were either illogical or (more often) the result of dishonest thinking. Thus the eminent theologian Johann Salomo Semler, who applied to the Bible a very competent *apparatus criticus,* introduced the idea of " accommodation," according to which the Son of God, the apostles, and the saints suited their words to the needs of men of their time; therefore in our time, when needs had changed, they could be otherwise understood. On the other side Rationalism, seeing everywhere, *à la* Wolff, a pervading wisdom in nature, led to a ridiculous vulgarization of theology. It was no longer enough to talk of a " physicotheology," which from the universality of law and the adaptation of the world to definite ends had argued a wise creator; there were new inventions such as litho-, phyto-, melitto-, acrido-,

Utilitarian interpretation of the Bible

235

ichthyo-, testaceo-, insecto-theology which were supposed to give evidence of God in all the detailed phenomena of stones, plants, bees, locusts, fish, snails, insects; there were even a bronto- and a seismo-theology, which led to the knowledge of God through the proper understanding of thunder and earthquakes. The utilitarian interpretation of the Bible was especially favoured in Evangelical services; the Manger was used in sermons to indicate the value of stable feeding, the Easter visit of the women to the tomb to prove the value of early rising, and the entry into Jerusalem to point the undesirability of damaging trees by the cutting of young branches.

The Resurrection fraud

The whole attitude of the time towards religious history may be summed up in the much-discussed work of Hermann Samuel Reimarus, which only circulated in a manuscript in his lifetime and was published later in fragments by Lessing, who pretended he had found it in the Wolfenbüttel Library. The real author was not known until 1814. Starting with the thesis that " a single untruth which contradicts evident experience, history, common sense, incontrovertible axioms, or the rules of good morals, is sufficient to cause a book to be rejected as evidence of divine inspiration," he takes a jump of which the audacity becomes almost imbecility, and argues that the apostles invented the story of the Resurrection for their own benefit: after the incessant wandering about with the Messiah they had forgotten how to work, but had realized that preaching the Kingdom of God supplied nurture for the preacher, since the womenfolk had been only too glad to maintain the Messiah and his future ministers in comfort. They therefore stole the body of Jesus, hid it, and proclaimed to the world that the Saviour had risen and would soon return. Jesus, in agreement with the popular Jewish conception, had pictured the Kingdom of God as a powerful kingdom of this earth and himself as its future king, but he and his disciples had been bitterly disappointed; and the latter had therefore invented a new scheme, according to which Christ had to suffer and die for the salvation of mankind, but had thereafter risen to heaven, whence he would soon come to restore his kingdom.

That a hypothesis which made of the apostles a greedy band of swindlers could meet with such a welcome finds its explanation in that complete lack of historical and psychological understanding which is one of the most conspicuous characteristics of the whole period. But the second assumption, that Jesus had simply intended to bring to pass the Messianic kingdom hoped for by the Jews, shows almost more misunderstanding. This absurdity has seldom been put forward with the crudity of Reimarus; but the nonsensical linkage of the Gospels with the Old Testament, which we have often alluded to before, gave and still gives opportunity for such misinterpretations. An unprejudiced study of the Bible must lead to the conclusion that Jesus did not merely transform the Messianic idea, extending it, spiritualizing it, filling it with deeper meaning, and raising it to a loftier height — which is the attitude of a good many theologians and laymen today — but that he absolutely refuted and abolished it: in other words, that he was *not* the Messiah. As a matter of fact, he never once called himself by the name, and the few passages which are commonly thought to prove it are at best ambiguous and only show that he was called so by others. It is impossible to enter into details here; but Moriz de Jonge — a comparatively unknown scholar with strange ideas that sometimes border on the pathological, yet a man of extraordinary knowledge — has submitted this question to an exact textual criticism and has come out at the most remarkable conclusions; and moreover no less an authority than Wellhausen says: " Jesus did not appear as the Messiah, as the fulfilment of the prophets, he . . . was not the Messiah and did not even wish to be." For the ordinary reader two simple considerations should suffice: if Jesus was the Messiah, why did he do nothing of what was expected of the Messiah? and secondly, if Jesus was the Messiah, why did the Jews not recognize him as such, and why do they refuse to do so even to the present day? That the world must not, cannot, be conquered by the sword, but only by the spirit, was a wholly new idea, which had occurred previously to neither Jew nor pagan. In short, if the Messiah was to be the Christ, the anointed, the king — which is certainly the right Jewish attitude — then Jesus was nothing more or less than the embodied Antichrist.

Lessing himself did not share the ideas of the " Wolffenbüttel Fragmentist "; rather he hoped by publishing the exposition of this " genuine opponent of religion " to arouse a genuine defender. But the defender failed to appear, for the age could produce only a short-sighted literal religiousness or a misty-sighted free-thinking religiosity. Of the latter, Lessing had an even greater abhorrence than of the former. " Orthodoxy," he writes in 1774, " was, thank God, more or less done with; there had been a sort of partition wall between it and philosophy, behind which everyone could go his own way without obstructing others; whereas nowadays — the wall is torn down, and under the pretence of making us reasonable Christians we are turned into unreasonable philosophers. . . . It is a patchwork made by bunglers and semi-philosophers, the religious system which they would nowadays put in the place of the old and which claims far more influence over reason and philosophy than the old." Hamann also saw that the Enlightenment had brought little light: he called it the northern lights or the cold barren light of the moon; and Schleiermacher, looking back upon it, summed its whole position up in the cutting words: " Philosophy consisted in this, that there is to be no philosophy, but only an enlightenment."

Lessing Lessing represents the final summing-up, but also the successful disruption, of the ideas of the German Enlightenment. His heyday lasted only half a generation: *Laokoon* appeared in 1776, *Minna von Barnhelm* and the *Hamburg Dramaturgy* in '77, *Emilia Galotti* in '72, *Nathan der Weise* in '79, and the *Education of the Human Race* in '80. His death marked the close of an epoch, for in that same year *Die Räuber* and the *Critique of Pure Reason* were published. He is one of the comparatively few men in Germany who without creating anything absolutely complete, and without saying the last word on anything, yet scatter fruitful seeds in all directions and make everything that they touch to stand out vital and ever fresh. His *Laokoon,* which marked out the limits between poetry and painting with a hitherto unimagined sharpness and lucidity, not merely taught the æsthetics (which would have been a success of little importance), but opened the eyes of artists; and it is especially noticeable, in a work which appeared under the imminent shadow of Winckelmann's Classicism, that it not only rejected the waxwork ideal of Greek Stoicism, but laid it down that we should imitate the Greeks by doing as they did: namely, by expressing what we are and what we experience. To the Hamburg National Theatre — an enterprise which began with lofty aspirations, but collapsed very soon through the dull conservatism of the public, the cliques and jealousies of the actors and the timid and fussy assertiveness of the patrons — German literature is indebted for *Minna* and the *Dramaturgie*. In his dramatic technique, which reached an almost unrivalled height in *Emilia,* Lessing proves himself a master of veiled exposition and exact intergearing of scenes, a brilliant analytical writer, an economical and therefore highly effective generator and distributor of dramatic eruptions, and, in virtue of all these things, a sort of ancestor of Ibsen. Like him Lessing belongs to the small group of Germanic dramatists who mastered the supreme artistry of the French and raised it to higher levels by adding, as their national contribution, vitality and individual characterization. But he lacks the note of enigma, the background terror which makes Ibsen's painting of souls so suggestive. He has not the pictorial quality, and his poems have far more the character of a fine clear-cut engraving; he directs and controls just a little too consciously, and Schiller was right in calling him the supervisor of his heroes. He himself realized his own defect with the superb clarity which infused his whole life and work: in his *Dramaturgie* he says: " I am neither actor nor poet. Often indeed men do me the honour to acknowledge me as the latter, but only because they do not know me. I do not feel in myself the living source which springs and works up through its own force in rays so rich, so fresh, and so pure; I have to press everything from within myself by pump and pipe. I should be poor, cold, short-sighted indeed, if I had not to some extent learnt humbly to borrow foreign treasure, to warm myself at others' fires, and to reinforce my vision by the glasses of art. I am always ashamed and depressed if I hear or read anything in disparagement of criticism. It is said to suppress genius: and I flattered myself that I got from it something very near to genius." In the pulsing dialectic, the electric tension and printed tragedy of his Faust fragment his dramatic potency, with its force and its limitations, is most clearly exhibited. In this Faust was to experience his temptation in a dream and was then to be purged and saved, but the brilliant conception was never carried out. Indeed, with the purely rationalistic means at his disposal it was hardly capable of accomplishment, for a man of such clear understanding, a man who possessed in the highest degree what Nietzsche called intellectual probity, was too conscientious and too honest ever to dream. And this word is to be taken as literal fact, for, as Leisewitz wrote to Lichtenberg, " he often assured me that he had never dreamed." His life ran its course wholly upon the illuminated half of our soul-sphere.

Lessing's last and deepest work is the *Education of the Human Race,* in which he treats the history of religion as a progressive revelation of God. The first stage is Judaism, the childhood, in which education is carried on by immediate concrete punishments and rewards; the second stage, the adolescence of humanity, is in the Christian religion, which directs " a generation more proficient in the practice of reason, no longer by hope and fear of temporal rewards and punishments, but by nobler and worthier motives." " And thus Christ was the first sure and practical teacher of immortality." But a third age is yet to come, " the manhood of full enlightenment and of the purity of heart which loves virtue for itself." The Bible is not the basis of religion, but religion the basis of the Bible, and Christianity is older than the Old Testament. And in that he introduces the idea of evolution into the treatment of history, and treats each of the great religions as justified at its own stage; in that he rejects the shallow " rational Christianity," remarking that it was a great pity that none could tell where it was rational and where Christian; in that he thinks of his own age, which seemed to the complacent philosophy of his time as the object and climax of all history, as nothing more than a halting-place in the progress of the divine scheme — he has passed far indeed beyond the Enlightenment.

Lichtenberg With Lessing should be mentioned Lichtenberg, one of the secret classics of German literature, for whom one would willingly exchange Wieland, who was never anything more than a clever man of letters. Goethe once said of Kant that when he read him, he felt as though he were entering a brightly lighted room; and there are few German writers of whom this would be truer than of Lichtenberg; except that his room still has all sorts of half-obscure angles, projections, and passages which lead to the most appalling haunted chambers.

It is a justifiable assumption to make of significant minds that they should be, as it were, a sort of focus of their age; and since all rays concentrate in them, it should be easy to follow each beam from the focal point and thus explain the time from the man, and the man from his time. This attempt would fail with Lichtenberg. His period was one of the most fertile and intellectually active that Germany has ever experienced, but he was never in any sense its focal point. What, then, is the proper position, in the midst of all this breathless activity, of this eager agile spirit who took so keen a part in every sphere? He was, quite simply, the *ideal public* of the whole movement. He was, in relation to his age, not a burning-glass, but only a magnifying mirror which registered its qualities with extreme and merciless sharpness.

Hardly ever do we find his name mentioned by his contemporaries with the emphasis it deserves, and in the minds of his fellows he never lived for what he was. He had neither the inclination nor the capacity to set the wheels of literary history in motion. He resembled rather the Goethe in later years, who sat over plants, stones, and memoirs rather than mix himself up with literary propaganda, until the passionate realism of Schiller brought him back to actuality. Lichtenberg's outward life flowed on in the writing of papers on physical and literary subjects, among a few little girls and a few good friends. Amidst such everyday affairs his life-work grew, but he himself knew it not.

That work is his diaries. " Merchants," he says, " have their ' waste-book,' in which they enter from day to day anything they buy or sell, in any sort of order. . . . This method is worthy of imitation. I need a book in which I can write anything, just as I see it or as it enters my thoughts." These disconnected entries, to which he himself attributed no more value than as a kind of gossip for his own use, contain the sum of his genius, a genius that for vigour and lucidity, concentrated capacity for thought and delicate sensibility, has few equals. Such works must, from their nature, lack a real conclusion, for they possess inherently an indefinite extensibility. Emerson too, among many others, committed his thoughts to such diaries, but he had the will-power to collect them as essays of smaller or greater length. In some places the joints still show through, so that he has been accused of illogical thinking. Lichtenberg could not make up his mind to write up his fragmentary thoughts, he was far too critical for such a task; and his " waste-book " only appeared after his death.

The destiny of books is as illogical and as irrational as that of men, or at least *seems* so. They obey an obscure law of their nature, which no one knows. None can tell how books come to birth, least of all their authors; they lead a strange, inconsistent life through the centuries, and they receive their share of popularity and unpopularity without just reason. There are authors who weary themselves for years with a problem or a poem, unnoticed by the world; doubt seizes them, and their work seems futile, when suddenly in an obscure corner of their mind there appears a thought, to which they have never attached importance, and this one little thought becomes a torch that shines through the ages.

These posthumous immortalities, which are recognized only after the death of their creators, are not the worst of their kind. Lichtenberg could only see his inability to reach a conclusion as a defect: "The delayer, the procrastinator — there is a subject for a comedy that I ought to work up. My worst fault has always been putting things off." What he took as a lack of energy, however, posterity is more inclined to regard as an indication of supreme intellectual power. It was just the extraordinary fullness and vitality with which new impressions and observations streamed in on him that prevented his coming to a conclusion. Perhaps he felt that for a man of such unlimited receptive power as himself it would be a sort of treachery to impose an arbitrary limit on his material. An infinite spirit stood face to face with infinite nature and was satisfied to let its richness pour into him. It is no matter of chance that so many writers leave their best work to the end, or never accomplish it at all: they are too enamoured of it not to feel they must achieve something better, not to want to see it perfect. "If only," said Lichtenberg, "I could say everything which I have thought together, as it is in me, and not separated, I should certainly have the applause of the world. If only I could mark out canals in my head, so as to accelerate the internal traffic between my stocks of thought!" But he could not, he could say things only as they were in him, so that he could not experience the separate unseparated, or set up artificial channels between thoughts which were not naturally connected in him; he could only think things as they were in his brain. The work of trimming and sandpapering, which is fundamental to every system, he did not understand.

"There is nothing," says Lichtenberg, "about which I should more like to hear the *secret* voices of thinking men than about the substance of the soul; I do not want the openly expressed ideas, which I know well enough. They belong not so much to psychology as to a collection of statutes." Man in his peculiarities, in that which *differentiates* him, in his multitudinous secret riddles, in his twists and turns, lives in Lichtenberg's notes. They are the most splendid collection of psychological documentation imaginable. Soul-testing is here for the first time scientifically practised as a branch of empirical knowledge of man, not indeed in the form of those physical measurements and logarithmic series which can never penetrate to the depths, but in the spirit of exactness and objectivity. Lichtenberg is a master of minute observation, a specialist in the integral calculus of the soul, a practical Leibnizian who can trace everywhere in fact and can describe the " *perceptions petites* " whose existence Leibniz had postulated theoretically. " I am greatly distressed not to have put into words a thousand tiny feelings and thoughts which are the true supports of human philosophy. A scholar too often writes what anyone could write and omits what he alone could write and thereby immortalize himself."

Lichtenberg's restless and uncompromising passion for truth and self-criticism has its outward expression in the perfect simplicity and naturalness of his style, in which only Lessing and Schopenhauer are his equals. His language functions with the sureness and clearness of a precision-tool; every phrase, even the most incidental, astonishes by its classical economy, its perspicuousness, and its weight. His thought illuminates things almost to the point of decomposing them and yet has that peculiar sort of shrewdness which is the privilege of genius.

There is always something timeless about men who are so extraordinarily natural, and consequently the historical traits of his time are not readily applicable to Lichtenberg. He belongs with them only in that he was their perfect contrary. He was the complement of his age, and men of this type, whenever they occur, are always the strangest and most noteworthy. Lichtenberg was the clear shadow thrown by the Enlightenment, and it is one of the many paradoxes of cultural history that the shadow has remained longer and more clearly visible than the light.

He was one of those minds that are too lucid and too sovereign to be very active. There is a peak of thoughtfulness at which it is no longer possible to act; to have seen wholly into a subject, to have penetrated it utterly, means to have done with it. The blindness and the limitations of the human spirit are perhaps not such great ills as pessimists would have us think; maybe they are nature's defensive arrangements to enable us to remain capable of living. For uncertainty is one of the strongest impulses to living, and as soon as a man attains the abnormal levels of clarity, the natural consequence will be that he loses the more potent impulse to action, even action in the intellectual sphere. Everything about him, men, achievements, knowledge, crises, become wholly transparent, so that he is satisfied with their tranquil contemplation. He has reached knowledge and has no further needs. " That which we know," says Maeterlinck, " concerns us no more."

For this reason Lichtenberg never developed any passionate opposition to the sins of his time; he kept himself always in the reserve line as a cool Mentor. In this he differs from Lessing, with whom in other ways he has most in common. If he was annoyed, he would, at the worst, become sarcastic; yet even his bitterest satires have an undercurrent of good humour and indulgence, just as, on the other hand, his most serious statements always have a delicate, barely noticeable trace of irony and jest — that contempt which never leaves the true thinker, the deep conviction that nothing is worth taking seriously, which made even so tragically wrestling a spirit as Pascal's cry out: " *Le vrai philosophe se moque de la philosophie.*"

The true philosopher is far more nearly allied to the artist than is generally thought. Both of them feel life as a game of which they seek to determine the rules, and that is all. The one not less than the other is a discoverer and a creator, but while the artist seeks to create as many and as manifold individuals as possible, the thinker depicts only one — namely, himself — but that one in all its variety. Every deeply felt philosophy is nothing more or less than an autobiographical novel.

What prevented Litchtenberg from passing out of this realm into the freer world of poetry, and especially of satirical comedy, was not any defect, but an excess. His never-resting critical faculty debarred him from wholly free creation. In this as in other things he was akin to Lessing. He too would never have written any plays

if there had been another to do it better. But since he had not only
to mean things, but practically to express his meanings, he was
compelled to produce a set of paradigms, which were worth as
much and as little as all such exemplars: from the didactic point
of view much, from the artistic little. He was the inspired producer
of the German poesy and never wished to be its inspired actor.
But even on the stage the producer has occasionally to interfere
and play the part himself, not because he thinks himself a first-
rate actor, but because he knows that all theoretical explanations
in the world can give no living picture of what he means, and that
when all is said and done, he is the one who can do it best, because
he is the cleverest. That is the weakness and the strength of Lessing's dramas; he was too clever to write pieces.

If Lessing's literary activity expressed itself outwardly,
Lichtenberg's work was concentrated inwardly. Both fought, the
one amid the hubbub of the world and its ideas, the other in quiet
communion with himself and his thoughts. Hence both should be
mentioned together, for together they are the genuine signature of
the German Enlightenment, which in these two men really de-
served the name. Yet it would be wrong to say that Lessing's fame
has obscured Lichtenberg's, since the German public knows
nothing of Lessing either.

In another way, too, Lessing and Lichtenberg burst the barriers of the Enlightenment. Like Frederick the Great they put
themselves royally beyond all creeds, rejecting and tolerating all
simultaneously, while Nicolai and the rest of his type showed
themselves as doctrinaire and intolerantly persecuting as Orthodoxy had been. Particularly the " smelling out of Jesuits " which
made that order responsible for all that was dark, violent, and
treacherous on earth, led in almost every country of Europe to the
most ruthless measures of oppression. The signal was raised by
Pombal, the regenerator of Portugal, whose all-embracing program included the annihilation of the Jesuits as one of its chief
items. An attempt on the King's life gave the excuse: all their
property was confiscated by the State, and all members of the
order declared rebels and foreigners and banished for ever. There
were, of course, plenty of other ways in which Pombal took the
most energetic steps to raise his country as quickly as possible
to the level of the central European powers. He abolished the

*Catastrophe
of the
Jesuit Order*

Inquisition; established industrial schools, in which all idle youths were retained till they had learnt a trade; set in order the state finances by dismissing numbers of lazy courtiers, so that there was always money in the treasury; set up an Exchange, a great Staple-house, an Arsenal, and an Academy of Sciences; encouraged street sanitation and the circulation of books — and all this against the will of the aristocracy, the people, and even of the King, who was only kept docile by fear of conspiracies and attempts on his life. After Pombal's death the whole structure collapsed.

Five years after the expulsion of the Jesuits from Portugal, the same fate overtook them in France. The King hoped to save them and suggested to the Pope that he should reform them; but he replied in the famous words: "*Sint ut sunt, aut non sint.*" The other Bourbon states soon followed suit: Spain (where a revolt in Madrid was made the excuse), Naples, and Parma. In the end Clement XIV had no course left to him but to dissolve the order. Next year he died, and his death was immediately attributed to the Jesuits. Finally the only sovereigns who tolerated them officially were the Greek Orthodox Catherine and the Protestant Frederick — who could not let the chance of a gibe pass by and wrote to Rome that the Pope's writ did not run in the lands of the King of Prussia.

In the circumstances the Jesuits had no other course but to carry on under all sorts of shams and disguises and to turn their power into wholly subterranean channels. Particularly they tried to insinuate themselves into all kinds of other societies, sometimes even when these were of diametrically opposite tendency. They were to be found among the Freemasons and Illuminati, and their capacity to be anything, to change themselves into anything, which was discussed in the last volume, was once more displayed most convincingly: they became even free-thinkers and " friends of the light."

The Illuminati

The founder of the Illuminati, the Ingolstadt professor Adam Weishaupt, had himself been a pupil of the Jesuits, though he afterwards became their bitterest persecutor. The two main principles of this new order (which soon spread over the whole of Europe) had been learnt from the Jesuits: namely, strictest organization and most rigid secrecy; indeed, the whole order was a sort of antithesis and counterpart of Jesuitry. Very soon, however, dogmatism, vanity, mystical formulæ, and pomposity penetrated the order, which became one of the main fields for the political *arrivisme* that in those days, owing to the absence of any parliament, had still to take refuge in such forms. In 1784 the order was banned in Bavaria as a result of Jesuit manipulation, but the exiles found a ready welcome elsewhere. The importance attached to it may be gauged from a remarkable book of Karl Friedrich Bahrdt, an adventurer and doubtful littérateur who yet for a while enjoyed some reputation. His *Briefe über die Bibel im Volkston* appeared in 1782; in this he depicts the coming of the Saviour as a subtly staged comedy of the Essenes, whom Bahrdt would have us believe to have been a secret society, with " lodges " everywhere even in those days and with tendencies and practices unmistakably suggesting those of the Illuminati.

While the Illuminati, who died out within a few decades through spiritual sterility, are hardly heard of nowadays, one of their most active members has retained a certain fame to this day. This was Freiherr Adolf von Knigge, who published his *Über den Umgang mit Menschen* in 1788. Knigge was an unscrupulous pen-pusher and one of the earliest of that class of writers who orient themselves purely by the commissions of publishers or the whim of the public; and he shared the lot of all such authors who write only to please, in that within half a lifetime he was already a deadly bore; for there is nothing more uninteresting and more uninspiring than a man who thinks and creates what is wanted by others. His *Umgang mit Menschen* alone was an exception, and he himself says in the preface that he had not scamped it as he had scamped some of his other works. " I am not writing a book of compliments, but putting down the conclusions of an experience gained over no short span of years." And in truth the work is not at all what it is generally assumed to be — namely, a manual of good tone — but a contribution to the practical philosophy of life. It treats, in homely fashion, but not without a certain refinement, of social intercourse with all and sundry: with the different temperaments and ages, classes and professions, with parents and children, betrothed and married, friends and women, creditors, debtors, teachers, pupils, guests, hosts, princes, courtiers, scholars, artists, enemies, tradesmen, servants, and neighbours, even of

Knigge

intercourse with oneself and with animals. It is pleasant and smooth, and, though broad and banal, it had a veiled humour and a very sound knowledge of the surface of humanity. It contains a vast mass of useful hints, which, though often obvious, are always cleverly expressed. On the moral side, nevertheless, they are occasionally rhetorical or hypocritical; for it is perfectly evident that when the author preaches uncompromising honesty, striving for perfection, contempt for show, and the like, he is only playing to the nebulous Enlightenment that was fashionable, knowing perfectly well that such characteristics have no place in society, where, so far from being high ethical qualities, they are definite handicaps. Most of his maxims can claim to be valid even today; for instance: conceal your resentment, do not boast overmuch of your good fortune, do not expose the weakness of your neighbour, give others the chance to shine, show an interest in others if you want them to show an interest in you, let each man be responsible for his own doings unless he is your ward, never try to make a man ridiculous, remember that everyone wants to be amused. There are even occasionally subtleties, as, for instance, when he warns us against assuring a man that he is kind-hearted or healthy, for both of these are regarded by some people as an offence; or when he advises us not to use unmeaning phrases, such as that health is a valuable asset, skating is a cold occupation, every man is his own neighbour, time flies, the exception proves the rule; or when he tells us to respect other men's convictions, since we must never forget that what we call enlightenment may to others be obscurity. It is not too much to say, in fact, that this most famous book of the German *Aufklärung* is well worth quotation by anyone and certainly does not deserve its fate of being read by almost no one.

Apart from the Illuminati and the Freemasons, there was a whole mass of other secret societies of a less harmless character, for instance the Rosicrucians, whose real or pretended members were responsible for some very serious swindles. For, so far as the masses were concerned, the whole age was far from being so enlightened as the philosophical output makes it appear. The miraculous phenomena of electricity and magnetism by no means encouraged a scientific attitude of mind among the half-educated; rather they encouraged the belief that the lucky experimenter might at any time make the impossible possible. Everyone believed in the magnetic cures which apparently endowed people with the powers of the prophets, the so-called mesmerism, on which Mesmer did very good business in Paris, Vienna, and elsewhere. Great popularity was also enjoyed by the wonder-cures and devil-exorcisms of Gassner and the invocation of ghosts by the innkeeper Schrepfer — who ended in suicide. The two most prominent representatives of this business were men of whom everyone has heard — Casanova and Cagliostro. The first, who was at least as famous as an international crook as he was as a seducer of women, wandered about the world as a cabbalist, astrologer, and necromancer practising rejuvenation cures, gold-making, and soothsaying. To Cagliostro magical arts and shams of all kinds were a means of livelihood; when his servant was asked if the Count was really three hundred years old, he replied that he could not say, as he had only been in his service for a hundred. The technique of these masters of sharp practice were dealt with effectively and in factual detail by Schiller in his *Geisterseher;* " their only capital," said Chledowski, " was their faith in human folly, and it was a capital which paid high interest."

But this period, in which soberest rationalism and crassest superstition, audacious charlatanry and true prophecy moved side by side, produced the polar complement to Cagliostro in the seer Swedenborg, whose figure, unrecognized and misunderstood by contemporaries and posterity, strides through history as a superb riddle. During the greater part of his life his face was turned towards worldly concerns. His original occupations in which he has considerable achievements to his credit had been mineralogy and mathematics, engineering and mining technique. Then suddenly in his fifty-fifth year he received the revelation, and from that time forth he had dealings only with the higher worlds. There are many proofs that he possessed abnormal occult powers: he learnt details from the dead which could not possibly have been known to him previously; he told the Queen of Sweden things which no one knew but herself, and in Gothenburg he saw the complete course of a big fire which broke out at the same moment in Stockholm, whence news only came two days later to confirm his story. Whether he was in continuous and special communication with angels, we cannot of course test, but he at least believed it. His

249

mission, as he conceived it, was the fulfilment of the Christian Church, the universal and victorious establishment of truth and love among men, which he called the new Heavenly and Earthly Jerusalem. The Trinity, Justification, and the Fall he regarded as allegories. The Other Side he saw in his visions as a duplicate of this side, repeating all earthly relations, only more clearly and more spiritually, without the coarseness of corporeality, yet so alike that some spirits did not notice the passage from one to the other. Probably this kingdom, too, which we should today call the astral world, was to him only a transition stage. Emerson called him the last of the Fathers; Kant, on the other hand, in his famous satire *Träume eines Geistersehers,* which appeared in his lifetime and represented him as the enthusiast and arch-fantastic, did him far less than justice.

Prussia's " premature rot "

In the successor of Frederick the Great, his nephew Frederick the Second, mysticism — though of the false sort, to be sure — ascended the throne itself. The new King, a man of some gifts, but lacking in energy and fond of pleasure, soon found his Tartuffe in the unscrupulous Wöllner, and his Cagliostro in the wily Bischoffswerder. The latter won him over to the Rosicrucians, while the former converted him to obscurantism, upheld by wild rites which took place in his house — at one of these the shade of Julius Cæsar, represented by a ventriloquist, appeared to enter into conversation with the King in person. Under Wöllner's influence Frederick William issued the reactionary Edict of Religion and Censorship, under which even Kant suffered, in that he was forbidden to express himself openly on religious subjects. The shortsighted and uninspired measures of the new government were so little suited to their times that they were not even obeyed by the executive officials. When the Prussian censor passed the closing sentence of a satire which ran as follows: "Woe to the land whose ministers are asses!" and was brought to book by Wöllner, he replied: "Should I perhaps have made him print: 'Well for the land whose ministers are asses'?" Frederick William, as often happens with such superficial types, combined with his mysticism a violent sensuality. He was a fine big man of excessive vitality and was called " the Fat " by his people, and, less pleasantly, " the Lump of Fat " by Catherine of Russia. The former wife of the chamberlain Rietz, created Duchess of Lichtenau, played the part of the Pompadour and acted not only as the official mistress, but also as a sort of manageress of the harem. Furthermore the King, though duly married to a princess of Hesse, was morganatically married to two other ladies, a Fräulein von Voss and a Countess Dönhoff. Mirabeau, in his *Histoire secrète de la cour de Berlin,* described him (not unfairly, though quite without sympathy) by saying that he was made up of three fundamental qualities: dishonesty to every man (which he took to be dexterity), an egoism which felt itself injured on the slightest provocation, and a worship of gold which was not so much avarice as a passion for possessing it. This portrait omits several more pleasant traits, but, on the whole, history has justified Mirabeau in describing the condition of Prussia at that time as one of " premature rot " and in prophesying for the State a rapid decline.

We have already mentioned that the eighteenth century saw an unusual number of personalities of importance and individuality on thrones. Among these must be included Joseph II, although the ordinary picture of him, as it appears, not only in popular plays, but in school-books, is nothing but an empty, false cliché, produced on the same principle as the faith, hope, and charity wrappers put round our boxes of soap. *The People's Kaiser*

For the half-educated the Emperor Joseph is surrounded with the radiant aureole of Toleration. But this eighteenth-century toleration, as we have shown, has its peculiar quality, and this was especially marked in him. While, in general, the *fortiter in re, suaviter in modo* may be taken as the basic principle of wise government, Joseph II exactly reversed the phrase, for he carried out the mildest, most liberal, and most kindly purposes with the most intolerant harshness, impatience, and narrowness. A fierce doctrinairism, sharpened by the hereditary Habsburg wilfulness, was the decisive element in his reforms, so that in many ways he appears as a *distortion,* nay, a caricature, of Frederick the Great. Schlözer, the most influential and competent publicist of the time, bluntly called his system " Stuartism," meaning thereby that in the self-sufficiency and arbitrariness of his rule he differed not at all in principle from the Stuarts. He was democrat and despot in one, and all the worse a despot because he had at his command (or so he thought) the forces of the moral sense. The interferences with private life that are apt to spring from despotism are often

251

infuriating, but they are as a rule only capricious and occasional; on the other hand the oppressiveness of a democracy may be less irritating, but far more fundamental and all-pervading. But if both are united in one man, the last shred of liberty vanishes. Whereas in England, France, and America liberalism was the demand of the *Tiers État,* the expression of the rising middle-classes as they became conscious of their power, in Austria — as Hermann Bahr acutely observed in his *Wien* (from which we have often quoted already) — it preceded the development of those classes; it was " not a natural growth, but an importation and an attempt to extract the principles of politics not from an inward necessity, but from foreign text-books."

Thus, when we compare Frederick II and Joseph II a little closely, the ordinary view has to be reversed. The strict " Old Fritz " appears as the idealist and the artist, as the liberal and the individualist, while the good Emperor Joseph, with all his freedom of thought, was not in the least what Nietzsche meant by a " free spirit," and his régime, for all his modern ideas of humanitarianism, was very far from being a humanitarian one. He intensified the rigour of the mediæval criminal law, he built up still further the Austrian secret-police system, and he used the censorship in a very reactionary spirit; for instance, the shocking *Räuber* was banned throughout his reign. While the King of Prussia enunciated the famous doctrine that journals, if they are to be interesting, must not be checked, Austria knew nothing of any liberty of the press, and the people were limited for their news and views to the *Wiener Zeitung,* which contained nothing but official notices and inspired articles. Only about the Emperor himself was it permitted to speak and write as one liked.

For in Austria it usually happens that the more serious currents of thought tend to express themselves in the form of a morbid or exaggerated fashion. Thus in those contemporary tendencies which really found their most brilliant expression in Frederick the Great — " absolutism in the interests of the people," *Realpolitik,* centralization, Germanization, uniform treatment of all citizens — the Emperor Joseph was an extremist. Above all, his centralization of administration — that idea which has proved so fatal for Austria — wrought much evil. There can be no doubt that in a kingdom consisting of several different nations a wholly centralized administration is a monstrosity; it may be questioned indeed whether it is beneficial even to the most homogeneous State; witness France, where in every period and under every government the rage for centralization has known no bounds.

When Frederick heard the news of Maria Theresa's death, his first words were: " *Voilà un nouvel ordre des choses!* " The new order made itself felt in almost every sphere; the nobility was put on an equality before the law with the middle classes. Spanish ceremonial, like Spanish court dress, was abolished; even on the most formal occasions the Emperor never wore anything but his simplified uniform, even without the stars of his orders, and on his travels he preferred the Werther costume, which was despised by the more conservative even of the middle classes. All processions and pilgrimages were banned, holy days considerably diminished, various brotherhoods broken up, monasteries and church property secularized. These drastic activities led the Pope to take the sensational step of visiting Vienna in person, where the Emperor received him respectfully, but where he achieved nothing. To provide a substitute for the extensive charities of the clergy state hospitals, poor-houses, and foundling hospitals were set up out of the proceeds of the confiscated property, but these new institutions had no very good reputation. The universities were robbed of all their privileges and completely officialized, to their considerable detriment; for the new education decree changed them from homes of scientific research to mere training centres for future officials, and only those subjects which could serve this end were taught, and taught by miserably paid professors. On the other hand, much was done for the elementary schools, whose number and standard were considerably raised, but even these were dominated by the mechanical regulations of the Josephine compulsory enlightenment: the arrangement of lessons was pre-arranged in such detail that at every minute Vienna knew which page of the text-book was being read by the children throughout the kingdom. " Good God! " cried Mirabeau, " even their souls are to be put in uniform! That is the summit of despotism! " The idea was to metamorphose, at a moment's notice and without consulting anybody's wishes, a clerical population into a liberal, a peasant and bourgeois society into a bureaucratic.

But most ill-timed of all were the attempts to force into a

unitary state the whole variegated mass of Germans, Poles, Czechoslovaks, Serbocroats, Ruthenians, Roumanians, and Italians, which could only hang together, if at all, as a federal state. "The German language," ran an Imperial edict, "is the universal language of my kingdom"; it was the obligatory medium of intercourse in all schools and offices. The aim of this forced Germanization, which extended to all the provinces with the exception of Belgium and Lombardy, was merely centralist, and not at all nationalistic — for the Emperor, in accordance with the fashion of the time, was cosmopolitan-minded — but it aroused nevertheless the bitterest resentment. The same object was subserved by the abolition of all corporations and guilds, all aristocratic privileges and provincial rights, in fact every trace of self-government. The Church, too, which the Emperor hoped to reform on Anglican or Gallican lines, only provoked his enmity because of its autonomy. He was no bigot like his mother, who demanded from every subject, even from Kaunitz, the oath of conformity, but he was a good Catholic: his anti-clerical measures, which have brought him most of both popularity and hatred, were only the outcome of his passion for centralization, of his apotheosis of the State, or rather of himself. The clergy were to be no more than officials, as though the cure of souls were just a variant of forestry or the postal service.

The régime of velleities The worst, however, was that all these extreme projects were only half carried out, so that they merely created unrest and discontent without gaining the advantages of a completely new system in compensation. The haste with which they were undertaken impaired their efficiency and yet, paradoxically, increased their unpopularity. That is what Frederick meant when he said that the Emperor took the second step before the first. Even today memorial tablets or pictures in many a peasant home serve to remind us that the country-folk regarded him as their greatest benefactor: yet even the abolition of serfdom was only a half-freedom, for the peasants were left under the justice of the manor, which made them subject to the whim of their lords. The Emperor's efforts to encourage trade and industry were equally incomplete: it is true that he set up free trade at home, but he did not do away with the tyranny of mercantilism, for all foreign goods were liable to heavy import-taxes, and the export of raw materials was forbidden. His attempts at reducing the burden of taxes also remained no more than velleities: for in actual fact, owing to the eternal deficit and the unfortunate Turkish War, he was compelled to allow for more expenses than his predecessor. This war was one of his worst blunders, even in its mere intention, for if he hoped to carry through such radical reforms quietly, it was imperative to spare his realm from all foreign disturbances. Worse still, he had no military ability at all and as a consequence no appreciation of the talents of his generals — Laudon, for instance.

His diplomacy also, though it was meant to be that of *Realpolitik*, was anything but successful. It was based on the elementary principle of pocketing everything and giving nothing for it. It included the annexation of Bavaria, the conquest of Alsace, expansion in the Balkans, and acquisitions in Italy. And all this at once and without the smallest concession to Prussia, France, Russia, or any other power. The result was that Bavaria was not exchanged for Belgium, but that both were lost; that no agreement was come to with Prussia, so that the main burden of the French invasion on the Rhine had to be borne by Austria; and, finally, that he won no foothold in the Balkans and went away empty-handed at the Second Partition of Poland. Even while he was co-regent this monstrous fashion of conducting diplomacy had led to serious loss. The oldest line of the Wittelsbachs had died out and Bavaria fell to the Palatinate, whose ruler declared his readiness, in return for monetary compensation, to support the claims of the Emperor to a great part of Bavaria. The Austrians marched in. But Frederick the Great immediately mobilized and in his turn marched into Bohemia, where he and Laudon lay inactive against each other until Maria Theresa, behind her son's back, concluded the Peace of Teschen, by the terms of which Prussia's claim to Ansbach and Bayreuth was recognized and Austria got nothing but the Inn district. The soldiers nicknamed the war the " Potato War " or the " orchard stunt," because it had consisted solely in the requisitioning of supplies. This was the moment that Joseph chose to bring forward his scheme of exchanges: Austria was to get Bavaria, and the Elector Palatine Belgium as the " Kingdom of Burgundy." The result was that he drew upon himself not only Prussia, but England, who felt herself bound to resist, on the principle that Belgium must never be seized by France and must therefore always be in the hands of a strong military power. On his side Frederick established the "Fürstenbund" after the model of the former Schmalkaldic League; it was joined by Saxony, Hanover, and numerous smaller states, and thus the union of Germany in defence of the established order, which had proved unattainable against Richelieu and against Louis XIV, was brought about by the unskilful tactics of the very monarch who was the Empire's titular head. So it befell that, only a year before his death, Frederick (though actuated only by a particularist motive) did the whole German people one more notable service. The exposed Netherlands, though they still threatened the Empire on the north flank, were of very problematic value to Austria (and, in fact, were soon lost) whereas a rounded-off Bavaria would have had great staying power. Such an acquisition would have thrust the Habsburg state into the middle of the Empire and have formed an almost invincible south German power. Not merely Prussian hegemony, but any solution of the German question that did not include Austria would have been made impossible by it, and the alien domination of Germany by the Habsburg rulers would not only have been perpetuated, but in course of time would have become real instead of nominal.

At the end of his reign Joseph saw his lands threatened on all sides: revolt in the Netherlands, risings in Galicia, Hungary, and Transylvania, discontent in the German Hereditary Provinces and especially in clerical Tyrol, hostility in the French Revolutionary government, the offended Pope, and the distrustful Italian dukes, continuous failure against the Turks, and danger of a vast northern coalition of England, Holland, Sweden, and Poland. He himself, shortly before his death, wrote to Kobenzl that there had never been a more critical time for the monarchy. And deliverance from these perils was due only to his brother and successor, Leopold II, a steady, cautious, and prudent politician and a master of clever hedging, or "temporizing" as it was then called, and at the same time one of the queerest Habsburgs who ever held the throne. Of small build, weak and ugly, he was the victim of overwhelming sexual passion, kept an international staff of mistresses and a pornographic museum, and died after two years' reign, from excessive indulgence in erotic stimulants.

At bottom Joseph II was merely a specially clear-cut speci-men of the typically Austrian bureaucracy, that sort of worldly wisdom which is quite satisfied when everything has been set down precisely on paper, and thinks that a thing has only to be written down to happen. The Josephine reforms were the harmless but highly dangerous amusements of an emperor, mere models and fitments, sketches of *décor* and scenario, figurines of reorganiza-tion that were never carried out. The Potemkin villages which Catherine showed for him in Gherson he saw through at once, for all his life he had pretty fair powers of observation; but these at least existed, if only as scenery, whereas his own were only on paper. His whole reign consisted of one enormous mass of circu-lars, ordinances, edicts, which followed close upon one another, crossing, contradicting, exaggerating. And on top of all these was a whole network of secret police, spies, and confidential agents to supervise their carrying out, to note their reception, and to register opposition.

His chief quality, in fact, notwithstanding his apparent ideal-ism and passion for "uplift," was an extreme ordinariness, dryness, chilliness, and prose. In contrast to Frederick he was completely uncultured, and literature was for him only a means to "Enlightenment" as he understood the idea: that is, the ex-tension of useful knowledge and liberal ideas. The free-thinking writings, which flourished under his patronage, were nothing more than the very lowest type of pitiful pamphleteering, and Herder said of him that fundamentally he regarded the whole publishing industry as cheesemongering. He did not go to see Voltaire when he passed near Ferney, and he confiscated the German edition of his works. *Werther* was produced in Vienna as a Prater firework display, in Linz as a tragic ballet, but the book itself was banned. The stage was dominated by the crudest clowning: its wit may be gathered from a price-list which lays down as payment one gulden for every jump into the water or over a wall, and thirty-four kreuzer for every box on the ears, kick, or drenching. The Viennese national and court theatre, "next to the Burg," which was insti-tuted and richly endowed by the Emperor, was quite out of touch with the spirit of the time and satisfied its ambitions by the per-formance of inane melodramas and farces like those of Schröder, Iffland, and Kotzebue.

So he really satisfied no one, neither Reaction nor Enlightenment, neither the middle classes nor the privileged. The reason is to be found not in his intentions, which were good, nor in his ideas, which were reasonable, but in his lack of real knowledge of men, or, we could even say, of imagination. He could not put himself into the minds of his subjects and thus understand their real needs. And so, for all his energy and uprightness, the question soon began to be put — was indeed the title of a pamphlet which appeared in 1787 — "Why is the Emperor Joseph not loved by his people?"

Nevertheless it is a sound instinct that has led posterity to select just this man from a long list of more able rulers and to seek in him something unusual, a sort of heroic or legendary figure. He had a quality which is very uncommon among the kings and rulers of the earth: he was modern, up to date. On an ancient legitimate throne he was a reforming, transforming revolutionary. And it is just the fact that he, like others, had to experience the truth that only genius is entitled to begin a revolution in this world that makes him a tragic and moving figure. Eternally seeking and yet never reaching fulfilment, this stepson of destiny has been surrounded with an atmosphere of romance and poetry. Humanity has always, and surely with a sort of justice, been more faithful and felt more kindly towards the wooers of life who have failed than to successful men. Everyone still hears of the Emperor Max, the last of the knights, while his far more powerful successor Charles V is exiled to the history-books; and for many a year the most popular king of Bavaria will be the fantastic Ludwig II, whose most notable achievement was that he wasted the public money on futile and tasteless theatricals and finally abandoned the claims of Bavaria to the hegemony of Germany. In these and similar matters humanity shows itself capable of great fineness of feeling; after all it is only in its individual examples that it is apt to be intolerable, and as a whole it certainly has its good points.

The end of Poland By the side of Frederick II and Joseph II we have the figure of Catherine II, who, like them, displayed a most powerful monarchic activity. She gained the throne by a *coup d'état* which she had herself staged, though in all probability she was innocent of the death of her husband. Her government was purely absolutist, and the legislative assembly that she summoned to help her was a mere comedy, a concession to the spirit of the age. She differed from Joseph II in the clearness of her vision, which never contemplated the impossible, and in her lively interest and understanding of the intellectual life of her time. She corresponded regularly with Diderot, d'Alembert, and Voltaire and other literary notabilities, whom she tried to attract to her court by rich gifts and pensions, and she was herself an authoress. Like Frederick and Joseph she attended to all details of government with inexhaustible energy. " Madame," the clever Prince de Ligne said to her one day, " I know no cabinet that is smaller than the Russian; it extends from one side of your head to the other." Her prudent advances and retreats, coupled with her tenacity, made her far more successful in her Balkan policy than Joseph. Her aim was Constantinople; she failed to win it, but it was under her government that the three partitions of Poland were brought about.

The catastrophe of the Polish Kingdom was long overdue. It was incapable of survival, if only because with its enormous extension it had a disproportionately small and moreover poor coastline. In addition, its form of government was impossible. The king was elected — on almost every occasion by a disorderly vote — and had practically no power. The *liberum veto* allowed every provincial deputy to cripple the measures of the government; there was even a rule that when one single law was rejected by any such vote, everything that had previously been settled was nullified, and it was of course easy enough to buy one such veto. Even at the beginning of the century it was common to talk of the " royal republic " of Poland, but it might as well have been called the " royal anarchy." The right of armed resistance was constitutionally guaranteed to the nobility, the *Schlachta*. The population consisted of a few great families of colossal wealth, a hopelessly insolvent beggar-nobility, and as to nine-tenths of the rest a serf population destitute of any rights whatsoever, in whom the nobility (as Georg Forster says in his *Ansichten vom Niederrhein*) had eradicated the last trace of a thinking faculty. Between the two, there were only Jesuits and Jews, and almost no middle class. Brandy, gambling, and syphilis were the three powers which had dominated this " chivalrous " people for generations — even abroad the Poles were notorious as the most reckless of all gamblers. Their corruption was proverbial and very greatly assisted the partitioning — indeed, the powers concerned had a common fund for this purpose. While the peasants were decaying in the most wretched poverty, the few wealthy lived in the most extravagant luxury: for instance, Prince Karl Radziwill in 1789 gave a feast to four thousand people, which cost two hundred thousand pounds in present money values. There were no post, almost no apothecaries or schools, and only itinerant craftsmen; on the other hand there were still wolves everywhere.

At the First Partition Poland, which had been about half as large again as France, lost a third of its area. Russia gained the most territorially, but lost in trade, for until then almost the whole of the Kingdom had been as good as a province of Russia. Prussia gained the valuable connexion between East Prussia and Pomerania, but did not yet get the port of Danzig or the fortress of Thorn. West Prussia undoubtedly benefited by the exchange of masters, for immediately after 1772 serfdom was abolished, the Bromberg Canal was begun and everything done for the raising of culture and material well-being. Even from the national point of view the incorporation was not wholly unjust, for the country had previously belonged to the German Orders, and the cities had a considerable residue of Germans. Austria did best by the annexation of Galicia and its valuable mines. Maria Theresa always regarded this act of violence as a blemish on her reign and probably really did suffer pangs of conscience about it; Frederick looked at the business more coldly and said: " She wept, but took her share." Austria did not share in the Second Partition, but not through generosity, only because of her unfavourable political position. The third, in 1795, led to the complete break-up of Poland.

Cosmopolitanism

This event, almost unique in modern history, produced no sort of outburst of public opinion, for the people of the time were cosmopolitan-minded and therefore the violation even of a whole nation did not appear to it as such. Even in Germany the present conception of patriotism was quite unknown. Thus Lessing writes: " I have no notion of love of country, and it seems to be at best a heroic weakness, which I am quite glad to do without." Herder asks: " What is a nation? " and answers: " A huge un-tended garden full of weeds, a gathering-place just as much of folly and error as of virtue and greatness." Goethe in his youth wrote: " If we can find a place in the world in which to settle with our possessions, a field to feed us, a house to cover us, is not that our fatherland? And are there not thousands in every state who possess this much? And are they not living happily within these limits? Why, then, this useless striving after a feeling which we neither can have nor would like to have, and which, with certain peoples, and at certain moments only, has been and is the result of fortunately concurring circumstances? Roman patriotism! May God save us from that as from any monster. We should have no stool to sit on, no bed to lay ourselves down in." And even as a matured man he comments thus on the recent establishment of the Rheinbund: " a split between the coachman and the groom on the box which aroused more feeling in us than the division of the Roman Empire." The author of an " article from Katzenellen-bogen " in Schlözer's *Staatsanzeiger* certainly expressed a general feeling when he wrote: " Others may deplore the fact that our rulers have no authority on the Ganges, but I regard it as a bless-ing for our country that the Hanseatic League has been broken up, that the German Admiral of the Sea under Ferdinand II was stifled at birth, that the Peace of Westphalia has divided Ger-many for some centuries to come into so many small states, each with its own interest, that in one case position, in another size, has made it impossible for them to launch vast merchant fleets. How foolish it is to run after pepper on the coasts of Malabar when our hands are full at home! " Lichtenberg summed the whole matter up in his effective style when he said: " I would give much to know for whom really the things are done which we are told publicly are done for the Fatherland."

Schiller, also, is no exception, though text-books and leading articles for a hundred years have pointed to him as the re-awakener of German patriotism. He uses the love of one's country in his poems merely as a valuable dramatic subject, without ever giving it a German nationalist colouring. *Wilhelm Tell* describes the heroic struggle of a people for its home and its liberty, and the *Maid of Orleans* the heroic resistance of a country against its conqueror; but the people is the Swiss, and the country is France. Only two of his plays take place on German soil: the one represents the criminal state of things at a petty court, the other depicts a group of young people who formed themselves into a band of robbers in a Catilinarian desperation. On October 13, 1789 he wrote to Körner: " The patriotic interest is important only for immature nations, for the youth of the world; it is a narrow, trivial ideal to write for but one nation; this limitation is for a philosophic spirit simply unbearable."

Moreover, patriotic tendencies were not looked upon by the governments concerned with any satisfaction, for they immediately scented republicanism; and since in those days the general idea was that true patriotism had only existed in the Classical age, while at the same time no one could picture the Greeks and Romans as anything but republicans, there was something to be said for this association of ideas. In general, political publicity existed only in the form of forbidden pamphlets. Censorship was as rigid as it was useless, and only made the banned books more popular. In some cases, indeed, the ban was the first thing that drew attention to the book; and therefore towards the end of the reign of Maria Theresa her government lit on a method of truly Austrian futility and forbade the publication of the index of forbidden books. Schlözer's *Staatsanzeigen,* which has been mentioned above, the only independent political journal appearing in German, was published in the free city of Göttingen, which, as a result of the personal union of Hanover with England, was almost an English city; and it had such influence that it was always to be seen on the desk of Joseph II, while Maria Theresa used to ask when important decisions were being discussed: " What will Schlözer say about it? "

Educational mania   Cultured circles, in fact, occupied themselves on the whole more with the details of internal administration than with questions of constitution or foreign policy. Particular importance attached to the works of the Marchese Baccaria and, above all, his *Dei delitti e delle pene,* in which he advocated, with noble enthusiasm, the abolition of torture and the death-penalty and pleaded for a public, impartial, humane administration of justice. It was translated into almost every civilized tongue, and in several European states it compelled a reform of the law. The magic word which was to solve all the social, ethical, and economic problems was " education " — not only for the child, but for the " people," peasant, middle class, and proletariat; and the goal of this discipline was to be the realization of paradise, of universal brotherhood, happiness, and freedom. This faith in the universal power of education marks one of the characteristic traits of this new culture, which in the main was the creation of teachers and ministers. Everywhere there sprang up " Philanthropines " — that was the name given to the reformed schools and other institutions for popular culture and enlightenment. Unfortunately the movement got into the hands of publicity-seeking muddle-heads and charlatans, but nevertheless the main ideas — above all, the increased attention paid to physical training and the freer methods of teaching — were put into practice almost everywhere. At the head of all this movement was Pestalozzi, the real discoverer of modern educational method, which aims at a simultaneous training of heart and head and seeks to take as its starting-point, not the intellect of the teacher, but the soul of the child. Pestalozzi's ideas never reached clarity in detail, being dominated after the fashion of the time by various abstract and nebulous ideas, the chief of which was a theory of " naturalness " in education, which was so wide and so vague that in practice it could mean anything or nothing. The idea came from Rousseau, who provided his age with the greater number of its slogans : " *Laissez faire en tout la nature* " was his doctrine in *Émile*.

The Physiocrats

Long before Rousseau this same principle had been applied to political economy (which was then reckoned as part of national education) by Boisguillebert: " *Qu'on laisse faire la nature!* " — let the economic life, he demanded, develop freely, unhampered by any state interference. Fifty years later d'Argenson based his system of " laissez-faire " on this postulate. The classic of the movement was Quesnay, Louis XV's physician, who repeated the demand of " *laissez passer* " in his *Tableau économique* and in his *La Physiocratie* (1768) founded the Physiocratic school that dominated the whole of the rest of the century. The implication of the word was that nature was to rule without restraint, because prosperity and progress can arise only from the natural sources of economics. Mercantilism was rejected, for it is not trade and industry that are productive, but only land and soil: " *la terre est l'unique source des richesses.* " Consequently the most important class is the landowners, who alone control a truly net output, and the landworkers, who are the true "productive class." The industrial and commercial classes, on the other hand, are "sterile," for the value of their product is always equivalent to its costs of production and they cannot increase the materials of production themselves; they are thus, as Turgot developed the argument, mere salaried workers, paid servants of the agriculturists. Freedom of exchange and competition lead of themselves to natural prices: that is the "*ordre naturel*," to which the real order of things ("*l'ordre positif*") must be assimilated as far as possible. The path to this end lies in the removal of all existing state restrictions, interference, and burdens, of the corvées, most of the taxes, regulation of prices, and especially of corn-prices, for they are all anti-natural. The new doctrine seized upon all thinking classes like a fever: the salons became the centre of heated arguments about monopolies, protective tariffs, and encouragement of agriculture; and political economy became the fashionable science. "About 1750," said Voltaire, "the country grew tired of verse, of tragedies, comedies, romances, operas, romantic tales, still more romantic moral discussions, and disputations about charm and curtsies, and began to argue about corn." But on the whole things did not go beyond arguing, and, as the reader will have already observed, the physiocrats or (as they were frequently called) economists merely put one specialist view-point in the place of another.

Conception of the machine man   It is the merit of the Englishman Adam Smith that he built up on these foundations a more tenable and comprehensive theory, which has maintained its hold to some extent to the present day. His magnum opus: *Inquiry into the Nature and Causes of the Wealth of Nations,* lays down two factors in production, on the one hand work, and on the other soil and climate. The value of all goods is decided by the amount of work expended upon them, which settles their natural price; this is not the same as the market price, which depends on certain other factors and especially on the relations of supply and demand. He further distinguishes utility value and exchange value; in the same product the one may be high, and the other almost zero: for instance, air and water have a very high utility value, but almost no exchange value, and, *per contra,* diamonds and ostrich-feathers have a definite exchange value and a very small utility value. The magnitude of the national wealth depends on the quantity of goods which have an exchange value, which in its turn depends on the quantity of work invested: work thus gives us the true price of goods, money only the nominal price. Smith is, therefore, not a pure physiocrat, for he recognizes all work, and not merely agricultural work, to be creative of value and productive, and of landowners he even says that they reap where they have not sown. To him the most important class is the capitalists, who encourage industry more than others, by investing their money in production and giving opportunity for work. His practical demands and conclusions are, however, in agreement with those of the " Economists ": he insists on complete freedom of trade and communication, removal of burdens on peasants, of serfdom, of price-control, and guild restrictions. The ideal means to increase production was to him the most thoroughgoing division of labour: in other words, the mechanicalization of work. He did not yet think of machinery, but only of a most intensive specialization of manual labour. One worker, he says, can produce ten pins in a day, but in a factory ten expert workers who adapt themselves to each other can produce forty-eight thousand pins in the same time. Thus, though the age of machinery had not yet dawned, he had a clear vision of the new ideas, which suppose that men are to be regarded only as the subject of industry, or even as its *object,* as exchangeable articles or wheels in the machine.

In the *Acta Eruditorum* of 1690 Papin, in describing his experiments with the steam-boiler, had chosen the title " New means to create considerable motive power at low prices." Thus even in his case the economic motive was already in the foreground. In 1712 Newcomen built an apparatus for raising water on Papin's principle; Arkwright invented the mechanical loom in 1769, in which year James Watt also patented his steam-engine; in 1786 Cartwright succeeded in constructing a mechanical loom, and in 1784, with the patenting of the " puddling " process (that is, the production of steel from crude iron), the most important prerequisite for the perfecting of machinery was met. By the end of the century, machines were pretty well distributed throughout Britain, though it was considerably later that this could be said of the Continent. So once again we are met with the fact, often before alluded to, that in human natural development the idea is always primary, which the corresponding reality follows of necessity. First came the idea of the " machine man," and after that there was nothing else but to invent the appropriate machine — or rather to reinvent, for the steam-engine had been known in antiquity, but had been regarded, quite rightly from the point of view of the classical world-outlook, as a toy.

The
" School for
Scandal "

English literature reached one of its highest points at this time. The *Letters of Junius*, perhaps the most effective political pamphlet of all time, hammered into every mind the ideas of liberalism with as much malice as energy. Goldsmith was writing his *Vicar of Wakefield*, Sterne — one of the most remarkable geniuses in the world's literature — was busy with *Tristram Shandy*, Fielding was ridiculing Richardson's characters in his novels, satirizing their pharisaism of untruth and indecency, the empty bleakness of their tradesman's virtues which were nothing but office correctness, and always making his rascals come out on top, as being far more human and genuine because they do not suppress their impulses or hide them under hypocrisy. Sheridan's comedies, too, preserve the life of contemporary London society in a pure and vigorous sparkle of wit. All these authors have the clear gaiety of men who stand above all their situations, and their wit is never forced: they simply cannot help being clever. They open some window of their brain and immediately there streams out an amusing cloud of innumerable paradoxes, follies, epigrams, and buffooneries. Sheridan's *School for Scandal*, for instance, could be used today as an education in graceful maliciousness.

" You cannot deny Miss Vermilion to be handsome. She has a charming fresh colour." " Yes, when it is fresh put on." " Oh fie, I'll swear her colour is natural: I have seen it come and go." " I dare swear you have, ma'am; it goes off at night and comes again in the morning. And what's more, her maid can fetch and carry it." " But surely now her sister is — or was — very handsome." " Who? Mrs. Evergreen? O Lord, she's six-and-fifty if she's an hour." " Now positively you wrong her; fifty-two or fifty-three at the utmost, and I don't think she is more." " Ah, there's no judging by her looks unless one could see her face." " Well, well, if Mrs. Evergreen does take some pains to repair the ravages of time, you must allow she does it with great ingenuity; and surely that's better than the careless manner in which widow Ochre chalks her wrinkles." "Nay, now, you are severe upon the widow. 'Tis not that she paints so ill, but when she has finished her face, she joins it badly to the neck, so that she looks like a mended statue in which the connoisseur sees at once that the head's modern, though her trunk's antique." "Ah, madam, true wit is more nearly allied to good nature than your ladyship is aware of." "True, I believe they are so near akin that they can never be united."

It will be admitted that this conversation has no sign of age, but might have been written yesterday. That is one of the pleasures the satirist gives to his reader; he notices with satisfaction that mankind a hundred and fifty years ago were as bad a lot as they are today.

While in almost every sphere English life was reaching a climax, the British Imperium, which was even then more or less a world-empire, suffered a painful shock in the loss of America. The first English colony in the West had been Virginia, founded in the reign of Elizabeth by adventurers who established plantations there at several points, but were chiefly concerned with the search for gold — instead of which they discovered tobacco. In 1620 the arrival of the *Mayflower,* in which the " Pilgrim Fathers " sought escape from the religious persecutions of the High Church, began the Puritan colony of New Plymouth, so called from the port of departure; to it was united the somewhat later foundation of Massachusetts, also a Puritan colony, with Boston as its capital. The chief sources of maintenance for the colonists were fishing and also shipbuilding, for which timber, the wealth of the land, offered enormous resources. The expulsion of the Dutch from New Amsterdam (which was henceforth known as New York) and the founding of Pennsylvania by the Quakers have been mentioned above. Here the chief town was Philadelphia, founded in 1682; in the south the colonies of Carolina and Georgia were added, and finally all these districts formed a continuous strip along the east coast.

The administration was managed by the mother country on strict mercantilist principles. The colonists were forbidden to begin new industries, or to export their raw materials elsewhere

The revolt of North America

267

than to England; this, as all competition was thereby eliminated, depressed prices very considerably and aroused bitter resentment. Also, as a result of her victory in the Seven Years' War, Britain had herself provided the most necessary prerequisite for defection; for the colonies, freed from the manace of absorption by French, were no longer dependent on British protection. The introduction of taxes on a number of British imports led to the decision to boycott all goods on which taxes had to be paid to England. As a result London cancelled these ordinances except for the tea-duty, which was still to be maintained. But the excitement had gone too far. The people stormily demanded representation in Parliament, and the battle-cry echoed through the land: "No taxation without representation." In 1773 some patriots, disguised as Indians, threw a whole cargo of tea into the water, and next year a Congress of deputies in Philadelphia decided to break off all commercial relations with Britain. War became inevitable. Under the leadership of George Washington an army of volunteers was formed which fought with varying fortunes against the English professional forces, part of which consisted of German subjects sold for the service. The Declaration of Independence was issued in 1776 by the thirteen United States, and it contained among other things the pregnant clause that all men are born free and equal. The war lasted eight years and ended with the recognition in the Peace of Versailles of the independence of all the States. The Americans began at a disadvantage, for their militia, in spite of its physical adroitness and knowledge of the country, had only the tactical value of a levy of white Indians. But the army of the confederation found an organizing genius in the Prussian colonel Friedrich Wilhelm von Steuben; and the entrance of France, Spain, and Holland into the war gave it a very unfavourable turn for England. These diplomatic successes were due, in the first place, to Benjamin Franklin, who appeared in Paris as negotiator and played in a masterly fashion the then so sympathetically regarded rôle of simple citizen and straightforward republican. His unadorned clothing, his unpowdered hair, his modest manners fascinated the salons; he was compared with Fabius and Brutus, Plato and Cato, his picture was on sale everywhere, so that, as he wrote to his daughter, his features were as well known as those of the Man in the Moon. He knew perfectly well that all this was only a fashion, but he used it like a shrewd business man for his own purposes. Ladies wore hats and did their hair *à l'indépendance, à la Bostonienne, à la Philadelphie, à la nouvelle Angleterre;* men went about in coarse cloth and thick shoes *à la Franklin,* and with thick stick and big round Quaker hat *à la Penn.* The Marquis de Lafayette, who had taken part in the war, hung two tablets on his wall: the one contained the American Declaration of Rights; the other was empty, but had the superscription " The Rights of France." The French government had its revenge on England in the Peace of Versailles, but the revenge cost it its own existence six years later.

The atmosphere of the time was condensed to a still higher tension of electricity in the *Marriage of Figaro,* which was performed a year after the end of the American War. That the piece, which had had to face all the trouble of the censorship for years, was at last passed for performance indicated already the victory of the Revolution and the capitulation of the government and old society, though at the moment it saw in this distant lightning nothing more than an amusing flash of rockets. The privileged classes applauded as loudly as the middle classes when Figaro spoke the famous words: " *Monsieur le comte . . . qu'avez-vous fait pour tant de biens? Vous vous êtes donné la peine de naître, et rien de plus.*" At the first performance the crowd was so great that three persons were suffocated; and the play ran for more than a hundred nights, which would mean about ten times as much today. Figaro has the sub-title " *la folle journée,*" and its production really did mark one of the maddest days in French history. Beaumarchais himself said there was one thing more foolish than his own piece, and that was its success, and Napoleon afterwards remarked that in *Figaro* the Revolution was already on the march. The impudence of Figaro, nevertheless, is a different thing from that of Rousseau. It is still of the Rococo, graceful, jewelled, amiable, and full of irony towards itself. It is the impudence of the lackey, who is still in the service of the butt of his impertinence, so that his self-expression and his movements are still in the same forms as those of his master; in spite of all apparent unbridledness, he is still constrained. Beaumarchais connects by countless threads with the Ancien Régime; his gods are money and pleasure. He took part in numerous commercial enterprises, he was the inventor of performing-right royalties, and his hero Figaro is only a cynical money-maker. On the other hand, he was akin to Rousseau and Chamfort in that his attacks were nothing but an intellectual pre-revolution, a play of ideas, born of the love of sensation and paradox, a marionette-show with no intentioned consequences. Reality passed him by as it did Chamfort, and as it would have done Rousseau if he had lived long enough. Mirabeau, already, could fling at Beaumarchais the words: " Expect nothing from the future except the privilege of being forgotten." During the Revolution he barely escaped with his life.

The polemics of Chamfort, though still only half-earnest, were already more aggressive. In his *Pensées* he says quite openly: " The nobility, we are told, is a stage between the king and his people. Yes, in the sense in which the dog is a stage between the huntsman and the hare." And again: " I regard the King of France only as the king of about a hundred thousand people, among whom he distributes the sweat, the blood, and the skin of more than twenty-four millions." One morning he remarked to the Duc de Lauraguais: " I have completed a work." " What, a book? " " No, no book; I am not such a fool. But I have got the title of a book, and the title is everything. I have already made a present of it to that puritan Sieyès, who can carry it into execution as he likes. He can write what he will: it is only the title that will be remembered." " Well, and what is this title? " " ' What is the Third Estate? Everything. And what does it possess? Nothing.' " In actual fact Sieyès did give this title to the famous pamphlet which had such a colossal effect — only he added a third clause: " What does it demand? To be something," which in reality weakened its epigrammatic vigour — so that the author proved quite right, all that was remembered of the pamphlet was its title. A second catchword of the Revolution, equally lapidary and inspiring: " War to the palace, peace to the hovel," had its origin with Chamfort. But in general, far from being an admirer of the masses or of public opinion, he said that " an individual can never be so contemptible as a corporation," and again: " The public! How many fools must be got together to constitute a public? " Of the National Assembly of 1789 he said: " If you look at the greater part of the deputies, you get the impression that they have destroyed prejudices only in order to acquire prejudices, like people who pull a building down to get the material." One of these malicious epigrams led to his imprisonment: for when he saw everywhere the general proclamation: " *Liberté, Egalité, Fraternité ou la mort!* " he added: " *C'est la fraternité de Caïn.*" He was set at liberty, only to be imprisoned a second time, when he attempted suicide. It is not certain whether he died as a result of this attempt or of a long-standing bladder trouble.

As for Rousseau, the history of the origin of his first work is extraordinarily characteristic of the man. The Academy of Dijon had set for a prize essay the subject: Has the revival of science and art contributed to the purification of morality? Diderot asked Rousseau which line he should take, and Rousseau replied: " Naturally, the affirmative." " That is the *pons asinorum,* every mediocrity will go that way. But the opposite view gives new scope to thought and style." Rousseau took the tip, and in his essay (which won the prize) he made the sensation he hoped for. Once he had made up his mind to take the opposing view, he went far beyond the question set, and sought to prove, as he lashed himself into a foam of fury against the whole of human civilization, that it has not merely not improved morality, but has corrupted it, and had been the cause of all human misery. What should we do with artists apart from the fatal luxury which brings them up? Should we be less numerous, less well governed, less flourishing without the men of learning? On the contrary, it is science and art, and they alone, which have made us put talent above virtue." Some years later the Dijon Academy set another prize theme: What is the origin of the inequality of men, and has it any natural basis? Rousseau wrote an essay on this subject also and attracted still more attention than with the earlier, for it was precisely because a blind and wild resentment spoke in him that it was a success. The origin of inequality, which is a scandalous crime against nature and justice, he again finds in civilization, in political and social conventions, which are the arbitrary creation of men. The only condition worthy of man is his natural condition: " If nature has determined us to be healthy, I dare to assert that the condition of reflection is an unnatural condition and that a man who thinks is a degenerate animal." " The first man who enclosed a piece of land and had the audacity to say: ' That is mine,' and found men simple enough to believe him, was

Rousseau's conception of Nature

271

the true founder of civic society. How many crimes, how many wars, how many privations and terrors would mankind have been spared if someone had pulled up the boundary stone, filled up the trenches, and cried to his fellows: 'Take heed of listening to this deceiver; you are lost if you forget that the fruits of the earth belong to all, and the land to none'!" All civilization means division of labour — that means inequality, and inequality is the root of all evil. Against all this, Rousseau demands the Return to Nature; he hates civilization chiefly because it signifies a change, or, in his view, perversion, of the original nature of man. We will not approach the question whether nature or civilization is the normal and suitable condition of the individual when he has reached the historical stage, and whether the state of nature is really possible or even conceivable for modern man; instead we will follow Rousseau's own principle and examine his own ideal exemplar, nature. In nature we come upon division of labour and inequality *everywhere*, and as organisms develop physically and intellectually, specialization increases. Complete absence of specialization is strictly not true even of the unicellular algæ and infusoria, but only at the still lower level of the membraneless "Monera." Higher types of life, on the other hand, have a rigidly specialist, aristocratic, and hierarchical organization, with the brain governing and despotically controlling the whole body politic. That it only seldom plays this part in monarchical governments is not the fault of the *form* of government.

Rousseau's conception of nature, in fact, was not at all a scientific, but a literary conception. To him the word meant, not a general idea created out of exact and precise observation of the physical world, but a romantic sentimental something, based on memories of a poor operetta or a deceptive travel-book. France, however, understood him only too well, and within a few years the principle of specialization was denied so emphatically, that Lavoisier was guillotined for devoting himself too one-sidedly to chemistry.

Héloïse, the Contrat, and Émile   The next important work of Rousseau was his novel *Julie, ou La Nouvelle Héloïse*, which also strikes a new note. It is the first psychological study of love in a modern romantic sense as a real passion, a tragic catastrophe, as a fatality above man and a force of elemental nature. But here, too, he spoils himself by calculated

272

effects, the propensity to façade and superfluous rhetoric; and the Marquise du Deffand — who combined the taste and acuteness of a Diderot with the intuitive psychological tact of the clairvoyant that only her sex possesses, and who may, therefore, be called the critical genius of her time — said of the book that there were splendid passages in it, but that they foundered in an ocean of chatter. *Héloïse* was followed shortly by the *Contrat social*, which proclaims the doctrine of popular sovereignty with a fanatic energy and intransigence such as had never before been known. It maintained that the existing government had been established, not by a treaty, but by a mandate received from the people; that its members are, therefore, not the masters, but the servants of the people, whose mandate was valid only so long as it pleased the people to continue it. From time to time a general plebiscite should decide if the present form of government is to be retained and if its executive officials should or should not be entrusted further with the administration. Christianity is unsuited to be a state religion since it preaches humility and subjection, and thus favours a régime of force; the sovereign people must thus settle upon a new religion. Numbers alone are decisive; if I am in a minority, that only shows that I have made a mistake in assuming an opinion to be the general will when it was not so. Anyone who refuses to submit to this general will must be coerced by the whole corporate body, which simply means that the corporation forces him to be free. Since the " sovereign " is nothing but the aggregate of all individuals, it can never will to do them any harm, for it is inconceivable that the body should want to harm its members. These treacherous sophisms were actually to control events a few years later: the " sovereign " lifted itself up, and — without willing them any harm — compelled all who had erred to be free. The agent of this compulsion was the guillotine.

Almost contemporaneous with the *Social Contract* was *Émile, ou De l'éducation,* the finest part of which is the well-known *" Profession de foi du vicaire savoyard."* With an obvious challenge to Voltaire, it exposes the superficial conception of Christ formed by the Enlightenment, which regarded the Saviour as an ambitious sectary, or at best a Classical sage of the type of Socrates: " Is that the note sounded by an enthusiast or fame-hunting sectary? What gentleness, what purity, what wonderful

273

sweetness! What nobility in his principles! What deep wisdom in his sayings, what presence of mind, what keenness and effectiveness in his answers, what lordship over the passions! Where is the man, where the sage, who can act and suffer and die like this, without weakness, without ostentation? . . . If Socrates proved himself a wise man in his life and death, in Christ we recognize the life and death of a God." Apart from this, as we have already mentioned, *Émile* preaches the vague and imprecise idea of a return to nature as a panacea for all the defects in the educational methods hitherto practised. The child is to learn everything "naturally," by its own thinking, its own observation, and its own good luck: an engaging maxim, which may be fascinating in a ceremonial oration, but is as good as useless for practical guidance. Rousseau urges with the greatest emphasis mothers to nurse their own children, and fathers to educate them, for only one who takes the duties of a father on himself has the right to be a father. And Rousseau had just sent his fifth child to the Foundlings' Home.

In all these works Rousseau reveals himself as, not a constructive thinker, but merely a gifted journalist, with now and then a lyrical suggestiveness, and a virtuosity in landscape-painting, which was quite new at the time. In fact he was the real inventor of the romance of wild nature; in his *Confessions* he says: " I have made it clear already what I mean by a beautiful landscape: never one of plains, be they never so beautiful. What I must have by me is torrents and rocks, pines, dark forests, mountains; rough tracks leading up and down, and awesome precipices."

The main object of all his writings is to attract attention at all costs, and to use every means to discount by every device anything that is purer, finer, and healthier. In this he was certainly not intellectually normal, but was swung hither and thither by three or four *idées fixes*, which, however, the rush of his eager dialectic enabled him to work up into the finest gossamer webs of deception. The fatal lack of humour, which is common to all abnormal minds, is united in him with the stolid seriousness of the plebeian mind which takes everything in a precise, literal, and narrow sense because he has never lived with anything but irritating and obstinate reality. And the fact that a people and an age which had regarded things as intellectually tolerable only if said with wit and

274

irony, taste and grace, now applauded the complete opposite of all this marks the last stage of decadence which the *Ancien Régime* could reach.

As to Rousseau's moral character, it is so repulsive as to be enough by itself to deny him the name of genius. We will say nothing of his double change of faith, which in both cases was due to self-interest, and as little of his youthful thievings, although the way in which he tried to make innocent persons responsible for them makes them still uglier. His incredible meanness towards Voltaire seems to have been the result of a sort of persecution mania. Though Voltaire had shown him every kindness on every occasion, he suddenly wrote to d'Alembert his open letter *Sur les spectacles*, in which, a complete Tartuffe of malice, he denounced Voltaire as a corrupter of morals, simply because he had a special theatre at Ferney — an accusation which came particularly ill from a composer of seductive songs and lewd novels. Voltaire, nevertheless, when Rousseau was banished from France and Switzerland and could not find a refuge, wrote him a letter of delicate consideration, in which he offered him permanent hospitality on one of his estates. But Rousseau continued to pursue Voltaire throughout his whole life with the venomous jealousy of the upstart. His behaviour to Frederick the Great was similar: when the latter instructed his deputy in Neuchâtel to offer him a considerable sum of money, together with corn, wood, and wine, and a villa thrown in, he answered with the lying honesty of a republican phrase-monger that it was impossible for him to sleep in a house built by the hands of kings, and he wrote to the King: "You are willing to give me bread; is there none of your subjects that has need of it?" And after he had achieved this ridiculous and tactless impertinence, his mistress accepted all the presents behind his back. Hume took him to England and got for him a delightful asylum and a pension from the King; the result was again a series of scandalous attacks from Rousseau, to which Hume replied with the admirable remark that as Rousseau was the worst enemy of his own peace, fortune, and honour, it was hardly surprising that he was Hume's also. When Madame d'Épinay, who had provided him for years with a delightful country-house in the wood of Montmorency, journeyed to Geneva, he spread abroad the calumny that she was going thither in order to bear a child secretly in

Rousseau's character

Switzerland. His relations with Diderot, d'Alembert, and Grimm were equally unfortunate: first the suspicion of secret plots and then ingratitude and calumny — so that even the mild and excellent philosopher d'Alembert could not restrain the remark that Jean Jacques was a wild beast who should only be approached with a stick and behind the bars of a cage. Voltaire spoke the final judgment: "A doctor ought to put Jean Jacques through a blood-transfusion, for his present blood is a mixture of vitriol and arsenic. I hold him to be one of the unhappiest of men because he is one of the most spiteful."

But the most repugnant of all his qualities was his pharisaic deceitfulness, and one refuses most emphatically to count among the artists a man who played so vulgar and dishonest a comedy throughout his whole life, even if one brings oneself to acknowledge as poetic talent a capacity for unusually skilful and blatant swindling. His whole life was an unpleasant pose and an insistent hypocrisy. *Héloïse* begins with the statement that the author regrets that he does not live in an age which would allow him to fling his book into the fire. After the furore created by his first effort, he declared ostentatiously that he scorned authorship and hoped to spend the rest of his life as a worthy and honest music-copyist; and he was, in fact, a music-copyist, but never a worthy one — for his copies are careless and unusable — nor an honest one — for the whole business was a posture. He did not object to his work being overpaid by curious snobs, though he knew quite well that the payment was not made for the worth of what he wrote, but for his temporary notoriety. Thus he really lived on his reputation as an author and in the doubly hateful form of humbug that shows itself off as proud independence. Presents, of course, he never accepted; they always came through the excellent Thérèse Levasseur. He fell in love with the sister-in-law of his benefactress Madame d'Épinay, the Countess d'Houdetot, who was unhappily married and already in love with another man, and pointed out to her with emphasis the immorality of her action: obviously it was only virtuous to deceive a husband if the lover were Rousseau. We have mentioned above that he sent all his children into the Foundlings' Home, but that, according to him, was only a virtuous action, for, he says, as a convinced citizen of a Platonic republic he regarded his children as common property and had not felt justified in withholding them. One day he decided, in his contempt for civilized gentility and unjust luxury, to assume the " simple " costume of an Armenian; but, with its embroidered jacket, silken caftan, lined cap, and many-coloured girdle, it amounted to a noisy and affected theatrical attire, the exact opposite of simple, and far more luxurious than ordinary clothing. When Voltaire wrote: " You must restore your health with me in your native air, enjoy freedom, and drink with me the milk of our cows, and eat of our vegetables," he replied with an affectation of which the tasteless insolence bordered on the ridiculous : " I should prefer to drink of the water of your springs rather than of the milk of your cows."

His melodramatic masterpiece is his *Confessions*. The very introductory words give the tone that runs through the whole book, a sophisticated mixture of obscurity and false humility, of self-glorification combined with a calculated self-depreciation. " I am undertaking a task which has never had, will never have, its like. I shall show my fellow-men a man in his true nature; I am that man, I alone. I know my heart and I know mankind, and I dare to think that I am unlike all other men that exist. If I am not better than they, I am at least different. . . . Eternal God, let each man unveil his heart before thy throne with equal honesty, and then let any of them say that can: 'I was better than this one.' " The program of the whole work lies in the sentence: " For all my misfortune I have only to thank my virtues . . . he that is not my ardent sympathizer is unworthy of me." Naturally Rousseau only confesses just as much as suits him, and even this much only in the light that seems to him both most advantageous and at the same time most sensational. The vaunted honesty of these confessions consists of thumping lies, hypocritical self-reproach, and some few misleading though honest autosuggestions. The many occasions on which he speaks of his own defects with a striking frankness spring partly from a passion for effect, partly from the knowledge that for the world, and above all for a world which likes its game high, it is his vices that make a man most interesting — doubly so if he plays the rôle of repentant sinner. This method, which differs from that of the cheap feuilleton only in its greater subtlety, achieves everything at once: the halo of the moral hero who passes judgment on himself, and the fascination of the devil-of-a-fellow with a past.

The phenomenon of Rousseau signifies in literature the irruption of exaggerated and brutal plebeianism. Hitherto the efforts of the middle classes had been to climb into the higher strata of society, to attain and, if possible, to surpass the refinement, restraint, and elegance of their manner of life. But Rousseau scorns " society," or rather adopts the virtuous rôle of one who scorns it. He stays down, and therein lies his originality and his strength. But his ordinariness is not simple nature, which would be uninteresting, but an advertising, posturing, exaggerated nature: he puts the rouge on inches thick, and by these means produces on his artificial and theatrical age an effect that is loud, striking, and theatrical from the outset. He performs a peasant drama to the salons, a task for which he was predestined as no other has been, for he united in himself the qualities of a real proletarian and an abnormally gifted amateur actor, the sincerity which is necessary to convince and the theatricality which is requisite for winning popular applause. Everyone was delighted with the piquant effect of seeing among the crinolines and the ample silk coats an unshaven yokel in short sleeves, who used his hand to blow his nose, spat in the corner, and called a spade a spade. An age whose only apperception-form was affectation could not, of course, realize that this was only a new shade in affectation.

Rousseauism During the generation between 1760 and 1790 the idea of the " *bon villageois* " which Rousseau had invented ruled in all cultured circles — a mixture of the school-book character and the light-opera figure, gnarled, honest, kindly, devoted to his master, beribboned and straw-hatted, unsophisticated, jolly, and modest. That the real peasant is the opposite of this — a hard, gloomy, greedy, and suspicious animal that jealously guards its home and its gathered supplies and defends them with tooth and claw — was not realized or had been forgotten. Rousseau with his sublimated cult of nature had met the requirements of this *blasé* society to perfection. Everything had been tasted, everything rejected, when suddenly by Rousseau's agency the charm of " naturalness " and " simplicity " was discovered: just as the gourmet whose tongue knows every delicacy to satiety suddenly begins to value the taste of coarse country bread and bacon, of fresh milk and fruit.

Henceforward it was the rage to have in one's park huts, mills, moss banks, grazing cattle, and even artificial jungle. Lambs were led by silken cords through a mild nature. This fashionable enthusiasm for country life was even responsible for the death of Louis XV; on a walk which he was taking with the Dubarry in the surroundings of the Trianon, he noticed a cow-girl plucking grass for her charges, who so delighted him in her country simplicity that he took her home to supper; next day she died of plague, and ten days later the King himself fell a victim to the same disease. Since Rousseau had urged mothers to suckle their own babies, it became the fashion in high society to do so with the utmost ostentation; and the fiftieth performance of *Figaro,* at the suggestion of the popularity-hunting author, was given in aid of poor nursing mothers.

The return to nature moreover demanded that everyone should feel the utmost unselfish and noble sentiments — for natural man is always warm, devoted, and delicate in his feelings — and should show them openly in public. Girl friends had to go always arm in arm and kiss each other as often as possible; when an author read his works aloud, it was the fashion to interrupt with sobs, and expressions of delight, and, now and then, fainting-fits. It even occurred that married people embraced in public, and brothers and sisters addressed each other familiarly. When the famous actress Clairon visited Voltaire at Ferney, she knelt before him: whereupon his only course was to kneel also; at last he interrupted the ceremonial with: " And now, mademoiselle, how are you? "

The painter of Rousseauism is Jean Baptiste Greuze, whom Diderot so excessively admired as to set him up against Boucher. Just as chattering and theatrical, as assertive and pseudo-sentimental, as Rousseau, but more charming and less affected, he illustrated the favourite subjects of this self-satisfied emotional philanthropy in numerous genre paintings: the noble people, the honest farmer, the fruitful and tender mother and wife, family happiness, the blessings of true religion, of industry, of contentment and piety. But his honourable women are mothers in a play, and his innocent exposed maidens are exhibitionists; it is once more the prurient keyhole-erotic of Fragonard, intensified by a modish pretence.

The German "Genius Period," which began, roughly, in the seventies, also goes back to Rousseau in essential traits. There was, as Goethe said retrospectively, a ferment of ideas. "The epoch in which we were living may be called the challenging age, for we made demands on ourselves and on others which no one had yet lived up to. The loftiest, most sensitive, and intelligent, in fact, had suddenly realized that the immediate view of nature, and action based thereon, was the best that man could wish for himself, and was not hard of achievement. . . . When now men advanced to its realization, it became clear that the easiest way out of the business was to call in the aid of genius, which by its magical gifts would solve the problem and meet the challenge." The watchword "genius" had been first used in this sense by Gerstenberg, who also wrote the first important drama of this school. The meaning of the word has been best expressed by Lavater in his *Physiognomy:* "The character of genius and all its works is *apparition;* as angels do not come, but are here, do not go away, but are away, so also with the work and the effect of genius. That which is unlearnt and unborrowed, which can be neither learnt nor borrowed, the inwardly individual, the inimitable, the divine, that is genius; the inspirational is genius and is called so, will be called so, at all times, among all peoples, as long as men think and feel and speak. Genius flashes and creates, it does not construct, just as it cannot itself be constructed, but is. Inimitability is the character of genius, instantaneity, revelation, and apparition, givenness; that which is given, not by man, but by God or by the Devil." The highest praise that could be — and often was — extended to a man at the time was to call him an "original genius" or a "Nature." What was demanded was no longer the handling of definite rules, but the "full heart," and the feelings were placed far above the reason — but yet associated with reason; for the whole of the impetuous youth which had made it part of its program to exude at all costs, was a strange mixture of naïveté and reflection, eld-wisdom and childishness.

The prelude to this extremely interesting movement, which introduced a completely new quality into German intellectual life, is the period of Sensibility, whose beginnings came about twenty years earlier. Gellert's chief demand, repeated time and again in his letters and writings, had been the "good and sensitive soul," and this fashionable softness and sentimentality was called, round about 1750, "delicacy" and "sensibility." Lessing translated Sterne's *Sentimental Journey* as *Empfindsame Reise*, and this expression not only made itself at home, but became very soon a sort of life-motto. Side by side with it was Rousseau's conception of "*la belle âme*," which lies open to every gentle and refined sentiment. Then the word "feeling" came, and extended its domination, with a power that is attainable only by a word that becomes the fashion over every sphere of life. Men were intoxicated by it, shouted it to each other like a watchword that is at the same time a secret inspiration. "Feeling" was the indispensable, but also the completely adequate, legitimation of everything. What was the foundation of love, friendship, harmony, all human relationship? — Feeling. What is the core of religion, what is the fatherland, what are life and Nature? — Feeling. What forms the painter, the poet, what gives the impress of true humanity? — always Feeling.

The inevitable consequence was that this feeling of everything from out of the inner wealth of the heart, which is a capacity and a talent that the gods rarely give, was in the thousands who wanted to keep up with fashion just an external parade and artificial show. One had to be always stirred, always moved, agitated, carried away, one must live in a perpetual condition of emotional high tension. In France this play with noble sentiment produced the Revolution; in Germany it had the more harmless consequence of a one-sided unworldly culture.

One of the first and most beneficial results of this cult of sentiment was that it broke down, in part, the partition walls which the stiff tradition of the seventeenth and eighteenth centuries had erected between men. Even Lessing, in other respects a warm and successful defender of the natural, addressed his best friends in formal terms; and in the elementary schools of Joseph II (which as little as his other reforms meant a real attainment of freedom) the children were strictly forbidden to say "thou" to each other. Goethe and Lavater on the other hand spoke familiarly, thee'd and thou'd each other at their first meeting; and this became the ordinary method of address among men who felt themselves intellectually in relation (a thing which was very easy at the time). Equally readily people took to calling each other "brother" and "sister." An indispensable part of even the smallest park was the Temple of Friendship, in which friends swore eternal loyalty. Men wallowed in the idea of a purely spiritual union of man and woman, and " soul-love," which rested on a community of noble impulses, became the fashionable form of flirting. We commonly meet, especially in poets, the " lady of one's thoughts," a supernal being inwardly reverenced, who had no existense save in the imagination. Tears welled up at every letter received, at every book opened, at the mere thought of nature, or friendship, or a bride, or oneself; in fact weeping was universal. In Miller's *Siegwart*, the most successful novel of the time, even the moon weeps. The early careful and well-articulated style was completely transformed, and language became the means for the expression of momentary emotion, almost to the point of meaninglessness; it is filled with dots, exclamation-marks, dashes, question-marks, violent interjections, and sentences which break off in the middle. This is undoubtedly a sort of Early Impressionism, acquired but to be lost again. This condition of passionate search, eternally dissatisfied, but uplifted by a Promethean consciousness of its new discoveries, is expressed for us in the concrete present in a letter written by the youthful Goethe in 1775, wherein he describes to a lady who is one of the " friends of his soul " how he passed the day, and he closes with the words: " I felt, through it all, like a rat which has eaten poison; which runs to every hole, swallows every drop of moisture, devours everything eatable that comes its way, while its heart burns with a consuming inextinguishable fire."

The period manifested the pathological condition of all epochs when something new is coming to birth, and at the same time the dual quality of all times of transition; hence its contradictions. Thus, for instance, the English garden transplanted to Germany, though it owed its existence to the enthusiasm for the Return to Nature, was nothing but an artificial attempt to collect in one spot everything that nature meant to these people — meadows, brooks, grottoes, clumps of trees, gentle sloping paths, the little wood with its inevitable clearing — with a host of accessories that formed a grotesque bric-à-brac of every conceivable reminiscence and whim, Greek columns, Roman tombs, Turkish mosques, and Gothic ruins. On top of all this was the universal and particularly tasteless and unnatural habit of scattering inscriptions which preached the text for each of these intended effects. Similarly hypersensibility and coarseness were strangely mingled. In the same Werther period, which saw something superhuman in every beloved, there was, as Magister Laukhard relates in his autobiography, a queer form of ovation, still common among the students at Giessen, which sounds more like Grimmelshausen: they went, after duly filling themselves with beer, to the front of a house inhabited by women, and relieved themselves there, to the accompaniment of whistling like that of a carman to the accompaniment of his horse's staling.

This enthronement of sentiment was bound to work itself out quite as much in licentiousness as in refinement. The fossilization and narrowness of the former laws of art and politics led to the conclusion that rules of any sort are to be thrown overboard. In *Werther* we read, with obvious irony: "You can say much in favour of rules, about as much as you can in praise of bourgeois society." Actually the youth of the time had the same contempt for the bourgeoisie as was held later on by the French Romantics, the poets of Young Germany, the Naturalists, the Expressionists, and, in fact, every youth-movement. This led to the rejection on principle of any and every calling; the one ambition was to be just a man. " Profession of scholarship — profession? Pish!" said Goethe's brother-in-law Schlosser in 1777 in the *Deutsches Museum,* " Good heavens, look at your professions, teachers, lawyers, ministers, authors, poets — professions everywhere and men nowhere. Why do you so seldom find wisdom, experience, knowledge of humanity in your professional men? Just because they form a profession." The ideal that hovered before the generation was a gifted amateurism, interested in everything, but tied to nothing definite and having as its one speciality the study of life.

One very marked characteristic of this period was its passion for the silhouette, which took the place of the Rococo's porcelain mania. These black portraits were to be found everywhere, in books and albums, on the walls and as medallions, on glasses and cups — and sometimes they were literally life-sized. The art of cutting-out became a popular and admired accomplishment, which even famous artists practised, and the favourite amusement at the family table. The peculiar quality of the age, its shadowy indicativeness, combining definition and abstraction, its schematism and love of outline, its union of darkness of feeling and daylight

Silhouette and circular letter

of reason, not to mention its amateurishness and dilettantism, found expression in this pastime: Lavater built up his science of physiognomy (rather a doubtful one in any case) for the most part on collections of silhouettes, which he gathered with the greatest zeal. This new form of soul-study compares roughly with our present-day graphology: its founder asserted that it was possible to read a man's character from his face and, as Lichtenberg remarked bitingly, found more in the noses of contemporary authors than the intelligent world did in their writings.

Letter-writing, again, became a positive mania. This was of quite a different kind from that of today, being anything but a private and intimate business — in fact the effusions and items of information which were consigned to paper were meant from the start for a wider circle of readers. The lack of proper newspapers, the strict censorship, the eagerness to disentangle one's own and others' souls, made the " circular letter," which was often read in dozens of different places, one of the dominant forms of intercourse. " For there was such a general openness of heart that it was impossible to speak or write to one individual without imagining our words to be directed to a larger number . . . and thus, since political discussions were of little interest, the moral world came to be pretty widely known." Letters were called " soulvisits "; one fell in love by letter and corresponded passionately with people with whom one never became personally acquainted.

It was indeed a literary age through and through; all word and movement, all love and hate took literary form. All the important expressions of life were done in writing, everything by paper for the paper's sake. State, society, religion, everything, became just a subject for literature; all classes were seized with an absolute mania for reading, lending-libraries were opened, and it was an essential part of one's turn-out to have a book in the pocket. Frederick the Great told d'Alembert that he would rather have written *Athalie* than won the Seven Years' War, and immediately after the appalling disaster at Kolin he composed a number of verses and epigrams. Madame Roland at the foot of the scaffold asked for pen and paper, to write down certain notable thoughts which had just occurred to her.

The frock-coat In the same way the costume of the time displayed a mixture of extravagance and naturalism. For a time hair was dressed so high that ladies had to remove the cushions from their coaches. At the French Court a frigate in full sail was seen as a coiffure. The Marquise de Créqui tells us that in 1785 Marie Antoinette appeared with her hair dressed *à la jardinière,* with an artichoke, a cabbage, a carrot, and a bundle of radishes on her head. One of the court ladies was so taken with this that she cried out: " I shall only wear vegetables in future, they are so simple, and much more natural than flowers." Huge hoods also came into fashion again, the so-called *dormeuses* or *baigneuses.* In the name of philanthropy, a vigorous opposition was set up against powdering, on the ground that the enormous use of wheat flour raised the price of bread for the people, and the hair actually began to be worn unpowdered, though this fashion was not universal. Men's pigtails became shorter every year, and the old full coat, which even during the Rococo had been slightly cut away, was then transformed into the frock-coat proper. This was modelled on the English riding-coat and came into fashion about 1770 as the swallow-tail. In its beginnings, however, it was by no means the serious dignified ceremonial dress that its survival is today, but an affected and provocative article of clothing, favoured especially by the revolutionary youth and worn in vivid colours such as scarlet, azure-blue, and violet, ornamented with gold or copper buttons. From the free America, towards the end of the period, came the top-hat and the big round felt hat. The Werther attire consisted of high boots with tops, yellow leather breeches, yellow waistcoat and blue frock-coat; the neck and hair were left free, which shocked the older generation particularly. Even women of the emancipated sort appeared with the Werther hat, waistcoat, and coat, the notorious " *caraco.*"

The gods of the time were those to whom Werther prayed, Homer, Ossian, and Shakspere, who was erroneously regarded as a book-dramatist. In 1760 the Scottish poet James Macpherson published his *Fragments of Ancient Poetry, collected in the Highlands,* bardic poems, purporting to be translated from the Gaelic of the time of Caracalla. In 1762 these were followed by a second work, *Fingal, an old epic poem, by Ossian, son of Fingal."* Doubts were already cast on their authenticity by Johnson and Hume, but it was not till 1807, eleven years after Macpherson's death, that the forgery was conclusively proved. But this really mattered little,

Ossian

285

and only paper-souls like Johnson or furious sceptics like Hume regarded it as a problem of importance. The real genius of these play-acting pieces lay in the very fact that they did not reproduce the old folk-poetry faithfully at all; but were just what the wishes of the age imagined and wanted nature-poetry to be, delicately primitive, artificially picturesque, mirroring the sadness of over-civilized minds. No genuine bardic poems have ever achieved the colossal success of these. They were translated into French, Italian, Spanish, Polish, Dutch, and about half a dozen times into German; Alwina, Selma, and Fingal became favourite baptismal names; bardic schools sprang up, and even Napoleon rated Ossian above Homer. Pallid melancholy and wild-natural disorder appeared to the time more poetical than clearness and form. The fascination and grandeur of the hitherto disparaged Gothic was rediscovered; Horace Walpole, son of the Robert Walpole already mentioned, rebuilt his home at Strawberry Hill as a mediæval castle and wrote the successful Gothic thriller *The Castle of Otranto*. Herder glorified the simple manners of the German past, and Goethe waxed enthusiastic over Strassburg Minster.

Sturm und Drang

It is to be noted of the poets of the "*Sturm und Drang*" movement that without exception their greatest vigour was shown when they were still young. This is true even of the classics — Herder, Goethe, and Schiller. The movement was preluded by Gersten-berg's *Ugolino* in 1767, a splendid dramatic study which was full of colour and movement, but was found repellent owing to the coarseness with which it discovered a sort of morphology of hunger. Gerstenberg was about ten years older than the other "Original Geniuses" and died as late as 1823, at the age of eighty-six, but he produced nothing of note after this promising beginning. The Göttingen "*Hain*," a group of idealistic young people which was founded in 1772, sought to revive the old scaldic poetry and was enthusiastic for liberty, fatherland, virtue, and Klopstock. The members of the real "*Sturm und Drang*" group, with which the Hain was in reality only externally connected, were all born about the middle of the century; they were often called Goetheans, since Goethe was looked on as the leader of the whole movement, though in fact (as everyone knows) he very soon withdrew from it. Their products were published anonymously, and it is delightful to see how even skilled critics blundered in the attribution of various works. Lessing believed that Leisewitz's *Julius von Tarent* was by Goethe, and Wagner's *Kindermörderin* by Lenz; some of Lenz's poems have found a place in almost all editions of Goethe, his *Soldaten* was generally regarded as a work of Klinger, while Klinger's *Leidendes Weib* was still included by Tieck among Lenz's collected works; Klinger's *Neue Arria* was assigned by Gleim and Schubart to Goethe; Lenz's *Hofmeister*, too, was by Klopstock, Voss, and the world generally attributed to Goethe, some even holding it to be his most important drama. As a matter of fact, Lenz is, after Goethe, by far the most interesting poet of the generation; Goethe called him a " rare and indefinable individuality," and Lavater summed up Lenz's strength and weakness admirably: " he spills over with genius." In some ways he reminds us of Wedekind; there is a fierce and yet cold sexuality in his works, an incoherent stream of thought and image to which precisely he owes his highly dramatic atmosphere; there is a naturalism, which is almost pathological and caricaturish and gives his figures a peculiar staring brightness and waxwork fixity; there is a moralism, which has no moral basis and does not shrink from the most repulsive motives: thus in the *Soldaten* the heroine is a harlot, and the *Hofmeister* closes with the hero's self-castration. Lenz's plays, though he himself, in the knowledge that they represented a mixed genre, called them comedies, fully satisfied the demands which he made on the drama in his *Anmerkungen über das Theater* of 1774: namely, that it must be a curio-cupboard. This apt remark actually comes from Goethe, whom Lenz tried to copy in everything. He fell in love with Friederike Brion and Frau von Stein, was a close friend of Schlosser and Cornelia, most successfully imitated the tone of the young Goethe in some of his poems, and wanted to enter, like him, upon a court career — hence Karl August called him the ape of Goethe. But he was diametrically opposite to Goethe, if in nothing else, in his extraordinary lack of human understanding and psychological insight, which, after his brief heyday, plunged him into the obscurity of madness and oblivion.

The basic quality of Klinger, too, was an overleaping and yet only artificially induced immoderateness. Wieland called him a drinker of lions' blood, and he himself wrote in a letter of 1775: " I am torn asunder by passions which would overwhelm anyone else . . . every moment I should like to fling humanity and all that lives and breathes to the chaos to devour, and to hurl myself after them." His figures live in a permanent ferment; his language is choked in a thick jungle of exaggerated metaphors and meaningless phrases. He went later on to Petersburg, where he became a general and a favourite of the Tsar, wrote mild but popular novels, and died at an advanced age. Of his youthful poems he said in 1785: " I can laugh as well as anyone at my earlier work; but so much at least is true, that every young man sees the world more or less as a poet and a visionary. He sees everything in a higher, nobler, completer form, albeit more confused, extreme, and exaggerated."

Heinrich Leopold Wagner was a rough, uncouth, but vigorous Naturalist. His drama *Die Reue nach der Tat* had a great success under Schröder, who gave it the flashy title of *Familienstolz.* He died in 1779. The painter Friedrich Müller, known in the histories of literature as " Maler Müller," wrote a Faust fragment and a play *Golo und Genoveva,* colourful, half-realist, half-lyrical successions of scenes, more tasteful, but duller than those of the others. The weakest, most moderate, and therefore most successful of the group was Leisewitz.

In 1773 appeared Bürger's *Leonore,* one of the most powerful of German ballads. This poetical form in fact reached full bloom at this time: it derives from the " Moritat " of the fair-booths and is thus a popular, vivid, and vigorous type, a sort of epic-lyric pendant to the drama of the " genius " period. The first musician who could match effectively the mysterious dark colouring of the ballads was Johann Rudolf Zumsteeg. Schiller wrote a somewhat one-sided critique of Bürger in the *Allgemeine Literaturzeitung* of 1791, which made a great stir and was applauded by Goethe, but upset the author of *Leonore* considerably, although in a good many places it expressed a real admiration and only refused him the supreme degree of artistic ripeness.

Two-dimensional poetry

This generation of talented but ineffective nature-poets, who dominated the German public for about a decade through the passion, novelty, and variety of their visions, was called at the time " *kraftgenialisch,*" a term that expressed fairly accurately the fact that their poetic force made them relatives, but no more than relatives, of genius. For genius is always a seer and stands in face

288

of the complex, chaotic, and apparently illogical phenomenon that we call life, as an initiate. And therefore the genius is to all other men as a connoisseur to a dilettante. All the *Sturm und Drang* poets, however, were just geniuses who had stuck fast on the threshold; they had no adequate intellect and training to back up their fantasy and creative power — an artist being, so to say, made only when he has completely dominated and controlled his own being. These men's abilities were never balanced, and consequently their effect is as of something violent, inorganic, and confused, and their originality was not fertilizing, but estranging. Their aim was to be the heralds of certain definite thoughts and to preach certain ideals of life; but unwittingly the Messianic gesture became to them only Herostratean. Their whole genre was always a little schoolboyish, and they never produced anything more than a high-grade poetry of adolescence. Nevertheless, or rather because of this, the " Genius period " must be called the flowering of German poetry, and in the literal sense of the word, for it never fructified; the flower was broken off by Classicism.

We may perhaps get a clearer understanding of the whole movement if we compare it with those of Naturalism and Expressionism. The differences are not as great as might appear from the noisy programs in which each of the three proclaimed itself as unique. The thing was at bottom the same in all three. In each the challenges of youth are flung against everything traditional. The movement bursts every bond of form, or thinks it does so, for in fact it creates for itself a new form; it is always a movement from below, stands for the right of a hitherto oppressed class, is " agin the government," and has as leftward a tendency as possible — in 1770 Democratic, in 1890 Socialistic, in 1920 Communistic. For its artistic creed it likes to give itself some great patron, whom it imitates in some essentials and misunderstands in other essentials: for the " *Originalgenies* " this patron was Shakspere, for the Naturalists Ibsen, for the Expressionists Strindberg. For preference they take as the object of their poetry something that infuriates the philistines: madness, murder, blasphemy; incest, rape, and harlotry; brawling, drinking, and spitting. They are fond of making the stage a social judge whose decisions are advertised in a mixture of provocative cynicism and convulsive ethic.

In this the *Sturm und Drang* poets remind us more particularly

of the Expressionists, with whom they also share the peculiarity of being poets with a two-dimensional fancy: they saw
everything as linear and in the flat. This is perhaps the real reason
why they are always accused of having artificially constructed their
characters. Of course they did, but in itself that would be no reproach, for up to a point every dramatist must be a builder. Their
weakness was that they were constructed in two dimensions, or,
to put it in a more usual though less definite way, were conceived
lyrically. Thus there was always something picture-bookish about
them, though they were not necessarily wrongly or imperfectly
drawn. The impression of stiffness and false perspective arose from
the fact that they were composed for the stage without being suited
to it. We always feel something lacking; and that something is the
third dimension. We get the same impression as we do from a first-
rate reciter who tries to turn actor. There is one inconspicuous hall-
mark that characterizes almost every author who sees in lines —
he has a passion for the line that interrupts the text: namely, the
thought-dash. The *Sturm und Drang* poets also used this typo-
graphical expedient and by immoderate use of it completely wore
it away.

Hamann   The prophet of the whole movement was Johann Georg
Hamann, a uniquely interesting curiosity of literary history. In the
firm conviction that our deepest impulses have their birth in the
realm of chiaroscuro, he created for himself a wholly new language, all made up of inklings, mysteries, and secrets, which
possessed a hitherto unheard-of suggestiveness, though often an
almost impenetrable obscurity. He spoke himself of his " stupid
profundity," his " grasshopper " or his " accursed sausage " style,
declared that he was unable to understand his own earlier writings, and described his whole productivity as mere lumps, fragments, whims, and fancies. He was the complete opposite of the
Aufklärer (the " lying, showy, mouthing false-prophets," as he
called them), who on their side looked down loftily on his confused
riddling. But could Mendelssohn, Nicolai, and their clique ever
have written, or even have felt the truth of, such brilliant sentences
as, for instance, this of Hamann's: " To drive the good inward, the
evil outward, to appear worse than one is, to be better than one appears, that is what I hold to be duty and art " ? In Socrates he
honoured, unlike Mendelssohn, not the moralist and dialectician,

but the secret mouthpiece of the Daimonion, and the Socratic non-knowing he interpreted, in the sense of the genius-idea, as a profession of Irrationalism. From the poet and thinker he demanded the " heart-warmth of wilfulness "; for " thinking, feeling, and understanding all depend on the heart, and a little enthusiasm and superstition not merely claim some indulgence, but are a yeast necessary to set the soul fermenting towards the heroism of philosophy." Poetry was to him the history of the human heart, philosophy self-knowledge: " Nothing but self-knowledge descending into hell prepares the way to the divine in men." His basic idea was the *coincidentia oppositorum* of Bruno, which he searched for and elucidated everywhere, in the mysterious union of body and soul, reason and feeling, in language which is nothing but incarnated spirit and concrete thought, in the Christian mysteries of the Trinity, the Incarnation, and Salvation.

So fundamental and ever-present a conviction of the paradox, the inner contradictoriness and organic illogicality, of all creation leads of necessity to the standpoint of irony. And in fact Hamann, like Plato and Pascal and Shakspere, was an ironist of the highest quality. He even goes so far as to regard the world as the product of divine irony, and the Bible, the Word of God, as the classical example of ironical literature. And even in the position, full of inconsistencies, which this thinker — complex and primitive, modern and old-fashioned, universal and one-sided, admired and misunderstood — took up in his time, and still holds in the history of philosophy, there is something deeply ironical.

On Hamann's theory that poetry is the mother tongue of the human race, Herder built up his whole poetic and philosophy of language. In the Introduction to Volume I an attempt was made to estimate the importance of this extraordinary man. He was to this extent the polar antithesis of the Enlightenment, that whereas it sought to adapt all the past to its narrow and philistine standpoint, he possessed in the highest degree the capacity to suit himself with eager sympathy to even the strangest and most dissimilar phenomena. " We are always writing for the academic type, we compose odes, heroic epics, church and kitchen songs, which no one understands, wants, or feels. Our classical literature is like a bird of paradise, as highly coloured, as well-behaved, all flight, all height, and without a foot on German soil." According to him,

Herder and Jacobi

291

poetry is the higher, the nearer it is to nature, and therefore the finest poetry has been written by the oldest peoples, the wild children of nature; while in the atmosphere of civilization it does not thrive. Popular poetry is full of freshness, vigour, clarity; it does not speak, but paints; it does not argue, but discharges itself in bold leaps and throws. To justify this view by concrete examples, he translated the " Voices of the Peoples " with a wonderful sympathy of genius — French, Italian, Spanish, English, Scottish, Danish poems, Norse bardic songs, and German folk-songs, the indigenous nature-poetry of all nations, even of Greenlanders and Lapps, Tatars and Wends. He discovered the splendour of mediæval art, the lofty power and simplicity of Dürer, the oriental witchery of the Old Testament, which he looked upon as a collection of national legends; but he saw all these things, not in isolation, but in their environment, as products of their age, their nationality, and their ethic. The Enlightenment described Shakspere as a genius ruined by his neglect of rule, Lessing said he was the genius who made his own rules, but Herder explained him as the vivid copy of the Elizabethan era and its peculiar life, its state, and its theatre, its society and philosophy.

The Irrationalist movement, inaugurated by Hamann and extended by Herder, continued and, as it were, culminated in Friedrich Heinrich Jacobi, the friend of Goethe's youth. He made his starting-point the confutation of Spinoza, proving that he was an atheist and fatalist, and that any method of mathematico-logical demonstration like his must necessarily lead to fatalism: conceptual thinking always gives us stones for bread, a mechanistic nature in place of a living God, rigid necessity in place of freedom of the will. Our organ for knowing the world is not reason, but feeling, the " capacity for the supersensible " which lies in each one of us. We can never prove by the reason that things exist outside of us; we only attain that certainty by an original and immediate faith. " We have nothing on which our judgment can base itself but the fact itself, the datum that things really are before us. Can we find a more proper word to express this than ' Revelation ' ?" But a being that is revealed supposes a being that reveals, a creative power, which can only be God. The existence of God can never be a consequence of the idea of God. God does not exist because we think him, but we are sure of him because he really exists. Cognition can never comprehend real Being, it can only grasp our idea of a thing and not the thing itself. That we apprehend (*wahrnehmen* in the literal sense, take for true) things, is an indeducible, inexplicable, and, therefore, truly miraculous fact.

Jacobi is today almost forgotten. And yet there is no more comforting, no more human, in fact (let us say outright) no truer philosophy than his. Everything, if we regard it rightly, is ultimately an act of faith, a divine revelation, an incomprehensible miracle: the world, my ego, everything great and small. In each case, even for the simplest assertion, faith is needed, and on this faith we live. The shoemaker who does not believe in his activity and the objects he deals with will never produce a good pair of shoes. The moment we withdraw our faith in things, they fall into nothingness like tinder; the moment we believe in them, they exist, real, inexpugnable, indestructible — even, in a sense, immortal.

Inner faith and devastating scepticism, intoxication of feeling, and ice of logic, wild rejection of law, and strict observance of method, all imaginable polar contrasts were united in this over-fertile age. And to cap it all, it saw the beginnings of the two " Dioscuri," the two who were in fact contraries and antipodes. The great and lasting achievements of the age go by the titles of *Götz, Werther*, and the *Urfaust; Räuber, Fiesco*, and *Kabale*.

" A remarkable man "

The young Goethe is described as follows by Lotte's fiancé Kestner, in a letter to a friend: " He has great talents, is a true genius and a man of character. He has an extraordinarily vivid imagination and thus usually expresses himself in images and similes. He himself says that he always expresses himself mediately (*uneigentlich*) and could not possibly do so in terms of himself. . . . He is strong in all his emotions, but has much self-control. His thought is noble, free from prejudice; it goes on as it will, irrespective of fashion and the ways of life. He hates all compulsion. . . . He has done his chief work in the fine arts and sciences, or rather in all the sciences save those that are called the bread-winning ones. He is, in fact, a remarkable man." The remarkable part about him was that he was capable of doing all that the others merely desired to do and indeed could not even desire clearly. *Götz* was a triumph such as there had never been before in what we must admit to be the genuine dramatic aptitude: namely, in the art of skilful omission and tightest compression, of breathless yet controlled gallop of pictures — that which Expressionism has again made into its norm, but has only mastered in cold externals. *Werther* is perhaps the unique example in the whole history of literature of a work which had a colossal and essential contemporary success and yet remained as an immortal. The reason is that, though Goethe in this romance echoed the time with an amazing subtlety and certainty, yet he also mirrored, with an equally amazing honesty and penetration, his own experience and humanity in its greatest depths. For that reason, as long as humanity produces men who are noble, but unrooted, so long there will be readers of *Werther*. And that is why on the contrary almost nobody nowadays reads *Héloïse*, which was an almost greater success; for it is the work of a highly gifted journalist who seems at his highest almost indistinguishable from a poet, whereas *Werther* is a pure poem which, though written only to relieve its author of a devastating experience, happened to have the qualities necessary for a " novel of the season." Rousseau intends to prove something; Goethe intends nothing at all.

On *Werther* Lessing wrote to Eschenburg, the translator of Shakspere: " Can you picture any Greek or Roman who would have taken his life in such a way and for such reasons? Certainly no Greek would have done it, still less a Roman — if only because gunpowder was not then discovered." But that was just the novelty in Goethe's work, that it portrayed, for the first time and with irresistible drawing, the disaster of a " sensitive," who died, not for love, nor from any blow of destiny, but simply from life. Goethe's achievement in *Werther* is his discovery of *fundamentally unhappy* love, and therein he expresses the feminine qualities of the age, for this is the specifically feminine type of love. But as regards his own personal case, in *Werther* he liberated himself from his love by making it objective, to a certain extent making it independent of himself, a self-existent being. The purifying and redeeming function which art played in Goethe's life is not unrelated to his peculiar attitude towards the women he loved, which is a psychological problem by itself. He broke off the affair with Käthchen Schönkopf, deserted Friederike Brion, and cancelled the engagement with Lili, each time without visible reasons. Even his feeling for Lotte was no unhappy love in the ordinary sense — he felt that Lotte was gliding over to him from her betrothed, and at that moment he drew back. In 1787 he fell in love with a beautiful blue-eyed Milanese girl, Maddalena Riggi, who also was already betrothed, and then a lengthy illness removed her from his mind. When he saw her again, the engagement had been broken off, but that very fact lost him to her; and she waited in vain for the declaration she expected. He left all of them in the lurch except two, Frau von Stein, because she was already married, and Christiane, because she was not dangerous to him. Even from Frau von Stein he eventually separated himself, and again without tangible reason.

We might perhaps explain this enigma of conduct by referring it to Goethe's mental structure as a whole. Firstly, in everything, even in women, he sought for the Prime Phenomenon, and thus no single woman could permanently satisfy him. Secondly, as artist — that is, as eternal wanderer — he stood in fear of woman, in whom he necessarily saw the stabilizing, anchoring principle. But the deepest reason perhaps is that every passion, at its moment, became objective to him, turned into a real figure, obliged him to draw from it real consequences, whether in the form of marriage or in that of an enduring " alliance of souls." If he had not been a poet, either he would have forced himself into a " normal " attitude, or else these conflicts would have killed him. But he possessed the safety-valve of his art, by which he achieved his own reaction: in it we find the fire of his passion stored up, but hardened into a cool lava-mass.

The years from 1770 to 1780 may be called the Age of Goethe. But *only* these years. At that time he really was looked on as the leader of German youth and was made answerable in addition for all the noisy extravagances and mad absurdities of the new movement. Almost all his innovations were effective, made disciples, and were treated by admirers and opponents alike as an art with a program. After this he never had the same broad and clear influence. It was especially in *Werther* that people recognized themselves; even Napoleon read it seven times. A hail of copies, continuations, dramatizations, commentaries, counterblasts, and parodies spread over Germany, and it was even translated into some of the non-European languages. *Werther* was shown at the fairs as a wax doll, and pilgrimages were made to the grave of his original, the young man Jerusalem. Every sensitive youth played

295

with the idea of imitating Werther's end and several actually did shoot themselves; every sensitive girl wanted to be loved like Lotte: "Werther has been the cause of more suicides than the most beautiful woman," said Madame de Staël. But the work that really did give the richest expression to the spirit of the time was not recognized by it at all: this was the *Urfaust*, written between 1773 and 1775, but only published, and then in an altered form, in 1790. And for all this productivity, amazing in both content and comprehensiveness, one has the impression that it was not the essence of its author, and that, in reality, his poems were by-products, organic but secondary secretions. The deepest and mightiest work of art which Goethe created was his own biography.

The young Schiller With Schiller, on the contrary, we are forced to the conviction that his whole genius flowed into his pen, and that his life was put into his thoughts and creatures almost without residue. This is not in the least meant to imply a different valuation, but simply to express two polar, but equally justified, poet-types.

Among Otto Weininger's posthumous works is a small essay in which Schiller is held up as the archetype of the modern journalist. This conception is right in so far that later journalists have often guided themselves by Schiller, but apart from that it is based on a misjudgment (which, for that matter, has become more or less typical in Schiller criticism), for the custom has grown up of arguing from the disciples to the master, so as not only to make him responsible for them, but at last actually to confound him with them. Now, Schiller is not at all the man to found a school; one can talk of a School of Rembrandt, Hegel, Ibsen, but not of a School of Schiller. It is impossible to imitate Schiller, or, rather, if he is imitated, he becomes intolerable. If another poet copies Schiller's pathos, it becomes phrase-seeking and exaggeration; if he follows his technique, it is artificial and inane; and if he repeats his ideas, they become fine-sounding platitudes. Schiller as orator would have been only a leader-writer, as characterist only a feuilletonist, as compositionist a stunt-reporter, but for the fact that he was Schiller. But this is not the place to go more closely into this question.

A contemporary report of the first performance of *Die Räuber* at Mannheim says: "The theatre was like a lunatic asylum, with rolling eyes, clenched fists, hoarse uproar among the audience. Strangers fell sobbing into each other's arms, women tottered, half-fainting, to the door. It was a universal disruption into chaos, out of whose mists a new creation is emerging." The scenery, arranged by the producer Freiherr von Dalberg, was, for those times, splendid: Schiller was specially delighted with a moon made of a bright metal mirror, which on Karl's oath: "Hear me, thou moon and stars," moved slowly over the horizon and spread a "natural and terrible light round about." The same Dalberg had, however, extorted from Schiller two fairly foolish modifications; the play closed with Amalia stabbing herself, and Franz being thrown into the Tower of Starvation, and the costumes were those of the time of Maximilian I. Schiller was quite right in saying of this weak and false re-dating of his work, which breathed essentially contemporary feeling, that it made of his drama a raven in peacock's feathers.

Schiller judged his first work with an acuteness and scepticism which perhaps does not sound quite genuine, because it is too deliberately exaggerated, a mixture of pride, contempt for the public, passion for exaggeration, and desire to mystify. Yet it offers almost a unique example of youthful self-criticism. When he begins the first draft of the preface with the words: "It may seem at first reading that this play will never gain the franchise of the theatre," we today hardly believe our eyes, for there is no German drama of which it can be asserted with more reason that it won the franchise of the theatre; but from the contemporary standpoint its author's misgivings were not so ridiculous. Just because it was so dramatic, its form was bound to seem new, unusual, and apparently so untheatrical that it might easily have been taken for undramatic. In a critique written in the *Wirtembergisches Repertorium*, in which he discussed his own play under the initials "K . . . r" (five years later everyone would have taken this for Körner), he declares that Franz's intrigues are appallingly crude and romantic and that the whole play halts in the middle; of the style and the dialogue he says they "ought to be more consistent and in general less poetic" — at one point the style was lyric and epic, at another even metaphysical, in a third biblical, a fourth flat; of Amalia he remarked: "I have read more than half the piece and do not yet know what the poet wants in the girl, and cannot imagine what could happen to her; no future destiny is hinted at or prepared, and her lover, moreover, does not say a word about her until the end of the third act. This is nothing less than a mortal blemish in the play; on this side the author puts himself well below mediocrity." And the résumé ran: " If one cannot notice in the beauties of the work that our author dotes on his Shakspere, one can notice it definitely enough in the extravagances." In a second criticism-disguise under the name of a " Correspondent in Worms " he added: " If I am to express my opinion openly, this piece is no piece for the theatre. Take away the shooting, the burning, the scorching, and the stabbing and so on, and it would be wearisome and heavy for the stage." A Frankfurt journal published a rejoinder which took up arms eagerly for Schiller against his own too harsh criticism.

These defects of the *Räuber,* which have since been commented on *ad nauseam* by far less competent critics, did not in fact reduce the forcefulness of the play in the least. This is obvious, even from the fact that the numerous and feeble adaptations of it (against which there then was no legal protection) could not weaken its effect. In the arrangement of Plümicke, which had an uninterrupted success on the Berlin stage, Franz revealed himself as a bastard, and Schweizer, unable to endure the thought that his captain was to die at the executioner's hands, killed first Karl and then himself. In France the play appeared (in a very much altered translation by La Martellière) under the title: *Robert, chef des brigands;* in this, Kosinsky appeared at the end with a pardon from the Emperor, who elevated the robber band into a " Free Corps of light troops " and made Robert their captain. La Martellière even wrote a continuation: *Le Tribunal redoutable, ou La Suite de Robert, chef des brigands.* Schiller himself planned an epilogue in one act: *Räuber Moors letztes Schicksal,* by which (as he wrote to Körner in 1785) he intended to set the play going again. The most absurd achievement in this direction is perhaps that of a Frau von Wallenrodt in her work *Karl Moor and his comrades after the parting at the Old Town, a picture of sublime human nature as a counterpart to Rinaldo Rinaldini:* in this, Amalia and old Moor come to life again, — the one having only fainted and the other only been slightly wounded — and then liberate Karl Moor, who had offered himself for judgment, by their pleading with the Emperor; whereupon Karl and Amalia marry, and all the robbers are persuaded to take up an honest bourgeois way of life.

Fiesco also appeared in Mannheim with an altered conclusion: Verrina aims a blow at Fiesco, who parries it, breaks the sceptre, and cries to the people, who kneel before him in joy: " Rise, men of Genoa. I have made you a present of the monarch — embrace now your happiest citizen." He behaves still more nobly in the adaptation of Plümicke, who in this case also produced a successful pirated edition for Berlin: he catches the dagger in the same way, but immediately offers his bared breast to Verrina, who draws back in agitation; in the end the old Doria appears, ready to accept his bitterest enemy as a son and to crown him with the ducal hat, but Fiesco wills to die as rescuer of his country and plunges the dagger into his own heart.

Iffland had even the tactlessness not only to produce in Mannheim a two-act farce, *Der schwarze Mann,* in which Schiller's indecision over the conclusions of his dramas was openly burlesqued, but even to wear a Schiller mask in playing the part of the poet " Flickwort " — whose commonest remark was: " Only over the catastrophe I am still uncertain " — though he himself had been partly responsible for the concessions that Schiller had made in the *Räuber* and *Fiesco.* But, after all, Schiller was only showing the true theatrical temperament in this very fact of not taking the destiny of his characters too seriously and concerning himself less with psychology and logic than with vigour of effects, atmosphere, and picture. He was, in fact, first and foremost a dramatist, even in his philosophical dialogues, for instance in the *Spaziergang unter den Linden,* which, although it is a purely theoretical discussion, he would not let go without an effective curtain. "WOLLMAR: Death has put his despotic seal on every point in the eternal universe. On every atom I read the desolate inscription, 'Past!' EDWIN: And why not 'been'? Even though every utterance is the swan-song of a happiness, yet it is also the hymn of all-present love. Wollmar, under this lime-tree my Juliet kissed me for the first time! WOLLMAR (*starting back*): Under this lime-tree I lost my Laura!"

On the other hand he was no lyrical poet — as to that he was just as clear in his own mind as he was about the defects of his

Schiller as a didactic

299

dramas. Thus he said of the Laura odes, for instance, that "the whole lot were overdone," and it is only because German pedagogues are remote from art that these have found a place in the anthologies. Some of them in their unconscious humour remind us absolutely of Wilhelm Busch: for instance, these lines from *Gang nach dem Eisenhammer:*

> "Tell, rascal, or prepare to die!"
> Sternly he spake and terribly.
> "Who dares aspire to Kunigonde?"
> "Oh, no, I'm speaking of the blonde."

Nor was he at the time even a good story-teller: thus he leads off his story *Eine grossmütige Handlung aus der neuesten Geschichte* with an utter clumsiness: "Plays and novels open to us the finest traits of the human heart"; and he suddenly interrupts the story thus: "The girl — but no; of her we will tell at the end." In all the epic works of this period the description never crystallizes into pure creation, but fluctuates between didactic poetry in the style of Gellert and feuilletonism in the style of Vulpius. The author was continually putting in his own comments, demonstrating, and moralizing with advice or awful example, and disturbing us by making us peep into his workshop. Think of passages like this in *Verbrecher aus verlorener Ehre:* "The following part of the story I pass over altogether; the merely terrible has nothing instructive for the reader." And, in general, the artistic vision of the young Schiller was still altogether clouded by the Enlightenment, so that he saw the chief aim of poetry as the moral improvement of the public — as he himself said a thousand times — and it was only in his dramas that he failed to carry his principles into practice; there the magnificent creative urge was stronger than his didactic intentions. Even to the stage, however, he attributed in principle a utilitarian object: that we should make the acquaintance of rascals so that we may guard ourselves against them. "We must meet them or avoid them, we must destroy them or become their subjects. But henceforth they cannot take us by surprise, we are prepared for their attacks. The stage has given us the secret of showing them up and making them harmless." This was also the source of his fondness for the black-and-white technique, the contrast of pure angelic figures like Louise and Amalia and double-dyed villains like Wurm and Franz Moor — to which, however, his plays owe a good deal of their effectiveness.

Even into music this didacticism penetrated for a time; witness Haydn, who, with Mozart and Gluck, formed the age's triumvirate of great composers. All three lived in Vienna and (as is the rule with genius in that city) were inadequately recognized. Gluck had been Hofkapellmeister under Maria Theresa and yet it was not till he was in his sixties, in 1774, that he had his first great success, with the performance of *Iphigenia in Aulis* in Paris, although there he had first to overcome the firmly rooted tradition of Lully and Rameau. Even while the rehearsals were going on, the dispute was continued in the " *cercles,*" the " *assemblées,*" and the coffee-houses between the Gluckists and the Piccinists — the followers of Niccolò Piccini, the gifted protagonists of the Neapolitan style. Long before the first performance the theatre was besieged, and middlemen tried to make many times the price of admission; when after a succession of sold-out houses an attempt was made to put on a performance of Rameau's *Castor and Pollux,* almost no one went to it. Even the Dauphine, Marie Antoinette, who had far less interest in intellectual life than in the gaming-table and her dressmaker, was enthralled: when she was riding through the Bois de Boulogne one day, she suddenly wheeled her horse with the exclamation: " *Mon dieu, Gluck,*" dashed after the master, and overwhelmed him with compliments; and the surrounding crowd was deeply moved and cried: " What a kind beautiful queen we shall have one day!" In the same year *Orpheus,* which had had only a moderate success in Vienna, was welcomed enthusiastically in Paris. But full victory did not come till the *Iphigenia in Tauris* in 1779; the earlier opponents were struck dumb and even Piccini became a Gluckist.

In the dedication of *Alceste,* which was addressed to the Grand Duke of Tuscany (later the Emperor Leopold II), Gluck says: " It was my object to banish all the abuses which had made their way into Italian opera through the vanity of singers and the weakness of composers and had transformed the finest and most glorious of all spectacles into the most ridiculous and wearisome. . . . I have endeavoured to remove all those excrescences against which common sense and good taste have so long been fighting in vain.

. . . I have further thought it my chief task to aim at a beautiful simplicity and have avoided making play with artistic trickery at the cost of clearness." In actual fact these words do contain the Gluckian reform. He liberated opera from the arrogant and absurd dominance of the *aria di bravura* and humanized it and deepened it by his honest truthfulness, vivid characterization, and genuineness of feeling. Yet a Classicistic coldness and self-consciousness barred him from attaining his final aims. His under-painting of recitatives, his grand finales and monologue arias and "*Intradas*," which were "to prepare the audience for the action and, so to say, herald its content" (in Italian opera there had been no sort of connexion between overture and drama), remained dominant for generations. His work represents, in opposition to Metastasianism, the victory of simplicity, of naturalness and sincerity; but on the other hand, just because of its architectonic clarity and impressive cleanness of line, it meant also a reduction and devitalization — a victory of that conception of art which was destined to play a grandiose and fateful rôle in the cultural life of Europe, and which we shall have later to treat in much more detail.

What Paris was to Gluck, London became to Haydn; there his symphonies brought him an overwhelming return in the form of money, social recognition, and public honour. His church music, though often attacked for its worldliness, is yet deeply Catholic and still almost Baroque: it affirms the world — but only on the underlying basis of transcendence. In his world-famous oratorios the *Creation* and the *Seasons* speaks the century's Rousseau-idea of nature, but refined by the gentle purity of an *anima candida* of true simplicity.

Mozart's equation of life

Mozart, too, lived in Vienna in just as poor circumstances as Gluck and Haydn had at first done, but refused, nevertheless, an invitation of Frederick William II, who offered him a well-endowed position as court musician in Berlin. Almost all his operas were performed for the first time in Vienna, although they seldom ran for any time, owing to petty and nasty intrigues: at the first night of *Figaro* the Italians of set purpose sang so badly that the thing failed, although it was at once a wild success in Prague. Mozart's work is, perhaps, in its many-sidedness and scope, the most astonishing achievement in all European artistic history. He was in everything a master, and Haydn, who was his devoted friend, said of him : " If Mozart had written nothing else than the violin quartets and his *Requiem,* he would have been immortal for those alone." His output included operas, symphonies, sonatas, and cantatas, church music and chamber-music : in all more than six hundred works. And the depth of his output is on a level with its extensiveness, a wealth of ideas pursuing and crossing each other, yet never confusing or disturbing ; copious and controlled as only in the case of Shakspere, with whom he shared too the same strange mixture of seriousness and humour. All this he poured forth, in a life of not quite thirty-six years, at a breathless terrifying *prestissimo* that makes us feel as if he foresaw that little time would be given to him, and reminds us of Schiller and Nietzsche, who also worked at such extreme pressures. We must, in fact, assume that every man has his specific inner tempo, which a mind capable of observing all the facts could probably express by an equation of one sort or another. There are certain obviously eruptive natures that are carried away by so tremendous an acclamation that they accomplish the whole span of their life and activity in half the normal period. It seems almost as if Schiller in his *Demetrius* fragment, Nietzsche in his *Antichrist* fragment, had fulfilled their last potentialities, like a steam-engine whose pressure-gauge has come to a stand at its maximum. The same is true of others who have been torn from the world too soon, of Kleist, Novalis, Raphael, Alexander the Great. In the psychological sphere the clock is a very inadequate meter ; the true measure of time here is the number of impressions and associations. Ideas *en masse* may crowd in upon the spirit so thickly that in a comparatively short time it accomplishes a man's whole destiny. An inkling of this lies in all geniuses who died young : the dramas of Kleist are written in a fever ; Novalis, tragically prophetic, gave his work the title of *Fragments;* Raphael painted night and day ; Alexander, with a dazzling impetuosity, tore through the war and peace history of a whole dynasty in thirteen years.

With Mozart, too, it is impossible to picture any development beyond *Figaro, Don Giovanni,* and the *Magic Flute,* and the history of the art up to this day would justify the assertion that they represent the climax not only of Mozart's music, but of man's. These three marvellous works of German honesty and simplicity are married with the silvery lightness and dreamy fancy of the

Rococo, while in the last of them the Enlightenment, also indefinitely deepened, finds musical voice. There was another genius, too, in whom the Enlightenment culminated, though in everything else he little resembled Mozart. His first epoch-making work was published in the same year as Mozart's first secular opera; 1781 saw the first performance of *Idomeneo* and the first edition of the *Critique of Pure Reason*.

In Kant there are two individualities whom we must distinguish, one bound to its time, the other timeless. In his views of law and State, society and church government, education and conduct, he remains completely on the footing of the Enlightenment; whenever he sets foot in the empirical world, he coincides fairly accurately in essentials with the leading spirits of the century: in physics with Newton, in theology with Leibniz, in æsthetics with Schiller, in historical philosophy with Lessing. But as a philosopher —that is, as an investigator of human cognition—he was a unique and miraculous phenomenon, a brain so formidably big, of such superhuman sharpness of discrimination, of such power to think things out to the end, as has once only appeared on this earth. He has a unique place not only in his times, not only in humanity, but in philosophy as well. Confucius, Buddha, Heraclitus, Plato, Augustine, and Pascal, and all other philosophical minds of the rank that confers immortality have created sublime thought-poems, but Kant was anything rather than a poet; he was a pure thinker, the purest that has ever lived. His work is not the individual vision of an artist, who carries us away by the force of his imagination, but the universally valid formulation of an investigator, who overpowers us by the force of sheer sagacity and observation. *His* system at least Frederick the Great could not have called a romance. Himself he said he was the historian of the human reason: one might also call him its inspired oceanographer, vivisector, and detective.

Yet at once we must add a correction. He was no poet, no realizer of self-created worlds, and he was an artist, if at all, only in respect of the clear lucid structure of his system; but at the same time he possessed fancy, and a type of fancy which in this extreme or even absurd form had never yet existed. He was the first to lecture on " physical geography," which was his most popular and his favourite course, and which he held almost every other term. In this, although he had never travelled beyond the environs of his native town of Königsberg, never seen the sea, or a world-city, or lush vegetation, or a single mountain range or great river, he described all the regions of the world with such liveliness and vigour in every detail that all who did not know him took him for a world-traveller. He once gave so accurate and definite an account of Westminster Bridge that an Englishman who was present said he must be an architect who had spent several years in London. This, in fact, was the peculiar type of his fancy, that he could visualize what he had never seen, and, for that matter, *what no man had ever seen.* This region, in which only he could see corporeally, clearly, and exactly, was human reason, and this was the gift that makes him unique in all human history.

It might appear that there was a double Kant in yet another sense than this.

There was one Kant who with unparalleled analytical power penetrated and broke up everything, a radical and revolutionary, a nihilist and merciless iconoclast of all hitherto existing world-conceptions. But there was also another Kant, who was nothing but the *petit bourgeois* of a provincial city remote from the world, Old Prussian, Protestant, pedantic, narrow, and conservative, who capitulated to the power of the State, the dogma of the Church, and public opinion, who lived day after day with the same exact allocation of hours, who left his home, returned from the university, ate his dinner, and went his walk so punctually that the neighbours set their clocks by him.

The " All-mutilator " and the " All-veiler "

Yet the reconciliation of these two apparently hostile souls in Kant carries with it the sense of his whole philosophy — to what extent we can for the moment only suggest. He showed realities as *theoretically* unproved and unprovable, or even as error and phantom, but at the same time as *practically* desirable, valuable, and necessary, or even as fact and certainty. The empirical world is unreal, phenomenal, but faith in it is a categorical imperative: and in this one proposition his *whole* philosophy, both the theoretical and the practical, is contained. With such a method of proof, by an exhausting but inevitable route, reality which was but now denied is again affirmed, and in all its details, including the world of " common sense." If one's thoughts have penetrated thus far, one can — nay, must — live by the clock — the world-clock, which is no doubt merely fictitious and phenomenal, but must be believed in, at the cost of a logical contradiction, as a mortal duty.

Furthermore, in the depths of Kant's clear soul there still lives, half hidden from himself, a deep religious and pietistic element which both posits and fuses these contradictions: he has a deep humility before the Creator — we have no right to set up his existence and that of the world as a scientific axiom, and so make them dependent in any way on our minds. In his doctrine of the antinomies, as is well known, Kant showed that all rational proofs of the existence of God fail, for if we deny God, we are landed in atheism, and if we affirm him, in anthropomorphism. Thus we can say neither that God exists nor that he does not. In reality his piety was speaking and he meant: Who are we that we should say there is a Creator?

The legend of these reputed "two Kants" not only figures throughout the record of his later fame, but was widespread even among his contemporaries. The most brilliant and most witty expression of it is Heine's, in his *History of Religion and Philosophy in Germany*, where he attempts to prove that Kant only wrote the *Critique of Practical Reason* to please his old servant Lampe. "After the tragedy comes the farce. Immanuel Kant so far has played the inexorable philosopher, he has stormed heaven and put the whole garrison to the sword, the Lord of the world swims unproved in his own blood . . . and then Immanuel Kant takes pity and shows that he is not only a great philosopher, but a good man; and he reflects and then, half in goodness of heart and half in irony, he says: 'Old Lampe must have a God, otherwise the poor man cannot be happy; and men are meant to be happy in the world, so the practical reason tells us — well, then the practical reason may, as far as I am concerned, vouch for the existence of God.' Upon this argument Kant distinguishes between theoretical and practical reason; and with the latter, as with a magic wand, he revived the corpse of the Deism which theoretical reason had killed." In this conception, even thus mellowed by graceful wit, is disclosed all that shallowness of "Young Germany" which could only assimilate as much of Kant as its own spirit understood: that is, its easy and unessential polemic against clericalism. But even as late as the beginning of this century Haeckel in his popular *Miracles of Life* drew up a table of the Antinomies of Immanuel Kant in which he set out the contradictions which were held to exist between his first and his second main works; there were two columns with eight points in each — " Kant I " the " All-mutilator " and " atheist by pure reason," and " Kant II," the " All-veiler " and " theist by pure reason."

On the contrary, the view that Kant himself was frightened after the event at the destruction wrought by his *Critique* and tried to make good the damage is untenable; one has only to read him without prejudice to see that the *Critique of Practical Reason* is clearly foreshadowed in the already mentioned chapter of the *Pure Reason* that treats of rational theology. Moreover, Kant himself expressed his view quite unequivocally in the preface to the second edition of the *Pure Reason,* which appeared *before* the first edition of the *Practical Reason:* " I had to eliminate knowledge in order to make room for faith; and the dogmatism of metaphysics . . . is the source of all the unbelief that disputes with morality and is always very dogmatic indeed." Kant established faith firmly against any attack from science, because he withdrew it once and for all from the scope of the theoretic reason. Judgments such as " right " or " wrong " are quite meaningless when applied to the content of religious consciousness, just as the Nietzschean immoralist stands beyond true and false.

In trying now briefly to set forth the fundamental ideas of the Kantian philosophy we must begin by stating that it is not, as its professorial manner and didactic structure might mislead us into supposing, a doctrine imparting a new knowledge, but a call to a moral and spiritual reflection which demands a new *being*. It is a way and not an end, and in order to take it in the right spirit we need, not only a certain interest and understanding of philosophical problems, but a definite temperament, an innate direction of the will towards truth and purity. For this reason numbers of clever and educated men have declared themselves unable to understand Kant, while many simple unphilosophic minds have found in his thoughts, which have penetrated into them by strange channels, the highest consolation and deepest illumination. " Philosophy," says Kant, " cannot be learnt. Mathematics, physics, history can be learnt, but not philosophy; it is only philosophizing that can be learnt." A philosophy that can be learnt would to him

The Critique of Reason

be no philosophy; it would be merely "historical" and not philosophical knowledge.

Further, I must ask the reader to be patient if he fails to understand some things at first glance; much will only be cleared up by what follows, and this time it will be advisable to read the text twice.

Philosophy is knowledge: that is perhaps the one thesis on which philosophers have been agreed. This knowledge takes place through our means of knowing, and in the modern age two main philosophical tendencies had grown up: the Sensualists had put the chief weight on sense-impressions, the Rationalists on the functions of the intellect. The common activity of the senses and the intellect forms what we call "experience." Now, so far, philosophers had sought to test the sense-impressions and the conclusions of the intellect with respect to their character and trustworthiness, but had taken the fact of experience for granted. It is very common, even in ordinary life, to call a sequence of thought that is based on the acceptance of unproved data uncritical. The whole philosophy so far had been in this regard simple and credulous, uncritical and dogmatic. But the Kantian philosophy is *critical,* and in the great struggle of the Rationalists and the Sensualists it aims at being the unbiased arbitrator and at being to the old academical metaphysic what chemistry is to alchemy, or astronomy to astrology. Kant puts the whole problem further back and asks whence all experience comes. How is it possible? How is knowledge itself known? One can only know a fact when one knows all the conditions from which it arose. Because Kantian philosophy seeks out what precedes the birth of our knowledge, it calls itself "transcendental" — which must not be confused with "transcendent," being rather its opposite. Transcendental means what lies this side of experience, precedes it; transcendent is what is beyond experience, overlaps it. The subject which the critical philosophy investigates is reason independent of all experience, reason as it is before all experience, as simple potentiality of experience; and hence it is called "pure" reason. The three basic faculties of pure reason are perception, or the faculty of receiving sense-impressions; thought, or the faculty of conquest; and reason (in the narrower sense), the faculty of ideas. By the activity of our reason there arises what

Kant calls the " phenomenon " : that is, the world as it appears to our consciousness; while that which is at the base of these phenomena is the "thing-in-itself," the thing as it is apart from our way of comprehending it, which in itself can never be known by us. On the whole, this terminology is unfortunately chosen, it is artificial and scholastic, vague and difficult to understand — indeed, capable of being misunderstood — and could have been easily replaced by terms more popular, more manageable, and clearer: thus, for example, he sometimes calls the thing-in-itself the " transcendental object," though, since it is beyond all experience, he should have called it the " transcendent object " — even if such an expression were permissible in any case, for it contains a *contradictio in adiecto,* in that something which transcends our consciousness can never become an object to us.

This wilful terminology, combined with the grandfatherly, twisted, and tedious style which Kant chose for his chief works, has frightened many off the study of his philosophy. Heine speaks of his grey, dry, brown-paper style; Schopenhauer of his " brilliant dryness " and of the " unclear, indefinite, inadequate, and sometimes obscure " language of the *Critique.* On the whole, however, these books are not so much badly written as just circumstantial and without artistic intention. The sentences are ground, but also polished; long-winded, but also strong-winded. Kant was not a classical prose-writer of the rank of Schopenhauer, but a first-class author who was very well capable of expressing himself smoothly, clearly, and even amusingly. Herder, who attended his lectures for two years, praised them thus : " Jest, wit, and good nature were all at his command, and his instructional lectures were a most delightful way of spending one's time." His favourite authors were Cervantes, Swift, Montaigne, and Lichtenberg, and the style of his earlier works is, with all its profusion of thought, clear and concise, often charming and humorous. But in the *Critique of Pure Reason* he went in for a completely new style of writing, which keeps coldly and rigidly to business, never admits the slightest mitigation, and scorns all consideration for the reader. His motive in this can only have been a deliberate intention, partly because he regarded the subject as too lofty to be satisfied by a merely pleasant presentation, partly because he wanted by his very form to put up a wall between himself and the popular philosophers.

The starting-point of Kant's philosophy is to be found in Hume, who, as will be remembered, had asserted that the causation-idea, association according to cause and effect, did not arise from experience, but was added by our thought to the events, so that of a *post hoc* we make a *propter hoc*. Kant took up this line of thought, but only to penetrate much deeper: he showed that the idea of causality was indeed something not contained in the things themselves, but that it was not imported into them *a posteriori* after experience, but was in ourselves before all experience, *a priori* — since through it experience first becomes possible, since in fact it *makes* our experience. It is the same with the idea of substance, of which Hume had also asserted that it had been discovered by ourselves and of our own will through mere observation of the constant association of certain properties and of the other Categories of "pure" reason-concepts, called so by Kant because they exist independently of our experience, which only comes into existence through them. The fundamental error of Hume had been that he confused the Categories with the ideas of kind, which latter do only arise from experience, since they are taken from, abstracted from, the individual objects.

The whole *Critique of Pure Reason* is in reality nothing but the application of this main idea to all spheres of cognition. The *a priori* forms of knowledge are: first, our forms of intuition — namely, space and time — which are the bases of the absolute validity of our geometric and arithmetic judgments, and are treated in the "Transcendental Æsthetic" (answering the question how pure mathematics is possible); secondly, the forms of thought, the twelve Categories or basic concepts of the understanding which make valid the universal axioms of the understanding and are dealt with in the "Transcendental Analytic" (answering the question how pure science is possible). Complete necessity and universality are only possessed by these pure intuitions and ideas, which are before all experience, since they spring from the human soul and its fundamental powers, while judgments which are obtained from experience only possess "assumed," "comparative," or "inductive" universality. Of them we can only say that, so far as has been perceived, there are no exceptions to this rule. Obviously by this method Kant turned the whole of the earlier philosophy upside down. It had been taken for granted that truth could only be won from experience, but Kant said that experience only gives conditioned and approximate truth, while absolute truth can only be found previous to experience, outside it, and without it.

Space and time are no properties of things, nor yet built up out of our observation of the external world; on the contrary, what we call the external world has time and space as precondition. The fact that things are simultaneous or successive already assumes time as pre-existing, just as space is assumed in the juxtaposition or separation of things. Space and time are the form in which things appear, in which they must appear, without which they cannot appear at all. Space and time cannot be thought away from out of things, but, on the contrary, space and time can very well be thought without any phenomena. All actual or even possible objects of our experience exist under the dominion of these two forms of intuition; but then it follows, also, that this dominion only extends as far as our experience, it is absolutely valid only within the empirical world of the human being. What we call reality, the observed world as it is brought to us by our perceptions, by the transcendental, *a priori* faculty which precedes all experience, is in fact only appearance, an ideal world in which things exist merely as phenomena of our consciousness and not as they are " in themselves," and thus they possess, as Kant says, at the same time empirical reality and " transcendental ideality."

Our data are, in the first place, only formless sense-impressions, which then are ordered by our " intuitive reason " in space and time, and by this means become phenomena. But these phenomena, again, have to be ordered and brought into a legitimate relation. This task is solved by the " thinking reason," or intellect, with the help of " pure concepts," by means of which appearances become experience. Perception only gives us the objects, and they have to be thought by means of concepts. Percepts without concepts are blind, concepts without percepts are empty. Since the understanding is the faculty of judgment, there arise from the separate forms of judgment the Categories, by means of which it grasps the world, and of which there are twelve. Kant worked out this table of the Categories, to which he was deeply attached, with the greatest care, but we need not go into any greater detail, since it does not mean much more than a clever scholastic game; it does not affect the main ideas of his system, and it is by no means unassailable, for by no means all the concepts which it arrives at are " pure " in the Kantian sense. They are particularly obnoxious to the finely critical remark that Paulsen made about Kant's doctrinal structure in general: " Many handsome and upstanding parts of his system are a little like the artificially inserted boughs of a Christmas-tree in the market-place."

How is Nature possible? Far more important — nay, the very centre of the Kantian philosophy — is the immediately following and difficult doctrine of " Transcendental Apperception." We have been told that things appear to us, not only in juxtaposition in space and succession in time, but also in settled and necessary relationship; and that the relating takes place by means of the concepts of our understanding, the result being what we call experience. But in experience things appear to us only in an actual and not in a necessary relation. Yet the relations affected by our intellect occur with the claim and character of strict necessity and universality. How can that be? Simply because we ourselves, owing to our unitary constitution, accomplish the synthesis through the " transcendental *a priori* unity of apperception." The world which is given to our senses in the first place as a dark chaotic manifold is apperceived from the first as a unity, by the unity of our consciousness; thus it *is* a unity and a *necessary* one. That the world we picture is always the same can only be explained by the unity and immutability of our " pure " consciousness, which exists before all the world and so forms the " highest principle " and the " radical faculty " of human knowledge. The unity of our ego is the true foundation for the unity of the world; " nature " becomes to us an object; the object of experience, the content of consciousness, a visible and duly ordered ensemble, because we have made it into this object by the already present faculties of contemplation and understanding which are in our soul. " Relating," says Kant, " cannot lie in the objects and cannot be extracted from them by our perception, but can only be an arrangement of the intellect," which itself is nothing else than the facility of

312

a priori relating. Our intellect, of its own activity, generates spontaneously, by means of a faculty which Kant calls "productive imagination," definite relations and laws, the so-called "laws of nature." "The intellect does not get its laws out of Nature, but prescribes them for her." That is the answer to the question: how is nature possible?

This conclusion represents the highest point of the *Critique of Pure Reason*. There follows the "Transcendental Dialectic," the theme of which we have already briefly touched upon: the refutation of the previous theology, cosmology, and psychology, the disciplines which sought to prove the existence of God and the soul, human freedom, and continued existence after death, by logical methods. It puts the question: how is metaphysics possible? And the answer is that, since metaphysics deals with transcendence, which can never become the subject of our knowledge, it is impossible as science, but possible and real as an unending problem set before man. God, the soul, freedom, immortality are "ideas" which can be neither proved nor disproved; they are matters of faith. As phenomenon, as empirical being, man is subject to the laws of causality, but as "thing-in-itself" and noumenal being he is free and knows no law, but subject only to moral "judgment": as such, however, he can only *think* himself. Our reason is incapable of proving that man is free, that he has an immaterial and immortal soul, that a being of supreme wisdom and goodness rules the world, but it may and should — nay, in virtue of its metaphysical disposition, must — look upon the world and on man *as if* it were so. Ideas do not give us laws like the Categories, but only maxims, guiding lines; they are not "constitutive," but merely "regulative" principles, not a real object of our intellect, but an ideal of our reason, the reason in the narrower and higher sense, which is nothing else than the faculty of forming ideas. In the same way science, as knowledge of the totality of the world, is only such an ideal of our mind, unattained and unattainable, which yet we must ceaselessly aspire to. The value of "ideas," then, consists, not in their realizability, but in their directing all our thought and action. God, freedom, immortality, the whole kingdom of science are problems which the noumenal ego puts before the empirical ego for solution.

The *Critique of Pure Reason* has put and answered three questions. The first is: how is pure mathematics possible? And the answer is: through our perceptions, our faculty of pure intuition, which makes the impressions or sensations — the only thing which is actually given — into phenomena by ordering them in space and time. The second question is: how is pure knowledge of nature possible? And the answer is: through our intellect, the faculty of " pure " concepts, which out of the phenomena, through ordering them under the Categories, makes up our experience. The third: how is metaphysics possible? is answered thus: through our reason, the faculty of ideas, which has the unending problem of creating science out of our experience. To the inclusive question to which the three may be reduced — namely, how does reality come into being? — the answer is: by pure reason.

Question	Faculty		Form	Product	
How is pure mathematics possible?	Sensation		Intuition	Phenomena	
How is pure science possible?	Intellect	Pure Reason	Concepts	Experience	Empirical Reality
How is metaphysics possible?	Reason (in the narrower sense)		Ideas	Science	

The human reason in the exercise of all its faculties is a merely forming force: space, time, the Categories, the Ideas are all forms which are brought to the content which is put before them; the " stuff " of our reason is the sensations, of which we can only say that they " affect " us. Since reason prescribes laws for the whole of reality, it follows that these laws are, for us, inviolable, and further that they are valid *only for us*. What the world really is, apart from our methods of comprehension, we cannot even imagine, since everything that comes before our consciousness is straightway phenomenal and possesses transcendental ideality. We can only say that there is something " at the base of " the appearances; that behind the things, beyond our capacity for experience, there is still something more, the Thing-in-itself. This

314

Thing-in-itself, which is not included under the space- and time-forms of intuition nor under the thought-forms of substance and causality, is a mere limit-notion; it marks the frontier at which our knowledge ceases.

Kant compared himself with Copernicus, and the *Critique of Pure Reason* does in fact mean a complete reversal of the hitherto existing world-picture. Only he really reverses it in an opposite way to Copernicus. For Copernicus said that man had till then believed the earth was the centre of the universe, all of whose movements were regulated according to it, whereas in reality the earth is only a tiny satellite of the sun and the great universe of worlds, and its path is regulated accordingly. Kant took the opposite path: hitherto man had believed that his knowledge was regulated by the objects of the external world; in reality the whole world has to be regulated according to him and his knowledge, through which alone, in fact, it can acquire existence. Nevertheless both systems have the same point: in our first volume we indicated that the new astronomy, which stands at the opening of the New Age, while it did reduce the earth to a tiny spot of light and extended the universe to terrific dimensions, at the same time raised man to be the power that pierces and unveils the cosmos; so that a finite but impenetrable magic-world was replaced by an infinite and yet calculable mathematical-world. In the same way Kant hurls man down to the depths of powerlessness and darkness and proves to him irrefutably that he is separated from knowledge of the " true " world, the world-in-itself, by insuperable barriers; but at the same time he makes him the creator and absolute lawgiver of the empirical world, whose enormous expanses can no longer make him fearful. The *Pure Reason* thus marks at once the lowest subjection and the highest triumph of human reason: man is a vanishingly small point in the universe, but this cipher imposes its laws on the universe.

The final chapter of the *Pure Reason* forms the transition to Kant's second great work, the *Critique of Practical Reason*, which appeared seven years later. The ideas of freedom, immortality, and divinity are inaccessible by theoretical paths, since they are beyond our experience, but they are unattainable by the practical, since by our moral will we can make them (not, of course, objective, but at least) subjective and personal certainties and

The primacy of Practical Reason

315

can make them objects of faith. The *Pure Reason* deals with the laws of our knowing, the *Practical Reason* with the laws of our action. Now, just as the laws of theoretical reason only possess rigid necessity and universality because they are not drawn from experience, but existed before all experience, so the laws of the practical reason can only claim unconditional validity if they are not abstracted from our empirical life, if (since the *content* of our action always comes from experience) they have a purely *formal* character.

As the theoretical reason dictates laws to the phenomenal world, so the practical gives to itself the moral law, which runs: " Always act so that the maxims of your will can be valid as principles of universal application." Either practical principles contain precepts which are only valid upon certain conditions, as, for instance: " *If* you want to be a master, you must train yourself," in which case we have a Hypothetical Imperative; or else they have an unconditional validity independent of all assumptions, as, for instance: " Thou *shalt* not lie," in which we have a Categorical Imperative. The moral law is such a Categorical Imperative, it is absolute and unconditioned, independent of all assumption, valid everywhere and always, before all experience, without any empirical confirmation, it is valid even if it is never or nowhere put into practice. " Morality is not the means to make us happy, but the means to make us worthy of happiness." We must observe the moral law from a feeling of duty, and not as an inclination, for if it were followed through inclination, it would be done for its own sake. Here we are at the summit of Kantian moral philosophy, on the raw pure glacial heights of absolute ethics.

The moral law within us says: " thou shalt," and from this " shalt " the " canst " must follow, else the demand would be absurd. As a sense-being man is subject to the necessities of nature, as a moral being he is free. In this form metaphysical ideas gain a new reality. We must will absolute moral perfection; and since this is unattainable at any period of our earthly life, our moral consciousness demands immortality. For similar reasons our practical reason demands the existence of God, freedom, and the soul. These ideas are not axioms of the pure reason, but postulates of the practical reason.

The action of the moral law within us is proof of the possibility, even the reality, of human freedom. Our moral faculty is to our knowing faculty as the noumenal is to the phenomenal world: the latter depends on the former, and hence Kant says that the practical has the primacy over the theoretical reason. The sense-world is through and through phenomenal, the appearance of a noumenal world that is its basis; in the same way our own physical existence, our empirical character are simply the appearance of our noumenal, our moral, existence. What is our moral ego then? It is nothing else than the " Thing-in-itself."

The *Pure Reason* had laid down that "intelligible" entities, ideas, things-in-themselves, could never be known or cognized, but only "thought" and believed. The *Practical Reason* asserts that they shall and must be thought, and believed, and made regulative of our being and action. For our speculative reason they are mere possibilities, desirabilities, ideals, hypotheses; but for our moral reason they are realities, necessities, categorical commands.

The *Critique of Practical Reason* is the crowning of the *Critique of Pure Reason*, without which it would have been a mere torso and question-mark. For, in fact, only unfairness or lack of understanding could see a contradiction between the two works, which are as organically connected as the two parts of *Faust* or Dante's *Inferno* and *Paradiso*. In both it is fundamentally the same view and method that controls the line of thought. Kant says of the Categorical Imperative that it " lies latent in our disposition," so that the moral law is as much *a priori* as the natural. Our conceptions of good and evil no more originate in experience than our intuitions of space and time do so. As a knowing being, man gives laws to the external world; as moral being, he gives laws to himself, legislator and subject in the same person. It is he who makes his own physical and moral worlds. Our theoretic reason *thinks* the world a unity intuitively ordered and related by law; therefore it *is* an intuitive and ordered world. Our practical reason *wills* man as a free and moral being, and therefore he *is* moral and free.

We must forgo a discussion of Kant's other works, and will only mention, as to his third main work, the *Critique of Judgment*, that he was the first to define the Beautiful exhaustively and convincingly; it is only since his day that there has been a science of æsthetics. Here too he showed that beauty is no idea which we get from experience, but a *judgment* or predicate which we bring to it: it is not the things that are æsthetic, but our ideas of them.

With this the construction of the system was accomplished in its three main divisions. Kant's philosophy contains, as he himself said, an "inventory," an inventory of what at all times and by each one of us — that is, necessarily and universally — must be *theoretically known, practically willed, and æsthetically felt*. And the outcome is the conclusion that truth is a product of our understanding, morality a product of our willing, and beauty a product of our taste. The answer in each case is as surprising as it is obvious: we are reminded, if the comparison be permitted, of the solutions in detective stories which the reader would never have discovered for himself, but, once given, feels as convincing necessity: the way to them is very complex, but they themselves are compellingly simple.

The general result of the *Critique* was defined by the Abbé Galiani, one of the cleverest men of the eighteenth century, in the words: "the dice of nature are loaded." This conclusion is, in fact, devastating; and yet (it is difficult to put intelligibly what can really only be felt) all the typical figures of the time, which to themselves seemed so confused, so contradictory and problematic — Werther, Rousseau, and even man as conceived by Kant — convey to us the impression of a benevolent and truly Classical linearity, for they are so completely symmetrical and geometric in their structure, they fit into so perfect and comprehensive a scheme, like the Canon of the human figure that we see in the atlases of the art-schools. Everything seemed, to men of that time, to be tottering, and the Kantian discoveries seemed to break up the whole external world into a mere shadow-play of the mind; and yet how well-ordered and peaceful today do we feel its pigeon-holing of the world-picture under time, space, and causation! One thinks of nice uncles who bring children three big boxes, in which all the contents of their small world are tidily and lovingly packed. Even the unfortunate Werther seems to us nowadays an enviable soul-logician, for, after all, he had so definite a line, so clear an aim; and *the erotic-in-itself* was not yet a problem. But it seems to be a law of the psychology of history that whenever mankind actually reaches a fresh foothold, it feels itself to be tottering. And if there is any proof at all that such a thing as progress does exist, it may be found in the fact that we nowadays attribute primitiveness to the highly complicated eighteenth century.

To finish with the Kantian philosophy itself, its criticism, as is well known, fills whole libraries and is the subject of special institutes; there is even a " Kantian philology," a very precarious and almost hopeless science, since, as we said above, Kant is by no means consistent and simple in the use of his own expressions, and even the fundamental word of his whole study, the word " reason (*Vernunft*)," is a confusing and ambiguous term, since he uses it both for the whole of our knowledge and for the faculty of the ideas.

Of his important contemporaries, Hamann was Kant's most violent opponent; in his view, Kant was nothing but an extreme rationalist, thinker, speculator, " sitting behind the stove in his night-cap." The first effective objections to the *Critique* were those of Jacobi, who analysed with great clearness the contradictions inherent in the Kantian " Thing-in-itself." It is supposed to underlie our world of phenomena as their cause, and thus should fall under the category of causality; yet on the other hand causality may only be applied to phenomena and never for things which lie beyond our experience. Thus, says Jacobi, we cannot enter into the Kantian system *without* the assumption of knowable, and therefore real, things, and we cannot remain there *with* it: " to remain therein with this presupposition is a flat impossibility."

The remaining attempts to controvert Kantian phenomenalism rest mostly on misunderstandings. Thus, for instance, idealism has been confronted with what academic philosophy calls the " objective mind ": namely, the precipitate of human creative activity in super-individual creations of permanent significance and effect, such as right, morality, speech, science, and art: these having obviously a reality independent of our subjectivity. This, however, is to confuse the concepts of " objectivity " and " reality " It is quite possible that an immense mass of ideas should have the most irreproachable and irrefutable objectivity within the consciousness of all mankind without our being in a position to

319

say anything about their reality, if by that is understood something which is valid even beyond our imagination. Philosophical idealism does not assert that the external world depends on the caprice of the individual subject, that it is a purely personal imagining, but only that it is given to us in an apperception-form which is found only in human consciousness and can only be proved there. This apperception-form, whether we call it earthly, anthropomorphic, temporal, or what you will, is subjective; but in this case the "perceiving subject" is not the individual with his changing personal perceptions, but the imaginative life of all men, their consciousness as a species from its origins and (we can add, without limitation) to its furthest days. Paradoxical as it may appear at first blush, this form of intuition of ours, just because it is so subjective, is of the highest objectivity. For though it is valid only for spiritual organizations of our kind and disposition, it is for that very reason absolutely binding for all creatures of that type. The very fact that humanity, as far as we can trace its history, in all its creations — even in those which can only be explained as the result of collaboration of countless individuals — has always been subject to the same ever-recurring apperception-forms proves definitely that what we call the world and its history has purely the character of a phenomenon.

The transcendental philosophy has, however, also been attacked from the other end, by proving (or anyhow arguing) that our forms of intuition of space and time have not at all the universal validity which Kant supposes. It is, in fact, not self-evidently certain that space, as we conceive it, is the only possible space, or that it is common to all cosmic beings and has, as it were, an intermundane significance. Our space-conception — the Euclidean, as it is called — rests on the axiom that the shortest distance between two points is a straight line, and that consequently a plane can always be laid down through any three points in space. But this assumption is simply a human prejudice; for it is quite conceivable that there should be beings obstinate enough to believe that the foundation of their geometry is the curve. These creatures would live in a spherical world and would feel as comfortable and as much at home in this spherical world as we in our world of the plane. It is also theoretically conceivable that there should be "flatlanders" living in two dimensions and capable of getting on very well with this fraction of our *a priori* equipment. On the other hand spiritualism is based on the assumption of a fourth dimension. At the time of the wonderful discoveries made by Gauss and Riemann of the non-Euclidean geometries, it was believed that the transcendental philosophy had received its death-blow. But so far are they from refuting it that they in fact constitute its confirmation. For Kant maintained that Euclidean space was *our* idea — ours only, but for us the one possible and necessary conception. Other spaces are thinkable, but not imaginable. Kant's doctrine of the a-priorism of space would only be refuted if a man appeared who could visually imagine a non-Euclidean geometry, a flatland life, or a four-dimensional world. The same is true of the extraordinary discoveries of Einstein; they prove unambiguously that many times are possible, and that the idea of an absolute time valid for all parts of space is a human fiction. From this numerous investigators concluded that the transcendental philosophy was no longer tenable. For instance, in his admirable *Lectures on the Physical Basis of Natural Science* Franz Exner says: " If we ask ourselves what remains of the absolute concept of space and time postulated and set up by Kant, we must answer, almost nothing." But surely Kant's epoch-making achievement was just that he *destroyed* the idea of absolute space and time. His whole system is anticipated Relativity, and Relativity is nothing but the exact, scientific establishment of the Kantian doctrine by methods which were not yet at his disposal. The idea of time is for Kant not only something relative, but something which apart from our faculties of imagining has no intelligible sense. We cannot even think an " absolute " time, let alone represent it to ourselves, and an absolute space — that is, a space which exists unconditioned and independent of our apperception — would be, in the Kantian sense, a phenomenal Thing-in-itself and, therefore, nonsense.

It would, therefore, be hardly going too far to say that, in its main outline, the Kantian system is inexpugnable. In detail, however, as we have seen, it is not free from contradictions and ambiguities, and that, unfortunately, in respect of precisely its two cardinal ideas: namely, phenomenon and thing-in-itself.

Kant propounded his theoretical philosophy twice, once in the *Critique of Pure Reason*, once, two years after, in his

The impossible Thing-in-itself

Prolegomena to any future Metaphysic which is to present itself as science, which puts forward the doctrine in a much shorter form and is, as it were, the piano score of it. If we followed our empirical world to its origins inductively, as Kant does in his *Critique of Pure Reason,* we see how out of the stuff of our impressions or sensations arises intuition, out of it experience, and out of this again (by indefinite approximation to limits) science. Our impressions must thus be given to us as the indispensable prerequisite of all knowledge. There is no doubt that we build up our world of appearance with the help of imaginings, our world of experience with the help of concepts, and our moral world with the help of ideas, but we do not manufacture our sensations. All that we produce is the forms; the stuff which is worked up into these forms is not our product. It is the fundamentally primary, for the stuff must exist before the form. There is, therefore, after all, something objective at the bottom of our activity of knowing, which compels us to deny to it the character of complete subjectivity. In a word, Kant attributes to the phenomenal world an ideality that at bottom is no ideality.

If we take the opposite path, the *deductive,* as Kant did in the *Prolegomena,* we find, when we have abstracted from our knowledge the ideas and concepts and intuitions, a last remainder, the thing-in-itself, whose unknowability and unimaginability Kant always emphasized, but whose reality and existence he never disputed. But what reality can a thing have which is wholly inconceivable to us? If an object is so wholly outside the possibilities of experience, we cannot say *what* it is; we cannot even say *that* it is. We can never know anything about it, but only have faith in its existence — with the aid of our practical reason. In a word, Kant attributed to things-in-themselves a reality which at bottom is no reality.

The Kantian system thus hovers between Idealism and Realism, Subjectivism and Empiricism: it is "double-ended" (as Jacobi aptly said of this dual character) and makes possible two opposite misinterpretations. If we put ourselves at the extreme left, as it were, and misunderstand it from the real end, we shall see in it a revised Sensualism *à la Locke;* if we stand at the extreme right and misunderstand it from the ideal end, we shall confuse it with the radical spiritualism of Berkeley.

The centre, in which all the difficulties meet, is the Thing-in-itself. It is, as Solomon Maimon, one of the deepest and clearest of the Kantians, remarked only ten years after the publication of the *Critique of Pure Reason,* neither knowable nor unknowable: if we say it is inconceivable, we cannot possibly talk of it; but if we say it is conceivable, it ceases to be a thing-in-itself. It is an impossible idea, a no-thing; it is not like x, as Kant taught, but like $\sqrt{-a}$.

There is only one way to complete the transcendental philosophy: the Thing-in-itself must be dissolved. This was the problem set and solved by the Romantic philosophy. But before we turn our attention to it, we must study the third of the main currents of which we spoke at the beginning of this chapter, Classicism.

CHAPTER II

THE DISCOVERY OF THE CLASSICAL

"Nothing modern is comparable to the Classical: a man may not measure himself with gods." (Wilhelm von Humboldt) — "The wisdom of the Greeks was truly bovine." (Luther)

"Greece was the cradle of humanity, of peoples' love." (Herder) — "Humanity is a thing so un-Greek that the language has no word for it." (Wilamowitz)

"Hellenism, what was it? Intellect, moderation, and clearness." (Schiller) — "To discover noble souls, golden means, and other perfections in the Greeks was made impossible for me by the psychologist that lived in me." (Nietzsche)

"None but the Greeks have been healthy in body and soul. Our world is a vast pest-house." (Rückert) — "The whole of Greek culture was mined and perverted by hysteria. The Greeks were mad." (Bahr)

"The foundation of knowledge will always be the glory of the Greeks." (Lotze) — "Their spirit lacked the patient care to rise from the particular limited fact to general truth." (Dubois-Reymond)

"The ancients lived for this world, earthly reality was everything." (Curtius) — "It is a strange notion that the Greeks centred their thoughts only on this world. On the contrary, there is probably no people that has thought so much and so fearfully of the other world." (Rohde)

"Their temperament led the Greeks to think of life as a pleasant journey." (Taine) — "We are dealing with people which in the highest degree felt, and was necessarily conscious of, its suffering." (Burckhardt)

"Everyone finds in the Ancients what he needs or wants — and, above all, himself." (Friedrich Schlegel)

The Gentleman in the post-coach

On Wednesday, 24 September 1755, a tall, rather old-looking gentleman, of a sallow complexion, with hasty and clumsy movements and a professorial look, mounted the post-coach at Dresden, to travel via Bavaria and Tyrol to Italy. On 18 November he entered Rome by the Porta del Popolo, and with that entry more or less took possession of the Eternal City. The gentleman was the Prussian littérateur Johann Joachim Winckelmann, author of a small treatise on art, dealing with the imitation of Greek works, which had had a very favourable reception in specialist circles, and this passage of the Alps and entry into Rome was one of the most important events of modern cultural history — quite as significant for the history of German culture and literature as the Hohen-

324

staufen journeys to Rome had been for the history of German politics and religion — and at the same time the starting-point of one of the most fateful of all aberrations of the German spirit, which dominated it for many decades and turned it in a very peculiar way out of its normal course of development.

Winckelmann was by profession archæologist, historian and philologist, critic of art and literature, philosopher, museum director, archivist and librarian, dragoman, cicerone, and connoisseur; in actual fact, however, he was never anything more than that as which he had begun his academic life: namely, a university rector and pedagogue. He is one of the mightiest schoolmasters that the world and the German people have ever known, and one of the most preposterous: like all born teachers, very useful in the mass and depth of his learning, but harmful in his misguiding one-sidedness and obstinate dogmatism.

No people has had so extensive and varied a history as the Greeks. The reason lies in their unique genius, which allows us to make literally anything out of them. One of the main differences between genius and talent is that the latter is unambiguous, the other manifold, manifold like the world, which it mirrors completely in itself. As there are countless conceptions of Hamlet, so in the mutable minds of delighted posterity the most diverse explanations and valuations of the Greeks have been put forward: all are false and all are true. The inestimable value of Hellenic culture for humanity lies in the fact that it has always been able to act as the ready mould and fine vessel into which each age and every man could pour his own ideal. *The Genius among peoples*

But what is an " ideal " ? It is that which one both is and is not. No one can set up as his ideal anything which he does not bear latent in himself; nor yet anything that he has already realized, or even that he ever can realize. An ideal is at the same time our ego and our non-ego, our complementary polar opposite, our Platonic Other, towards which, through all our earthly course, we strive as vainly as indefatigably. These two contrary tendencies — to find in one's ideal both oneself and one's second higher self, one's complementary other — continually mingle together so as to make of the psychology of idealism an almost impossibly confused problem, the more so as the discrepancies are usually visible only to outside observers. For instance, the Enlightenment on the one hand saw the Greeks as rationalistic popular philosophers of the eighteenth century, and on the other hand praised their naturalness and force, their unity and simplicity, as the foil of the rational artificiality and multiplicity of the present. The school of Burckhardt, which culminates in Nietzsche, saw the Greeks as a tragic and romantic people, but also saw them as masters of life and virtuosi of the will-to-power, and their whole culture as the successful effort to cure themselves of the disease of romanticism.

Augustan, Carolingian, and Ottonian Renaissances
The first great " Rebirth of the Classical " occurred even within the Classical period itself, in the Golden Age of the Emperor Augustus. Then for the first time art set itself the since oft-repeated task of itself attaining mastery by imitating the recognized masterpieces of Greece. Thus Virgil copied Homer, Horace Archilochus and Anacreon, Ovid Theocritus, and Livy Thucydides; and because everything they did was second-hand, artistically worded and calculated, they achieved the waxwork perfection which made them into school-authors, even in their own lifetimes. Though the Romans wrote out more or less indiscriminately the authors of every age, and though in point of cultural level their closest affinity was with the Alexandrine age, they soon got into the habit of regarding Periclean literature as the only standard. At the same time they decreed to be alone Classical a style in architecture and sculpture that was refined almost to vacuity. And this too was possible only because it was " received," taken over; for a living style which is the child of its own time can never be classic.

These traditions, with certain variations, dominated the whole Imperial age. Then came the chaos, and when the obscurities began to clear somewhat, there followed towards the end of the eighth century the second great Renaissance, the Carolingian, in which Charles the Great sought to revive both the Roman Empire and the Roman culture. His hope was to make of Aachen a " Christian Athens," but in fact what was read at his court was almost exclusively the Latin authors, Ovid, Virgil, Sallust, Suetonius, Terence, Martial, Cæsar, and Cicero. For sons of the nobility attendance at the Latin school was compulsory, and the Emperor even thought, for a time, of making Latin the popular language. The Ottoman Renaissance, which falls in the second half of the tenth century, is of a somewhat different character. The son of Otto the Great, Otto II, had married the Greek princess Theophano, and the child of this union of German and Greek was Otto III, who dreamed of a Roman world-theocracy of German emperors and died at the age of twenty-two, reminding us in his parentage, his meteoric career, and his early end of Euphorion. He knew Greek perfectly, preferred the Byzantine dress and etiquette, and was, as his master Gerbert — the light of learning of the age — declared, more Greek and Roman than German. Yet the Ottonian Renaissance succeeded as little as the Carolingian in bringing Greek literature and art within the sphere of central Europe; the famous authors of the age are at both periods wholly under Latin influence. Ekkehard's *Waltharilied* is a shadow of Virgil, the dramas of the nun Hroswitha are modelled on the comedies of Terence, and Einhard's *Vita Caroli Magni* follows Suetonius even in detail. The Greeks were studied, if at all, in Latin translations; only the Irish understood a little Greek, and the Monastery of St. Gall for a time possessed *"Ellinici Fratres"* as a curiosity. That Greek literature was rescued to survive into modern times was due almost wholly to the Byzantines.

As for the Italian Rináscita, we have pointed out in the first volume that it also was predominantly a reawakening of the old Roman culture, an attempt to return to the art and attitude of the national ancestors; that Greek was unknown to Petrarch, the first great propagandist of the Classics, and even later was only studied in the Platonic Academy at Florence, and that, generally, out of the whole Classical inheritance all that was taken over was a stock of external (and moreover misunderstood) decorative elements: all sorts of minor *appliqués* of architecture, mechanically turned flowers of rhetoric, and pompous cheap allegory. It was frequently and emphatically maintained that Italy had always stood higher than Greece, and there was a definite bias against Greek studies. The Humanistic ideal was the " educated " Romans of the later Republic, whose culture was really based on political, military, and agricultural efficiency, but who affected a second-hand passion for scholarly poetastering, rhetoric, and philosophizing: a Romanness already enfeebled, dissipated, and decadent, which playacted about its own past. Greek civilization, on the other hand, as conceived in the Renaissance no less than in the Middle Ages, was a picture that had reached them first via the Romans and then via themselves; that is, at three removes from the original.

The same is true of the refurbishing of the Antique under Louis XIV; it is purely Latin, and the Greeks of Racine, Puget, and Poussin are Romans with Greek nicknames.

Even the *scavi* — the excavated ruins of Herculaneum (from 1737) and Pompeii (from 1748), and the remains (discovered about the same time) of Pæstum and Agrigentum, which, preserved for thousands of years in a protective desolation, for the first time unveiled to the modern eye the complete form of a Greek temple — were still viewed, under the influence of the place of discovery, with Roman eyes. In Germany during the first half of the eighteenth century Greek was still a theological subject and was learnt, so far as it was studied at all, in order to read the New Testament. Even then it was included among the oriental languages. Homer and Herodotus, Æschylus and Sophocles were read here and there, but never in the original, and many of the learned only knew them by name. Greek literature, said Winckelmann, had been almost driven forth from Germany.

But now, by the genius of this one man, Hellas was to rise up like an enchanted isle from the sea of the past, no doubt only as a deceptive mirage, but yet with a pure and clear-cut splendour that became the delight of his age.

Winckelmann's famous proposition that the only way for us to become great, and even possibly inimitable, was to imitate the Greeks ourselves provoked Klopstock to reply: " I must not imitate, and yet your words of praise tell always only of Greece. Yes! Let him who has the fire of genius in his heart imitate the Greeks ; for the Greeks discovered! " In fact, how could any thinker or artist more openly display his own and his age's poverty than by the advice to imitate anything, however great? Yet Winckelmann was a spirit anything but devoid of idea or of fancy ; rather he was a genius of invention, just as the Greeks had been. He too invented something — namely, the Greek.

The mis-set class-theme

We know today that Antiquity was not antique. Read Greek literature without preconception or minute scholarship, and you will find that Plato and Demosthenes were less old-fashioned than Mendelssohn or Professor Unrat, and that the gestures of Euripides' Medea must have been less classical than those of Charlotte Wolter. What the so-called humanistically trained minds have retained of Antiquity is a few lifeless pieces of costume : lyre and peplos, wreath of laurels or myrtle or olive. They are like Faust, who held in his hands nothing of Greek Helen but an empty robe: the rest was cloud. We know today that the Greek with the bright eyes and the Roman with the bronze forehead never existed, for the quite simple reason that it is impossible that such men could have lived at any time or in any place. We know, too, whence the German Classicists got their æsthetic and their idea of history: from the teaching and example of the generation that preceded them — a generation of physically and spiritually underfed schoolmasters, of stunted bookworms and twisted pedants — from the dusty corners of the library and the study, the ill-lighted stuffiness of small provincial streets, the poor warped and thwarted life of the miniature-world of the German Baroque. Today it is that world and not the Classical that we feel as a piece of past history: in its worm-eatenness, its odour of wood paving and oil-lamps, the anæmia produced by its non-albuminous fare and its pathetic-contemptible attempt to acquire seriousness and profundity by a stiff parade of knowledge and pretentious accumulation of proper names and book-titles. Everywhere, despite the love for the unadorned and the praise of Classic simplicity, ornament and trimming obtrude themselves. And what, in fact, was understood by this much-vaunted " simplicity of the Ancients " which was to be their luminous exemplar? Nothing but the enforced spiritual and bodily helplessness of the German house-tutor, subrector, and travelling companion. Fortunately, they were not at all simple, the Greeks and Romans, but very complex, incalculable, and fastidious; above all, men of a " late " period. But these other men, members of a beginning age that had but recently reawakened to intellectual life, first confused some bad plaster casts and corrupted scholia with the Greeks, and then further confused the caricature and marionette of Greek culture that they built up therefrom with — themselves! A people whose most prominent quality lay in a highly irritable and mobile faculty of uptake, in an almost over-developed gift of sight, were newly discovered and " understood " by a group of men who had actually never yet learnt to make use of their eyes and had built up their whole conception of the world at second hand from descriptions, extracts, and opinions about opinions.

Most grotesque of all, however, was the effect; it was as if a one-idea'd but amazingly efficient schoolmaster entered a class-room and, by his teaching, forced the minds of his pupils — all of them lively, talented, inquisitive children — once and for all into an oblique and receding path. All classical poetry became *work-shop poetry:* the dramas, stories, poems, treatises of the Classicists all have, as it were, tiny windows, the atmosphere of interiors, arti-ficial or, at best, indoor lighting, strong lines, but pale colours. Everything is narrow, badly ventilated, curtained over, half dark, alcoved; and all this was supposed to be imitation of the Greeks, who created and produced their plays, their sculptures, and their paintings in the open air, who pursued their artistic sport, their philosophy, and their rhetoric in the streets, who never held their political meetings or court sittings, their divine worship or theatri-cal performances under cover and were, in fact, "*plein-air*" crea-tures *par excellence.*

Schiller, one of the most powerful of German temperaments; Goethe, whose whole life, thought, and creations were an organized seership; whole generations of German sculptors and painters, who were by their innermost gifts cut out for Naturalism; even the leaders of the nominally anti-classical Romantic school — all, all took up the Classicist task-work. Napoleon, wild, hundred-eyed child of reality, had nothing more urgent to do as Emperor than to spread the empty veneer of the Empire style all over Europe.

The "Classical" Greek

Were we to believe this conception of Antiquity, the chief occu-pation of Greeks and Romans must obviously have been to read hard at Winckelmann, just as Rousseau's children of nature must have known the *Contrat social* by heart. This remarkable return to the Classical is only intelligible as a fundamental urge and last effort of the age to find — in a world of pure measure and propor-tion, clear order and easy oversight, self-limitation and avoidance of complication — relief and rest from its own problems, from the fluctuating formlessness and confusing multiplicity of its own strivings, situations, and outlooks. Classicism was born of the fears of modern man.

But it is on the other hand highly remarkable, a sort of invol-untary irony at one's own expense, that the ideal of the Classical was found in Alexandrinism, the sugary, lush, and literary sculp-ture of the Greek Baroque: men, in fact, instinctively made for that which was most closely akin to themselves. The Greek decadence was taken as the Classical ideal; a Greek that was no longer Greek, as the strong fabric of Hellenic being — such was, unconsciously, the heart of the Classicist theory. Winckelmann took as the " flower " of Greek art works like the Belvedere Apollo, the Belvedere Hercules, the Niobids, which are in truth the over-ripe, withered, and even rotting fruits of the Hellenic creativeness. Whenever the word " Greek " was mentioned, everyone thought at once almost inevitably of the Laocoon, the magnificent and heartless virtuoso-effort of a melodramatic self-consciousness, a mixture of brutality and sensitivity, of uninspired calculation and exaggerated refinement — such as can appear only at times of brilliant decadence.

Still, out of these works a blissful innocence was able to abstract the ideal of " noble simplicity and still grandeur," which, by the way, has no place in Greek *life*. Down to the beginning of the fifth century Greek culture has something stiff, rigid, hieratic; even, if the word be permitted, Gothic. Art and poetry are pious, angular, archaic, the men have stiff, gold-worked robes and barbaric ornament, pigtails and plaited beards, the women chignons and corkscrew locks. Yet at the end of the century, so swift is the tempo of Greek development, there is complete naturalism in State, society, clothing, philosophy, and drama, and in the next century Alexandrinism is already beginning. Where is there room, then, for the " Classical " Greek? The reasons which enabled this phantom to materialize we shall have to examine more closely. For architecture and sculpture they lie in the erroneous assumption of achromia, the dead colourlessness of buildings and figures: for poetry, in the loss of the musical accompaniments which must have played in this connexion a similar rôle to that of the painting with the sculpture; for prose, in the decay of the characteristic cadence, the tempo, the jargon; and in sum this fiction was, firstly, a phenomenon due to the clarifying, intensifying, concentrating, and foreshortening effects of distance; secondly, a result of the introduction of one's own traits into an alien being; and thirdly, a consequence of confusing life with the work of art, whose function (and precisely at the highest levels) is just the contradiction, the compensation, and the reversal of life. Yet it remains always a riddle how this conception of the Greeks arose, for a being of so fundamentally different a structure would, one would think, manifest itself to an unprejudiced age in a myriad ways. Think only of the Platonic dialogues, the philosophic biographies, the Characters of Theophrastus, the whole of the Old, Middle, and New Comedy, and all the Greek history, which is the most turbulent, chaotic, and scandalous in the world.

The " romantic " Greek

It will, of course, never be possible to describe exactly what Hellas really looked like in olden times, but we can say what it was *not* like, and that is what the eighteenth century took it to be. It was multi-coloured and fragmentary, nervous and iridescent, uncontrolled, tumultuous, and quite definitely not enlightened; its centre, Athens, a box of colours in the middle of a bright picturesque nature, determined to outshout even that nature, a charming playbox of a city, such as has never been seen — and, unfortunately, never attempted — in later times, packed with delicate and delightfully daubed life-size dolls of stone and clay, colossal figures brilliantly and loudly gilded, flashing faience, coquettish knick-knacks, and charming curious terracottas; and among all these things men who played with anything and everything, not merely with their oratorical and physical exercises, with their art and erotic, but with their science and philosophy, with their justice and political economy, with their states and wars, and even with their gods, always in motion and emotion, speaking in enormous quantity and at enormous speed — which of itself suffices to kill the Classicist idea — but at the same time observing the extreme of refinement in intonation, pronunciation, order of words, and rhythm of clauses; their drama a mixture of ballet, marionette, and popular concert, their real theatre the daily parliament, their women ornaments for decorating interiors, their philosophers original buffoons and swindlers, and their religion an organized carnival and excuse for wrestling- and running-matches, processions, and banquets.

Through their cardinal characteristic, a vast power of fantasy, the Greeks, more than any other people, were predestined to *lying* and *suffering*. One may even go to the length of saying that the tendency to lie was endemic among the Greeks; only a few exceptions fought against it, always uselessly and often nervously. Ethic there was not, whether individual or social, save in a few unworldly philosophers — the majority had not an inkling of such a thing — and if one were not quite certain that " Classical masters " do not understand a word of Greek authors, one would have not only to cut these out of school curricula, but forbid them for private reading as unmoral in the highest degree. But on adults the impression the Greeks make is that of beautiful beasts of prey, whom one appraises from a purely æsthetic point of view, or certain drama-figures of which one admires the fine characterization without approving the characters. In any case, the average Athenian himself regarded the Greek culture, even of the Periclean Age, as a degraded compound of democratic chatter, soap-box strategy, sporting jargon, and onion prices.

Goethe is responsible for the well-known remark that the Romantic is the morbid, the Classical the healthy. Without troubling to discuss the accuracy of this thesis, one can probably say anyhow that the Greeks were Romantic and unhealthy in their life, its manifestations and institutions, Classical and healthy in their poetry and thought. They were indeed absolutely forced to it, for they could never have carried the luxury of a Romantic art and philosophy, which would have involved them in an immediate collapse. The relation of life to its product is always, as we have pointed out, that of positive to negative. It is not a matter of accident that the sickly, highly sensitive, and gentle-hearted Nietzsche set up the ideal of the superman, while on the contrary the healthy, happy, and most egoistic Schopenhauer taught a philosophy of pessimism and negation of the will; that a strong sensualist like Wagner preached spirituality, while Rousseau was a fanatic of the primitive, the idyllic, and the " good." If we judged the " *Fin de Siècle* " only by its art, we should hardly argue from Ibsen, Maeterlinck, Altenberg, George, Khnopff, and Klimt to an age of technocracy, bourse domination, militarism, and imperialism. It is the same with the Greek ideal of *sophrosyne:* the tempered wisdom, clear sense, and controlled passion. They spoke so much of it because they had it not. Of their taste, on the other hand, of which they had as much as all other peoples old and new put together, they never spoke.

In the centre of Greek history, chronologically as well as intellectually, stands the mysterious figure of Socrates, who had a good deal to say to his fellow-countrymen about these things. Nietzsche, as everyone knows, saw in him a typical decadent, even a criminal, and called his dialectic the victory of mob-resentment;

Socratism

333

already ninety years ago Carlyle, without any detailed knowledge, led only by his gifts of instinct, expressed the opinion that Socrates with his eternal logic-chopping heralded the end of the true Greek culture. Alexander Moszkowski, in a very amusing little study, *Socrates the Idiot,* sets him up as a worthy imbecile, a futile pedant of speech and acrobat of words, who suffered from a sort of " echolalia " of logic. The eighteenth century, for its part, made of him a perorating Quaker who incessantly spouted wisdom and nobility, and even dared to compare him to Christ. Others have seen in him a parallel with Kant, which is equally ridiculous, for, while the *Critique of Pure Reason* is the revolutionary deed of a supreme spirit which overthrows all previous thought because it looks down on it, Socratism, set over against the grandiose cosmic fantasies of Ionic nature-philosophy, represents only the triumph of practical everyday comprehensibleness over the obscurity of real inwardness. All these different conceptions can be reduced to a common denominator which Nietzsche hinted at when he said: " There was only one choice, either to crash or — to be absurdly rational." Socrates' effort was nothing more and nothing less than to save Greece by preaching reason and virtue, two wholly un-Greek qualities; while he remained all the time enough of a Greek to have the good taste to clothe his moral lectures in the form of an exquisite irony. That is the meaning of the Socratic " Know thyself ": know what you lack — moderation, modesty, self-control, self-criticism — and strive for them as your redeeming antithesis. But Socrates was Athens, Athens was Greece, and Greece the world. Thus Socratism stands for the self-knowledge of the ancient culture; in him it looks itself in the face, and shudders. And no wonder that the Greeks smashed this mirror, for *they could not endure to look into it.*

The plaster Greek   As the teaching of Socrates, so Greek art owes its subsequent fame especially to the fact that it is the representation of calm clarity and noble self-purification, a contrast phenomenon, but not at all to the extent we love to imagine. The whole misty picture of the Classicism of Greece would presumably never have arisen if its polychromy had been known at the very outset. When it was at last discovered, the notion of colourless temples and statues had, from centuries of enthusiastic copying, definitely established itself in the modern consciousness, so that, though today we know *of* the painting, we really know nothing *about* it, because in every big city there are countless monuments and public buildings which owe their existence to the mistaken idea of classical achromia, and these contradict the new knowledge by their constant manifest counter-assertion. This obsession of ideas that are as unnatural as they are incorrect goes so far that white sculpture — which after all only owes its existence to an inadequate knowledge of Greek art — has been played off against the real Greek sculpture, which has been thought to need excuses for its polychromy. Thus for example Friedrich Theodor Vischer says in his *Æsthetic* — a fundamental and still unsurpassed work of enormous scope and inexhaustible content — " Every addition of colour to the modelling of the pure form, if it does not content itself with a few hints, is excluded by the very idea of pure sculpture. . . . So if an art which in other ways occupied a high place paints its statues completely — that is, with all the colour values as displayed on the living body — the explanation must lie in special conditions in the history of art "; and with the Greeks, he says, polychromic treatment certainly exceeded the limits conceded by the expression of " a few hints." " Even in the face of the unique faculty of the Greeks for the comprehension of pure form as such, and the glorious perfection of the art which was based on this faculty, we cannot sacrifice this view. . . . We must seek another way out, by a comparison with Greek drama. Here poetry and mimicry were united with music, song, and dance in a way which can never serve as a model. . . . Yet the great tragedies are no less great, although we can never imitate them in their use of these art-forms in combination. And as we enjoy what is left, the pure poetic beauty of Æschylus and Sophocles without the recitative and song and marchlike dance of the chorus, and make it part of our poetry, so we can strip the great sculptures of the colour, which, as a perishable addition, has its justification only in a particular moment of art-history, and which has been cleaned off (as from the Greek temples also) by air and rain." Now, quite apart from the remarkable deduction that colour is a transitory part of Greek sculpture because air and rain might wash it off, this description contains a very instructive unconscious avowal of the fatal transformation and falsification that our Classicism introduced into Greek art. For indeed it did make it bloodless and boring, really did take its

335

colour from it. So, for that matter, it did from the poetry, by unjusti-
fiably taking the mere libretto that alone had survived, and treating it as something self-sufficing, with the result that here also
one holds in one's hand only a pale, lifeless fragment of marble.

But the Greeks were very far from the *modern barbarism* of
leaving wood and stone unpainted; gaily, and with a very natural
and very artistic feeling, they tinted everything that came under
their hands; and our white sculpture and architecture would have
seemed to them an art for the colour-blind. The eyes, too, were as
a matter of course painted on, or, still better, represented by jewels,
crystals, etc.; and it speaks volumes for our utterly uncritical imitation of Greek monuments that because no traces were immediately found, we started the bizarre convention of ignoring the
organ of highest soul-expression altogether. The " Greek head "
with pale plaster cheek, without the flash of the eye, without a look
into the world, is the most speaking symbol of the neo-German
Humanism.

The Greek
plastic Now, a real Greek statue must have made a magnificent impression. First of all, the marble was rubbed with a pink or brown
dressing of oil and wax which gave it a warm flesh-coloured tint.
The reproach of the art-historians that the splendid material must
have thus been spoilt deserves little attention; as the Greeks knew
the value of their marble, presumably this treatment would only
enhance it — that is a question that may be left to their own judgment. The lips were painted red, the hair black or yellow, or made
gilt by metallic *appliqué;* the dress either was left white (in which
case, however, the folds at least would be coloured) or was likewise
painted, the inside and outside with different tints. Helmets and
crests, weapons and shields, ornaments and sandals were of metal,
and preferably gilded. The painter and sculptor were not necessarily the same person: thus Praxiteles' statues were painted by
Nicias, who was almost as celebrated. The chryselephantine
statues, like the lost Zeus statue of Olympia, Phidias' colossal work,
were wonderfully coloured: the core was of wood, the ivory by
skilled treatment was made so thin and elastic that it fitted the
core almost like a coating of lacquer: its natural tint already ap-
proximated it to flesh-colour and it may be that it was slightly dyed
as well. The robes and attributes were of richly painted gold plate,
the hair and beard of variously tinted gold, the eyes of flashing

jewels. On the temples the frieze and metopes were delightfully coloured, like tin soldiers, on a background of gleaming red or blue, the " drops " and other details were gilded, the echinus and the gutter of the roof ornamented in many colours after the fashion of our modern enamel-painting. On the Hecatompedon, the old temple of Athena on the Acropolis, made of porous limestone, which was destroyed in 480 B.C. by the Persians, and only rediscovered in the " Persian rubbish-heap " in our eighties, the men still had their bright-blue beards and hair, grass-green eyes, and red bodies. Painted relief, however, was always regarded, through the whole of Antiquity, only as a side-line of picture-painting.

In the light of a blazing sun, a hitting blue sky, cinnabar-red hills, sulphur-coloured rocks, poison-green trees, and a sea that flashed in a hundred changing shades the Greeks were predisposed already to be one of the most colour-loving — nay, colour-drunken — of peoples. Their poetic and philosophical fantasy always lived in an atmosphere of rich, strong colouring, and in their dress they loved loud and violently contrasting hues: purple and sky-blue, saffron and scarlet; even gleaming white had with them the character of a colour.

Their painting, as to which we have only scanty information — perhaps very fortunately so, for it is hard to say what its example might have led to in modern European art — seems to have had a strictly conventional character till right into the fifth century, and if relief was a sort of painting over moulding, painting must in its turn have been a sort of two-dimensional coloured plastic. As in the drama, the chief reasons for this limitedness lay partly in the primitiveness and conservatism of technique, partly in its orientation towards religious cultus. The frescoes of Polygnotus, who flourished in the second quarter of the fifth century, showed no thrown shadows, no chiaroscuro, no modelling, and were nothing but coloured-in outlines; nor did he know anything of perspective, recession being shown by superposition. It was only in the second half of the century, at the beginning of the Peloponnesian War, that Agatharchus discovered " *Scenographia,*" a scene-setting kind of perspective, which became the height of fashion when Alcibiades had his house decorated with such pictures. About the same time Apollodorus was at work, called the shadow-painter because he was the first correctly to observe and reproduce light-relations.

Greek painting

337

And already in Zeuxis and Parrhasius, the younger contemporaries of Apollodorus, we have obviously illusionist painters; for even if the story be not true that Zeuxis deceived the birds with his painted fruits, while Parrhasius deceived Zeuxis with a painted curtain, it still shows the kind of powers that were attributed to these painters. Zeuxis, too, was the first to paint the female nude, a subject which only occurs in sculpture a generation later. Here again we meet with the law that has been mentioned more than once, that painting seems to precede sculpture in its development; Greek sculpture, at the height of its expressive ability, should thus be regarded as the posthumous child of the Periclean Age, and the parallels to Euripides and the Sophists are not Phidias, Polycletus, and Myron, but Scopas, Praxiteles, and Lysippus. At the beginning of the fourth century the transition was made from tempera painting to encaustic, which by the use of wax colours aimed at greater brilliance and glow and played almost the same part in Classical painting as oil has in modern. At the end of the century quite modern movements break in, and Alexandria had its rhopographs and rhyparographs, its painters of trivialities and of filth.

Alexandrinism   Alexandrinism, considered in general, affords an excellent example of the necessity of entirely reversing the traditional picture of Hellenism. The Periclean Age having held everyone under a continued hypnosis, the Alexandrine period of Greek culture has been passed over for two thousand years, being treated either as decadence or simply as non-existent. It became the custom, even, to reduce the word " Alexandrinism " to a term of reproach: and when a professor or littérateur used the word, it was to imply that he was discussing an artistic or intellectual movement which was bloodless, affected, mechanical, artificial, professorial, and uncreative; in short, one like himself. Actually, in this conception as in so many others, one trait, and that not even the most important, has overshadowed the rest.

In reality the Alexandrine period, which includes the three last centuries (and more narrowly the third century) B.C., developed the Greek national gifts to their finest and richest expression. Greek culture became a world-culture, spread over the whole area of the Classical civilization; and it is not till this period that what we regard as the specifically Greek spirit, the nimble, quick, free, many-sided quality, developed to its fullest. If a deeper interest in

338

the Alexandrian age has only recently awakened, there is an obvious, one might say an egoistic, reason for it: it is very like our own.

The original Greek attitude to things never recognized " professions," but only an ideal unity and the claim of " Kalokagathia " to incorporate them all. Specialism was banausic; it was hated if only because it makes a man ugly, cripples body and soul by inartistically exaggerating one quality. But suddenly, at the turn of the fourth century, a number of new, hitherto un-Greek types begin to prevail within the Classical culture-area, the virtuoso who is an artist by profession, the athlete who is a professional gymnast, the officer, bureaucrat, diplomat, man of letters who is soldier, official, politician, savant, and author by profession; each one, in contrast to the objectivity and even anonymity of the earlier time, reveals his own ego as " author." Whereas the presentation of tragic and comic dramas had been till then (as with mediæval Passion plays) a matter for the whole citizen body, there now arose everywhere specialist dramatic schools, the so-called " Guilds of Dionysiac artists." In politics we have imperialism and its complement, cosmopolitanism. The favourite form of government is absolutism, but enlightened absolutism: Antigonos Gonatas called monarchy an ἔνδοξος δουλεία, a glorious servitude, which sounds quite Frederician, and the Diadochi loved to give themselves names such as *Euergetes*, the Benefactor, or *Soter*, the Saviour; in fact even the heads of philosophic schools, such as Epicurus, were given such honourable titles. The outer forms of government include the usual apparatus of strong dynastic rule — privy council, court etiquette, audiences, decrees, edicts, standing army, royal sanctity, oaths taken in the name of the king's " Tyche." The new ideas arise of " subject " and " private " citizen, though (as generally happens) this person had more personal freedom and security under the unlimited monarchy than under an incalculable democracy. Quite new, too, is the dawning of a sort of humanitarianism; in war a primitive international law begins to be recognized, and even, not seldom, an almost chivalrous romanticism; the position of slaves and the justification of slavery become subjects of serious thought, with, as its counterpart, the development of a *free* working proletariat. In the Polis the individual had regarded himself simply as a part, member, and organ of a narrow special community which was all in all to

339

him; now, as the Stoa taught, the true State is the cosmos, and the duties of a citizen and father begin to be looked upon with the eyes of the Cynic philosopher whose portrait Epictetus, a few centuries later, limned so shrewdly: " The Kingdom of the Cynic is well worth denying oneself wife and children for its sake. He sees all men as his children. Is it really the greatest benefit for mankind to bring a few snivelling children into the world? Who has done more for humanity as a whole: Priam, who begot fifty wastrels, or Homer? You ask me if the Cynic will take part in politics? You fool, can there be a greater political problem than his? Is a man to make speeches on taxes and revenues before the Athenians when his duty is to converse with all men, be they Athenians, Corinthians, or Romans, and not about taxes and revenues, about war and peace, but about happiness and misery, good and evil fortune, slavery and freedom? "

Hellenistic megalopolitanism   As both cause and consequence of this cosmopolitanism we find the devouring extension of a world-economy such as the ancient world had never hitherto known. The conquests of Alexander the Great had opened up the trade of the East, and India, Persia, China sent in a wealth of hitherto unknown articles of luxury. Men began to venture on to the open sea instead of nervously hugging the coast as they had always done. Main roads were built, after the Persian example, to provide land communications for the vast caravan trains. Hotel-keeping, till then quite unheard-of, began to flourish. Countless banks, chief of them the almighty central bank of Alexandria, extensive cartels grouping large-scale business men, shipping companies, were established; there were even world-exhibitions. A complicated tax system, for which Egypt provided its age-long experience, spread its net over a stupefied humanity; there were stamps and fees and taxes for everything. A highly subdivided industrialism spread: there were bakers of coarse and of fine bread, pig-butchers and beef-purveyors, basket- and matting-plaiters. Engineers began to play an important part in warfare: ballistæ, catapults, mobile batteries came into use, and King Demetrius, called *Poliorcetes* (the Stormer of Cities), built his famous " city-taker, " a machine of nine storeys, fifty metres high, which ran on wheels, was armoured like a tank, and defended by hundreds of men and any number of rocks, beams, bullets, and fire-arrows, and could be brought accurately into position against any objective. Huge ships for war and commerce were built, and there was the same competition in increasing tonnage as there is today. The great passenger ship *Syrakosia* of King Hieron held three hundred marines and six hundred sailors and a proportionate number of saloons, bathrooms, towers, and batteries. A sort of artillery was developed on elephants, of which Seleucus I had a depot of five hundred at Apamea. The new metropolises and residences — all of the same physiognomy, with straight roads cutting each other at right angles — rapidly developed to the proportions of our modern megalopolis, even to the mammoth monstrousness of their public buildings: the Colossus of Rhodes was 32 metres high, the Mausoleum at Halicarnassus 44, the eight-storeyed lighthouse on the island of Pharos 160 (its modern analogue, the Statue of Liberty at New York, measures with the base only 93).

In literature, too, mass production becomes common, though in the individual work an almost exaggerated brevity was demanded — " a big book, a big evil," said Callimachus, one of the most famous of the Alexandrine poets. It is a frank " art-for-art's-sake " that arises, an art that prefers the sensational and precious, the esoteric and complex, the curious and artificially archaic, and makes itself the expression of a sort of Rococo of literary sensibility. Lyrical poetry, in Rousseauian fashion, becomes bucolic, painting discovers landscape — even though both are still wholly Classical, in that they have none of the modern subjectivism that transfers its own feelings into dead nature, and so are not yet able to produce " atmosphere." Yet the most complete naturalism prevails: on the stage we have the triumph of Menander, who, with equal elegance of language and of dress, created the type of the comedy of manners, that mixture of cleverness and sentimentality which was the glory of the French during the last century. He too puts the noble courtesan in the centre of his play, and a shower of flashing epigrams conceals the cold inanity of the structure. A rhetorical mannerism, whose object is above all to dazzle, dominates not only the stage, but history and the arts as well, and penetrates even into everyday life. Architecture's first aim is to illustrate; sculpture is genre and purest realism and has attained to a brilliant virtuosity of technique. The so-called New Attic dithyramb is already on the way to program music and as much attacked as in our own day. There are already vaudeville artists, and Herondas

Hellenistic " Art for art's sake " and professional science

of Cos writes *Mimiamboi,* parodied and realistic cabaret scenes from the ordinary life of Ionia. But the favourite literary form is the Diatribe, which corresponds more or less to our feuilleton.

The greatest glory of the Hellenistic period was its science. The conception of the " scientific man " derives from Aristotle, whom his teacher Plato had called (not without an intention to disparage) the " reader." As in art the " artist " and the " connoisseur " came forward, so in literature there is the " educated man," who with his fellow-highbrows forms a sort of sect with a kind of secret language and secret knowledge of its own. A whole set of sciences was then, and only then, founded; Aristarchus of Samothrace established critical philology, Dicæarchus of Messene (in his Βίος Ἑλλάδος) cultural history, Duris of Samos the history of art, Polybius pragmatic history, Theophrastus the physiology of plants, Apollonius of Perga trigonometry and the theory of irrationals. Euclid not only produced, in his *Elements,* the classical text-book of geometry, but also gave the first systematic presentation of optics, the theory of propagation of light, and of " catoptrics," that of its reflection. Archimedes stated the formulæ for the circumference of the circle and volume of the sphere, gave a theory of the lever (on the basis of which he constructed pulley-systems), and discovered the fundamental " principle of Archimedes," which enabled him to calculate specific weight. Surgery, pharmacology, and anatomy (aided by vivisection practised on criminals) first received scientific form: zoological gardens, collections of antiquities, encyclopædias, huge libraries were established. In short, that mysterious thing we call Culture was given the quality of elephantiasis, which it possesses to this day. There were also astronomical charts, already fairly accurate, with calculations of solar and lunar eclipses; and about 250 Aristarchus of Samos taught that the earth turned on its own axis round the sun, which stood immovably as the cosmic centre. About the same time the geographer Eratosthenes, who knew of the spherical form of the earth, maintained that it was possible to reach India from Spain. The discovery of atmospheric pressure led Ctesibius to the idea of shooting bullets by compressed air out of small guns. Hero of Alexandria invented not only a coin-in-slot machine for obtaining holy water, a mechanical door-opener, and a taximeter carriage, but also screw-presses, water-engines, and cableways which were steam-driven. Thus at that moment men stood at the threshold of the heliocentric system, the discovery of America, and the invention of the steam-engine.

Another thing, too, came into the world — the emancipation of women. Queens made history, women philosophers and novelists made literature, and poets began to write for a feminine public. The feminine soul was discovered, and with it sentimental love. The " lady " is a discovery of the time, and she begins to move freely and takes part in everything, even in sport. That age first knew the meaning of coquetry, gallantry, and fashion; men kissed the hand of women, and in all seriousness contemplated suicide for unhappiness in love. Yet another great power arose, that of paper; it became the custom to say everything in writing and at the greatest possible length. A rather feminine, over-civilized trait shows itself too in the beardlessness which was then universal; one of the Seleucids who did not follow the fashion became so conspicuous that he got the nickname of πώγων, the Man with the Beard.

The most exquisite delicacies, culinary and intellectual, were brought from every part of the world, and the excess and over-refinement of pleasure induced a *blasé* attitude of boredom and satiety. Over this fine-nerved, busy, and all-knowing world brooded a vast leaden nihilism. " When man feels no more joy and no more pain, the winter of the soul is thawed " — in these words of Epicurus the age discovered its formula. The three dominant philosophies, however much they disputed between one another, all came out at the same end even by different channels: the Epicurean worship of *ataraxia* (immovability), the Stoic ideal of *apathia* (lack of feeling), and the Sceptical demand for ἐποχή (the suspense of judgment) all have at bottom the same intent. Thus we get the grandiose spectacle of a universal world-nausea, which gripped Classical mankind like an epidemic until in a distant despised province a Hero of a new kind was born, the son, not of Jupiter nor of Jehovah, but of the true God; who understood more of philosophy than Plato and more of conquest than Alexander, and by whom this mankind was redeemed.

It is only because the Alexandrine age, in its immense expectation of a new God, forms a sort of ante-room to Christianity that our reason can comprehend it a little; and pre-Christian peoples — let us not harbour any delusions about that — are in the ultimate depths of their soul unintelligible to us. Herman Grimm says in

343

his magnificent biography of Goethe: " We never get over the alienness of Greek life. It is said that among the quadroons, the otherwise wholly white descendants of Negroes, the half-moons of the finger-nails remain dark. In the same way, however akin to us Homer or Plato, even Aristotle and Thucydides may appear, something like this half-moon on the nail reminds us of the ichor, the blood of the gods, of which a last drop flowed into the veins of the Greeks." The Greeks are to us the exotic people *par excellence*. The reason that even today we are not properly clear about this lies in the well-meaning but foolish self-complacency and credulity of our schools, which for centuries have been in the hands of hopelessly mediocre and psychologically untalented syllable-mongers. Still, now that such a work as Spengler's *Decline of the West* has torn up foundations, many eyes will have been opened to the fact that a hopeless gulf separates us from Antiquity.

If we want to gain some sort of picture of this fundamental difference of Greek culture, we ought probably to take as our starting-point their pre-eminent musicality. It was not the plastic arts that stood in the centre of Greek life, but music. The singer was supposed to be inspired immediately by the gods, and conversely every prayer was a song; even field-warfare depended on song, which was regarded as the most trustworthy method of maintaining tactical unity: the piper was the most important person in the infantry attack, and likewise in the galley. The Herms which pointed the wanderer's way gave their guidance in hexameters; if *we* attempted to revive this custom, it would quite rightly be regarded as a foolish and tiresome snobbism, but the Greek felt musically and metrically even in things of everyday life. Music had such power over the soul that it was used for therapeutic purposes; Pythagoras healed the sick by song, and Plutarch tells of a sick girl from Argos who asked the oracle for healing remedies and was told to dedicate herself to the Muses; having followed the advice, she recovered her strength so much that she became a sort of Peloponnesian Joan of Arc, who repulsed a Spartan invasion at the head of a women's corps. Even the dead were thought to be sensitive to the sound of music: on the oil-flasks which were put into the grave, the survivors sought to cheer the shade by a figured flute-playing. In ordinary life music had the same educational significance for the soul as gymnastics had for the body; and gymnastics in turn were really a sort of rhythmical education of the body, the Greeks being profoundly convinced that only a musical soul could be healthy, strong, and fair. Plato says in the *Republic* that ugliness and bad morals are related to defective rhythm and harmony. The man physically and morally beautiful, in whom the ideal of *kalokagathia* was realized, the well-ordered State, and the whole cosmos were represented under the figure of a symphony. *Nomos* means law and melody, and every Polis was *thought of* as a piece of chamber-music. Musical innovators were regarded as political revolutionaries. The rhythm of the temple and its parts, columns and architraves and roof, is strictly musical; the pediments are built up metrically and symmetrically like verses which rise and fall. The same musical geometry lives in tragedy, with the surge and ebb of its action and the exactly corresponding changes of its speech; and even paintings were probably composed in higher and lower relation to a central point. We must not forget, too, that all the poets were in the first place composers. A song really was a song. Tyrtæus, Pindar, Alcæus, and Sappho sang their poems. A new lyric poet was, above all, the inventor of a new cadence, taking the word in its literal sense. Epics, too, were originally sung, and later on were at least recited dramatically. Even the orators chanted in a way which would have struck us as very unpleasant. The three great tragedians were renowned above all as tone-poets; Euripides, who was bitterly attacked and enthusiastically praised for his bold transformation of the musical drama, played much the same rôle as Richard Wagner. Tragedy was a sort of aggregate art-product unified by its music; by which we must understand, not a huge orchestra like that of the modern operas, but a kind of *inner* rhythm, for the instrumentation was such as we should call very simple, not to say scanty. Greek music knew no stringed instruments played with the bow, and trumpets were used only for signals. It was in essentials simply vocal music, the instruments being used mostly for accompaniment and only in a very limited degree for solos — in fact the entire orchestra for a tragedy consisted of one citharist and one or two flute-players. But, above all, Greek music throughout rejected polyphony, and the chorus always sang in unison. The solo word-parts moved amongst rhapsodies, choral antiphonies, duets, and monologue arias. It was only in Hellenistic times, when a new,

345

un-Greek spirit pervades every sphere, that the actors ceased to sing and the chorus was pushed away into the entr'actes, which in those conditions is its true place. To make it speak in unison — as Schiller tried to do in the *Bride of Messina* and as people still try to do now and again — is artistic and psychological nonsense. Music, in short, is as inseparable from Greek poetry as colour from its architectural and sculptural work; to separate them is to produce a monstrosity by elevating a spoken libretto to the rank of a dramatic ideal.

The Greek language The language also has a marked, and even a unique, musicalness in its vitality, its fineness, its modulation and melodiousness, variety and colour, force and elasticity, and, not least, in another element that we may in a certain sense call musical (since the tone-world is something immediately intelligible to everyone): namely, its noble popularity. Greek, though it was the first language in which the highest scientific and philosophic problems were discussed, has almost no alien words; and yet at the same time it has the ability to express the most abstract ideas plastically, to put the purest concepts in tangible concreteness, to move, in the true Platonic sense, among the intuited ideas. Add to this its extraordinary wealth of forms, of which a good many are peculiar to it — the optative, the aorist, the double verbal adjective, the middle, and the dual: the last two especially have a wonderful subtlety, for what you do of yourself is as different from what you do for others as it is from what others do to you, and what you do *à deux* is a very different thing from what you do alone or with a number. This formation, which goes through all the tenses and moods, may perhaps have been determined by the great part played by the erotic life. Further, by the numerous particles (unsurpassed in number by those of any other language) speech acquires at once a structural unity and a power of nuance, a clarity and atmosphere, and above all an indefinable element of playful, hovering irony, which is equally unsurpassed. No doubt these subtle shades of expression are generally quite untranslatable, or translatable only by the aid of the keenest thought and finest sensitiveness to language; and the ordinary philologists' translations, which are content to reproduce every part of the sentence simply verbally and, worse still, uncouthly and mockarchaically, do not exactly fill the bill.

346

The Greeks' feeling for language as a musical phenomenon is proved by their amazing feeling for false pronunciation or emphasis or order, which is recorded in many episodes and has an analogy only in the delicate sense of Italian audiences for errors in singing. This was, in fact, the secret of the Greek style; they had been trained by centuries of organized listening and seeing to the highest sensibility and discrimination.

We mentioned just now the central rôle played in Greek life by its erotic. But we must not think in terms of modern or mediæval love. There were two cardinal differences: the first was an absence of sentimentality, though it is doubtful how far this absence is to be equated with naïveté. Freud, in his work on sexual aberration, says: " The most fundamental difference between the loves of the Ancients and our own lies in the fact that the Ancients put the emphasis on the urge itself, and we on its object. The Greeks honoured the feeling and were prepared to glorify even a second-rate object by it, while we depreciate the impulsive activity in itself and only excuse it by the virtues of its object." This is the reason, also, why in Antiquity unhappy love existed only as a pathological phenomenon (the Greeks regarded the rare cases of it that occurred much as we do an infectious disease), since such love must be centred on a definite object, whereas the " impulse " itself never fails and never deceives; thus the two chief sources on which the complex of unhappy love is nourished did not exist.

Far more important, however, is the fact that the erotic of the Greeks was almost entirely restricted to homosexual affection. The reason for this has been attributed to their splendid, but almost madly exaggerated, cult of the body in everlasting gymnastics, riding, boxing, wrestling, races, and discus-throwing. Perhaps the powerful influence of the East might also have counted. Be this as it may, pæderasty reached an unparalleled extension and intensity with the Greeks. With the Dorians, in Sparta and Crete it was literally a part of public education; in Athens it was punished with *atimia* (that is, deprivation of civil rights) only if it was a matter of assault or rape: that is, under conditions in which the normal sex-act would also be counted as disgraceful. There were public male-prostitutes, and they even paid taxes as such. Since the murder of the Athenian tyrant Hipparchus by Harmodius and Aristogiton, who were lovers, pæderasty acquired an almost heroic glamour. Alexander's love for his Hephæstion, taken from him in the flower of youth, was clothed in an atmosphere of poesy. At the courts of the Diadochi it was viewed with disfavour, not on moral grounds, but only because any association of men was thought to veil a conspiracy. In battles these pairs of lovers were of the highest value, and they formed, as it were, the smallest tactical unit. The famous Sacred Band at Thebes, which counted as the finest force in Greece, consisted entirely of pæderasts. Not only were almost all famous Greeks, from Solon to Alcibiades, homosexuals, but many of the gods and heroes, such as Apollo, Poseidon, Heracles, and Ganymede were regarded as such. But most conclusive is the fact that the Greek art and philosophy play round this theme so fondly. " Right it is," says Pindar, " to cull love's blossom in due season, in life's prime; but whosoever has seen the rays flashing from the eye of Theoxenus and does not swell with longing, his black heart was forged of steel and iron at a frozen flame, and Aphrodite honours him not. Either he is busy with all his might about gold, or else, sacrificing his heart to woman, is borne along every path. But I, for the goddess's sake, waste away like wax of holy bees under the heat of the sun, when I look at the young blooming limbs of boys." Note that love of woman is here put on a par with love of gold, which was always despicable and especially so for the aristocratic Theban, and that Aphrodite is regarded as the goddess of love of boys! The feminine antithesis to Pindar is Sappho. She too prays to Aphrodite for help in the hardness of her love for a girl, and paints for her beloved her own passion in contrast with the unemotional coolness with which a man hears the sweet voice and dear laughter of his bride: " My heart beats, my voice fails, fire runs beneath the skin, the eyes see not, the ears buzz, sweat flows off me, trembling seizes me, and, fading like withered grass, I am as one dead." The notorious " Platonic " love, too, is a supersensual sublimated love — our use of the phrase is quite correct — but it is exclusively homosexual. " There are two goddesses of love," says Pausanias in the *Symposium,* " and, therefore, also two forms of Eros. The Eros of the earthly Aphrodite is earthly, universal, common, and casual. And everything common worships her. Both sexes, man and woman, had part in the creation and birth of the earthly Aphrodite. The higher love comes from

the heavenly Aphrodite and she is the creation of a man. Therefore all youths and men who are seized with this love strive after
their own sex, full of longing for the manly; they love the stronger
nature and the higher mind." The Stoics included the difference
of sex as one of the many "*adiaphora,*" the indifferent things of
life. But this really says too little: it was not an *adiaphoron,* since
in fact for the Greek man his own sex was far more important
than the feminine. Erotic, with all its attendant phenomena of
ecstasy, of jealousy, of devotion and protest, was only known in
the form of boy-love. The wife, on the other hand, is only a mother
or a dowry, and the hetaira a mere sex-object. It was not till Euripides that woman was discovered as a psychological problem, but
even he paints her rather as the subject than the object of passion.
Anyone who fell in love with a woman with the same feelings as
with a member of his own sex was regarded — even in Alexandrine times, when, as we have seen, sexual life was already looked
at with quite other eyes — as a lover blinded by the god to his
own ruin.

Now, this deep-rooted perversion in the Greek character is
" vice " enough already for most modern critics; but there can be
absolutely no doubt that in other respects also the national character of the Greeks was a real masterpiece of bad, and what we
call immoral, qualities. Probably the best way to put it is that
there was a *constitutional amorality* in the Greeks. When Œdipus
says to Theseus in Sophocles' *Œdipus Coloneus:* " I have found
piety nowhere in the world as with you, and mildness of heart and
absence of lies," the intention may or may not be to allude to the
past in contrast with the present, but in any case these words completely *counter*-characterize the Athenians and the Greeks generally. More, they disclose an involuntary *self-portrait,* in that
they show how completely they lacked understanding of what
they were and how bad they were. In the whole of Antiquity —
which was not over-strict in these matters — their quarrelsome-
ness and slanderousness, their avarice and corruption, their vanity
and boastfulness, their laziness and indifference, their vengeful-
ness and perfidy, their jealousy and Thersitism were notorious
and even proverbial. But it was their lying and their cruelty which
were worst. " I have no fear," said Cyrus the Elder about the
Greeks even of the good old days, " of men who have a place in

*Greek
amorality*

349

the middle of their city where they meet to deceive each other with false oaths." Plato complains that at least one example of perjury occurred in every lawsuit, since both parties were prepared to swear. Even Zeus, the loftiest of the gods, perjured himself time and again. There never was such a thing as Greek humanity, and the first faint stirrings of it betoken the collapse of Hellenism. It is a piquant irony of cultural history that the first of the moderns who consciously returned to the Classical called themselves Humanists, and that even today the studies dealing with Antiquity are called " *humaniora,*" the more human. In cold truth there were customs prevalent in Greece that were so devilishly inhuman as to arouse — and not infrequently — the abhorrence even of barbarians: think only of the fate of captured cities, even purely Greek cities, where it was habitual to devastate the whole land in the most brutal manner, to burn down all houses, kill the men, enslave women and children, or even cut off the hands of the whole population. Think of the treatment of slaves, who were compelled to work sometimes their whole lives chained in quarries and mines, who as witnesses were tortured and could be even tendered for torture by their owners; think of the Spartan St. Bartholomew massacres, the famous *Krupteia,* in which at regular intervals part of the subject population was rooted out. It is significant for the " moral insanity " of the Greeks that they have no word for the morally reprehensible, for κακόν means both wicked and ill, the κακός both depraved and wretched, πονήρος both the vicious and the unfortunate. The Greeks did not distinguish between one who was bad and one for whom things go badly, but reckoned ethical defects simply among the other countless calamities of life. Even blasphemy is mere fate, whether this be the *Heimarmene* of gods with their capricious partiality and jealous rancour; the brazen *Ananke* who rules blindly; the inflexible *Moira* who has long ago determined everything; the *Alastor,* the spirit of expiation who avenges the deeds of ancestors; or some unsuspected *Agos,* a fault which brings a curse in its train; or under a more enlightened interpretation the effect of a given character, which must be as it is, or of overpowering passion, which is a misfortune like any other illness. But the fate-goddess of the Hellenistic Age is *Tyche,* who distributes chances indiscriminately, the luck of the gambler.

350

Nietzsche called the Greeks the "state fools of ancient history." And in fact almost every form of human association, caricatured to its final consequences, was experienced, and in the process proved futile, by these men. First aristocracy: in Homer there are *only* nobles, the people are nothing but voiceless supers and vacant background. Then the Tyrannis, an absolutism of the "*l'état c'est moi*" type, but without an ever-present etiquette or an insuperable clergy such as kept the omnipotence of the Bourbons within bounds; in Sparta the military communism with its strictly uniform life, rationed meals, exclusively national education, complete equality of women, prohibition of alcohol and travelling, iron pocket-money and threat of death for the possession of silver. Finally, the extreme democracy, which was no real parliamentary government and knew nothing of equality and universal suffrage, but in which the whole populace voted noisily, not merely about laws, but about the whole administration; with a jury consisting (in theory at least) of the whole people, with officials appointed by lot, and the executive in war entrusted to ten *strategoi*, elected annually, but daily changing round in the supreme command. We can imagine how things must have gone on in this mad hive of the Polis, which even from the beginning, and still more as time went on, was a pretext for class justice, minority tyranny, party cheating, and "patriotic" extortion. The fallacy of every democracy, clearly seen already in Herodotus when he said that the majority was taken as the whole, was elevated in Greece to an all-consuming national delusion. The development shows up in the change of the word "demagogue" as its meaning passed from that of a leader of the people to that of a deceiver of the people who works with any and every means of basest mob-swaying. Since the Greeks had none of that love of truth which we set up at least as an ideal postulate, and equally lacked anything of the modern sense of honour, any man who was foolish enough to appear in public or make himself somehow conspicuous became — by the very fact of doing so, and irrespective of whether he was acting for good or for ill — the natural and obvious butt of the most scandalous slander, indiscretions, and calumny, not to mention private and official chicanery of every kind. Above all, he was handed over defenceless to the refined befouling technique of a comedy that makes our present-day pamphleteers, press gunmen, and keyhole-poets seem almost harmless. Ostracism, which could banish any citizen by plebiscite, was expressly directed not only against traitors and the sacrilegious — categories which in themselves were capable of wide enough extension — but against any outstanding individual. And in fact it did hit a large number of prominent citizens, or forced them to precautionary flight, whether they were victorious men of practical life like Alcibiades, fruitful students like Aristotle, brilliant fashionable thinkers like Protagoras, or quiet researchers like Anaxagoras. Goethe once said that there was nothing that humanity needed more than efficiency, and that there was nothing that it knew less how to tolerate. The Greeks, who established once and for all the canon of the human body, were equally thoroughgoing in the standardizing of the human soul. They gave *Classical* expression, too, to that elementary fact of human nature, the attitude which men adopt towards every intellectual superiority, and which is comprised in the words: "We need you, genius, but we find you tiresome. We should not like, Phidias, to do without your statues, but it is really an impertinence on your part to be so eminent a sculptor. It is insolent of you, Themistocles, to be so great a general, and of you, Aristides, to be so just, and of you, Socrates, to be so wise, for we cannot be like you; yet we, the people, the masses, the average, the common people, are what really matters. Every one of your activities is an offence to us, for each of you proves afresh that he possesses more beauty, generosity, and wisdom than those in all of us together. We know that we cannot do without you, but that does not prevent our regarding you as a necessary evil, which we will endure only so long as we must." That was the attitude of the Greeks, as it has been (if less clearly and concretely) that of all times and all peoples, and especially of all democracies.

Life in a Greek city must have been absolutely intolerable from the modern standpoint; the Terror under the Jacobins or in Russia today can give only a feeble idea of it. In the first place there was always the possibility for everyone of being enslaved through robbing, war, or debt; this actually happened to two such outstanding men as Plato and Diogenes. But even the free were far from being in the true sense free, for they lived under the hidden threat of mob-caprice, and greedy sycophancy, in a perpetual state of being on bail. As for intellectual life, there was, it is true, no official censorship — a fact by which the scandalous licence of the comic stage chiefly profited — but there was a secret one which was far more oppressive and inhibiting: namely, the tradition which laid on both poets and artists the most burdensome restrictions as to choice of form and content alike. Over the philosopher and the scientist hung always the liability to prosecution for impiety. The three most conspicuous thinkers of Pericles' time — Socrates, Protagoras, and Anaxagoras — were victims of these *asebeia* charges, the last-named because he had taught that the sun was a glowing rock. There was indeed no professional priesthood to make the persecution of these heresies a life-work, but none was necessary to that end, for the State, a religious institution through and through, performed the function. Thus the pride of liberal historians in the fact that Greece had no State Church is sadly wide of the mark: its Church — and an exceedingly superstitious, intolerant, and despotic Church — was the State. Moreover, Greece did possess in the Delphic Oracle an institution that was very like a Church.

For that matter, they even possessed, though only as a by- or under-current, a sort of theology: the Orphic, Dionysiac, or Chthonic religion, which has long received inadequate attention (and precisely because it was *not* the orthodox), though as one of the deepest expressions of the Greek soul it must have played a part similar to that of Mysticism in the Catholic world, Pietism in the Lutheran, and the prophets in Judaism, even if different entirely in kind from these. About 600 the Thracian Bacchus came to the Greeks as the Stranger God, and they called him Dionysus: about 550 began the Orphic sects, who traced themselves to the Thracian minstrel Orpheus; about 500 Pythagoras proclaimed the Orphic wisdom which, from Empedocles and Heraclitus down to Plato and Plotinus, accompanied Greek thought like a dark shadow. All these schools have an ascetic and spiritual quality in common: the idea that the body is the tomb of the soul, that the earth is only a preparation for a higher life, and that by apotheosis, mystical union with the divinity, man can find salvation. The Eleusinian mysteries were only distantly connected with these currents, and they held out for their adepts far more solid advantages, in life wealth, and after death liberation from

The Greek religious-ness

Hades — and Hades was particularly unattractive to the Greeks, who believed and yet did not believe in him (as in everything else that concerned their religion) on account of his darkness and silence that contrasted so uncomfortably with their earthly existence of dazzling sunshine and exaggerated chatter.

The Orphic movement discloses certain impulses towards a true religiousness, though its esoteric doctrine was certainly intelligible only to a few. But the Olympian religion was nothing but a superficial story-telling, an empty cult-ritual, a childish fear of demons and ghosts; in fact, at bottom no religion at all. It is incomprehensible how the Greeks have been credited so often and so emphatically with a special piety. Certainly their whole life rested on a religious basis, but it was a very thin and fluctuating one. Government, justice, war, commerce, even erotic and social life, sport and theatre, were under the patronage of gods and took the form of a sort of permanent liturgy. But this was the very thing that at once turned itself into something trivial, worldly, and irreligious. Moreover, there was no real faith even in their own caricatures of gods, who in very principle were operetta figures. Men felt quite definitely that their gods were of their own making. The famous remark of Herodotus that Homer and Hesiod created their theogony for the Greeks " only yesterday or the day before " and had given the gods " their names, offices, and honours just like their form," is in *our* sense of the word a piece of atheism. The Pythagoreans, on the other hand, taught that Homer would have to pay in the underworld for the silly stories which he had spread abroad. Heraclitus said of his fellow-countrymen: " They pray to pictures — as though it were possible to converse with houses." Xenophanes wrote: "If bulls and lions had hands like men, could paint and carve, the beasts would fashion gods in their own image, the gods of horses as horses, of oxen as oxen." These are three voices from the Greek Middle Ages; but after Pericles' time scorn of gods and doubts of their existence actually became the intellectual fashion. Protagoras put at the head of his work *On the Gods* the sentence: " Of the gods I cannot say whether they are or are not." When Diogenes was asked what happened in heaven, he answered that he had not been there. Epicurus made the oft-quoted remark of the gods that " they do not heed men, otherwise they would not be blissful ";

he did not, however (as one can see from these words), deny their existence; indeed, he sacrificed to them in traditional fashion, which is the more remarkable in that he was one of the most downright of the ancient materialists. The Platonic school of the Newer Academy, had similar ideas: it was just as possible that the gods should be as that they should not be, so it was best to keep to custom and continue their worship. This was the typical Greek attitude, first of the cultured and then even of the people; neither their existence nor their power is proved, but " one cannot tell " — more or less the attitude of many people today towards Spiritualism. In the Hellenistic period theological rationalism took on forms which only reappeared in the nineteenth century. The David Friedrich Strauss of Antiquity was Euhemeros, who taught that the Olympians were men of early times who had done great service and been raised to divinity, and the Stoics said that all the traditional mythology was an allegorization of natural forces. It was only the reverse aspect of Euhemerism that the Diadochi began to proclaim themselves gods: even Demetrius Poliorcetes had had the Athenians sing songs to him of which it is hard to say whether they are the product of a refined Byzantinism or a naïve cynicism: " How fair that the greatest and dearest of gods dwell in our city! Now the festal day gives us both Demeter and Demetrius: she to perform the lofty mysteries of the maiden, and he is there, happy, fair, and laughing as beseems a god. Hail, thou son of mighty Poseidon and Aphrodite! For the other gods are far away, or have no ears, or are not, or care not a rush for us; but thee we see, not of wood or stone, but real, before us, and thee we honour."

The criticism of the poets restricted itself mostly to reproaching the gods that they saw the world's injustice and heeded not. Already in the middle of the sixth century Theognis is asking: " Who will take note of the gods when he sees how the wicked rolls in his wealth while the just man starves and withers? " Even Æschylus, filled though he was with genuine faith, makes Prometheus cry to the almighty Zeus, who is towards him an unjust tyrant, in wildest words: " And why has the Titan to suffer so horribly? Only because he loved humanity too well." The motive that this tragedy, for all its basic conservatism, so overpoweringly expresses is the jealousy of the gods, which does not even wish men to be happy. Sophocles is even more emphatic when he makes the chorus sing in the *Œdipus:* " How shall man protect his own heart from impious thoughts in such times? If such doings bring honour, why do we dance still before the gods? " But Euripides is already a Sophist. To him destiny is neither wrath nor love of the gods, neither Moira nor the dæmon of the family, but man himself. His *Weltanschauung* could be summed up in a single phrase which is attributed to his contemporary Hippocrates, the great physician of antiquity: " All is divine and all is human "; and, generally, he holds that " if gods sin, they are no gods." But when he looks down upon the world created and ruled by man, a deep resignation takes him. " Even as they come, I take the gifts of today and of tomorrow with a calm heart. Faith and hope are dead and my soul is dark."

Greek
pessimism This brings us to the question of Greek pessimism. Now, in Greek national character there are two apparently contradictory qualities. The one is a cheerfulness, playfulness, light-heartedness, and sensuous worldliness, which impressed even Antiquity itself: it is seen in the ordinary form of greeting, χαῖρε, be glad, whereas for the Roman, who said *Vale* and *Salve,* strength and health were what mattered. The other is a bleak melancholy and scepticism, which did not merely express itself in dialectic and poetry, but was lived by them, for their whole being was impregnated with it as with some delicate tint or essence. Both rooted in their stern sense of reality. They lived almost wholly in this world — the other side was to them a misty and at bottom unreal shadow-world, and the Orphic doctrines of asceticism and metempsychosis seem, inside the Greek culture as a whole, rather like an alien spice — and therefore they enjoyed to the full the reality that they knew. But, being clear practical observers, they saw also the suffering and imperfection of existence with quite undeluded eyes. They were empirics and, therefore, pessimists. They knew what life was: a troublesome, incalculable, and thankless business. Moreover they were entirely unserious, because artistic, and therefore neither had their affirmative realism the brutal straightforwardness, wearisome objectivity, and leaden banality which it acquired later with the Romans, nor had their accusatory pessimism the metaphysical power over the last depths of the soul that it had for the Indians.

356

The piteous maxim that it is best ($\mu\grave{\eta}$ $\phi\hat{\upsilon}\nu\alpha\iota$) "not to have been born at all" passes in innumerable fine variations through all Greek thought. Even the Iliad says that of all things that live and move, man is the most miserable. Heraclitus says profoundly of time that it is a child, playing and exercising itself on the game-board, and that "this child has the king's power"; Thales declared that he remained unmarried "for love of children." Even the calmly smiling Socrates bursts forth in the *Gorgias* with "$\delta\epsilon\iota\nu\grave{o}\varsigma$ $\overset{\text{'}}{o}$ $\beta\acute{\iota}o\varsigma$ (Life is terrible)!" Aristotle, more scientifically, asks "what is man," and answers that he is a monument of weakness, the prey of the moment, the sport of chance, and for the rest mucus and bile. Menander says that he is happiest who earliest leaves the fair of life, and again: "If God after death offered you another life, you should pray to be anything, even an ass, rather than man." His contemporary was Hegesias, a philosopher who is said to have by his lectures persuaded many of his hearers to suicide, and so received the name $\pi\epsilon\iota\sigma\iota\theta\acute{\alpha}\nu\alpha\tau\circ\varsigma$. There was a treatise of his on the subject which bore the title $\overset{\text{'}}{o}$ $\acute{\alpha}\pi\circ\kappa\alpha\rho\tau\epsilon\rho\hat{\omega}\nu$, and it is significant that this word was actually a current technical term, which we can only render by a long phrase: "one who can endure life no more and therefore starves himself to death."

Yet already in Homer we find the counterpoise which the Greek was able to throw into the scales of destiny. Alcinous says to Odysseus: "Tell us why you weep thus and grieve in your heart, when you learn the fate which has befallen the Argives at Troy. For it was but the work of the gods; they wove this ruin for men that it might live in the songs of posterity." And Anaxagoras said that being born was to be preferred to not being born, if only that one might observe the heavens and the whole order of the world. The joy of form and observation, of singing and seeing, which the Greeks knew better than any other people, compensated all the sufferings of life. A misery that can be the theme of song is no more a misery, and a world that can be studied cannot be too bad.

Yes, the Greeks *were* idealists, but in a quite special, very unmodern sense, which perhaps only Goethe understood; and yet he too misunderstood them in making this the dominant quality in them. In an earlier chapter we tried to show that every Frenchman was a born Cartesian, and in the same sense it might be said

Greek idealism

that every Greek was a Platonist. In the Platonic philosophy the ideas are the immortal παραδείγματα, the originals and exemplars, after which all earthly appearances are formed as μιμήματα, imitations and copies. What fascinates us as the "beauty" of an object is the ἀνάμνησις, the dark remembrance in our soul, of its eternal archetype, which it saw before birth. Ideas are therefore something quite different from concepts, for we reach a knowledge, or rather an inkling of them, not by abstraction, but by intuition. Aristotle, the second most influential Greek philosopher, has a somewhat different, yet fundamentally similar conception. For him the *morphe*, the form, is in essence the same as the *Eidos*, the idea, and the *Hyle*, or material, is the *dunamis*, the possibility of form, while *energeia* is the realization of the material. *Hyle* means actually raw material, timber, and Aristotle illustrates the meaning of the *Eidos* by the function of a carpenter — which is the idea of the house. The form, therefore, exists first; it generates the house. Aristotle says quite emphatically that the idea, the universal, is πρότερον φύσει, the first in reality, and the individual only πρότερον πρὸς ἡμᾶς, the first for us. The conviction of the priority of the Idea is common to Plato and Aristotle. It is the Classical model of each thing, that which nature really aims at, but never achieves; it is, certainly in Plato, something quite concrete. It will be recalled from the previous chapter that Goethe had a similar idea before him when he thought of the *Urpflanze*. The canon of the beautiful human form, as moulded by the Greeks in their sculpture, corresponded to it in a way. The same character informs their feeling of tragedy. Nietzsche said in his *Birth of Tragedy:* "There is an assertion by someone or other that all individuals as individuals are comic, and therefore untragic: from which it might be argued that the Greeks *could* not endure individuals on their tragic stage." A dramatic art that individualized, that in any sense created something more than the idea, the *mask*, would have been to them not a higher, but a ridiculous, unworthy, and blasphemous form. For one must not forget the religious basis on which this tragedy rested. Alfred Bäumler says in his penetrating and suggestive introduction to a selection of Bachofen's works: "Every thought of everyday matters must be put away if we want to understand Agamemnon, Orestes, Œdipus Ajax, Antigone. They are in fact *shades* that rise up before us on the tragic stage. These heroes are not fetched from the highways, but conjured up from the grave. . . . Everything empirical, every thought of realism, is infinitely remote. The exposition-form of Greek tragedy is not to be explained merely from the idea (which admittedly exists) of a real superhuman greatness in the heroes of the past, but far more in a holy reverence in presence of the dead." Therefore: since the tragic heroes came forth from the grave, they could not be represented realistically like modern heroes, for they were part of a religious ceremony and could only be grasped as universal symbols. In this light we can see that the change from the older type-art to the "psychology" and character-drawing that we get in Euripides was a symbol of irreligion, the dramatic counterpart to the destructive dialectic of Protagoras and to Alcibiades' profanation of the Mysteries.

The Greeks had — connected both with their Platonism and with their musicality — a native eye for the geometry of things, their arrangement, division, proportion — an extraordinary gift of recognizing in everything the secret outline, plan, and style, the inner skeleton and diagrammatic scheme. They were eminently linear artists and, for all their nervous quality, the very opposite of impressionists. Γράφειν means both to write and to paint. They had no eye for half-tones, screened lighting, gradual transitions, and subtle shadows; and perspective was not yet known, as we can argue with certainty from the description of paintings that survive and the poets' descriptions of nature. The very character of their land, the crystalline brightness and clearness of the air, the sharp profiling of the hills, the strong, varied articulation of the coast-line, had pushed them to such a definite feeling for contours. In Athens the sun, on the average, is clouded over only twenty-five days a year. In Homer everything takes place in brightest daylight. Night was the most hateful thing known to the Greeks; and for the poetry of mist, of the autumn mood, of twilight, of moonlight, which plays so large a part in modern sensibility they possessed no organ at all. Further, the whole day was lived in the open. Consequently we must tacitly add the Greek landscape to all that the Greeks did and created — to their drama, their temples, their vases and pictures, their speeches and songs, their symposia and games — just as they themselves always accepted it, consciously or unconsciously, and with their style-sense composed everything into it.

In addition, every relation and dimension had for the Greeks something simple, comprehensive, and synoptic, therefore something limited, clear, and definite. The culture before them could still be viewed and scanned as a whole. The artistic and scientific tradition was neither old nor wide-ranging. Their circle of experience includes barely a dozen generations; two opposite coasts with an intervening sea (made practically an inland sea by its island-bridges and the barrier of Crete on the south); a homogeneous fauna and flora. On the peninsula at home, the isthmuses and steep mountain ranges produced still smaller centres of activity, and generally the slow, difficult, dangerous process of travelling and the distrustful isolation of the ancient peoples imposed a certain limitedness of horizon. Everything with them was *concrete* in the proper sense, " grown together," concentrated on the smallest area, pressed to the minutest form; and this made it possible for them, in all spheres of life, to be plastic, intuitive, and artistic. Conversely, it is today almost impossible to be artistic. It is no chance that the most powerful poetic currents in the last fifty years have come from physically limited Scandinavia and intellectually limited Russia. The Greek political idea was neither a vague philosophical idea, such as hovered in the minds of the eighteenth century, nor a nationalism or imperialism thinking in terms of the world and dealing with huge peoples, as is the case today. In fact, it was not at all an object of complicated legal reasoning such as has been indulged in by all modern times, even the Middle Ages and the Roman Empire, but meant simply and solely the particular Polis, a most visible, tangible, and objective creature: namely, a small city, a sharply demarcated human settlement with military, religious, political, and industrial centres — a fortress with a sanctuary, an agora, and a harbour. Measured by modern standards, Athens was a moderately important trading centre, Sparta a mountain hamlet, Thebes a largish village, and Olympia a little Oberammergau. These places were just big enough to be able to produce all the social and intellectual differentiations, and small enough to produce the most intimate frictions and interactions among all its inmates. The peninsula, so far as it was Greek, had about the area of post-war

Austria and about the population of Berlin. The distance in a bee-line between the most northerly point, Olympus, and the most southerly, Tænaron, was about the same as that between Berlin and Vienna and can be traversed by air today in three to four hours. The Greeks, too, had their World War, the Peloponnesian, but, though it lasted about as long as the Thirty Years' War, it was, in both its course and its objects, entirely simple and clear: namely, a seesaw struggle between Athens and Sparta for the hegemony of the peninsula, which, as we have seen, was an incoherent mass of cunning diplomacy, complicated troop-movements, and hopelessly incomprehensible territorial policies; the Greek world-war was neither religious, nor social, nor political, but simply chaos. In their physical appearance the Greeks were, measured by the standards of Nordic peoples, rather small, but wonderfully well-proportioned, as the result of a long tradition of physical training which they pursued with supreme persistence and deliberation: thus even their bodies were to a certain extent the product of a highly developed craftsman's technique — in fact, like everything else with them, well built. Their manner of life was simple, almost spare. A few tasteful vases and well-carved wooden chests satisfied their desire for luxury; a few fish and salt cakes, with figs and olives, constituted their normal meal; to mix two parts of wine to three of water was reckoned excess. It is all the same moderation — arising from the æsthetic, not the moral impulse — that we see in their use of architectural forms and poetic motives, in their stock of concepts and their stock of figures. They nowhere exhibit either the indistinctness or the over-distinctness of the moderns, with their too many possessions. Even their Panhellenic games and festivals — which were no monster-productions and moreover were very infrequent — had none of the inartistic, plebeian boost-quality which every public institution nowadays is obliged to display. This peculiar sobriety is perhaps the central phenomenon of the Greek culture, and one that has never appeared since. Greek simplicity — misinterpreted in the eighteenth century as " simpleness," dignity, purity of heart, but actually nothing but differentiation in the life-feeling and a certainty of the limits of the field of view — created the strong, clear, unbroken lines of the Greek life-form. They were very genuinely the people of the Mean. And thus their much-lauded prudence, self-control, and love of the mean imply only that they were in everything a people of good medium format, well-proportioned and natural life-size.

Nevertheless, Winckelmann's success with his invention of the " harmonious " Greek was due to the fact — it is the necessary precondition for every great historical achievement — that a strong personality and a strong current of the time happened to coincide. Moreover (as was briefly noticed in our first volume, in the chapter dealing with the Reformation), far from being the initiator of a new age, he was rather the concluding type of a departing age. He was the last great humanist, as Luther was the last great monk and Bismarck the last great Junker.

The last Humanist   Winckelmann is notable, if for nothing else, at any rate as being one of the most ready-made men who have ever been productive. Generally a creative personality means one that is always developing, never coming to an end, and always challenging contradiction, but he stands, from the very outset, like one of his beloved white marbles, as something in cold, pure, and unambiguous lines. One might say that everything which he was to produce as the final full fruit of a long life of deep, wide, and well-ordered thinking was known to him from the beginning — nay, more, before he actually knew it or had any scientific right to know it. One might perhaps propose the thesis that every pronounced individuality embodies only one of the periods of life, and holds that one fast throughout its career. The masses have a very sound instinct when they picture Schiller as always young, Louis XIV always as man at his zenith, Schopenhauer as always an old gentleman. Schopenhauer in youth, Schiller in middle age, Louis XIV in his grey hairs do not really exist in our minds. As for Winckelmann, he was, all his life, about fifty years old.

The way in which Winckelmann approached art and its history is so familiar to us today — even if we have never read a line of his — that we generally forget altogether how original it was in his own time. Winckelmann was, in a word, the first archæologist in the legitimate sense of the word, an eager investigator and connoisseur of Antiquity, for whom his knowledge was not an end in itself, but an organ for penetrating into the past. No detail escaped his vision — even if his interpretation of it was not always the right one — and moreover he was not above turning his attention to those questions of workshop-tradition and technique which play so great a rôle in art. Just as he was one of the first to look for the key to the understanding of ancient art-works in ancient authors, he was the very first to read a work of art like a text, with the eyes of a philologist, microscopically exact, cautiously testing, cautiously co-ordinating. Yet withal he never forgot the greater relationships: he regarded art as a growth, of which the character was determined by soil, climate, nurture, environment (anticipating in a sense the *milieu* theory of Taine); and he understood its history as the course of a typical development-series, which passes from the " archaic " style which is still hard and angular, via the " great," genuinely ideal, and the " beautiful " or flowing and gracious style, to that of the " decadence " which is imitation and artificiality. All these ideas he set forth in a witty nervous style, which really did recall Attic prose in its noble unadornedness and sturdy strength of meaning; and, in contrast with the springy impulsiveness and excitable elasticity of Lessing (who was only a decade younger), the impression he leaves on us is, in fact, Classical: that is, wholly unimpressionistic.

His chief work, the *History of Art in Antiquity,* is a history in outward form, but actually it is an æsthetic which, judging modern art by the standard of ancient, rejects it and demands an unconditional return to the antique. For Winckelmann there is practically but one art, that of sculpture; for painting only counts for him in so far as it is a sort of sculpture: namely, as outline drawing, as contour; this is " the chief aim of the artist," " drawing comes, for the painter, first and second and third," and " colour, light, and shade do not make a painting so valuable as noble contour." Even in historical development the most important motive has been " changes in the drawing." This artistic Spartanism, this (as it was then imagined) Dorian apotheosis of pure line, pure white, and sparing ornament, must be regarded as a natural reaction against the degenerate and outworn Baroque. In the eighteenth century only a few voices were raised against this reactionary (and, fundamentally, inartistic) purism. But one of these was Herder's, crying in indignation: " A painter, and yet not to be one? Shall he, then, turn the drums of a column with his brush? " And another was Heinse's, declaring emphatically that " drawing is only a necessary evil for the purpose of easily finding proportions, and the end and object of art is colour." Lessing, on the other hand, went so far as to wish that oil-painting had never been invented, and Georg Forster in his *Opinions from the Lower Rhine* voiced the general feeling when he cried: "What is colour compared to form?"

Winckelmann goes further, and admits in sculpture only the presentation of the human, or, to speak more precisely, the masculine, form. When he talks of beauty in general, he is always thinking, consciously or unconsciously, of the masculine. If he does discuss the feminine, it is the more boy-like qualities of the feminine form that he emphasizes. The Dutch school was intolerable to him, partly on account of its colour, but probably also because it was so pronouncedly heterosexual. Specifically feminine sex-characters like the breasts or the pelvis he never commented on as beautiful. His temperament was in fact manifestly homosexual. His friendships with handsome young men, which he cultivated throughout his life, had a definitely erotic character, though at the same time it appears that these relationships, like those of Socrates, were always sublimated. This abnormality of emotion, too, was probably the cause of his tragic end; for there is no other way to explain his deigning to have any close relations with the common-place and uncultured fellow who murdered him in Trieste for the sake of a few exhibition coins. He never, for that matter, made any secret of his peculiarity, for he had the magnanimous candour that he had learnt from the Greeks. Thus for example he wrote to an acquaintance: "Could you believe that I could fall in love with a girl? Yet I have, with a twelve-year-old dancer whom I saw on the stage . . . only I do not mean to be unfaithful"; and again: "I have never seen such fine beauty in the weaker sex as in our own. What beauty has a woman to show that we have not? If I had thought otherwise than I do, my essay on beauty would not have come out in the way that it has." He gives even clearer expression to the connexion between his art theories and his sexuality in the words: "I have noticed that those who have eyes only for the beauties of the female sex and find little or nothing to stir them in our own sex do not readily have the inborn broad and vivid feeling for art." This is the psychological key to Winckelmann's *Æsthetic*, given us by himself. The homosexual eye sees especially contour, volume, outline, linear beauty, and plastic; it has no sensitivity for dissolved form, misty values, purely picturesque impressions. And so, brought right out into the light, the whole *idée fixe* of Classicism is seen to go back to the sexual perversion of a provincial German antiquary.

What Winckelmann thought about modern art is expressed in many passages of his works, but nowhere more unambiguously than in a letter to his friend Uden: " The moderns are asses compared to the ancients, and that though we do not possess the latter's very finest works. Bernini is the biggest ass of all." The only exception was his friend Mengs, of whom he said in his history of art: " The sum of all the beauties I have described in the Classical figures is to be found in the immortal works of Herr Anton Raphael Mengs, principal court painter to the Kings of Spain and Poland, the greatest artist of his own time and perhaps the future as well. He rose out of the ashes of the first Raphael like a phœnix, to teach the world the beauty of art and to reach the highest flight of human powers in the same." Mengs, who also occupied himself deeply with the theoretical side of art and was called the " painter philosopher," was the father of that rationalistic, academic, " educated " painting of the gallery-copyists who flourished for many decades in Europe. His doctrine consisted, in essence, in the idea that art is superior to nature, since it can choose its subject freely and is not subject to accidents in what it produces, and that it can and must therefore unite all perfection in one form: uniformity in outline, greatness of form, freedom of attitude, beauty of limb, strength in the chest, lightness in the legs, force in the shoulders and arms, uprightness in the forehead and eyebrows, wisdom between the eyes, health in the cheeks, kindliness in the mouth — " that was what the Ancients did." The painter, thus, has nothing to do but seek out the best and finest details and put them together on a pattern-sheet. We have seen in the first volume that Raphael Santi had a theory like his homonym's, but he was saved from its most pernicious consequences by his genius and his race; in Raphael Mengs both these restrictions were removed from its play, and, to make matters worse, even in technical execution he regarded the emptiest eclecticism as the ideal, demanding a union of Raphael's line, Titian's colour, and Correggio's charm with the simplicity of the Antique. And thus there came forth under his brush those desperately learned and deadly dull groups, which (apart from being even in composition wholly superficial and untrue to the character of living figures) give us in place of human beings mediocre reproductions of antique statuary. To him the highest form was the allegory, and therein also he was only the sciolist pupil of Winckelmann, who had said: "The truth, delightful as it is in itself, pleases more and makes a more definite impression if it is clothed in a fable: what a fable in the narrowest sense is for children, the allegory is for men of riper age. . . . The more one finds of the unexpected in a painting, the more it moves us; and through the allegory it gives us both," and he demanded that the painter's brush should be "dipped in intellect." This recipe Mengs fulfilled in highest measure.

The Græcomania set in about the sixties, but only reached the level of a general European epidemic after about a generation. In England the two painters James Stuart and Nicolas Revett were immensely effective with their handsome publication: *The Antiquities of Athens*. In the German the excellent Göttingen professor Christian Gottlob Heyne lectured from 1767 on the "Archæology of the Art of the Ancients, and more especially of Greece and Rome." About the same time Wieland began his long series of novels of ancient Hellas, of which he himself said that their colour was borrowed from Winckelmann; Lessing remarked that *Agathon* was the first German novel of Classical taste, and Goethe said in *Dichtung und Wahrheit* that in *Musarion* he had believed that he saw the Classical alive and new again. Gluck also is a pupil of Winckelmann, not merely in his conception of Hellenism, but in his hatred of ornament and love of contour: "I intended," he says in the foreword to the *Alceste*, "to restore to music its true task; which is to serve poetry by its expression, without weakening the action by superfluous ornament. And I felt that — just as in the case of colour and the contrast of light and shade in a true and carefully constructed picture — its business is to give life to the forms without altering their contours." Hypnotized by Winckelmann's theory, the young and talented Asmus Carstens conceived the idea of discarding the brush altogether and painting pictures without colour — as had hitherto been the case only with the preliminary "cartoons," done usually in pencil, ink, or black chalk (with at the most a light tone) — and thus transferring the supposed achromia of Greek sculpture to two-dimensional painting. And in fact his figures do actually appear like white statues cut out of paper, and he even liked to begin by making models of the figures which he intended to paint. The remarkable thing in this experiment is that Carstens and his contemporaries never regarded it all as technical fooling or artistic bizarrerie, but as a legitimate and valid substitute for painting, which was thought to be destined to surpass it and replace it. In portraiture it was not possible to go so far, and the popular Angelica Kauffmann, the acknowledged leader of this art, contented herself with dressing the ladies who commissioned her as Sibyls, Bacchantes, and Muses. In France the last ten years of the *Ancien Régime* were dominated by a strict antiquarian, artificially simple and rectilinear style, which was called "*Louis Seize,*" although it appeared as early as 1760 and spread over other countries as "*Zopf.*" The Abbé Barthélemy worked a whole generation long on his *Voyage of the young Anacharsis in Greece,* which appeared in 1788 and for the first time gave a general picture of Greek life. In place of the towering coiffures there came a fashion *à la Diane,* and furniture, decoration, utensils, snuff-boxes, everything had to be *à la grecque.* Marie Antoinette played the harp in the Trianon wreathed with laurel and robed in Greek dress. At the famous suppers given by the painter Madame Vigée-Lebrun, the hostess herself appeared in a peplos as Aspasia, Barthélemy in a chiton as a rhapsodist, a Monsieur de Cubières with golden lyre as Memnon; the guests reclined on couches, drank from vases, and were attended by boys dressed as slaves, who served food, which, as an eyewitness relates, was "all genuine Greek." In the gardens were to be seen on all sides Isles of the Dead and Mausoleums, funerary and sacrificial vessels, lecythi, and shrouds. In this propensity for the symbols of mourning and of death we can see, already darkly presaged, the future.

Louis XVI, an insignificant phlegmatic being of a child's capacity and ability, was not among these people. He was interested only in work on his castles and in hunting. On July 14, 1789 he had shot nothing and therefore wrote in his diary, which he kept very conscientiously: "*Rien.*" This entry was one of the many mistakes as innocent, as fatal, of which his whole life was made up. For on this day the Paris mob stormed the Bastille, liberated the seven prisoners — of whom one was imprisoned for

" Rien "

madness, one at the request of his family, and four for forgery — carried the heads of the murdered guards through the city on pikes, and proclaimed the Sovereignty of the People. To the Duc de Liancourt, who brought him the news of these events late that night, the King, upset and still half-asleep, replied: "But, good God, that is revolt!" "No, sire," answered the Duke, "it is Revolution."

CHAPTER III

EMPIRE

> *" All who achieve real distinction in life begin as revolutionists. The most distinguished persons become more revolutionary as they grow older, though they are commonly supposed to become more conservative, owing to their loss of faith in conventional methods of reform. Any person under the age of thirty, who, having any knowledge of the existing social order, is not a revolutionist, is an inferior. And yet revolutions have never lightened the burden of tyranny; they have only shifted it to another shoulder."*
>
> *Shaw*

Side by side with that mighty spectral procession of mankind, now dimly discerned as by the light of a flickering flame, now hidden in complete gloom and darkness, there runs a brightly lighted gallery of clearly sculptured, proudly profiled character-figures which, throned solitary and motionless in their niches, seem entirely alien to the wretched crowd beneath them, but are nevertheless the bright lanterns by which we can get our bearings on the mighty stream of human life. These are the so-called great men. What is a great man? The question is hard to answer. It is still harder to discover how a man *becomes* such; as to that, paradoxically, one can only predicate that its definition is indefinability.

Yet, whether these questions are hard or are impossible to answer, great men *are;* that is wholly undeniable. Few certainties have so high a degree of certainty. And, instead of searching for the process of their becoming — a process which can never be completely established, because it is subterranean and takes place in the dark caverns of man's collective soul — we will content ourselves with putting down the result. This result is clear and plain enough, extraordinary as it is. These men were but yesterday

The Lanterns

as other men: individuals, separate creatures, cells in the great organism of the human race, units in the aggregate of millions; and suddenly they have become a whole genus, a Platonic idea, a newly-discovered element, a new word in the dictionary of mankind. Yesterday there was no aluminium — no one knew what aluminium was; today everyone knows, cannot help knowing, and must take account of this new word or sign *Al;* nothing is more real than these two letters *Al*. A man becomes a genius in the eyes of others by a precisely similar process. An individual has, overnight, become a concept. That process is just as great a mystery as the birth of any other marvel of natural creation. The crude intellect of the average man may have only the slightest understanding of concepts such as Socrates, Luther, or Cæsar. He may possess the most one-sided or distorted image of them; but he knows about them, he carries in his mind some kind of picture of them, they form a part of the stock of his associations just as much as the labels of everyday objects. And does he in fact know more of the other things? His understanding of the concepts "sugar" and "light" is no more and no less than his understanding of the concepts "Shakspere" and "Kant." But he uses them each and all, together: they are disintegrated, inexact, false; and yet they provide him with means to orient himself in the world and to be a little wiser. In the moment when a natural force emerges into light and becomes known to the consciousness of mankind, a word is found for it, usually an inexact and fortuitous word, but what does the word matter? Try to eliminate from the stock of ideas of the most ordinary man the concept "electricity" or "Bismarck." It is impossible in either case; he was, one can almost say, born with them, they rise involuntarily to his lips, they exist because real and true things to which they correspond exist. If he did not possess these concepts he would be deprived of a fraction of the means of communicating with his fellow-men; he would be to that extent a deaf-mute. We may, therefore, risk the statement that a man becomes great at the moment when he has become a concept.

The period of which we now speak enriched human speech with two of these concepts: Goethe and Napoleon, the greatest contemplative genius and the greatest active genius that the modern world has produced; the one, as Wieland somewhere remarked, was the counterpart in the world of imagination to the other in the world of politics. Emerson counts them among his six *Representative Men* — "Goethe or the Writer," "Napoleon or the Man of the World." Carlyle includes them in his six groups of *Heroes:* Goethe is the "Hero as Man of Letters," Napoleon the "Hero as King." They were alike in that neither remained true to the Revolution out of which they had grown: Napoleon because of his Cæsarism, Goethe because of his Classicism, both of which things are inherent tendencies of the cultural complex which in the widest sense of the word we may call Empire. That they should tread this backward path was probably inevitable, for, as Goethe himself said, "Great men are always bound to their century by some weaknesses."

In discussions of the French Revolution it is generally said that its greatest historical importance lay in the fact that it freed France and Europe by emancipating society from the domination of absolutism, of the Church, and of the privileged classes; and that the proclamation of the "Rights of Man" begins the era of intellectual independence, of legislation by the citizen for the citizen, and of unfettered economic competition. Now, it is quite true, of course, that certain emancipatory movements were set in motion by the Paris Revolution, but the view that constitutionalism, liberalism, socialism, and the other similar political movements of the nineteenth century arose from this one source is, stated in this crude form, false and misleading. The Revolution brought about the decisive victory of the bourgeoisie, but only at the outset; later it led to the decisive victory of the mob. The Revolution overthrew absolutism, but not for long, for on June 2, 1793 absolutism returned in the dictatorship of the Convention and the Commune, on April 1, 1794 it developed (not formally, but *de facto*) into the dictatorship of a single man, Robespierre, and by Napoleon's *coup d'état* of the 18th Brumaire the dictatorship became formal as well as *de facto*. Neither was it the Revolution that definitively broke up the old forms of hereditary monarchy, aristocratic domination, and the rule of the priests; these powers, alleged to be dead, experienced a partial resurrection under the First Empire, and an almost complete one under the Restoration in the reigns of Louis XVIII and Charles X. The French Revolution did *not* create equality; it only produced

371

another and more objectionable form of inequality in the inequalities of capitalism. The French Revolution did *not* bring liberty; it exercised the same narrow, cruel, and selfish censorship over minds as the *Ancien Régime*, but in the name of liberty and by much more Draconian methods. It asked every man if he was on the side of liberty, and if a perfectly unambiguous answer was not forthcoming it replied, not with *lettres de cachet*, but with the guillotine. Never before, either under Turkish sultans and Arab caliphs, or under Russian Grand Dukes and Spanish inquisitors, has there been such an unfreedom as under the " Constitution of Friends of Freedom," for never before was the death-penalty imposed for a whole series of quite passive qualities, such as culture, purity, tolerance, silence, even mere existence. Of the three slogans, *fraternité*, *liberté*, and *égalité*, the first was a mere operatic phrase, of which practical politics took no account whatsoever, and the two others were irreconcilable opposites. For equality is destructive of liberty, and liberty is destructive of equality. If all men are looked upon as identical and therefore subjected to the same rights, duties, and life-forms, they are no longer free; and if all may develop in accordance with their various individualities, they are no longer equal.

Nevertheless there remains to the French Revolution the high merit of having made the relation between the State and the subject, the ruler and the ruled, so to say more labile. The association of the two partners, outwardly still the same, became merely looser, much more easily breakable; from that time onwards a slight shock was often sufficient to produce complete dissociation. The European states became unstable combinations, after the manner of certain carbohydrate compounds which have a " free radical link." This " free radical link " has constituted since that time a latent threat to the structure of the State, ever ready to enter on new affinities and thus to change (or destroy) the character of the existing combination.

The nation of the extreme "The French nation," said Goethe, "is a nation of the extreme; it knows no moderation. It is the only nation of the world in whose history we find both a Massacre of St. Bartholomew and a Feast of Reason, the absolutism of Louis XIV and the unbridledness of the Sansculottes." The two extremes, between which the soul of France is hurled hither and thither, are pedantry and folly, and both have their roots in one and the same fundamental characteristic. The spirit of France may be briefly — indeed, summarily — described as consisting in an extraordinary absence of the sense of reality.

Pedantry and folly are not opposites, but merely different grades of the same relation to actuality. The pedant is a kind of tame fool, and the fool a kind of pedant run wild. Both have one-sided, incomplete, and therefore false perspective of life. They take, as it were, opposite positions on the thermometric scale. The pedant is at freezing-point, the fool at boiling-point.

One has only to attempt an unprejudiced examination of the French national character in its essential manifestations to find that pedantry is a persistent feature of the French, though one has to confess that it leads, in the highest products of the national spirit, to a most marvellous mastery of form. They have created a language excellently adapted to speech and written composition; a language in which it is impossible to express oneself badly; the only choice is to write correct and beautiful French or something incomprehensible, ridiculous, and absurd, and therefore not French at all. They have produced a classical tragedy in which vague, unclear, or confused writing cannot be. They possess a philosophical terminology in which illogical or vague thinking is impossible. They are the inventors of a centralized administration without which the Revolution in all its stages would have been unthinkable; for this system alone enabled the man who happened to have his hand on the lever of the machine to become the absolute ruler of all France, so that a country of twenty-five million inhabitants was ruled first by an idle oligarchy completely unfit to rule, then by a handful of empty-headed juristic doctrinaires, then by a gang of hysterical bandits, next by a set of thievish financiers, and eventually by the brain and will of a *conquistador* of genius. Even in the greatest period of their history, under Louis XIV, when they held not only the political, but also the intellectual hegemony of Europe, they produced nothing but pedantic creations of a monumental style, accurately compassed court poems, court paintings, and court philosophy. Method, program, mathematics, system, rule, *clarté*, have always formed the strength of the French, in complete contrast to the Germans, whose essential genius is brewing, soaring, experimenting, and centrifugal. But it is just these things that are the basis of the German's steady capacity for development and regeneration; he is never complete and rounded-off, and therein lies his greatness.

What, then, happens when the pedant is suddenly compelled by these or those circumstances to come to practical terms with hard fact? Will he correct his distorted picture of the world, his false sentiments, his biased concepts, his wrong perspective, in the light of reality and experience? No. Faced with the dilemma, he will prefer to force the facts to fit the theory. He does not admit that his thermometer is faulty; he merely alters the graduation. And when he reaches this point the harmless pedant is transformed into the dangerous fool.

This is how it happened that this magnificent and appalling leviathan of revolution leapt into the world, the wonderful and horrible monster whose blood-stained dragon's-body lurched for six years through the fairest country of Europe, destroying with its greedy maw human bodies and human dwellings by the thousand.

The starting-mechanism But we must attempt a more exact answer to the question of how in reality such a revolution arose. Taken by itself, there never was a more extraordinary and even nonsensical phenomenon. For nothing is more firmly rooted in men (even in the apparently most " enlightened ") than the belief in some authority or other. The atheist who regards the Church merely as a club-house would yet never dream of smoking his cigar in it, even without being explicitly forbidden to do so. And if any one of us today were suddenly to meet the Emperor William in a wood, would he not involuntarily take off his hat? Our experience, our logic, our intellectual convictions may conquer a vast number of prejudices, but our nerves, our perceptions, our muscles will continue to cling to the old ideas; the novelty has, as it were, not been discussed between the brain and the other parts of the body, and the lag often endures for generations. With our reason we believe that we no longer believe in things that our organism is still convinced exist; and the organism is the stronger every time. If this fact is to be observed daily in so-called thinking circles, how much more must it be the case among the mass of the people which lives wholly on its instincts! And in France, even towards the end of the century, circumstances were still particularly unfavourable for

374

so radical a change of attitude as this. No monarchy has ever been more fully recognized, no right of the ruler to absolute command over millions of men has ever been more unquestioned, than in France. No Roman emperor or Egyptian king-god, no Persian shah or Tatar khan has ever been so convinced of his absolute sovereignty as the king of the French. This conviction, however, was not atavistic, was no court convention, no megalomania; it was rooted in the convictions of the whole nation. The king might have his failings, his passions, even his vices, he might heap error upon error, and the people were in no way blind to these things, but they did not prevent anyone from looking upon him in spite of it all as a superior being, an exterritorial or even a supermundane individual, beyond the laws and the criticism of men, a radiant star whose orbit it would be folly to calculate by earthly standards. The *Roi Soleil* resembled the sun most of all in that his existence was a matter of course; the spots on the sun never led anyone to think he might be dispensed with or indeed could be done away with. And yet the worthiest among all these kings was suddenly, with the approval of the whole nation, brought to the scaffold, and everyone who called him anything but Citizen Capet was guilty of high treason. The disinterested spectator is strongly drawn to the view that the famous French nation must have been mad, either before the Revolution, when it revered a good stout fellow-citizen of moderate abilities as a divine being, or after it, when it forgot the purest, deepest, and loftiest sentiments of its ancestors and, in an attack of blindness, attacked its most sacred institution.

Now, the strange phenomenon of " Revolution " in the history of nations is not made any the clearer to us by the fact that we have ourselves participated in such a movement. This appears at first strange, but is in reality only too natural. The contemporary sees a historical event never as a whole, but by fragments; he gets his story in a number of arbitrarily divided instalments which appear at irregular intervals, and in some cases are missing. Moreover, distance has for the idea of time a different — indeed, a reverse — significance from that which it has for the idea of space; it does not diminish, but on the contrary acts like a magnifying glass. Hence movements observed at a certain time-distance acquire a clearness that is lacking for

375

contemporary observers; they appear, indeed, to take place much more rapidly than they really did, but this very fact makes them easier of comprehension. If we observe drops of water through a microscope, we see a multitude of small animals shooting about in it with astonishing speed. In point of fact these creatures, so far from being as agile as they seem, are actually moving slowly and idly. But the glass enlarges them some hundreds of times, and the speed of their movements is correspondingly magnified. Historical observation works similarly; events unroll themselves more quickly in proportion to their distance from us in time because of the time-microscope, which each one of us possesses without having had to buy it. Egyptian history, for instance, does not seem to us in any way longer than Prussian history; we have the impression of a few dynasties which ruled their little country with varying fortune. And yet that history is at least ten times as long. But for that very reason it becomes for us a manageable, luminous, and easily surveyed subject. This is the real reason why we understand more of the past than of the present, and not, as is often stated, the ability to place ourselves intellectually at a distance and therefore to judge more objectively; for the fact that it was spiritually remote from us would be a reason rather for our *not* understanding it.

If we are hopelessly puzzled by the present European revolution, we can at least console ourselves by the fact that the French Revolution was equally incomprehensible to its contemporaries, even the cleverest. None heard its approach, none sensed the subterranean rumble. Frederick the Great died shortly before its outbreak and did not see it. The famous traveller Arthur Young, who placed on record a series of the most admirable observations on France and the French, left Paris shortly after the summoning of the States-General, and yet he suggested that the coming change would increase the privileges of the nobility and the clergy; Wieland, in the *Deutsche Merkur*, expresses the hope that by about the end of the nineteenth century much will have been realized "which at the end of the eighteenth might be called, to give it the kindest name, the dream of an extravagant cosmopolitan." We have already seen what an idyllic picture Voltaire drew of the hoped-for reform of all conditions. Even Rousseau, too, in no wise contemplated a revolution of violence.

376

In answering our questions we must, I think, hold fast above all to the principle — which may be almost raised to the rank of an axiom of historical research — that the moment of origin of a historical happening can hardly ever be fixed with complete exactitude; on the contrary, it may almost always be taken as reasonably certain that the thing has *not* begun at the point in time which history assigns as its commencement. For example, it has been fully established that the Thirty Years' War did not have its beginning in 1618, nor the World War in 1914, nor the Reformation in 1517. The "Defenestration" in Prague, the murder of the Austrian Grand Duke, the nailing-up of the Theses at Wittenberg had in these three cases about the same significance as the release of the catch on a stopped machine, the sharp blow on a nitroglycerine container, the opening of the valve of a locomotive. A railway train maintains high speed for hours, carries heavy loads of men and goods to widely separated places. The true cause of this considerable performance is obviously not to be found in the release of a little steam. At the same time there *is* a specific chain of causation. The opening of the valve is the only possible means of setting in motion all the complicated and far-reaching movements that follow; in other words, the locomotive has a clearly defined structure, and this structure arranges for the release of the machinery of the locomotive only in one particular way. In the same way revolutions have their own specific starting-system, which remains, apart from a few variations, always the same.

This mechanism is a fairly simple one and has two elements. A revolution is let loose when the army refuses to act, which it does when the people have no food. This, putting aside all ideology, is the immediate cause of almost all revolutions.

In the school-books the cause of the great upheavals is generally alleged to be the unquenchable thirst of the People for Liberty. This certainly rests on false — indeed, the falsest of all — assumption. The people never desires liberty, firstly because it has no conception of it, and secondly because it would not know what to do with it. Liberty has value for two classes of men only, for the so-called privileged classes and for the philosophers. The former have won the ability to apply liberty to pleasant or useful ends through generations of careful "training"; the latter possess

377

liberty at all times and in all places, in every condition of and under every form of government. The great majority of men, however, who have not been made capable of freedom either by training or by philosophy, would fall into the most hopeless boredom if they were not diverted from themselves and their inner emptiness by a thousand imposed rules. Give a docker, a clerk, a gymnastic instructor, or a postman complete disposal of his time and his person, and he will become a melancholic or a rogue. And a point that is still more important, though generally forgotten, is that the more libertarian form of government nearly always makes the individual less free. Under the absolutism of the seventeenth and eighteenth centuries the citizen as such was condemned to almost complete nullity; on the other hand his private life was passed in a comfort, tranquillity, and undisturbedness of which we of today can hardly form any idea. Under the constitutional monarchy of the nineteenth century he obtained political rights, but along with these came the imposition of universal liability to military service — indubitably a much greater slavery than any despotism of earlier times. For there can hardly be a more grievous attack on personal freedom than the demand, implemented by statutory enactment and by prison methods of discipline, to submit to the control of one's person for three years, and to perform again in subsequent years, for some weeks annually, an unaccustomed and arduous piece of compulsory labour. But even constitutional monarchy tends in the course of events to give place to a freer form of government; the tyrant is entirely abolished, and the people reigns as sovereign. The result, however, is almost always that life, which has hitherto had the prison character only during the period of military service, is under coercion throughout its whole course. A free government of the people interferes literally in everything: it measures out the number of square yards of each man's dwelling and the beans that he may cook; it controls his use of light, his requirements in boots, his movements, and, if possible, his reproduction; it has the confessed or unconfessed aim of making human society into a boarding-school; of all this these very Jacobins provide the most striking proof. No State can commit so many follies and deeds of violence as the democratic State, for it alone has the *organic* consciousness of its infallibility, sanctity, and complete legitimacy. Even the most absolute monarchy has limitations of a hundred kinds, in the personal consciousness of responsibility of the ruler (which under democracy is always put on the intangible " will of the people "), in the court clique, in the Church, in the advisers and ministers and " government circles " that inevitably crystallize around every potentate. Moreover, the fear of dethronement, which is theoretically always possible, affects every sole-ruler. But a treacherous circular reasoning protects the rule of the " sovereign people " from any limitation — it is in the right because it is the collective will, and is the collective will because it is in the right.

Nevertheless the people, if it has very little feeling for liberty, has a very great reactivity to injustice. And, therefore, we must qualify what has just been said, by adding that the fact of the people's starving is not alone sufficient to cause a revolution; they must feel also that things might be otherwise. In short, every revolution, to be complete, must have an idea, or rather (since the masses cannot comprehend real ideas) what Weininger has called a " Henide ": that is, a dull and still inarticulate feeling, almost a premonition, of the state of affairs, which accompanies definite impressions half-consciously like a sort of broad border or fringe. Thus before a revolution there is generated among the people a sort of fringe-thought of a great unrighteousness, a disproportion and general inequality in the distribution of social burdens and privileges; these waves may remain underground for years — indeed, for centuries — but no politician should on that account think that they will not one day emerge to the surface! In the spiritual and moral life, as well as in the physical, there is something resembling a conservation of energy. Nothing is lost in our moral cosmos, and small, almost invisible injustices accumulate, as the microscopic silica shells hold up mighty reefs and mountains which change the face of the earth. The Bourbons had very gradually degenerated from strong hero-kings to splendid do-nothings, and, at the expense of millions of oppressed, joyless, and undernourished working people, reduced to animal status, they had made their court into a gilded glass forcing-house merely for the production of a few culturally useless and sophisticated luxury-plants. The people appeared to regard this as quite in order, but one day came a sudden shock which shattered the costly glass-house into a thousand fragments. The Habsburgs had maintained for centuries in central Europe a rule which in selfishness and narrowness was unprecedented by anything in earlier history, this rule also built up on the simple and convenient principle that the only divine right of the peoples was that of being ruled. For centuries on end the peoples seemed to admit this principle, until they one day unanimously declared that it was completely false and unendurable, was indeed not a divine, but a wholly infernal principle. So it may very well be said that every revolution has its birth at the moment when any fact of public injustice is changed in any human soul into a consciousness thereof. The first flash spreads with the same certainty and irresistibility as any other terrestrial light, though with far less speed. And thus it is, too, that every revolution bears within itself the germ of a counterrevolution, when it wanders, as it always does, from the path of justice. At the moment when men recognize that the most profitable thing a man can do on earth is to respect the interests of all other men, then and then only something resembling a stable form of society in all domains of life, public and private, intellectual and practical, becomes possible. Whether this society is oriented to the right or the left, whether it is absolutist or Spartacist, is just about as important as the hats or tableware which its subjects use.

The French Revolution had, among its many characteristics, one that was quite extraordinary. A revolution is usually a senselessly destructive, savagely animal, and horribly ugly spectacle: dead horses, bombarded houses, plundered shops, bridges blown up, charred and mangled human bodies. But the French Revolution, though horrible, does not seem to us ugly; it has for us a quality of dæmonic picturesqueness. What is it that converts a revolution from the raging chaos of greed and madness that is always part of its physical appearance, into an æsthetic phenomenon?

There are, I think, two reasons. One of these is universal in character. Events take on for us more or less the aspect of artistic phenomena when they have become historic: that is, when they are sufficiently distant. We regard them today with the disinterestedness which is alleged to be one of the chief prerequisites of artistic enjoyment. But this is because distance has a clarifying effect on objects. Paradoxical as it may sound at first, the further we stand from a fact, the deeper its effect on us, the greater its æsthetic pull. A plant seems to us more poetic than an animal, a child than a grown person, a dead man than a living man. The same naturally applies to the past. Even our own past has its own particular half-romantic character; we always think of past events, even when they were painful, with a certain envy, and we rather think that life was better then. Experience possesses much less reality than fiction. The events which history hands down are told, presented, thought over, their existence is in fantasy. But those which we live through as contemporaries are merely actual. Historical events come down to us in epic dress and have that aromatic, intoxicating, confusing effect which poesy always possesses and actuality never. When we live through an event, the deep spiritual impression that it might make is blanketed and nullified by the intrusion of a multitude of everyday details. Proximity is too great, the physical too importunate, for us to have a clear conception of the matter. Illusion, the mysterious effect of distance, is destroyed. That which *was* affects us more deeply than that which *is*.

But the second specially remarkable point about the French Revolution is the simple fact that this revolution was French. The Frenchman has the paradoxical and mysterious talent of making everything — God, love, liberty, fame, and everyday life — into a stage thrill, a sensational novel; he knows how to give everything a certain æsthetic presentation and a good and effective *décor*. The mere imposing ferocity of the instincts then let loose alone provided a dazzling spectacle to a Europe already fading out in dust of books and smoke of tobacco; Europe was awakened from its drowsy afternoon musings by a flaming torch reddening the sky with a magnificent display of colour.

In his report of the Convention session of January 16, 1793, which voted the death of the King, Mercier remarked: " *Tout est optique,*" a remarkably pregnant phrase. It seems that this whole French Revolution affected many like a ghostly puppet-theatre, like scenes in a magic lantern. No one has rendered this truly magic atmosphere more movingly and suggestively than Carlyle in his *French Revolution*, in which the strange shadowiness, the batlike uncanniness of all its events, and their so-to-say two-dimensional character, nightmarish and unreal into the bargain, are brought out with the most vivid effect.

Then, besides, there was the marvellous Latin perfection of form with which the drama was played. The public utterances of this wild horde of murderers and madmen, their speeches, pamphlets, manifestos, were always works of art. They might, without alteration or at most with a few cuts, be taken over bodily into a play. For example, when Robespierre, conscious of his omnipotence, had the effrontery to say to the Convention: "Who dares accuse me?" and Louvet rose, slowly took four steps forward, and, looking him in the face, replied: "I, I, Robespierre, accuse you." Or Danton, who cried before his execution: "Oh, my beloved wife, must I thus leave thee behind alone?" but forthwith interrupted himself: "Fie, Danton; no weakness, Danton!" Or the famous accusation of Camille Desmoulins in the Vieux Cordelier against Jacobin domination, which in its magnificent intensification would have made a show piece for Kainz (he pretends to be speaking of conditions under the Roman emperors, but refers, of course, to the present):

"In that time words became state crimes; from now on, there was but a single step to turn a sigh or a glance into a crime. It became a counter-revolutionary crime for Cremutius Claudius to call Brutus and Cassius the last of the Romans; it was a counter-revolutionary crime for Mamercus Scaurus to have written tragic scenes capable of a double interpretation; it was a counter-revolutionary crime for Torquatus Silanus to live ostentatiously, for the Consul Cassius Geminus to lament the unhappiness of the time, for that implied accusation of the Government; for a descendant of Cassius to have a portrait of his great-grandfather in the house; for the widow of Gellius Furca to have wept at her husband's execution.

"Everything awakened suspicion in the tyrant. Did a citizen enjoy the favour of the people, he was a rival of the Prince; suspect! Did he, on the other hand, avoid the favour of the people and remain sitting at the fire-side, this retired life showed that he was politically indifferent; suspect! Was a man rich, the people might be led astray by his expenditure; suspect! Was a man poor, none is so enterprising as the destitute; suspect! Was a man gloomy, melancholy in temperament, he was vexed that public affairs went well; suspect! Did a man enjoy himself and get indigestion, it was for joy that the Prince was indisposed; suspect! Was a man strict and virtuous in his way of life, he desired to humiliate the court; suspect! Was a man a philosopher, an orator, a poet, he desired to have a greater reputation than the Government; suspect! Was a man a victorious general, his talent made him the more dangerous; suspect! Suspect! Suspect!"

Asked for his name, age, and address before the Revolutionary Tribunal, Danton replies: "My age is thirty-five, my name is inscribed in the Pantheon of world-history, and my dwelling-place will soon be nothingness." Camille Desmoulins answers: "I am as old as the good sansculotte Jesus, a dangerous age for revolutionaries." In fact he was already thirty-four, but he reduced the figure a little for the sake of effect. When his fellow-victim Hérault-Séchelles desired to embrace him on the scaffold, Danton said, pointing to the sack containing the heads of the guillotined: "There, my friend, our heads will kiss one another." These are sheer scene-endings and *scènes à faire* such as hardly occurred to Sardou and Dumas in their best hours.

There was also much that was pitifully melodramatic. The painter David declared in the Convention: "Under a good régime women bear children painlessly." The Conventional commissary Ferry addressed the peasants of the departments under him with the words: "Noble friends of Nature!" and ends with the demand: "Good citizens are herewith invited to give the rural festival of harvest the sentimental character proper to it." The first number of the *Mercure de France* which appeared after the September massacres bore at its head an ode: "To the Shade of my Canary-bird."

The tragic operetta

Indeed, in observing the endless feasts of liberty and magnificent processions, the extravagant expenditure on decked-out noisy supers, on pinchbeck symbolical properties, on plaster and pasteboard and tin, it seems almost as if Revolution had been conceived by the French nation as a kind of tragic operetta. It often borders closely on the ridiculous. One day a countryman of a hundred and twenty years of age entered the National Assembly and aroused much emotion by his expression of republican sentiments. On another occasion Anacharsis Cloots appeared with a

383

train of " representatives of the human race," long-bearded Chaldeans, pigtailed Chinamen, bronzed Ethiopians, Turks, Tatars, Greeks, Mesopotamians, who offered their greetings to the Republic; in reality they were good Parisians cleverly disguised, painted lay figures of the brotherhood of man. On August 10, 1793, the first New Year's Day of the era of Liberty, there was a universal festival, for which David had projected a whole collection of gigantic fooleries: " Liberty " with a colossal Phrygian cap, the "People" as an enormous Hercules with a swinging club, " Nature " a more than life-size female figure from whose breasts water flowed. Simultaneously three thousand birds were let loose to the four winds with labels on their necks inscribed: " We are free, imitate us." Even in its most horrible operations the Revolution always maintained something of French *esprit*. Men and women were bound together and thrown into the water, and this was called " Republican marriage "; small craft were filled with " renegade " priests and sunk, and this was " vertical deportation "; even a word like " *septembriser* " has something striking, pungent, scientific. There is evidenced in all these things the power produced by centuries of intellectual development in the national consciousness, of clear ordering fancy, of bringing up the right word almost automatically in the right place, of thoroughly trained artistic eye.

Meanwhile everyday life, *fort comme la mort,* went quietly on its way, and the *esprit gaulois* did not allow its good humour to be spoilt. During the September massacres twenty-three theatres were open in Paris. Even the night-sitting which decided the question of the King's life or death was like a theatre performance. " The attendants in the neighbourhood of the Mountain," says Mercier, " were like the box attendants at the opera." The gentlemen provided ices and sweets for their ladies, who marked down each " yes " or " no " with pins on cards; there was betting on the result in the neighbouring coffee-houses. Duke Philippe of Orleans, called *Égalité* — great-grandson of the Regent, father of the later "bourgeois King" Louis Philippe, and perhaps the greatest rascal produced by the Revolution — devoured before his execution a breakfast of two dozen oysters, two cutlets, and a bottle of claret and went to the scaffold carefully dressed in the latest fashion, in a green frock-coat, light piqué waistcoat, yellow leather breeches, and new top-boots. Not a few ladies used their paint-box and powder-puff on the way to the guillotine.

In short, disregarding all questions of the moral or political principles involved, the *Grande Révolution* represents the strongest and most complete expression of the French nation to be found in its whole history, a nation fuller of contradictions than perhaps any other, so affirmative in its passionate joy in life and so negative in its dæmonic nihilism, so unchanging in its essential character and so incalculable in its different manifestations, fanatic and urbane, heroic and frivolous, sober and excitable, romantic to the point of absurdity and materialistic to the point of stupidity; a people of whom every imaginable bad thing can be said — that they are foolish, coarse, narrow, vain, malicious, greedy, often even devilish — but never that they are boring.

We will now briefly recall the course and the principal events of the French Revolution, in order to make a somewhat closer acquaintance with the character of the movement. Its immediate cause was an enormous deficit and imminent state bankruptcy. The only possible salvation would have lain in the execution of the reform program which Turgot — no less great as finance minister than he was as economist — had proposed to the King. The proposals included free trade in grain, abolition of the guilds and close trade corporations, and equal division of the land-tax on all properties. But he was forced to resign, and in taking leave of the King he prophesied: "The fate of kings who are ruled by courtiers is that of Charles I." At the outbreak of the Revolution France had about twenty-five million inhabitants, of whom twenty-one million gained their bread (if the expression is justified) by agriculture; for they alone had to bear the whole weight of taxation, and it left them so little that agriculture gave almost no return. Moreover, in the winter of 1788–9 there was an extraordinary rise in prices on account of a bad harvest and extreme cold. So finally the necessity common both to the extravagant court and to the starving people left no other course open but to summon to Versailles the States-General, which had not met for nearly two centuries, in order to discuss the necessary reforms. They began their sessions on May 5, 1789; as early as June 17 the representatives of the Third Estate, on the proposal of the Abbé Sieyès, declared themselves to be the sole National

History of the French Revolution

385

Assembly, *assemblée nationale*, merely inviting the other two estates to join them. When the grand master of ceremonies, de Brézé, commanded them in the King's name to leave the hall, Mirabeau replied: "Tell your master that we are here by the command of the people and will only yield at the point of the bayonet." Three days later the same deputies, assembled in the Tennis Court, took an oath not to separate until they had given the country a constitution. This was the first theoretical expression of the end of the unlimited monarchy and the rule of the nobility. July 14 brought the real victory of the people over royalty and aristocracy. On that day took place the capture and destruction of the Bastille, a tumultuary act of merely symbolical significance, but nevertheless of the highest importance, because during the proceedings the royal guard went over to the popular side, and because it gave the signal for revolt to all France. After this national guards were formed all over the country as engines of the people's military power, and communal councils as organs of its political power. On August 4, in the " St. Bartholomew of Abuses," the National Assembly, which now, self-charged with drawing up the Constitution, took the name of *Assemblée nationale constituante*, passed resolutions for the annulment of all feudal rights, equality of taxation, and the admission of all citizens to public office. A few weeks later, on the motion of Lafayette, there followed the Declaration of the Rights of Man: universal equality, freedom of the person, security of property, resistance to oppression, sovereignty of the people. On October 6 King and National Assembly were compelled by a revolt of the Paris mob to remove into Paris. The year 1790 brought further changes: abolition of nobility, introduction of the jury system, and (in accordance with Mirabeau's slogan *"il faut décatholiser la France"*) secularization both of the property of the Church and of the status of the clergy, who were now required to swear allegiance to the Constitution. In April 1791 the King decided to take refuge abroad, but he was stopped at Varennes and brought back. On September 30 the Constituent ended its activities, to change itself on October 1 into the Legislative Assembly, *Assemblée nationale législative;* its two principal parties were the constitutional-monarchist Feuillants (so-called after the Feuillants convent, where they held their meetings), and the bourgeois-republican Girondists (whose most prominent members came from the Gironde). The real political power, however, lay with the clubs outside parliament, especially with the Jacobin Club, and in the galleries of the Assembly, from which the mob shouted down the deputies and terrorized them with threats of denunciation. In April 1792 the Girondists compelled the King to declare war against Austria, which had already for a long time manifested a hostile attitude. On June 20 a noisy mob, the " procession of the black breeches," forced their way into the Tuileries, but retired after they had compelled the King, who appeared at a window, to don the red cap of liberty; a young officer named Buonaparte murmured in his own tongue: " *Che coglione* — what a blockhead!" Meanwhile Prussia had formed a coalition with Austria, and the supreme commander of the Allied armies, the Duke of Brunswick, published at the end of July a manifesto containing exceedingly unwise threats. This step, of which it was known the King approved, was one of the main causes of the second attack on the Tuileries, on August 10; the Swiss Guard, which defended the palace, was destroyed, the King suspended and taken to the Temple as a prisoner. In the " September Massacres " which followed three thousand imprisoned " suspects " were, after a brief hearing, delivered to the mob, who killed them with a cannibal brutality. By these proceedings the Feuillants were driven into the background, and in the Convention, the *Convention nationale,* a parliament of unlimited powers which superseded the Legislative Assembly on September 22, the Girondists formed the Right and the members of the " Mountain " (*les montagnards,* so called because they sat on the top benches) the radical-democratic Left. But once more the principal power lay with an outside body, the Committee of Public Safety, which through its power of accusing any citizen terrorized the Convention. Meanwhile internal and external difficulties increased. As early as the autumn of 1792 the scarcity of food was so great that Santerre proposed first that every citizen should live for two days a week on potatoes and secondly should hang his dog. The Duke of Brunswick captured the fortresses of Longwy and Verdun; the Republic seemed lost. But it was rescued by the skill and decision of General Dumouriez, who occupied the four outlets of the Argonne and thereby locked the door of France against the enemy. He wrote to the minister of war: " The camps at Grandpré and

387

Les Islettes are the French Thermopylæ, but I shall be more fortunate than Leonidas." The historic fiasco of the cannonade of Valmy — in itself a quite unimportant action — together with a devastating epidemic of dysentery, insufficient commissariat, and continuous rain demoralized the Allies and compelled them to retreat. On January 21, 1793 King Louis XVI was beheaded. Throughout this year there was "*la Terreur à l'ordre du jour.*" The Revolutionary Tribunal, an extraordinary court without jury and without appeal, raged against "suspects" in all classes of society. A royalist revolt in La Vendée was bloodily repressed after nine months of war. The leaders of the Girondists were imprisoned on June 2 and guillotined some months later; and with that the victory of mob rule over the Third Estate was decided. Towards the end of the year the Convention decided to replace Catholicism by the cult of Reason. There were now left only the "Dantonists," the moderate radicals (if the term is admissible), and the "Hébertists," the ultra-revolutionaries. Robespierre made himself the master of both by sending to the scaffold the Hébertists and, ten days later, on April 3, 1794 (the 14th Germinal of the year II, for the *style esclave* had been replaced by the Republican calendar) the Dantonists. The Revolution had now reached its culminating point, and the reaction began. Robespierre was overthrown on July 27 (9th Thermidor), and on the next day executed, and in the two groups of the Convention were now the Mountain, the party of the radical "Committees" and the moderate "Thermidorists." On May 2 (1st Prairial) 1795 the complete failure of a mob-revolt ended the Jacobin rule. Executive power was handed over to a Directorate of five; the Convention dissolved itself. The middle classes once more seized the helm, and the "Terrorists" were now hunted down as the "Aristocrats" had once been — both concepts being equally extensible, it only needed malevolence on the part of an accuser for almost every citizen to find himself arraigned. In the mean time the flood of the Revolution had crossed the borders of France; Belgium and the Rhineland were conquered, evacuated, and reconquered, Holland was "freed" and became the Batavian Republic. The peace of Basel in April 1795 gave France the left bank of the Rhine. In the same year appeared Kant's "philosophical project" *For Perpetual Peace,* in which he set forth the "preliminary articles" under which a perpetual peace of nations should and would be established. But the Treaty of Basel was only the first double-bar of a twenty years world-war.

The most important personality that emerged in the moderate phase of the Revolution was Mirabeau. With his strikingly tall, broad-shouldered, bloated, square figure, his great pock-marked head, crowned with a mighty lion's mane of unpowdered curly hair, and his huge buttons and shoe-buckles, his outward appearance suggested a peculiar, rather repellent but imposing elephantiasis. "His whole person," says Madame de Staël, "was the embodiment of force unregulated and unlimited." In his countenance, to use Chateaubriand's words, "there shone forth pride, vice, and genius. His eyes shot lightning flashes, his mouth thunder, his parliamentary speeches were conflagrations, cloud-bursts, eruptions, battle-symphonies, but skilfully composed, subtly modulated, and accompanied with economical but highly effective gestures. When he stood like a gigantic rock in the raging sea of enthusiasm and agitation, no appeal or contradiction could move him." Louis Blanc says: "There was in the National Assembly a fourth party, that party was a man, and the man Mirabeau." He formed that party which, alas, is almost always a one-man party, that of capacity and knowledge, of ability and intelligence. True, he also was no real political genius of the category of Frederick or Bismarck, Napoleon or Cæsar, but rather a passionate, elemental force. The Revolution itself is often described as elemental, but Mirabeau was a fruitful and intelligent force, and the Revolution was blind, aimless, and stupid, a merely destructive force.

It is always a sign of the creative gift in a man that he displays the capacity for seeing his data. Such a man was Mirabeau. All the others, from the learned Girondists to the bovine Hébert, had a " theory "; Mirabeau had none. He was intelligent and practical and therefore stood above all parties. He was not definable, followed neither doctrines like the educated nor slogans like the masses. He was for the Jacobins when they were against war, because he saw that war would only mean the victory of anarchy; he was against the Jacobins when they demanded radical democracy, because he saw that this must also lead to anarchy; he was against the King's coming to Paris, because he knew the danger of his giving himself into the hands of the people, and he was against his going to the frontier because he knew the danger of enraging the people; he thundered in one breath against feudalists and republicans, against clubs and *émigrés:* tendencies apparently contradictory, but in reality all serving one great end: the avoidance of hopeless chaos, and the creation of a modern monarchy which should be suited to the times, and of which the content should be, and the title should rest on, the promotion of national welfare and public order.

He did not shrink even from accepting large sums of money from the court, and yet he cannot be called corrupt. For he knew that they would not move him an inch from his clearly marked, straight path. He was a convinced monarchist, because he was a convinced Frenchman. " Good citizens who know the country and the nation do not want a republican constitution. They feel that France is monarchist by its geographical condition," by which phrase he obviously meant its spiritual-geographical condition. His whole program was contained in the words: " I want the re-establishment of order, but not the re-establishment of the old order." He wanted to see the King lead the Revolution in alliance with the people for their common victory over feudalism and the Church. Seeing the hypertrophied forms towards which the movement was tending, he recommended summoning the leading Jacobins to enter the ministry, which was in fact the only possible way of making them harmless. Unfortunately he died in April 1791. But even had he lived longer, he would not have been able to stem the movement of events, for the King was far too lacking in decision, too mentally lazy, and too much influenced by his foolish wife and the unteachable court party to place entire confidence in him.

The Cellar Rat, the Noble Brigand and the Headmaster And now the magnificent gutter-romance which so amazed and horrified Europe began its course. Its three principal heroes were: Marat, Danton, and Robespierre. Jean Paul Marat was a maddened cellar-rat, enabled by the failure of the public drainage system to creep from its latrine; furiously biting everything, filthy, maniacal, deformed, syphilitic, and filled with insatiable hatred of all who were washed, sane, and neither deformed nor syphilitic, he was the typical representative of the riff-raff of the Revolution, of the subterranean creatures emerging from brothel-taverns, tumbledown workshops, holes in cave or forest. George Jacques

Danton, a kind of " noble brigand " and bad copy of Karl Moor, was called the Mirabeau of the mob because of his pock-marked bulldog face, his booming voice, his strong vitality and joy of living; actually, he was by turns bloodthirsty and good-humoured, stupid and intelligent, like an untamed bulldog. Maximilien Robespierre was a headmaster turned demoniacal, who would under normal circumstances have exercised his tyranny on points of conduct; he brought nothing to the dictatorship but a conventional mind, a secondary-school education, and the reputation of a moderately successful place-hunter; he was head boy at school, and at any other time and in any other country would have become a struggling lawyer (as indeed he was at first), a magistrate's clerk, a book-keeper or a police spy; he actually became, what a head boy could never have become save in that time and that country, autocrat of Jacobin France.

The Jacobin Party is one great Rousseau, with a persecution-complex and a mania for persecuting, fanatical and pharisaical, phrase-drunk and doctrinaire, theatrical and pseudo-sentimental; but with this confused phantasmagoria of an over-heated imagination was associated in practice the very real reality of the guillotine. Its axe fell on all who did not by chance escape: on Catholics for believing too much, and atheists for believing too little, on the Dantonists for working too hard, and on Hébertists for working too little. As the regicide Barère expressed it later, one got one's neighbour beheaded in order not to be beheaded by him. Even during the moderate phase of the Revolution, Georg Forster, one of the most enthusiastic of the German admirers of the Revolution, had prophesied: " The world has still to face the tyranny of Reason, perhaps the most iron of all tyrannies. . . . The nobler the thing, the more devilish is its abuse. Fire and flood are as nothing compared with the disasters which Reason is preparing." Simultaneously with the absolute rule of Reason was established the reign of Virtue. Robespierre left no doubt of its meaning for him: " only the man of no possessions is virtuous, wise, and fit to rule "; " rich," " anti-Revolutionary," and " vicious " are synonymous terms. The most important of the Rights of Man that the National Assembly had proclaimed were security of life and property and resistance to oppression. But since oppression could of course only proceed from the dark powers of reaction, monarchy, nobility, and Church, there was a tacit reservation that resistance was only permissible against these; the sovereign people *cannot* be the oppressor, and consequently revolt against its will was the gravest of all public crimes. To avenge these, or rather to nip them in the bud, was the task of the Committee of Public Safety, which we can forgive the short-sighted enemies of the Revolution for regarding as an established and organized *un*-securing of all life and property such as the world had never yet seen.

But even the wise and virtuous who were ready to serve the Revolution were in constant danger of misunderstanding its meaning and intention, for it was easy to fall under suspicion of aristocracy under the severe rule of Reason, which demanded the removal of Strassburg Cathedral because it was so unrepublican as to tower above the other buildings; which sent Lavoisier to the scaffold because he was so unfraternal as to understand chemistry better than his fellow-citizens; and which permitted no golden-haired princess, but only a " beauty with assignat hair." It may be quite in order to imprison a girl because she is " suspected of having served a priest," even though the crime is only suspected — it is entirely logical, even, to give as the reason for the order of imprisonment against several persons: " they have intellect, and may therefore be dangerous "; Henriot, formerly a professional thief and now commander-in-chief of the National Guard, can justify the arrest of a hundred and thirty persons with the words: " These people are no Sansculottes, for they are stout and fat." But it is disconcerting when a six-year-old boy loses his freedom because he " has never shown signs of patriotism," and a pedlar because he greeted the municipal officials with " Good morning, gentlemen." And what is to be said of the imprisonment of a cobbler because he " was always such an aristocrat "?

The virtuous Robespierre did, indeed, do away with the materialistic cult of Reason and ordained the public worship of a " Supreme Being," he himself acting as high priest. But it was not advisable to have much to do with God; he who attended sermon or mass was lost, and the man who was caught receiving extreme unction was lucky to cheat the guillotine by his speedy death.

To enforce economic as well as religious equality, Reason discovered a very simple method, which hitherto the servants of princes had only not applied because of stupidity or malice. The income of each citizen was divided into a " necessary " part of a thousand francs per head per annum, and a " superfluous " part, of which a fourth, a third, or, where the sum amounted to more than nine thousand francs, the whole was taken. The superficial observer might think that this system had two drawbacks: possibly many citizens will not put forth their full effort if there is no sufficient incitement thereto, and possibly many citizens, though excellent republicans, do not possess the " necessary " portion. But of course in the ideal republic such possibilities do not arise; patriotism takes the place of reward as the incitement to work, and if good citizens do not possess the minimum income it can only be a case of aristocratic treason, which must be exposed. Equality, if not exactly liberty, is promoted by the decision that every inheritance is to be divided evenly among posterity, illegitimate children to stand on the same footing as legitimate. Further, the State fixes maximum prices for all garments, articles of food and drink, lighting, cleaning and heating materials; and it arrests anyone who offers or asks for a higher price. The production of goods is handed over to national workshops, in which the eager throng of manual workers are paid, not by piece, but by time (an arrangement which does not precisely tend to stimulate output), and the product is not lowered in quality, since every proletarian is virtuous, and whether qualified or unqualified is, *qua* good republican, a good worker. But as there are unfortunately many criminal persons who will not submit to the dispositions made by the central government, and as the peasant, in spite of the victory of democracy, shows himself recalcitrant, the Convention sends out its commissaries, who spread like a swarm of locusts over the provinces to execute justice; and these plenipotentiaries of the People's Will have six-horsed coaches, banquets with many covers, musicians, comedians, naughty ladies, and other amelioratives of their republican mission. The reactionary peasantry indeed lives on roots, just as it had done under the rascally monarchy, but the white bread eaten by the officials, the so-called " Commissary bread," is of such excellent quality that the *Roi Soleil* himself would not have despised it. But since even the most righteous will sometimes permit themselves mildness, the commissaries do not refuse the ransom which the suspects repentantly offer them; often, too, they succeed in rescuing for the cause of liberty such counter-revolutionary valuables as farms, furniture, carriages, and jewellery, by forcing up prices to the level at which competitive buyers are frightened off and securing give-away prices for themselves, arguing that " these goods could not fall into better hands than those of patriots."

The Assignats

But Jacobinism did not succeed in taking the final step to which these principles should have brought them: namely, the complete abolition of private property; or, rather, they did so only when the Revolutionary flood was already on the ebb. We refer to the remarkable Babeuf conspiracy in 1796, based on the motto: " *la propriété individuelle cause de l'esclavage.*" Its program went beyond Robespierre's, for it decreed, for example, that all citizens should be dressed alike and have the same furniture; all children were to be brought into a great house of education where they should receive the same instruction without any regard to their intellectual gifts; art and research-work were to be confined to such things as can easily be shared by all; all great cities were to be broken up, for they are a disease of public life. Babeuf had relations with the Mountain and was supported by the Paris workmen and the greater part of the army, and the plan was only defeated by treachery.

While Babeuf intended to abolish money by making the use of it punishable by death, the Revolution attained the same end by the introduction of the assignats. These were state land-bonds, mortgages on the nationalized property of the clergy and nobility; and their value (in spite of compulsory rates of exchange) fell so rapidly that a gold louis d'or was worth four hundred assignats in May 1795 and nineteen thousand in May 1796; some months later a newspaper calculated that the cheapest way of papering a large room was to change a gold louis into forty-five thousand paper francs. Liberty had turned France into a poorhouse and a desert. Half the land lay untilled, a majority of the population were unemployed, high roads and canals, dams and harbours were falling into ruin; hygiene, police, education, and street lighting disappeared, and the Parisian, thrown back to Merovingian times, saw wolves prowl on the outskirts of the city.

The Time Machine

In one of his Utopian romances Wells describes a traveller in time, the inventor of an ingeniously constructed machine with which he can sail in the time medium. He travels first into the

394

future, into a distant century, where he finds to his astonishment that mankind has split into two species: the *Eloi,* whose continuous leisure has brought them to the highest physical refinement and beauty, but at the same time to an infantine level of intellect; and the *Morlocks,* who by uninterrupted manual activity have become ape-like, cave-creatures, stupid robots. A certain adjustment takes place, as the Morlocks from time to time fall upon the defenceless Eloi and devour them. France was in a similar situation at the time of the Revolution. But in Wells's romance there is the time traveller to make himself master of the situation. It would be easy for him to subject the two degenerate races: the Eloi by kindness, the Morlocks by his energy, and both alike by superiority of intellectual power, an incomprehensible and therefore terrifying application of intellectual means. This rôle fell in France to Napoleon. The *coup d'état* of the 18th Brumaire brought down the Directory and set up the Consulate, which was already a constitutional (or hardly even a constitutional) monarchy. Its proclamation of December 15, 1799 declared: "The Revolution is at an end."

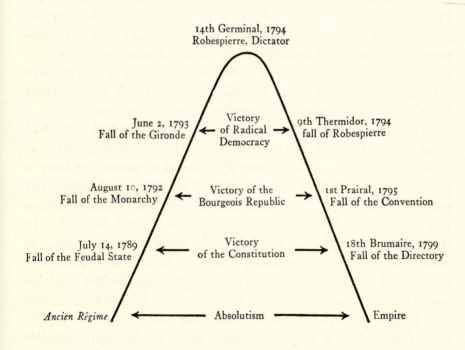

14th Germinal, 1794
Robespierre, Dictator

June 2, 1793
Fall of the Gironde ← Victory of Radical Democracy → 9th Thermidor, 1794
fall of Robespierre

August 10, 1792
Fall of the Monarchy ← Victory of the Bourgeois Republic → 1st Prairal, 1795
Fall of the Convention

July 14, 1789
Fall of the Feudal State ← Victory of the Constitution → 18th Brumaire, 1799
Fall of the Directory

Ancien Régime ← Absolutism → Empire

Looking back once again on the course of the Revolution, we observe that it was completed in regular form, describing a perfect parabola. It is as if an invisible pencil had put down beforehand on paper the equation from which it was constructed in reality.

By the storming of the Bastille, on July 14, 1789, the *Ancien Régime* was brought down, and replaced by the rule of the National Assembly, which meant the victory of constitutionalism over absolutism. The storming of the Tuileries, on August 10, 1792, resulted in the suspension of the King, or the victory of the Republic over the monarchy. The imprisonment of the Girondist leaders, on June 2, 1793, marks the sole rule of the Mountain, and with it the victory of proletarian over bourgeois democracy. With the execution of the Dantonists on the 14th Germinal 1794, the Revolution reaches its highest point in the dictatorship of Robespierre, and it then enters on its downward phase, the stages of which correspond exactly with those of the ascending branch. On the 9th Thermidor 1794 the Convention, as representative of radical democracy, vanquishes Robespierre, just as on June 2, 1793 he had triumphed over moderate democracy; on the 1st Prairial 1795 the Republic of the Third Estate triumphs over the Jacobins, as it on August 10, 1792 had triumphed over the monarchy; on the 18th Brumaire 1799 constitutional monarchy triumphs over the Directory as it had done on July 14, 1789 over the old feudal State. And the Revolution, which sprang from Bourbon absolutism, ends in the absolutism of the Empire.

Thus events shaped themselves just as a historical mind had already seen them in 1793, prophesying that the republican constitution would pass into anarchy, and that sooner or later a powerful man would appear who would make himself master not only of France, but of a large part of Europe. This prediction was made by an " honorary citizen " of the French Republic. In the later summer of 1792, just before the September massacres, the *Moniteur universel* announced that " *le sieur Giller, publiciste allemand,*" had received French citizenship from the National Assembly; other papers corrected the name into Gisler, Gillers, and Schyler; and in March 1798 " Monsieur Giller " got his certificate. And indeed it is only in the dramas of the young Schiller that the chaotic and yet secretly logical atmosphere of the Revolution has been captured. We have already compared Danton to Karl Moor; and the traits of other principal actors in the movement remind us of figures in Schiller's world: the cold, devilish reasoning of Robespierre and Saint-Just reminds us of Franz Moor, the poisonous hatred in Marat and Hébert of Wurm, the noble and oratorical republicanism of Roland recalls Verrina, and his sensitive, rather overdrawn wife reminds us of Amalia. (All the same, the reality often outdistanced any fiction: for instance, the colossally vile " letter scene " in which Hébert makes the eight-year-old Dauphin sign a protocol charging the Queen with sexual intercourse with him.)

Klopstock, also an " honorary citizen " of France, hastened to write a naïve poem (in which France, of course, is called " Gaul ") hymning the Revolution in the style in which Louis I of Bavaria was later to excel, and celebrating it as the new, refreshing, and even undreamed-of sun. Others who championed the Revolution in public or private utterances were Schlözer and Johannes Müller, Hölderlin and Jean Paul, Wieland and Herder, Schubart and Klinger, even the youthful Gentz and Baron von Dalberg, and at length Kant and Fichte; only Iffland and Kotzebue wrote silly parodies on it. But in the end almost all educated people shared the feelings of Schiller, who wrote to Körner shortly after the King's execution: " For a fortnight I haven't been able to read a French newspaper, so disgusted am I by these miserable butchers."

At this time the stars by which the German set his course were manufacture, domestic industry, and agriculture; everything, or at least everything essential, was produced locally. This both induced and presupposed a certain narrowness of outlook, spiritual exclusiveness, and mental inertia, but at the same time a warm intimacy and honourable self-sufficingness of normal life. Three-quarters of the population was rural, and most cities were not much more than big villages, agricultural towns. Great centres like Paris, London, or Rome did not exist. Moreover there were no machines or even machine-like tools; that is to say, there was no exact, plentiful, and cheap production and no easy, rapid, and extended means of communication. The uncertainty of far-reaching speculative undertakings, of transport, of world trade and political relations was, however, counterbalanced by a high

Sleeping Germany

397

degree of security in small proprietorship and small businesses, based on stability of the market, absence of competition, uniformity both of productive capacities and of demand. These conditions produced even in the " working " classes an atmosphere of reflectiveness and leisure which is hardly to be found anywhere today. At that period, in contrast to later times, the average middle-class woman was generally more active than her husband, but quite uninterested in intellectual matters; he on the other hand, thanks to his large leisure, could take a much greater share in all cultural things than he can today. There was also a relative absence of distractions and diversions and of the fuss of every sort that so completely fills our own hours of leisure; there were no big newspapers and mass meetings, no film-dramas and radio-dramas, nor telephone calls every few minutes, nor red-hot news by telegraph, telephone, and wireless; in short, none of the interruptions which break up our present-day life into fragments. The circumstances of daily existence encouraged subtle and imaginative thinking, introvert activity, as much as the environment of today discourages them. Out of this intellectual life arose the Classical age of German literature. Others sweated and hurried hither and thither, England toiled for bars of gold and sacks of pepper, America began to turn itself into the gigantic trust that we see today, France became a madhouse and a den of murderers, but Germany slept an honourable, sound, refreshing sleep. And what lovely dreams that sleep brought her!

Did the Classics really live?   A little girl once asked me: "Were the Classics ever really alive?" — a most revealing question. They have in fact been so hung about with hollow, false, and frosted phrases by the philistines who came after them that their figures pass before our mind's eye as empty, unreal, legendary personages; they have no more reality and individuality in our consciousness than, for instance, Knecht Ruprecht or King Drosselbart.

Even so soon as the War of Liberation Schiller's sentences were mottoes for gymnastic associations, and thus he became the " national " poet, and the pattern of the unworldly poetic youth living in an attic and devoting his whole activity to communion with his muse. The principal author of the legend of the " ideal Schiller " was his sister-in-law Karoline von Wolzogen, also his first serious biographer. Karoline was one of those susceptible blue-stockings then *à la mode,* and she had at one time cherished an unrequited love for her brother-in-law; this at once accounts for the fact that one of the very people who knew Schiller best has drawn the falsest picture of him, and for the fact that this picture became firmly fixed. After that, how horrible it would have been thought if Schiller's name was associated with blurbs or publishers' accounts! Or if one had dared to say: " Schiller had freckles and much too long a nose; Schiller's movements were impossibly ungainly and he was bow-legged; Schiller smoked and took snuff incessantly and was prone to drinking quantities of champagne; Schiller wrote on margins of the drafts of his plays notes of expected takings and expenses."

It was Schiller's fate to be turned into a lifeless piece of gala scenery, victimized even more than Goethe, because he was always the more popular of the two. Of Goethe, Herman Grimm says in his *Vorlesungen:* " If he had been shot from his horse at the cannonade of Valmy or otherwise carried off, his best friends would perhaps have opined, as in the case of Lord Byron, that his loss was to be lamented indeed, but that he had accomplished what was necessary for his poetic fame, and that it was doubtful whether any greater work was to be expected." Between 1787 and 1790 appeared Goethe's *Gesammelte Schriften,* published in instalments by Göschen in eight volumes; the subscribers numbered 600. The market for separate editions was even smaller; the number of copies sold were: *Clavigo* 17, *Götz* 20, *Iphigenie* 312, *Egmont* 377, and *Werther* (!) only 262; the publisher lost more than seventeen hundred thalers over the whole undertaking. On the other hand 3,500 copies of the first edition of *Wallenstein* were sold out in two months, although reprints appeared simultaneously in two German cities. But it must not be imagined that Schiller, either, was adequately appreciated in influential circles. In 1798 he was nominated honorary professor of philosophy at the University of Jena. In the draft of the letter in which he was informed of this, it was stated that the professional body esteemed it an honour to be more closely connected with him; but on riper consideration the expression seemed excessive and " honour " was changed to " great pleasure." The common German opinion of the Dioscuri was nicely hit by the Berlin engraver Clas when he put them on the same sheet with Kotzebue and Iffland, a production which sold largely at twelve groschen.

Two plaster casts
What, then, was the real significance of these two men, plaster casts of whose heads the German sets reverently on his table? They *lived,* and lived *symbolically.* That is their whole importance.

The life of the one was nothing but work, diligence, again work. Never resting, always moving, hither and thither, up and down; that was the manner of his existence. His whole intellect, real and physical organism, was just a giant motor which uninterruptedly accumulated, dispensed, and again accumulated power. And so he tore on breathlessly, an insatiable racer, until he collapsed exhausted in the middle of the race.

The other's life was nothing but growth, development, again growth. As a crystal slowly accumulates by silent " apposition," for ever adding new links in clear right-angled equal forms, so he grew, neither adding nor subtracting anything, neither slackening nor hastening the process arbitrarily. But when he had reached the greatest height and fullness attainable to man, he died; added no more crystals, but *remained standing,* radiant and clear-cut, with every facet reflecting light, an immortal human work of art, glittering for the coming centuries.

Panoramic ability
Goethe says in his *Maximen und Reflexionen:* " An English critic credits me with ' panoramic ability,' for which I am exceedingly grateful to him." In fact his *faculté maîtresse* could not be better described. He had a panoramic soul: a mind's eye which could see stereoscopically into things rich and full and was adept in perspective and chiaroscuro; and an encyclopædic all-comprehending moral sense. But precisely because of this miraculous gift his personality can never be reduced to a formula. Sometimes we think we have fixed him as something definite, but the next moment we have to admit that he was just as much the opposite of our definition. Hence much is talked about the " contradictions in Goethe's nature." And yet in fact his was the least contradictory personality imaginable; for he never set himself in opposition to what we call fate, neither to the fate about him nor to the fate upon him, neither in the world at large nor in his own life. He had the enthusiasm of a blue-stocking and the solid sense of a bureaucrat, could be the rough genius (even to the point of churlishness) and even the courtier (to the point of sycophancy), he

was pietist and atheist, German and cosmopolitan, mystic and materialist, emancipated and reactionary, a fiery lover completely absorbed in his passion, and a cold egoist entirely concentrated on himself: he was all things, because life is all things. He looked upon the whole world, inner and outer, as a mysterious laboratory in which dark powers arise and disappear, unite and separate, and he regarded himself as the passive spectator who has only to remain still so as not to disturb the magic play, and to report on it from time to time. His earthly life may therefore be described as an epic, perhaps the greatest and most perfect the world has seen.

Schiller on the other hand was a *dramatic* organism. His biography is a Schiller drama. His youth makes a powerful impression and is a masterpiece of tense and exciting exposition, and then the story proceeds through varied and violent conflicts at a breathless tempo — interrupted now and then by a rather declamatory philosophizing — up to the violent, tragic catastrophe, flickering out suddenly like a candle at the central climax of the action. He dies leaving the torso of *Demetrius,* the strongest first act in literature.

And when he was dead the Schiller drama continued to play itself out, uninterrupted, in the story of his fame. Here, too, it is all sudden, surprising turns. There was continual fighting for and against his reputation, just as if his plays were yesterday's first nights. It often seemed as if the success or failure of his works were a matter of a momentary conjuncture, mood, and tendency. Argument centred round him as if he were living, and there was never unanimity. He was dangerous politically and the saviour of his country, the mirror of noble poetry and a clear case of theatricality, a preacher of the highest moral ideals and a representative of an empty and outworn world of ideas. And with all this, in the resounding march of history, which puts the men and works of the past impartially in their proper places and finally separates the enduring from the merely temporary, Schiller was not definitely placed; he was all things at once, and the " for or against " remains unsettled. Perhaps he will never become a really permanent possession of culture; he will always kindle passion and call forth extremes in the minds and hearts of men. That may be his historical mission — a dramatic one.

Schiller once wrote to Körner: " I have really devised a drama

after my own talent, which has a certain excellence for me because
it is my own. If I venture into ' natural ' drama, I feel keenly the
superiority of Goethe and many other earlier poets. Therefore I
do not allow myself to be intimidated; for the more I realize how
I lack many and various talents or requisites, the more convinced
I am of the reality and strength of the particular talent which, in
spite of all I lack, has brought me to where I am. For without a
great talent on the one side, I could never have made good the
lack of others as I have done, and should never have attained the
influence I have on the finer minds."

This specific and fundamental talent which dominated
Schiller's work was his talent for the theatre. His poems create not
the real world, but another, freely composed: the world of the
theatre, which forms a complete realm of its own, with its own
psychology, its own ethic, its own logic — like Fairyland, which
also obeys laws evolved by itself. And to create an actuality of the
second order so complete and so faultlessly coherent, the author
must have also a sense of actuality, though one of a kind out of
the ordinary. In this world Schiller ruled unfettered and alone,
surveying, ordering, distributing, and directing; he is the absolute
Theatrarch. With a master hand he ranges the world of appearances in his theatre-system. Goethe and not a few others surpassed
him in the naturalness of their characters. The essential difference
is that Goethe describes his characters completely, models them,
as it were, in the round, even with their unessential lines; they lead
their own life and are to Schiller's creations as a massive theatre-
door is to a painted one. Schiller shows always only what he immediately needs, cross-sections; nothing is given merely for the
sake of characterization, every touch has its place in the general
scheme. Goethe creates men; Schiller creates figures. This would
be quite definitely a fault if he were not writing for the theatre, but
as he *is* doing so, it is not more a fault than the fact that movable
stage scenery is only painted on the side turned to the spectator, or
that an actor whose head alone is visible is not dressed in full
costume. There is hardly a single passage in Schiller's plays which
is not thought of in terms of the stage, for a space that has three
dimensions, but also only three walls. Goethe did not compose
specially for the stage, but placed his own personages and the
action in a real four-walled room and in true natural surroundings

that radiated colour from all sides; in short, in a world which can be viewed without disillusion from the back of the stage as well as from the footlights. His characters speak to themselves and to one another as if they were alone. But this was the very reason why he must be regarded, though under another aspect, as no more of a dramatist than were the poets of the *Sturm und Drang* period, discussed in the last chapter but one. They had one dimension too little, and he had one wall too much.

Schiller is known to have been inspired in composition by the smell of rotten apples. It may be said (without intending thereby anything derogatory) that the passion of his plots and the characters of his plays belong to that atmosphere. Their passion is entirely genuine, but there is something about it not quite fresh, a touch of the repellent and yet seductive flavour of the morbid and the preserved, of theatricality.

Technical considerations, as for example in the Bauerbach draft of Don Carlos ("tightening up the plot — ever tighter — apparent unravelling which only entangles all the knots still more "), are never to be found in Goethe's drafts, but Schiller was concerned with them to his very last days. Among these numerous annotations in which he appears like an actor at a rehearsal, intimate and unobserved, there are notes such as the following in *Demetrius:* " Must avoid repeating in this scene any point which has already arisen in the Diet "; " this act should be very successful theatrically "; " to avoid resembling the coronation scene in the *Maid of Orleans,* it must be introduced and acted on quite different lines." For a long time he hesitated between *Demetrius* and a similar subject from English history, Perkin Warbeck; before he finally decided he set out the *pro* and *con* in a detailed list, with remarks such as: " For Warbeck, happy ending, popular material, interests of the principal rôle, good début part." These are the ideas of a realist of the theatre.

Goethe thinks very little about the actors, but Schiller's stage directions are those of a gifted producer who never loses sight of the scene and the actors. Think for instance of Mortimer's extraordinarily effective first entry: " Mortimer, Paulet's nephew, enters, and, without taking any notice of the Queen, addresses Paulet: ' You are wanted, Uncle.' He retires, in the same way "; or the impressive silent byplay — an epitome of the whole drama

— when the Maid listens to Bertrand's report of the terrible danger that hovers over Orleans: "Joan listens with strained attention and puts on her helmet"; or of the expressive close of the first scene of the third act of *Wilhelm Tell:* "Hedwig goes to the gate and follows the departing guests for a long time with her eyes"; or the equally effective stage arrangement in *Demetrius:* "He places himself so that he can see a great part of the Assembly and of the public admitted to the session, but just so that he does not turn his back on the throne." In these and many other passages Schiller sees himself seated at the producer's desk. Even in his prose writings he remains a man of the theatre; even here he thinks rather of listeners than of readers, and the punctuation of certain phrases and passages (as Richard Fester has well said) "have, as directions for emphasis in listening, the precise effect of a producer's notes."

The Genius of the Thriller — Consequently the advent of Classicism constituted a really tragic moment in his artistic development. Without any clear conception of his own, he was forced in a direction fundamentally opposed to the bent of his character and to his methods of composition. It is well known that Goethe was anything but innocent in this connexion. The tendency of the time was the main reason, but it must be added that Goethe strengthened, sharpened, and emphasized the whole movement, and that it owed its final sanction to the weight of his suggestive and unique personality. He himself, it is true, was the least injured by this false orientation, but this very fact made his example all the more deadly. It belonged to his nature that, at bottom, he was incapable of being handicapped by anything, for he assimilated everything, good and bad, lofty and mean, alien or kin, and yet always remained himself; just as the human body builds a uniform cell-matter from the various kinds of food that it absorbs, so Goethe turned all material into Goethe, and nothing could permanently hinder his growth. But in this he was unique. Schiller's reaction was different; on the one hand he was much more violent and masterful, and on the other much more humble and impressionable. It was his nature to let himself be carried away and then to drag others along with him. Once seized with an idea, he was completely absorbed in it and did not rest until he had followed it up in all its implications and applications. When Goethe was confronted by new thoughts, associations, images, and leading ideas, he sought to possess them; Schiller in like case wanted to be possessed by them.

Schiller's Classicism reached its highest point in the *Bride of Messina*. Everything in the play is thin, pale, silver-toned, antiquarian, court-theatrical; it reminds one of the papery, anæmic " heroic landscapes " of the period, in which the very animals are pompous and dull. Even Wallenstein is slightly reminiscent of the abstract " representation " portraits of the period, which have more passion than individual likeness; around him, though invisible, are the Rigaud pillars indispensable to the portrait of a statesman. Even in *Wilhelm Tell* there is a good deal of conventional decoration. But, at the same time, it is manifest that in Schiller's dramas Classicism is only a bright varnish to suit the mode of the time. In 1801 he wrote to Körner: " Iambics do not help theatrical effect, but often hinder expression "; he had originally intended to write both *Wallenstein* and *Don Carlos* in prose, and in fact a prose version arranged for by himself was played in several theatres. In *Wallenstein* the Classicist misunderstanding of the Classical notion of fate had the worst results. The *Lager* is the highly original conception of a dramatic genius: the idea of writing a prelude to a tragedy in which the hero does not appear — and for that very reason is continuously and most impressively present — was indeed as engaging as it was compelling. In the tragedy itself, the idea of showing only the catastrophe, the last shadows of fate which show the hero against the background of a long earlier history packed with action and movement, was essentially a conception born of the theatre, but it was one that could only have been effective if it had been worked out with extreme concentration. Schiller forgot that *Œdipus*, the model that hovered before his mind, is only the *last act* of a tragedy, whereas Wallenstein has eleven acts and seventy-five hundred lines. *Don Carlos* suffers from a similar monstrous length. If the family drama is separated out (not so sacrilegious a proceeding as it seems, for Schiller himself composed it originally without Flanders, Freedom, and Posa), there remains an admirable drama of intrigue, full of force, tempo, and excitement, such as Schiller alone could write; even Otto Ludwig, the most inexorable of all Schiller's critics, has admitted the extraordinary merit of this part of the drama and has drawn attention to the fact that it formed the most instructive model for Scribe and his school.

And this really is Schiller's special importance in the history of the European theatre: he was one of the greatest geniuses of the thriller. We do not intend this term in any derogatory sense, but are thinking of the highest achievements in this category in Ibsen and Shakspere, Dostoievski and Balzac. Schiller had a passionate liking for poetical representation of dodges, *coups* and *contrecoups,* intrigues and cabals, and his imagination dwelt by almost exclusive preference in the atmosphere of the shocker. His youthful dramas are exclusively of this kind. Their " best-seller " character is indicated by the fact that their catastrophes lack inevitability. We have already pointed out that *Die Räuber* and *Fiesco* were often played — without detracting from their success — with a " happy ending," and Schiller himself altered the last scenes for the Mannheim theatre. Of *Kabale und Liebe,* too, a version was staged in which the President appears at the last moment with an antidote and repentantly gives his blessing to the lovers. For the prose version of *Don Carlos* Schiller composed another ending: Carlos stabs himself at the moment of his arrest, and Philip sinks down in despair on his corpse.

The *Geisterseher,* the first fragment of which appeared in *Thalia* in 1787, and the first volume in 1789, would have been one of the most grandiose thriller-romances of world literature. But we do not share the general opinion that Schiller left it unfinished because he could no longer find his way about in the tangled story; this would be in contradiction with his whole working method, which almost always proceeded from a settled and detailed general plan — in fact, such a proceeding would be improbable in the case of any author who set out upon a detective novel, for the story is unrolled from behind the scenes and necessarily follows a pre-ordained course. Plainly, he did not proceed with it because in the mean time he had adopted Classicism. But he retained till his death a secret liking for the thriller. Immediately after the completion of *Wallenstein,* in 1799, he thought for some time of a crime-drama with poison, kidnapping, and stolen treasure: *Narbonne oder die Kinder des Hauses* — on which he was engaged until 1805 — and of a more ambitious subject of the same kind: *Die Polizei.* " A monstrous and highly complicated crime, involving many families, and gradually pieced together by investigations that result always in fresh discoveries, is the main theme. It is like an enormous tree which has interwoven its branches far and wide with others, and to uproot which a whole area must be burrowed through. So Paris will be dug up, and all sorts of existence of depravity, etc., will by this means be gradually brought to light." The first act, which was to take place in the reception room of the Lieutenant of Police and was to show all the wheels of the great machine in motion, would certainly have been a genre picture of great variety and interest, such as a Schiller alone could have drawn. In his very useful *Literaturgeschichte des achtzehnten Jahrhunderts* Hermann Hettner remarks: "Who would care to have seen Schiller in the environment of Eugène Sue's Paris secrets? The spirit of beauty preserved Schiller from executing these plans." In fact this warning "spirit of beauty" and nothing else must be held responsible for the fact that Germany failed to produce that drama for which her strongest talents equipped her above all other nations.

The same spirit hovered over that alliance of the two Dioscuri which Hettner and other literary historians cannot praise highly enough. As is well known, Goethe and Schiller were at first mutually antipathetic. Schiller blamed Goethe for "a devotion to Nature carried to affectation," and declared: "His presentation of ideas is too sensual, it nudges one too much"; and finally also to Körner he wrote bluntly: "This man, this Goethe, is always in my way." In the memorial in which Goethe recommended Schiller for the Jena professorship he had nothing better to say than that he had "made a name by his writings," and he subsequently said plainly: "I hated Schiller." And when he looked back on the years of co-operation, he wrote to Zelter, in October 1824, nearly twenty years after Schiller's death: "I am looking through my correspondence with Schiller from 1794 to 1805. . . . I am enjoying it wonderfully, for I am learning what sort of man I then was. But the most instructive thing is the circumstances in which two men who forced themselves to adopt the same aims so squandered their time in excessive mental activity and external incitements and distractions that they produced at bottom nothing fully worthy of their powers, their dispositions, and their intentions."

In those ten years Goethe and Schiller co-operated in the

The Alliance of the Dioscuri

creation of two things, the Weimar theatre and the *Xenien*. The so-called "Weimar school" which arose from their exertions must, if report be true, have spread a perfectly appalling method of acting throughout Germany; it was manifestly the climax of the style described today (in a most unflattering sense) as "court-theatre" style. Goethe's fundamental maxim was: "The actor is always to remember that he is there for the sake of the public"; consequently he should not play with a "mistaken naturalness," as if he were alone. This principle, not in itself incorrect, was nevertheless taken literally and exaggerated almost beyond belief. The actors must always form a pleasant semicircle, must never speak towards the background, never turn their backs — or even their profiles — to the audience. The greatest stress was laid on cultivated delivery; excessively clear articulation, which eliminated the personality of the actor and the character of the personage, and a kind of sing-song declamation, which was considered the most beautiful possible — in short, it was the reduction of the art of acting to mere recitation and a number of fixed gestures. Consequently an unconscionable amount of time was taken up by reading rehearsals conducted personally by Goethe and Schiller — both of them, as is often the case with poets, being miserable readers. Schiller in particular was so bad that he on many occasions literally endangered the success of his pieces; he read *Fiesco* at Mannheim so badly that the audience, assembled in great expectation, went away after the second act, and the producer, Meyer Streicher, actually asked whether someone else had written *Die Räuber* and Schiller only put his name to it, for *Fiesco* was the very worst piece he had ever heard. He had a similar experience with Frau von Kalb, who told him after he had read *Don Carlos* aloud: "Dear Schiller! this is absolutely the very worst thing you have done yet"; and again in 1801 — when he stood at the height of his fame — with the *Jungfrau von Orleans*, which, according to the account of the actor Heinrich Schmidt, had had no effect, or rather a narcotic effect, on the audience. Nevertheless to the end of his life he considered himself the best interpreter of his own works — indeed, at one period of his youth he had intended actually to become an actor.

As for the *Xenien*, probably that room at Jena where most of the products of their collaboration were composed contained the maximum of wisdom, taste, *Zeitgeist*, power of speech, and knowledge of the soul that Germany could then produce — and everyone knows the result. The work was almost unanimously rejected by contemporaries; the leading papers, the *Erlanger gelehrten Zeitungen*, the *Neue allgemeine deutsche Bibliothek*, the *Oberdeutsche allgemeine Literaturzeitung*, Reichardt's *Deutschland*, Wieland's *Teutscher Merkur*, and almost all the others declared more or less bluntly that it was a failure. The general opinion was voiced most clearly in the *Kosmopolit*, edited by Voss, who (speaking of a prospectus which described the *Xenien* as " in its way a quite new phenomenon ") asked: " Who can maintain for one moment with regard to four hundred little poems . . . given to the public as a bouquet of delicate Attic wit, as a particularly nice *present*, but for the most part either coarse, or malicious, or dull and meaningless, and as poetry almost entirely without value, that they are, ' in their way a new phenomenon '? " And nine months later he maintained, in speaking of the whole collection, that amongst all the opinions he had heard expressed on the *Xenien* he had not heard one in their favour. It was left to the schoolmaster of a later generation to rave about them, on the simple principle that when each of two authors accomplishes extraordinary work by himself, what they produce in common must be twice as valuable.

Hebbel once wrote in his diary: " I had seen very little of Goethe's work, and I esteemed him perhaps the less because his fire was a subterranean fire, and because I imagined that between him and Schiller there was a relationship something like that between Mohammed and Christ. That there was hardly any relation at all could never have occurred to me." And in fact (as we have already remarked) they can be regarded as an absolutely classic example of opposed kinds of artistic productivity.

On June 5, 1825 Goethe said (to Eckermann, of course) in discussing the definitions of poetry: " What is there to define? A live feeling for states and the ability to express it make a poet." Schiller, on the contrary, wrote: " That alone is poetry which never existed in time or place." Two poles of the artistic world could not be more pregnantly described than in these sentences. But while Goethe's statement is clear to everyone at sight, Schiller's *mot* indicates the real paradox of the artistic nature. Emerson introduces his essay on Shakspere with the words: " If we require the originality which consists in weaving their web from their own bowels like a spider . . . no great men are original." Now, Schiller anyhow was exactly a spider like that; he drew all his material from himself.

Schiller, as is well known, had no knowledge about Switzerland but a few antiquated and colourless descriptions and some maps and views with which he adorned his room while he was working on *Wilhelm Tell*. And yet the whole of Switzerland is in *Tell:* all Swiss critics are astonished by the amazingly accurate portrayal of the country, its customs, its national civilization, its speech. Guide-books even today use Schiller's verses to orient and interpret by. The investigation of this problem has always been a favourite subject for the essayist. We may say, however, that Schiller not only did not need Switzerland for his description, but further that he was able to describe it so well precisely *because* he had never seen it. A careful tour through mountains and valleys would only have muddled him. The contradictory and confused external impressions would only have thrust aside his clear and powerful inner visions. A real Switzerland would have meant nothing to Schiller the poet.

There is a still cruder instance. In the *Musenalmanach* for 1800 appeared the *Lied von der Glocke*. People were surprised and delighted at the exactness and fidelity with which the processes of casting the bell were described. Eleven years earlier Schiller had worked on the material and (as Karoline has related) often visited a bell-foundry. But the poem would not go right, and he put the plan aside. One day, however, he came upon a thoroughly dull book, a technical encyclopædia by Krünitz. He read it, and the image was there! In the last chapter but one we drew attention to Kant as possessing, perhaps in an even greater degree, this ability to derive the liveliest and clearest mental images from books.

In life the relation of Goethe and Schiller was, strangely enough, just the reverse. Goethe said in his old age: " I am still a new-born child," and he was all his life passive, undecided, fundamentally aloof from the world, whereas Schiller, from his maturity onwards, was distinguished by very keen knowledge and resolute handling of the world around him. He was a virtuoso in managing the publicity engine (which he did to an extent that was rarer then than now), a master of blurb and prospectus; witness the preface to the selection from Pitaval, the prefatory matter to the *Sammlung historischer Memoires*, the announcements of the magazines that he published, the *Rheinische Thalia* and the *Horen*, both of which he edited with great skill, making use to some extent of some entirely modern journalistic dodges. In the *Horen* he calculated quite consciously on the snobbism of certain circles, writing to the publisher Cotta as follows: " Thinking is bad work for many people, but we must make him who cannot think ashamed to confess the fact, and praise us against his will in order to seem what he is not "; he arranged for the separate numbers of the *Horen* to be discussed at once, at Cotta's expense, in the *Allgemeine Literaturzeitung*, which (seeing that this was the most respected and influential of German reviews) would have been an unheard-of proceeding even today. When the *Horen* fell through, he gave serious consideration to the American idea of attracting the censor's prohibition by including a " wild politico-religious article " in order to turn the fiasco into cash.

If we carry the comparison between Goethe and Schiller a little further — although, if we are not mistaken, it has already been done here and there — the most marked difference will perhaps appear to be that in Goethe the extreme *optical*, and in Schiller the *acoustical*, types were embodied. Goethe says expressly: " Compared with the eye, the ear is a dull sense." All experience reaches him through the eyes. The sight of Strassburg Cathedral makes him a " Gothicist "; the sight of a cracked ram's skull leads him to his vertebral theory. With a dim feeling that Italy will bear fruit for him in new poems, he hurries thither to *see* it, and the idea of a Tell epic would have come to him, in an exactly opposite way from Schiller's, through seeing the Swiss places associated with the Tell legend. He wanted permanently to possess copies of the works of art that he admired; whereas Schiller did not even look at the originals of famous works of art when they were right in front of him. Goethe's poems are, as he has himself said, occasional poetry, and the same may be said of his dramas; with him the creative faculty grows out of concrete experience, and literary historians can put their fingers on the correlated passages in his life and his poetry. He had a great passion for everything to do with botany, but the cryptogams did not interest him, because their characteristics could not be studied with the naked eye; for the same reason he did not study astronomy. He turned aside from mathematic physics because it was likewise a science of the unseen, and from the Newtonian theory that white was built up from the colours of the spectrum because it contradicted visual appearances. He apotheosized the eyes so far that he never used spectacles because they were an artificial mode of seeing.

Music, on the contrary, had little attraction for him. He looked on it as a subsidiary art; the world of " absolute " music was closed to him. As is well known, he was as little in sympathy with the greatest musical composers of his time, Beethoven and Schubert, as was his friend the worthy conductor Zelter, in whom he saw the ideal composer of songs. But for Schiller music was the centre of all artistic activity, and especially on the stage. He declared that his poetic ideas arose always from " a certain musical mood of feeling," he repeatedly insisted that a dramatic work of art required for its completion music, and he gave it a large and dominating place in the dramatic economy. The climaxes of his later works especially are musically experienced and very often demand direct support from the orchestra. Indeed, some of his poetic dramas, such as *Tell* and the *Maid of Orleans,* may almost be described as opera with spoken words — which, however, is no reproach, save in the eyes of those art-Bolshevists who, void of theatre-sense, have recently had the imbecile impertinence to cut out from *Tell* (as being unessential padding) details such as the prelude, the chorus of the Monks Hospitallers, and the musical finale of the Rütli act.

Static and Dynamic

We might perhaps bring the contrast between Goethe and Schiller to another common denominator by describing Goethe as static, Schiller as dynamic. This classification has the fault of all formulæ, in attempting the wholly impossible task of bringing living organisms within a cut-and-dried definition; it also has the advantage of a formula in establishing two clear groups stretching beyond individual to general significance. For the " static " Goethe the pivot of life, thought, and philosophy is in being, in resting, in the eternal; for Schiller it is in becoming, in moving. In somatology it is the province of anatomy that forms Goethe's field of work, and he took little interest in physiology, which is concerned with changes in the body. But the only scientific treatise that Schiller ever wrote, his dissertation, was originally entitled *Philosophy of Physiology*. Goethe's principal botanical study was in morphology, the science of the enduring form of the plant; his "prime plant" is a powerful attempt to refer the different stages of plant-development to a unitary, permanent, fundamental principle, to make a being out of a becoming. The chief of his inorganic studies was mineralogy, for which he had a passion; but he took little interest in the basic science of all mineralogy, chemistry, because it is concerned with the metamorphosis of matter and is a dynamic science.

After all this it does not need closer inspection to explain why Goethe was so important as a lyrical poet, but never wrote real drama, while with Schiller the case is exactly the opposite; why Goethe took such keen interest in art, and Schiller in politics; why Schiller was one of the most intelligent and comprehending pupils of Kant (whose philosophy, as we have seen, had no other subject but the becoming of our understanding), while Goethe declared that he could not understand him. We will only mention one more apparent contradiction: Goethe was a great traveller and a great writer on his travels, just because he was static. For the travel-lover, although constantly on the move, always has his attention at any given moment concentrated on the permanent; the various descriptions with which travel-literature is in touch — ethnography, geography, archæology, geognosy — are essentially founded on principles.

The relation between the two can be reduced to the two cardinal notions, Nature and History; Goethe was one of the greatest naturalists, Schiller one of the greatest historians, of the time. *Nature and History*

In Goethe's poetry, too, Nature predominates. We always know about the weather, the time of day, the season of the year, and the latitude, even without the smallest direct mention of these things; the atmosphere breathed by his personages lies thick around them, envelops them as a particular tone envelops a picture. This applies even to the most abstract scenes in the Second Part of *Faust*. Schiller is not indifferent to the landscape, the physical environment. Indeed, he realizes that it is a very effective factor; think of the splendid close of the Rütli scene: "The empty stage remains disclosed for a time and displays the vision of the sun rising over the snow mountains." But the effect made is always that of something painted, which is added where it will increase the stage effect, as a piece of theatrical machinery to switch on and off. Hence, whenever it is used, it stares us in the face much more than is the case with Goethe. This is evidence against, and not for, Schiller's feeling for nature; for real nature is something that is always there, almost imperceptible. The lake in *Tell*, the thunderstorm in the *Maid*, the forest in the *Räuber* are almost dramatis personæ. On the other hand this equally proves Schiller's strong sense of the theatre, for on the stage nothing is justified that cannot also stand on the bill.

"History" dominates Schiller's works. Goethe is the dramatist of private life, Schiller of world-historical matters. All his pieces, even his "domestic" plays, have a big political background. It is more or less an accident that Karl and Franz Moor are only the sons of a small reigning Count, and that the President and Ferdinand live at a duodecimo court. They speak and act as if they bore distinguished names to be found in every book in history. But with Goethe the historical element is merely a question of names. Tasso happens to be called Tasso; he would interest us just as much if he were not identified with the author of the *Gerusalemme Liberata*, and Egmont, for his effect on us, might quite as well be a mere namesake of the Netherlands hero.

Dictation and Dictatorship

We have already spoken of the dynamic element in Schiller's life. His development proceeded with a haste and energy, a feverish hurry arising from a dark foreboding of having but little time. He was able to keep the mastery of the permanent physical and psychical state of crisis that we usually call genius by his remarkably clear and strong talent for disposing; his marvellous economy is the use of exactly and carefully distributed powers so as to give the impression of richness, superfluity, and lavishness. While working on one drama he was always already thinking of the next, and there was only the minutest pause for breath between the completion of one and the beginning of the new one. If, by way of exception, he had not decided definitely on a new subject, he felt, as he said, as if he were floating in a vacuum. He even tells us that he, in moments of physical well-being, detected a slackening of intellectual activity and will-power; here, once more, is that remarkable connexion between sickness and productiveness which was discussed in the first volume. The difference between him and Goethe is apparent in the external circumstances of their work;

in the latter part of his life Goethe almost always dictated, but Schiller never — he snorted and stamped, declaimed and gesticulated during composition in the most terrifying way.

Goethe did not take art excessively seriously. He had none of the artist's monomania (necessary in some degree) which makes his own small fragment of human activity the centre of the world. But Schiller had it, like the actor. With him work, in the modern sense, entered art in a way quite new to the time, meaning by "work" the overcoming of obstacles within and without and the ordering of all activity under a predetermined plan. But Goethe, for all his continuous, careful, and many-sided activity, did not "work" in this sense. He remained amateur, lover, and poet, thinker and investigator as the occasion moved him. His work seemed to arise from chance, even though in reality it came from deepest necessity. One day he discovers the intermaxillary bone, on the next he is writing his life-history, or a part of *Faust*, or perhaps a perfectly colourless report on mining or education. Everything is of equal importance, equal interest, to him. He makes no choice. He never allows himself to be pushed into anything. He knows that if anything is indispensable to him it will one day take possession of his soul. Paradoxical as it may sound, it is true that Goethe, this enormous intellect which reabsorbed and transformed almost the whole of human knowledge of his own and former days, was in fact not an active, but a passive nature.

Schiller on the other hand made everything out of himself. That is why, in a certain sense, he seems the more modern of the two. What would he not have done, with his unremitting talent for organization, with the means that would be his today: festival-theatres, giant publishing-businesses, popular institutes, journals with world-wide circulation! One can see him equipped with fountain-pen and typewriter, or as film scenario-writer and broadcasting speaker. Goethe is unimaginable in such circumstances; he is the last representative of the age of tranquillity.

So completely dynamic was Schiller that he may be said to have been nothing else. Movement was everything to him. And the vehicle by which he set himself and others in motion was idealism. Schiller's specific idealism is nothing but the overpowering expression of his immense temperament, of his extraordinary personal powers of tension. This idealism, elemental, unlimited, uncompromising, acted, as it were, quantitatively. His passionate optimism was such that he could only shout what he had to say. He could only write in capital letters. Oscar Wilde once said that a map of the world on which Utopia is not shown is not worth looking at, for it omits a shore on which mankind will always land; once arrived there, man looks around for a better land and directs his sail thither; progress is the realization of Utopias. Schiller preached this kind of human progress all his life. Utopia was the most important province on his map of the world. And in this sense Schiller offers a program for all poets, for without this program a true poet is quite impossible. His form could not be that of anybody else's Utopia, for it was proper only to himself, but his whole manner of vision, life, and being will remain an example for ever. His road was upward, away from the earth, from yesterday, from today. He looked away from " things," not into the unrealities of the past which never existed, but into the realities of the future which do not yet exist. That was the poetic in him. For a poet is in the last resort nothing more or less than one who understands more of the future than of the present.

In this sense it may also be said that Schiller was the strongest and purest Romanticist of his age, although he was so bitterly attacked by the Romantic school, who introduced into the intellectual life of the closing century a new variant.

What is Romanticism? One might imagine that the answer to this question is uncommonly easy. Romanticism, it will be said, is a heightening and colouring of existence, it is exoticism and fantasy and correspondingly a return to the art and philosophy of those earlier ages whose roots were in a more decorative and " poetic " spiritual life.

And this indeed was at first the idea of the poets and literary men who founded the Romantic school. But only at first. For the clock of history cannot be put back. You cannot return to the art or the spiritual constitution of earlier times even though possibly they were fuller and more beautiful, and we cannot go " back to the Antique," " back to Gothic," " back to the German Renaissance "; all we can accomplish with this vain desire is to invest the philosophy and artistic aims of the present with a particular colour.

This state of things could not in the long run remain hidden even from the Romanticists, and consequently — the more so as their recognition of it was still unclear — the whole Romantic movement and its philosophy became tangled, enigmatical, and labyrinthine, so that it is almost impossible to comprehend and define it. Anyhow the Romanticists themselves could not. Although they believed or professed that they were striving for a return to the forms of primitive cultures, they were in fact the most modern, complicated, and critical, even, it must be said, the least fanciful, men of their time. An intellectual and artistic movement which has for its motto a return to the ancient and the native, to childlike dreams and story-telling, to mysticism and naïve piety, was called into life by a combination of highly reflective, refined, and intellectual dialecticians, sceptics, and philosophers; and by the mere fact that the movement had a program it immediately acquired a character of second-handness, of something translated, substituted, interpolated; and this need not surprise anyone, considering that this generation was more enlightened and instructed, more subtle, and more introspective than any that had preceded it. In short, what emerged from all these intellectual efforts was not real Romanticism, but Romanticism as a noteheading to paper and (so far as concerns the most talented of the school) Romanticism as a cleverly staged comedy. The star of this theatrical company was Ludwig Tieck; literally so, for he was the most applauded declaimer and improvisator of his time, and it was universally agreed that if he had gone on the stage, he would have been one of the greatest of actors. This trait passed into his writings. The figures in his historical romances are actors in costume, and his lyrics are nothing but a magnificent, well-stocked stage-wardrobe of romantic metaphors and associations. He was the actor-genius of Romanticism as Friedrich Schlegel was its journalist-genius and Wilhelm Schlegel its professor-genius. In the light of this we can understand how it was that he became one of the most brilliant representatives of the genre (which in fact he was the first to bring to full development) of the artificial fairy-tale, which professes to be infantine, but is in fact satire. The Romanticism of Tieck and of almost all his fellows is merely a studio joke, a masked ball, at which the extreme rationalists are disguised as believers; Heine put it as accurately as maliciously when he said that Tieck lived in the same house as Nicolai, but one storey higher. All his work is conscious and mechanical, willed, and built up. His famous figure William Lovell, in whom he sought to represent the immoralist, is characteristic. Lovell presents himself as a waster and a rascal, declaring: " I myself am the only law in the whole of nature," and he conscientiously executes the task he has set himself; but we don't believe in a single one of the vices and crimes of this tutor in amorality. This is even more marked in Friedrich Schlegel's novel *Lucinde,* of which Karoline, Wilhelm's wife, remarked that it was the still-born child of the union of pedantry and sin. Rationalism was not, however, so serious for Friedrich as it was for Tieck, since Friedrich's principal activity was in the philosophical and scientific field. His fundamental fault lay elsewhere, in his moody, loose, rhapsodical method of thought and work. Although there was an abundance of original and fruitful ideas fermenting in him, he could never pull himself together to achieve a comprehensive unified conception. The meals he provided consisted of abundance of piquant and rare *hors d'œuvres.* At first he hoped to make a virtue of his defect, maintaining that " fragments are the proper form of universal philosophy "; but later on he wrote to his brother, with full self-knowledge: " Didn't you know that I always make good my want of inner strength by making plans? " and his brother said of him: " His whole genius really limits itself to mystic terminology."

Romanticist irony   In truth, we have before us the remarkable fact that a great intellectual movement, a quite new poetry and philosophy, grew from a few brilliantly fashioned, coloured, and polished catchwords and terms. Quite simply, we have to think of the Romanticists as the " moderns " of the end of the eighteenth century. The school was, as new movements are apt to be, very self-conscious, self-satisfied, and doctrinaire and most firmly convinced that it possessed the only right and final view of the nature of art; very busy, propagandist, and tumultuous, actively quarrelling with its predecessors and scenting antiquatedness everywhere; publicly defiant of public opinion, but secretly delighting in large editions and eagerly seeking to monopolize publishers and journals; but nevertheless, with its challenging offensive against outworn, stale, and exhausted forms, a powerful liberating force. The Romanticists had taken over from the *Sturm und Drang* the cult of the ego, the doctrine of the supremacy of sentiment, hatred of the En-

418

lightenment and of professionalism, enthusiasm for the German past, and a provocative praise of irregularity and illegitimacy. They resembled the Expressionists in that they possessed a detailed program (which, however, they were unable to carry into effect because of their self-consciousness and their impotence to create) and that they were intoxicated with their own affected and confused, though considerably cleverer phraseology, enveloping themselves and the external world in a mist of words. These deliberate attempts to do away with logic and order led eventually to complete obliteration of the boundaries between the different arts, between art and life, between philosophy, poetry, and religion, and between the different sense-impressions; colours were experienced as sounds, sounds as scents, and they dreamed of a poetic art which should have " at most a broad allegorical sense and an indirect effect like music." They had a special preference for the fairy-tale because of its independence of causality. " All poetry," said Novalis, " must be akin to the fairy-tale. The poet adores chance." The romanticizing of the drama consisted, according to Tieck, in breaking up the dramatic structure by the insertion of epic and lyric elements. In the Jena circle Romanticist often meant merely novelistic, and the novel was then considered the highest form of literary art, evidently because of that formlessness which the novels of that time (and precisely the best of them) exemplify. Jean Paul Richter, who was supreme in this style, was one of those figures that appear from time to time in the history of literature, an outsider and oddity who is yet both determinative and permanently significant. His wide outlook, arising from his inexhaustible store of ideas and observations, defied all strict definitions and formulation. Wilhelm Schlegel aptly called his novels monologues, and indeed his extreme subjectivity brought down everything that he observed and everything that he formed to private conversation. But he possessed something rare that lies between the Classical seriousness and the Romanticist art — humour. This is the rich, clear-flowing source of his solitary creativeness, which, however, dissolved and fluidized everything. But the Romantic school, to which Jean Paul did not really belong, proceeded from the theory that an art which produced complete illusion was no true art at all, for true art must have free play; they therefore laid down the principle that illusion must be broken down by irony, self-parody; and this is the sense of the famous "romantic irony," which eventually succeeded in raising everything to the power of two, laughing at its own jokes, and contemplating its own contemplations.

"Double Love"

This universal tendency to look calmly on everything, to make fun of everything, to find antithesis immediately everywhere, gave contemporary life an intellectual, but a frivolous, colour. The numerous — one may actually say, fashionable — " double loves " of the time showed that the ironic point of view also embraced erotic relations; almost always a woman stands between two men, or a man between two women: Karoline Schlegel between Wilhelm and Schelling, Bürger in a kind of double marriage between two sisters, Prince Louis Ferdinand of Prussia between the gentle Henriette Fromm and Pauline Wiesel, the "marvel of beauty and vulgarity"; and Novalis loved at the same time a living and a dead woman — Sophie von Kühn, who died at thirteen, and his fiancée, Julie von Charpentier, a situation which he sought to explain to himself by saying that it was only in the world of appearance that Sophie and Julie were two persons, but that in the world of reality they were one. Schiller hesitated long between the two Wolzogen sisters, Lotte and Line (in Weimar almost all the women were then Charlottes or Karolines), until the intervention of Fräulein Karoline von Dacheröden, who, however, had already divided her affection between Wilhelm von Humboldt and Karl von Laroche; and Laroche was unable to decide between her and the beautiful Berlin Jewess Henriette Herz, later the soul-friend of Schleiermacher.

Unromantic Romanticism

In the first volume we have tried to show that the whole history of modern times consists in nothing but the intensification and over-intensification of the rationalist principle in its application to all the departments of life. That is why we call this development the crisis of the European soul, and we are optimists enough to believe that this crisis has been surmounted by the health-restoring trauma of the World War, and that a new era has dawned. We have also on occasion pointed out that the so-called counter-movements that appear periodically in the course of the Modern Age were just as rationalist as the rationalism which they criticized. The truth is that at certain periods reason asserts itself naked and triumphant, while at other moments it has twinges of conscience — moral twinges, as being never wholly free from a utilitarian element; æsthetic, on account of stifling of fancy; religious because it is anti-mystical, earthly, and at bottom atheistic — and correspondingly seeks to hide itself from itself. Such counter-currents were the Baroque reacting against Humanism, Sensibility reacting against the Enlightenment, Romanticism reacting against Classicism, and the Neo-Romanticism of the end of the century reacting against Naturalism. Sometimes these " Romantic " reactions were much more rational, more thought out, built up, and conscious than the preceding " realistic " movements, which often broke out with the force of nature in their elemental drive towards charity, truth, and reality.

In their fight against Classicism the Romantic school proved unable to create an opposition style; and what they accomplished was rather the abolition of all style. And the most important and extraordinary thing is that Romanticism was really only a " sport " of Classicism. Rudolf Haym, in his standard work (still unsurpassed) on the Romantic school, calls Hölderlin a " side-issue of Romantic poetry "; the description could be inverted and the whole Romantic school called a side-issue of the Classicist poetry. Its whole artistic revolution was nothing but an affair of catchwords, twisting of points, and juggling with antitheses, word-fencing in front of a mirror, clever dialectical strokes, lashing into foam, and cold devil's advocacy: an artistic experiment on whether things could be done " differently." And really not even as much as that. Friedrich Schlegel says in his *Gemäldebeschreibungen:* " Serious and severe forms in definite outlines that stand out sharply; no painting in chiaroscuro and dirty colour, night and shadow, but clear relations and mass of colour as in a plain harmony . . . that alone is the style I like." Winckelmann might have written that, and indeed Friedrich says himself that his ideal is to become the " Winckelmann of Greek poetry." In precisely the same vein he declares Greek poetry to be the " canon of natural poetry," which is " an effective law and universal prototype for all ages and all nations," and he categorically demands a return to the Greek. Of his brother, Wilhelm, Goethe wrote to Heinrich Meyer: " So far as I can perceive, he is at one with us in his main and fundamental æsthetic ideas." The two brothers placed *Iphigenie* and *Tasso* far above *Götz* and *Werther* and regarded *Die Räuber* as a crude and barbarous production. In his lyric poems Wilhelm is the complete Classicist and indeed already an Epigone, in that he is a Schiller copyist, while Tieck's prose is very strongly influenced by Goethe's work. Friedrich's *Alarcos* and Wilhelm's *Ion,* both produced by Goethe, are of the most faultlessly Classical achromia and dullness. Schiller's dramatic theory, on the contrary, is entirely romantic. Propositions like this, for example: " Once for all, a man is only acting when he is a man in the fullest sense of the word, and he is only the complete man when he is acting," might quite well have come from Friedrich Schlegel. The avowed reason for the later violent antagonism of the Romanticists towards Schiller was the breach between him and the two Schlegels, who, however, continued to set the highest value on Goethe, although compared with Schiller he was without a doubt an " unsentimental " poet. Moreover, Franz Hemsterhuis, the " Batavian Plato," whom they venerated as the founder of the Romanticist philosophy, had declared that the Greeks were the ideal nation and that development since their time had been downhill. And so perhaps the highest, though over-clouded, peak of the Romantic irony is the fact that the Romantic school was quite unromantic.

Novalis The only real genius of the school was Novalis, who is amongst the others like a nightingale among a lot of cleverly constructed musical boxes; and even he is more important for his ideas than for his works. The bulk of his ideas are expressed in the *Frag-mente,* a comprehensive collection of aphorisms, of which only a part were published in his lifetime, under the title *Blüthen-staub,* in the Romanticist journal *Athenäum.* He had not adopted the aphoristic form from eccentricity or convenience, but as the only mode of expression organically suited to his temperament. The fundamental characteristic was a noble incompleteness, everything with him being groundwork, seed, nucleus. He himself was well aware of this; thus, he wrote in his diary: " I shall not reach perfection in this world," and again: " I am not to accomplish anything here, I am to be cut off in my flowering-time." He produced, indeed, the blossoms, not the fruit, of a philosophy.

For Novalis all knowledge is, in the final and highest sense, mystical. " Everything precious," so runs his noble saying, " is in a relation to mysticism. If all men were lovers, the difference between mysticism and non-mysticism would disappear." This mysticism culminates in requiring the mind to submerge itself in inwardness, and therein to build up a new world. The aphorism in his posthumous papers: "The world is not a dream, but it should and will perhaps become one," bears the superscription " Doctrine of Life's Future." Novalis means that we should strive to acquire a lightness of soul similar to that which we have in the dream-state, and the dream-capacity of penetrating the secret of every object and losing ourselves in it. At the moment when our thinking organ has our senses in its power, we can modify or direct these as we please; thus the painter even now controls the eye, the musician the ear, the poet speech and imagination: " our body is absolutely capable of being set in any desired motion by the spirit." Perhaps man will one day be able even to reconstruct lost limbs, or to kill himself, by mere will-power; he will be able to compel his senses to produce the figure he desires, to separate his mind from his body at will; he will see, hear, and feel what he will, how and in what connexion he will; and then for the first time he will be able to live his world in the truest sense. We have to *learn* this active, free use of our mind, our body, our whole world. All obstacles are there to be surmounted. In this direction lies our future.

If these scattered notes are taken objectively and literally, then " magic idealism " (as Novalis called his philosophy) appears as nothing but the abstruse conclusion that an uncritical mind has drawn from the Fichtean system, and Novalis an intellectual adventurer, a philosophical Cagliostro. But if one sees in these utterances the philosophical dreams of a deep and original poetic mind, then Novalis is the prophet of a spiritual fulfilment and higher development of mankind and is himself the most significant proof of the force and might of human fancy. After all, have we not daily experience of the fact that the mind is stronger than the body, that the body only exists to serve the mind? A century after Novalis the physician Karl Ludwig Schleich, in a series of exceedingly thoughtful, fruitful, and in many parts inspired works, brought forward experimental proof of the capacity of the mind to build the body, drawing attention among other things to the metaphysical power of creation in hysteria: as everyone knows, hysterical patients can merely by their will, their power of imagination, produce swellings, burns, hæmorrhage; and there is even a hysterical apparent death, and actual death through auto-suggestion. (And, for that matter, hysteria is indeed only an intensification of quite normal and everyday operations in which manifestly the thought creates the representation: the blush of shame, the pallor of anger, the goose-flesh of fright, the watering of the mouth at the idea of dainties, and so on. And every death from fright is a kind of death by autosuggestion.) All this urges us to the conclusion that every man is the poet of his own biography — the man of genius consciously so, and the rest of us following unconsciously an instinctive creative principle, somewhat as an alga builds its silica home. Our experiences and our actions alike are secretions of our will, of our noumenal ego, our soul, which, as the only true reality, sits enthroned, enigmatically creative, behind our visible life.

Schleier-macher　　We might, in opposition to a century-old professional tradition, put the proposition that Novalis — not Schleiermacher, not Fichte, least of all Schelling — was the most important philosopher of the Romantic school. What Schleiermacher did was to devote a most admirable intellectual energy to the attempt to build up a Romanticist theology. For him religion is neither knowledge nor deeds, but an emotional state, and indeed — to use his own rather cacophonous expression, a " *schlechthiniges Abhängigkeitsgefühl* " (absolute feeling of dependence). In this consists our consciousness of God. And because piety is an emotional state, it is altogether individual and extra-dogmatic, and the religious geniuses, the founders of religions, have been those persons who gave a new form to this dependence. Although this is rather a jejune interpretation of the phenomenon of religion, Schleiermacher's writings have inspired whole generations of Protestant theologians. He was also indubitably one of the first and most powerful dialecticians that Germany ever had. But fundamentally he was only a renegade disciple of the Enlightenment. He possessed merely the will to believe, just as he also leaned pretty strongly, but not quite whole-heartedly, to pantheism, often treating God and the Universal as identical concepts, and evincing the highest possible respect for Spinoza.

Fichte　　One of the most original and suggestive personalities of the age was Fichte. Even in his outward appearance and manner —

in his powerful thickset figure, his sharply cut features, his fiery and commanding gaze, his incisive voice, his rather dictatorial than logical discourse — he had much more of the founder of sect or a party-leader than a thinker and scholar. Anselm Feuerbach said of him: " I am convinced that he would be capable of playing the part of a Mahomet if we were still living in Mahomet's time, and would enforce his doctrine of science with sword and prison if his chair were a royal throne." And, in fact, Fichte did not tolerate the smallest contradiction, treated everyone who attempted to suggest the smallest modifications in his philosophy as an ass or a rogue, and got himself into trouble with everyone by his touchy and masterful ways. He had to leave the University of Jena, where he had had a brilliant success as professor, in a storm caused by an affair in which he was formally, if the authorities were factually, in the wrong. He even called Kant, who rejected his system, a " three-quarter brain." His lectures on the *Foundations of the Modern Age,* delivered in Berlin in the winter of 1804 to 1805, exercised extraordinary moral effect; in them he turned with high ethical passion against the " nullity " of the *Zeitgeist,* its empty free-thinking and its superficial pretence of enlightenment, its " rooted self-seeking," and its " complete sinfulness " — all of which failings were presently to lead Prussia to Jena and Tilsit. He displayed a most admirable courage in delivering his *Addresses to the German Nation* in the winter of 1807 to 1808, when a French commandant resided in Berlin; it was universally feared that he might suffer the fate of the bookseller Palm, and he himself expected it. In these addresses he demanded the moral regeneration of the nation as the prerequisite of the political, and it is not too much to say that these speeches formed one of the strongest factors that made the uprising of 1813.

As early as 1794 he had begun to develop his philosophical system in his *Grundlage der gesamten Wissenschaftslehre,* which treats of the origin of knowledge. His deduction starts from the critical examination of the Kantian theory of knowledge. According to this theory the cause of our sensations is in the Thing-in-itself — a rather precarious and contradictory concept, as we have already attempted to show. Fichte, on the other hand, declares that the absolute, the first, the primary and original, is not the Thing-in-itself, but the ego; this is the basic premiss and condition for every kind of experience, because it alone makes all experience possible. Since all thought, all empiria, the totality of all objects, is placed in the ego and only in it, the ego cannot be established by any other than itself. The existence of the ego is its own deed, and therefore not a thing-fact, but an action-fact. But how did the ego accomplish this original action-fact? Fichte's explanation is that by nature the ego bears the urge to production in itself, that the theoretical ego is based on the practical ego, whose nature is driving-power, will, striving. The existence of the ego is no proposition, but a requirement; no axiom, but a postulate; no decision, but a resolve. Hence the first proposition of the Fichtean philosophy: establish your ego! Without the ego there is no objective world, no Nature, no non-ego; the ego establishes itself and its opposite. The theoretical ego establishes a subject, so that the practical ego may have an object to oppose to itself.

In short, the world is the product of the ego. The ego carries out a series of operations, out of which arises what we call the outer world. But these operations of the ego take place unconsciously. We know nothing about this formative activity, just as in a dream creatures confront us with all the appearance of realities, beings completely independent of us, although they are nothing but the products of our mental activity. This unconscious world-creating activity of the ego is called by Fichte " unconscious production," and the faculty by which we carry out this production he finds in the imagination. Because production is unconscious, the world appears to us as something outside ourselves, as " non-ego," object: that is to say, as something existing independently of our subject. But what we think is our subject is in reality our product.

The whole of this deduction, however, refers to facts of the unconscious. Now, there is one human intellectual activity in which this mysterious process lies open for all to see. The faculty by which art produces its creations is likewise the imagination, and the result to which it attains is the same as that of the Fichtean " production ": when art has completed its action, its products too appear to be independent objects, realities which seem to have been released from the artist's ego. Nevertheless there is an important difference. Man accomplishes the creation of a self-coherent world unconsciously, but the artist creates with full consciousness. Here theory becomes actuality, and what every man does without knowing it, in the dark recesses of subconsciousness, the artist accomplishes as a being master of himself and in the full light of consciousness. Therefore Fichte said: " Art makes the transcendental point of view the common." His philosophy, rightly understood, is a radical philosophy of art. The Romanticists understood it and made Fichte their prophet.

The basis of the Fichtean system is an equation: Ego $=$ World. Schelling
If we reverse this equation, the whole world would appear as an ego, as a spiritual being teeming with life, as a many-staged realm of intellectual potencies, with conscious man as the highest of the stages. From this standpoint nature appears no longer as a dead mass, a rigid frame of the mind, but as a counter-ego, as undeveloped man, immature intelligence, stuff of our stuff and mind of our mind. Nature is not non-intellectual, but pre-intellectual, mind-unconscious and becoming, an ever-developing series of steadily more successful attempts of the non-ego to become the ego. This is the view of Schelling. Fichte said: Ego $=$ All; Schelling said All $=$ Ego and therefore described Fichte's system as subjective, and his own as objective, idealism. For him nature and mind are oneness of the ideal and real, of the subjective and the objective, though in nature the real, and in mind the ideal, predominate. Nature and mind, object and subject, stand to one another in the relation of *polarity*, whose fundamental law is: the identical splits itself in two, the opposites strive after union. All material and intellectual phenomena display polarity: magnetism and electricity, acids and alkalis, bodies in their mutual attraction and repulsion, plants and animals in their reversed relation to oxygen, the higher forms of life in their dualism of irritability (physical susceptibility) and sensibility (psychical susceptibility), the ego in its unconscious and its conscious activity, and art, which as a representative of the infinite in the finite is the " real and enduring organon " of philosophy.

The highly intellectual philosophy of Schelling, communicated in unpleasing and unhelpfully enigmatic language, is — in spite of its constant quotation of Kant and Fichte and the lavish use of the terms " critical " and " transcendental " — only a masked or, rather, unconscious return to dogmatism. There would have been no objection to this if Schelling had confined himself to being a poet like Novalis or an essayist like Friedrich Schlegel, or to building a grand encyclopædic structure of learning like Hegel. But to that he never won through, and the reason was that he became famous too rapidly and too early. Consequently he contented himself with launching all kinds of apocalyptic directives and suggestions, charcoal sketches and studies, programs and memoranda. Fichte's reproach to Kant, that he did not understand himself, really did apply to Schelling. The reason for his being thus unintelligible was not the depth of his ideas, but his failure to think them out to final clarity and therefore to make them comprehensible to others, and, further, the fact that he was not master of the enormous armoury of facts which he desired and needed. He helped himself out, therefore, with a dilettante eclecticism which tried to hide its shortcomings behind a high oracular manner. All the same, for some time his propositions found an enthusiastic public, partly because of the original, fruitful, and sifted ideas (or rather *aperçus*) that are scattered here and there in them, partly because there are always half-educated people who are disinclined to, or incapable of, hard pure thinking, and who therefore find an obscurity in which even the best can only move haltingly to be at once comfortable and terribly distinguished.

Chemistry recognizes certain bodies, " catalysts," which have the property of accelerating the tempo of a chemical process by their mere presence. A catalytic substance binds, by its affinity, a component of the compound, which it thereby splits, and delivers it over to a body with a stronger affinity: thus it simply causes labile intermediate products, without itself appearing in the products that it has evoked; in fact it merely provides the stimulus. The Romantic school was just such a productive disintegrator, source of intellectual chemical changes, and hastener of intellectual reactions. It provoked new combinations, changes of camp, and reconstructions without appearing in the stable " end-products " of the transformative process; it merely lent wings to development, not in itself productive, but a cause of production, an element of unrest, activation, incitement, disturbance. All this happened because the Romanticists were the neurasthenics, the unstable, the " pathological " elements of their time, possessing stability in an especially low degree and the faculty of psychic scent in an especially high degree.

Such a keen flair Schelling also showed in calling into being a philosophy that had a scientific orientation. For in the first quarter of the nineteenth century " natural philosophy " was all the fashion, and there was a whole series of important experimental advances to support it. In 1800 Carlisle and Nicholson carried out electrolysis, the decomposition of water by the galvanic current; this process was further investigated by Humphry Davy, who through its means discovered two new metals, potassium and sodium, by electrolytically separating the oxygen from potash and soda derivatives which had up to that time been considered elements. Davy was also one of the first to declare heat to be a form of motion. In 1811 Courtois likewise discovered a new element, which Gay-Lussac named iodine (after the Greek ἰοειδής) because of its violet-coloured vapour; to Gay-Lussac we owe also the famous *Recherche sur la dilatation des gases et des vapeurs,* in which proof was given that all gases and vapours expand with equal force under equal heating. In the same year as the *Recherche* there appeared also the treatise *On the Theory of Light and Colours,* in which Thomas Young, going back to Huygens, declared light to be a movement in the æther, and referred the different sensations produced by colours to the different numbers of vibrations which these æther-motions produced upon the retina. Théodore de Saussure (son of Benedict Saussure, the first conqueror of Mont Blanc) carried out botanical experiments with nutrient solutions, and by measurements (some of which were already of high accuracy) showed the parts played by oxygen, carbonic acid, water, salt, and various earth minerals in plant life. Monge, who was director of cannon-founding under the Convention and participated in Napoleon's Egyptian expedition, discovered the " descriptive " or " projective " geometry, which made it possible to project bodies on to planes, to reduce three-dimensional to two-dimensional forms, or, rather, represent them as such — a science of the greatest importance to engineers and technicians as well as to architects and painters. Cuvier, the favourite of Napoleon (who entrusted him with the reorganization of education), published his *Leçons d'anatomie comparée* in 1805; he was the first exactly to classify the invertebrates, dividing them into three circles of four classes each, and he set up his doctrine of the "Correlation of Organs," according to which all parts of a given animal-type condition one another and are in the closest correlation (in the carnivores, for instance, entrails for digestion, strong jaws and claws, means of rapid motion, sharp teeth and eyes). He also developed the "catastrophe theory," which divides the history of the earth according to its periodic transformations: in each geological epoch there arises by new creation a special fauna, which one day is completely annihilated by a catastrophe, to make way for another; the last great catastrophe he placed at five thousand years ago. This hypothesis has been completely abandoned by later science, but at that time it was universally adopted, and Lamarck found no support when in 1809, in his *Philosophie zoologique,* he put forward the opposed theory of Descent, which explained the development of animal life by adaptation and inheritance, the origin of the organs through use, and their degeneration through disuse. It is not difficult to comprehend that a generation which had experienced the sudden and violent changes of the French Revolution and Napoleon preferred to regard the catastrophe theory as the more credible.

Classical costume The other fashionable science was archæology. Antiques, seized from all countries, accumulated during the Revolutionary period in the Louvre, the "*Musée Central,*" later the *Musée Napoléon.*" In 1806 Joseph Bonaparte, as King of Naples, began new and intensive excavations at Pompeii. Lord Elgin, English ambassador to Turkey, brought to London the Parthenon sculptures (the "Elgin Marbles"), purchased by the State for the British Museum. The real founder of archæology in the modern comprehensive sense was Friedrich August Wolf. He was the first who insisted on matriculating as a student of "philology," but in doing so he defined the term from the first as "the knowledge of ancient humanity itself."

The universal interest in archæology was a natural result of the ruling Classicism. Rarely has there been so widespread and intense a passion for dressing up in the mode of ancient life-forms. The French Revolution lost no time in beginning to Classicize everything, but far less in the Greek than in the Latin form (which meant more to the Gallic soul), and since "Roman" and " Republican " were identical concepts in the minds of that age, political tendencies also found nourishment therein. There were busts everywhere of the " heroes of liberty," Brutus and Cincinnatus, Seneca and Cato; and Lafayette was called " Scipio Americanus." The Jacobins continually borrowed names for their political and economic measures from Rome and Sparta, and their badge was the Phrygian cap, *le bonnet rouge,* a red woollen cap of antique shape. The official sign of the French Republic, " *R.F.*," was copied from the Roman " *S.P.Q.R.*" (*senatus populusque Romanus*). The new names of the months and the names of the newly-founded republics were Greek or Latin; the harvest month was called Messidor, the hot month Thermidor, the fruit-gathering month Fructidor; Holland became Batavia, Switzerland Helvetia, Genoa Liguria, and Naples Parthenope. Babeuf changed his baptismal name into Gracchus and called his paper the *Tribune of the People.* Even playing-cards had to be antique; the knave of spades became Publius Decius Mus. The " Messidor " style of new buildings allowed only the Classical straight line, and perhorresced at every curve. Napoleon openly employed Classical reminiscences: such as tribunate, senate, plebiscite. He called himself First Consul and then Imperator, introduced the Roman eagle into the army, and copied the Emperor Augustus in all sorts of outward details. Even in questions of home and foreign policy he saw in his mind's eye the practice of the Roman Empire, with its levelling civil administration, its Prætorian Guard, and its metamorphosis of defeated princes into " allies." The Empire or Napoleonic style, which developed under his rule, is shy of colour, using only white and gold, sparsely ornamented hangings, dark mahogany and dull bronze fittings; its favourite decorative forms were the laurel-wreath and the lyre, medallions, crossed torches, stiff meander, egg-and-dart, and garlands of lilies — all " antique " motives. The permanent prevalence of a state of war is indicated by the taste for trophies of armour, floral tributes, and funerary urns. Sphinxes, caryatids, columns, and obelisks abounded not only on the façades of buildings, but in rooms. Bookcases and wardrobes, even night-stools, were Greek temples with capitals and architraves, the wash-hand-stands tripods, the stoves altars; in Hamburg even the gallows was built with Corinthian columns. Military head-dress took the form of the antique helmet. For some time ladies wore helmet-like hats, the forerunners of the "coal-scuttle" type which long held its own; their coiffure was the Greek knot confined in a hair-net. In their costume they sought to approximate to antique nakedness, using a single article of clothing, the tunic, which because of its shirt-like cut was also called the chemise, exposing neck, breast, arms, and legs, with the addition at most of a flesh-coloured knitted wrap or a Cashmere shawl, the draping of which was a difficult and carefully practised art; and on the naked feet were worn sandals or flat string-shoes. This costume was very un-healthful, as the tunic might only be made of light material (the chronic catarrh from which ladies suffered was called the "muslin illness"), but hygiene has never exercised a decisive influence on fashion, and it is mere self-deception to think that it does so today; for thin silk stockings and patent shoes give little more protection against chills than the Empire costume.

This radical change in costume hangs together with the tendency to "republican simplicity." The story of the Turkish woman who asked the crinolined lady: "Is all that you?" was passed round with delight, and high coiffures and high heels, small waists and stays counted as admissions of counter-revolutionary sentiments. Similarly, men abandoned powder and pig-tail, and the Rococo costume was driven out by the plain dark coat of the Third Estate, and the *pantalon*, the long sailors' trousers, of the Sansculottes. Under the Directory all sorts of allusions to the Terror were fashionable: ladies wore their hair shaved at the back and a thin red band round the neck, and since the population had been decimated by the guillotine, pregnancy was simulated by wearing a pad. In the wild jubilation of society after its long anxiety and privations, costume for a time adopted the most extravagant forms. The dandies, the so-called "Incroyables," wore monstrous double-pointed hats, frock-coats with enormous lapels, several ample stocks, hiding the lower part of the face, club-shaped walking-sticks, and ear-rings; the corresponding female dandies, the "Merveilleuses," wore their hair short and crimped *à la sauvage* and rings on their feet. It was then that the world-dominion of the top-hat set in. What horror was aroused by the first appearance of this grotesque article of attire is shown by a notice in *The Times* in 1796, which recorded

432

that one John Hetherington was brought before the Lord Mayor for gross misbehaviour and obstructing the street. It was proved that he had appeared in the street wearing what he called a silk hat, a high shiny structure calculated to reduce timid people to a state of terror; in fact several policemen testified that women had fainted and children wept, and that one of the crowd that assembled had fallen and broken his right arm.

The Classicizing spirit naturally attacked the arts also. In Italy the most powerful representative of the tendency was Alfieri, a fine draughtsman of literature, who abjured ornament in speech and psychology, admitted no episodes or subsidiary interests, and strictly observed the three unities in his plays — programmatic and tendentious, affectedly Laconian and Catonian in manner. In France the most influential artist of this orientation was Jacques Louis David. His pictures were the first to reproduce antique armour, costume, implements, and heads — with archæological correctness, but they are cold and staged for pathos, gloomy and rhetorical panegyrics on antique virtue, liberty, and patriotism. And when he painted contemporaries — the murdered Marat, Napoleon as General and Emperor, Barère demanding the King's death — they all became Romans under his brush. His contemporary was the great Talma, whose art, as described by eye-witnesses, must have been that of David translated into acting: his attitudes were compared with those of Antique sculpture, and Wilhelm von Humboldt says that his playing was one unbroken succession of fine pictures. Like David also, he was the first to demand historical correctness in his costumes, whereas Garrick was still playing Shakspere's heroes in powdered wigs, and Greek kings in doublet and feathered hat. In sculpture the Dane Thorwaldsen indisputably held the first place. In his marked talent for clear, pleasant outlines — a pure relief talent — the undramatic tedium of Classicism culminates in a genuine elevation and purity. Asked for the date of his birth, Thorwaldsen replied: " I do not know; on March 8, 1797 I came for the first time to Rome." His " Expedition of Alexander," which for some decades was placed on a level with the Parthenon frieze, was no doubt a technical masterpiece in command of form and severity of composition, but it was merely a stage procession, cold to the point of indifference, the figures so drawn to type as to be

433

almost indistinguishable, and in the case of women particularly, utterly dead and commonplace; simplification is carried to the point that the four horses of Alexander's chariot only show four hind legs. Führich declared that Thorwaldsen was "nothing but a player." We might even say a "court player."

We have already shown that at that time "Gothic" signified barbaric, rough, devoid of art. Heinrich Meyer, in Goethe's estimation the greatest art-authority of his time, said in 1799 in *Propyläen* that the sight of Gothic buildings made one "despise those who produced such works." The influential Karl Ludwig Fernow, also a friend of Goethe's, censured Michelangelo for the obtrusion of his personal will; and opined that with all his fire he never attained the union of genius and taste, any more than Æschylus, Dante, or Shakspere, or than Bernini and the other masters of the Baroque. The greatest devastations of Classicism are in the field of landscape-painting; its special weakness was for stylized versions of the Italian Campagna, enlivened by "picturesque" opera-brigands, with in the centre a grazing ass, gracious and dignified, which appears to have come straight from Weimar.

Goya   Wholly aside from all this stands the enigmatic figure of Goya, the irresistible suggestiveness and unique problem-character of whose work has only come to be fully appreciated in our own days. In his astounding paintings and etchings are united Baroque, naturalism, and Impressionism. His "*Caprichos*" conceive the world in terms of masquerade and dream. His portraits of the Spanish royal family rendered the ugliness of their models with a truth to nature which other painters would hardly have dared to use with private sitters; and his "Shooting of the Street-fighters," which anticipated the whole Impressionist movement, is known to have been Manet's model for the "Execution of the Emperor Maximilian." He is — like Herder, the *Sturm und Drang* poets, and the young Goethe — a proof that Impressionism would have developed out of Rococo in the eighteenth century quite naturally and inevitably had it not been forcibly thrust back by Classicism. Already at the turn of the century an actual theory of Impressionism was put forward (though he was not able to carry it out in his works) by the painter Philipp Otto Runge, who declared that the Greeks and the painters of the Renaissance had reached the highest point in form, but had never seriously studied the nuances of colour under the play of light, and that the representation of light and air was the great problem to be conquered by modern painters.

Beethoven, too, must be regarded as entirely aloof from the movement. He cannot be classed as a Romanticist or as Classicist, though both schools claim him. He is too big and timeless for such ordinary classification, like Michelangelo, with whom he has other characteristics in common; dæmonic ugliness, tyrannical roughness, mistrustful capriciousness, study of self, and misanthropic hatred of society, the mingled love and contempt of money, the combination of business ability with a helplessness that made him a prey to greedy relations; the attitude to patrons, whom he uses and solicits, yet imperiously, and as though they were far beneath him; the passionate eroticism, which, however, was confined to imagination and therefore never reached its goal: the unbending intransigence in artistry; the vast self-confidence and early realization that he is a figure of permanent significance, embittered by constant dissatisfaction with his own achievement; the colossal reach of his conceptions; his gigantic power of work and constant and successful search for new methods and new technique, stretching the existing forms in undreamed-of degree and reaching forward to beyond the bounds of art; and, lastly, the complete misunderstanding of him by his contemporaries. But he differs from Michelangelo by his fundamental kindliness and his illuminating and liberating humour — two qualities which the Roman, for all his high development, neither possessed nor understood nor valued — and by his piety, which in his case stretches to quite other abysses than those explored by the world-intoxicated Renaissance master. For him art was the " communication of the divine, a higher revelation than all wisdom and all philosophy," and music " more emotion than tone-painting "; and between his achievement of the highest in absolute music and this piety of his there is the very closest communion. Beethoven with Napoleon and Goethe makes up the great trinity of the age; but he is the noblest of the three. It is the dispensation of tragedy that, though he understood the two others, they did not understand him. Had Goethe understood the phenomenon of Beethoven, we might possibly have had the greatest and profoundest work of art of all time: a *Faust* composed by Beethoven; infinite

435

thought wedded to infinite melody. And if Napoleon had understood Beethoven, Europe might have another aspect today. As is well known, Beethoven originally dedicated his Third Symphony (the *Eroica*), *composta per festeggiare il sovvenire di un grand' uomo,* to General Bonaparte, and when Napoleon made himself emperor, he destroyed the dedication. Napoleon should and could have become the hero portrayed in this and the Ninth Symphony, the hero in the service of mankind; but he did not.

Malthu-sianism

England, too, developed in an isolated way, though in quite another direction from Goya and Beethoven. We have already shown that there, as the result of a much quicker and more intensive economic development, the modern machine man was conceived. England is also the birthplace of the so-called modern economic theories. Their founders are Malthus and Ricardo. The argumentation on which the clergyman Robert Malthus built was this: the yield from English soil might in twenty-five years be almost doubled, in fifty years trebled, and in seventy-five years quadrupled — that is to say, food-supply moved in arithmetical progression — but population showed a tendency to double in twenty-five years, to be fourfold in fifty years and eightfold in seventy-five years — that is to say, to increase in geometrical progression. This disparity could only be rectified by " checks " on population, by wars and epidemics, by existence in narrow streets and airless factories; and therefore all care for the aged, the poor, and the orphan was to be regarded as mistaken. Ricardo added the law that the natural rate of wages gravitated towards the minimum necessary for existence; if the workers earned more, there would be a compensatory diminution of population. Malthusianism thus took the opposite standpoint from that of Mercantilism, which maintained that a country would be richer and more efficient the greater its population, and sought to raise this by all possible means; Malthusianism on the contrary saw the greatest economic danger in a rising population figure. The bases of this theory, however, are not free from objection statistically, let alone philosophically. It ignores the fact that the productive capacity of the soil is far from exhausted and that new methods, new forms of transport, new sources of energy may any day be discovered; that matter is always ruled by mind, and that, as every man is the poet of his own biography, every people is the

436

poet of its own history; and that sociologically want does not lie in the absence of an adequate basis for food-supply, but in an inequality and unskilfulness of distribution due to human selfishness and stupidity. The absurdity of Malthusianism is cleverly illustrated by Franz Oppenheimer, who imagines Robinson Crusoe as a pupil of Ricardo, who, as sole master of the island, pays his man Friday the exact minimum subsistence-wage "strictly according to the brazen law of wages (probably the island is overpopulated!)," and adds: " In every country of the world the State has arisen from a few thousand or hundred thousand ill-armed, scattered, superstitious Fridays being subjugated by a few hundred or thousand well-armed, well-disciplined Robinsons, who thereupon take possession of the land." And Friedrich List touches the root of the matter when he says: " This doctrine would turn men's hearts to stone. But what after all would become of a nation whose citizens have stones instead of hearts in their bosoms? What but a complete decay of morality, and therewith of all productive power, all wealth, civilization, and might? " It is, in plain words, the most shameless and deceitful attempt to justify a capitalist philosophy that has ever been made. The legitimation of man's existence is not to be the eternal fact that man has a soul, but the question whether he is born into an adequate food-area! And this was taught by a Christian priest! But this is not, after all, so strange in Malthus's case, when we remember that English Puritanism is really a Jewish religion; and Ricardo was in actual fact the son of a Portuguese Jew.

Of course the English materialism, like every energetic and purposeful materialism, had its good side as well. The average standard of living of the people was far better than on the Continent; hygiene, sport, cleanliness were on a much higher level. The costume of the English was the healthfullest, simplest, and most rational in Europe; they were the first to have the sensible idea of dressing children differently from grown-up people. The furniture and arrangement of houses was appropriate, solid, and useful. At the beginning of the century in London most houses had water-closets; in 1814 the whole city was lighted by gas. The post was quick and punctual, the roads were in excellent order, while on the Continent they were just as neglected as in the mercantile period, when they had been allowed to fall into disrepair so as to compel visitors to a longer stay and to make it more difficult for the inhabitants to leave the country. There were already many bridges and other constructions of iron. In 1810 two hundred steam-engines were working in France, five thousand in England; in 1814 Stephenson built his first locomotive, and about the same time steamships plied on regular passenger services in English and Scottish waters.

This detached development of England was partly due to the Continental embargo decreed by Napoleon in 1806; its terms forbade all trade, all intercourse, all correspondence of the Continent with England and declared every Englishman in the French spheres of influence a prisoner and all English goods fair prize. British export trade sank by nearly one-half, the exchange value of the national paper by one-third, while the cost of living was doubled. The Continent itself was injured almost as seriously; on all sides factories and other undertakings were cut down and there were numerous bankruptcies. The prices of dyes and iron manufactures, of cotton, rice, spices, and colonial goods generally, reached fantastic heights. People drank coffee made from roasted acorns and smoked tobacco made from coltsfoot. A pound of sugar immediately after the Berlin Decrees cost a thaler and even two thalers, an enormous price when it is considered that a simple dwelling-house was to be had in these days for four hundred thalers. But in 1810 the price of sugar rose again by four hundred per cent. This led the Frenchman Achard to attempt the production of sugar from beet-root, and Kirchhof used potato starch for the purpose; but the technique was still imperfect, and on the removal of the blockade beet-sugar was again, for the time being, driven out by the cane product. The Continental embargo cost Napoleon the mortal hostility, not only of England, but of the whole of Europe, and to a greater intensity than all his conscriptions and requisitionings, his censorship and police regulations, his invasions and overthrowings of dynasties.

Napoleon's career developed in complete dramatic form, with exposition, development of action, climax, denouement, and " point of highest tension," and catastrophe — almost exactly in accordance with the scheme laid down in Gustav Freytag's *Technik des Dramas*. The brilliant Italian campaign of 1796 constitutes the point of departure, and there followed an uninterrupted series of triumphs over all the generals, nations, and instruments of war that stood in his way, won by his power of changing his soldiers (as a Prussian officer wrote after Jena) into superhuman beings. He suffered his first reverse in 1809 at Aspern; and even this he was able to announce as a victory because of his orderly retreat and the Archduke Charles's inadequate pursuit; and a fortnight later he compensated it by his success at Wagram. His victories at home were equally important. In accordance with his motto " the Romance of the Revolution has to be completed by the History of the Revolution " — he brought order and prosperity out of chaos in France; he guaranteed to the whole population freedom of religion and trade, juridical rights irrespective of party, civic security, extensive state provision for welfare and education; and he removed obstacles to the return of the *émigrés*. Though he revived nobility and titles of honour, he protected talent alone, and that whenever and wherever it was found. The climax of his career was reached in 1810. At this time Belgium, Holland, Hanover, Oldenburg, the left bank of the Rhine, the North Sea coast with the Hanse towns, the Illyrian provinces, upper Italy with South Tyrol, and central Italy with the States of the Church were French; the dependencies of France included the Confederation of the Rhine (consisting of Bavaria, Württemberg, Baden, Saxony, Hesse and the Kingdom of Westphalia), Switzerland, the Duchy of Warsaw, Spain under Joseph Bonaparte, and Naples under Murat; Austria, Prussia, and the Kingdom of Norway and Denmark were allied with France. In 1811 Napoleon said to the Bavarian general Wrede: " Three more years, and I am master of the universe."

Three years later, however, he found himself in Elba. For the year of his climax was also the year of the beginning of the denouement, when he divorced Josephine, his " mascot," and concluded the *mésalliance* with the house of Habsburg, the *mésalliance* of progress with stagnation, of reality with appearance, of genius with convention. And now follows the " declining action." What his intentions were in the Russian campaign he explained to Narbonne in the clearest words: " Finally, this way is the long way to India. . . . Imagine Moscow stormed, Russia beaten, the Tsar reconciled or fallen a victim to a palace conspiracy, and tell me whether an army of Frenchmen cannot then penetrate to the Ganges. And India only needs to see the sword of France for the whole edifice of her commercial greatness to fall into our hands."

But with this adventure his imagination had for the first time lost touch with actuality. Even during his preliminary marches an eyewitness stated: "Everything is lacking, even Jews." Of six hundred thousand men, fifty thousand reached home; of a hundred and eighty thousand horses, fifteen thousand.

At the beginning of the year 1918 C. H. Meray in his most suggestive but unfortunately little-known book *Weltmutation* prophesied that Germany must be defeated if she came into contact with the "foreign body" of America, for the organic process by which the giant "cell" Germany sought to overcome and absorb the cells of other European states would by that contact become pathological. In fact, at the moment when the Russian "foreign body" fell out of the World War, Germany was theoretically the victor. But only theoretically, for England, with a profound understanding of the circumstances, had already arranged for the entry of a new "foreign body." In the history of Antiquity we may see a similar process in the prime and the catastrophe of the Roman world-empire. The "organism" of Antiquity was the Mediterranean and its surrounding lands. Rome was never able to reach out beyond these, and with wise restraint hardly ever tried to do so. But with the advent of the Germans Rome came into contact with a new continent and collapsed. The Spanish world-monarchy had the same experience with America. And so too Napoleon, when by his Russian expedition he came into contact with Asia. He himself must have had a dim conception of it, when in 1813 he said to Marshal Marmont: "My chess-board is in confusion."

The "moment of greatest tension" corresponds with the Hundred Days. On March 11, 1815 there was a great ball at Vienna at Prince Metternich's. Suddenly the news spread: "He is in France." Everybody knew who "he" was. Dancing stopped, the talkers were silent, the orchestra played on in vain. The royal guests left the house in silence, the others followed. The lights went out, the city lay in a poignant darkness; there was world-war once more.

During the winter the French soldiers had already called

Napoleon *"Père la violette"* because they expected him back with the March violets. On his way from Cannes to Paris not a single shot was fired, all the armies sent against him going over to his side. Some men died for joy at the news of his landing. But the Emperor was no more the " giant cell " of former days. The mightiest of all dramas and destiny in modern history ended at Waterloo.

Napoleon himself had always been completely convinced that his whole destiny was determined and conducted by some sort of magic impulse. Once, when he had been nearly killed by a fall from a carriage, he said to Metternich: " I felt life fading from me, but I said to myself: ' I will not die,' and I lived," and another time, warned of threatened attempts on his life, he replied: " What have I to fear? I cannot be murdered." His Egyptian proclamation ran: " Is there any man so blind as not to recognize that my action is directed by fate? . . . The day will come when the whole world will see that I am led by a higher hand, and that human effort can do nothing against me." His contemporaries, friends and opponents, had long ceased to measure him by human standards; they regarded him as a dazzling irresistible manifestation of Nature with which it was idle to argue, magnificent to look on, devastating in its effects.

Napoleon and destiny

On one occasion Talleyrand said to Napoleon: " Good taste is your personal enemy. If you could have got rid of it by bombardment it would long since have been conquered." A true saying, truer than that finished court-intriguer could guess. Naturally Napoleon was without taste. Destitute of taste and tact, education and culture, he exploded the whole backward, corrupt, calcified world of feudalism and diplomacy, of drawing-room chatterers and paper strategists. A giant is not a pleasing spectacle. An earthquake, a volcano emitting lava and dust, is not a pleasant spectacle. No natural catastrophe, no elemental event, nothing beyond life-size is in " good taste." What is in good taste is the average, the conventional, the clean copy, the known. Any phenomenon which is not completely comprehensible confuses, irritates, and disturbs us. It has the bad taste to get on our nerves.

We only need to look at any single department of Napoleon's activity — for example, his generalship — to understand how this conscious and obstinate breach with the past dominated all his

Napoleon and strategy

441

actions. In the age in which he made his entry, Duke Karl Ferdinand of Brunswick was esteemed the greatest of generals. To him strategy was nothing more than a game of chess to be played as perfectly as might be. He did not really want war, he wanted only something of the " state of siege " sort. And this was (as we have already shown) the general attitude of the experts. Fundamentally they were only concerned with artificial manœuvres, with surrounding, cutting off, harassing the enemy, with all sorts of clever combinations and ingenious deceptions. There were people who thought the Duke of Brunswick a greater general than Frederick the Great. But he was a pure theoretician, a strategist who inspired respect only so long as there was no downright shooting and marching. Perhaps it was not too much to say that the twenty years of Revolutionary war were brought upon Europe by his fault, for upon him rests the responsibility for Valmy. He never saw anything but the obstacles, the dangers, the negative instances. His case throws light on two things : first, the theoretical and paper character of the whole period, which extended even to the most frightful of all realities, war ; and, second, the worthlessness and impotence of the so-called professional, which is forced to our notice in any and every imaginable domain. All great generals, with Napoleon at their head, have declared war to be a very simple thing, as all great artists have said of art, and all great physicians of medicine. Moltke, indeed, maintained that strategy was no science at all. On the other hand, the technical expert is always a complicated fellow. The Revolutionary generals knew nothing at all about strategy. They were amateurs enough to see in war a reality, a matter of furious attack, advance, and victory. They were uneducated enough to carry on war simply as war and to think that what mattered was the overwhelming of the enemy and not merely the theoretical refutation of his actions.

The management of the Revolutionary armies, which had already reached a high standard under Carnot, the " Organizer of Victory," was new in four ways : in the *levée en masse*, which turned the whole male population into soldiers (though only in theory, because under Napoleon it was still allowable to purchase a substitute) ; in the new tactics, which used columns for attack, instead of rigid lines of small depth, and replaced concentrated mass-fire by the " dispersed order " of skirmishers ; and in unhesitating expansion of the strength of armies, coupled with the change from magazine supply to the requisition system. To these changes Napoleon added others: the division of the army into several independent army-units (corps and divisions), self-contained, with all arms and resources; the brilliant application of reserves, in which he far surpassed Frederick the Great; and the full use of the "interior lines," which consisted in operating with his whole army on the inner flanks of the separate parts of the hostile army, which he then successively attacked and defeated in detail with superior numbers, even when his own numerical total was inferior to the enemy's.

"Victory is to be won first by the legs of the soldiers and only secondarily by their bayonets." That is as simple as all truths, and it proved equally difficult to be got into the human head. Since war is a kind of duel or boxing-match on a large scale, similar laws apply to it. Nobody doubts that in a close-quarters fight the decision is obtained by quickness and boldness; or, if he doubts it, he does so at the danger of his own limbs. Just as simple were the other fundamental principles of the new leading: arming of the population, supply by foraging, continuous penetration of the enemy's country, and dispersed-order fighting. It was (though in quite a different sense from that of Rousseau and the Revolutionary phrasemakers) a "return to nature." It is natural for every man at the moment of real or even imagined danger to fly to arms and seek to defend himself; it is natural to live from the soil wherever one happens to be and to spread oneself out as far as one can, and it is natural to go for the enemy when and where he is to be found. It was the old methods that were unnatural, cumbrous, and artificial: the voluntary recruiting system, magazine supply, hesitant and purely demonstrative strategy, linear tactics. But Nature is ever victorious, and therefore the Revolution was victorious over Europe. Moreover, Napoleon introduced a completely new factor, his unheard-of *tempo*. In the words of the editor of the Austrian official history of the 1866 war, "Napoleon conquered space with time." Or as he himself once said: "I have destroyed the Austrians by marching." The principle which he sought most constantly to impress upon his subordinate generals was: "*Activité, activité! Vitesse!*" And this principle was not confined to his generalship. He imparted to the whole of Europe a speeding-up process by which it was fundamentally transformed. He is the creator of the modern pace of living.

The Man of the Realities It is only necessary to compare Napoleon with any other personality of the Revolution to be aware of his incomparability. For example, there was a moment when Dumouriez had only to will it to become dictator of France. This was after the battle of Neerwinden. At that time he could have made an agreement with the Austrians which would have enabled him to disarm the Jacobin element of his army by the line troops (who were completely devoted to him) and to march on Paris, where he would have been received as a liberator by the overwhelming majority of a population embittered by the September murders and the mob Reign of Terror. He had long been turning over this plan in his mind, had taken the preparatory steps, had made inquiries everywhere, had entered into negotiations with Austria and Paris; but he lacked energy to take the last decisive step. This shows that three things are necessary for practical genius: survey of the given situation, recognition of the necessary measures, and action at the right moment, which usually only comes once. Dumouriez lacked only the third of these necessaries for a Napoleonic career, and that amounts to saying that he lacked them all. Napoleon himself said: "The same thing cannot be done twice in the same century," but an elemental force of a completeness and strength of Napoleon does not emerge twice in a thousand years.

And yet there was something in his influence and his character which deters us from giving him that unconditioned veneration which we so willingly bestow on other and lesser heroes. Why? What hinders us from seeing in Napoleon one of those great models on which we should like to form our own existence and will?

Taine introduces his characterization of Napoleon (one of the most brilliant examples of French Impressionism) with the words: "Napoleon belongs to another age. . . . In order to understand him, such balanced students of history as Stendhal and Madame de Staël go back to the minor Italian tyrants of the fourteenth and fifteenth centuries. Bonaparte is descended from the great Italians of that time, from the men of action, the military adventurers, the usurping founders of life-sovereignties; he inherited by direct descent their blood, their inmost essence, their moral and intellectual constitution." Now, Napoleon certainly did not belong to the eighteenth century, but instead of placing him in the fourteenth or fifteenth, it would be equally correct to place him in the nineteenth or, if you like, in the twentieth. Perhaps he was really only a colossal condottiere; if so, he was one who had a knowledge (or at least the elements of a knowledge) of chemistry, geography, and, above all, psychology — and he possessed the capacity, unheard-of in France, of reckoning with data.

Goethe said that Napoleon was the greatest intellect the world has ever known. Sieyès said of him: "He knows everything, he wills everything, he can do everything." And he himself said of himself: "My great talent consists in my clear insight into everything; even my special type of eloquence is based on my seeing the essentials of a question from all sides. The perpendicular is shorter than the diagonal," and: "Different affairs are all grouped in my head as in a desk. When I want to break off with one, I close its drawer and open another one. They never get mixed up, they don't confuse and tire me by their manifoldness. If I want to sleep I close all drawers, and I am at once fast asleep." Another time he compares his head to a dove-cote: "When I wish to arrange anything, I open the proper outlet, shutting all the others; when I want to sleep I shut them all." This capacity made it possible for him to do with from three to (exceptionally) six hours of sleep; otherwise he worked uninterruptedly — "even at meals and at the theatre," as he himself said — and it is probable, indeed, that he went on working in sleep. This faculty, in which lay his essential difference from other Frenchmen, explains his immediate and immense success. He himself was quite clear on the matter. "The French," he once said to Metternich, "are an intellectual people; intellect runs about the streets. But behind it there is no character, no principle, and no will; they run after everything, they can be led by their vanity, and, like children, they must always be provided with a toy." (In almost literal agreement with the words of Goethe to Eckermann: "The French have judgment and intellect, but no stability and no piety.") Napoleon openly spoke in this sense as early as 1797: "You Frenchmen do not know how to desire anything seriously. Your vanity must always be fed. What was the origin of the Revolution? Vanity.

And what will destroy it? Also vanity "; and later, more shortly and plainly: "Triflers play a great part in France. Good sense plays none at all." He taught his people to think in terms of reality and to act clearly; he taught them to turn their eyes on things instead of illusions and phrases, and to orient their course constantly by facts. Emerson was well advised when he opened his essay on him with the following words: " If Napoleon is France, if Napoleon is Europe, it is because the people whom he sways are little Napoleons." But the reverse could also be said: namely, that he was the leader of his time because he succeeded in *making* little Napoleons out of all the men of his time.

Nevertheless we have to admit that the principal reproach against Napoleon is precisely that he was so completely a type of the new men whose destiny it was to rule the coming century. He was, perhaps, the most complete empiricist that ever lived; and this was the essence of his incomparable genius as of his catastrophal weakness. For he was so complete an empiricist that he was nothing else. He was not a moral and metaphysical phenomenon; ethics and ideology meant nothing to him. This absence of all ideology was his fundamental defect, and it was this that made his domination a transitory one.

And so one is almost tempted to say that this adamantine and argus-eyed hero was a *touching* spectacle. He knew everything, could do everything, held everything in his mighty hand — only not himself. He was stronger than the whole world; but not stronger than his own deeds. He forgot that *even* the greatest man — indeed, particularly the greatest man — exists for mankind only. His success went to his head just as if he had been an ordinary banker, minister, or actor. And so his empyrean flight became a miserable descent into hell.

The Stage-manager of Europe Madame de Staël said of him: " He is a skilled chess-player, and his opponent is the human race, whom he is determined to checkmate." But his dæmonic temperament made him more than a master of chess; rather, a great stage-manager, one such as the world has perhaps never seen. Even his outward appearance was incomparably theatrical: the master of Europe in the crumpled hat and worn cloak of the common soldier in the midst of glittering generals, dignitaries covered with orders, and bejewelled women. Many episodes in his life make superb theatre-scenes: for example, when, throwing his watch on the ground, he addresses his brother Lucien: " Since you will not obey, I will smash you like this watch," or when, at the Opéra, an attempt on his life has been made with an infernal machine, and he remarks: " The rascals wanted to blow me up, did they? . . . Bring me today's libretto." The tradition that Talma taught him his poses is so little in accordance with the facts that it is rather the reverse that is true: Talma himself declared he had drawn the most valuable lessons from the glance, play of gesture, and bearing of the Emperor, who had indeed been his model. The man to whom the present work is dedicated, the greatest captain of a modern stage-history,[1] has been compared with him innumerable times.

Perhaps Napoleon's success and popularity are partly to be ascribed to the fact that he was not an entirely great man. Men of genius are only partially recognized by their contemporaries. In the less civilized ages they are even scorned or annihilated, which is inherent in the nature of the case. In order completely to understand Plato, Beethoven, Dante, Dostoievski, one would have to be a kind of negative print of Plato, Beethoven, Dante, Dostoievski, a true photograph capable of collecting and conscientiously recording all the rays emanating from those suns. This want of intensity can only be made good extensively by full and long exposure. Napoleon is the only man of genius who is at once and completely comprehensible, because the vulgar and average qualities that he had provide a sort of vernacular for the translation and communication of his meaning. He was a liar, a rowdy, an egoist; brutal, sensual, shameless; his whole bearing had something magnificently vulgar, parvenu-like; his marriage to the daughter of a Habsburg reminds one of a stockbroker who tries to ennoble himself by marrying into a ruined aristocratic family. He gave offence in society by his uncouth barrack-manners, he delighted in malicious indiscretions and mean gossip, he permitted himself unseemly jokes about women and boasted like a commercial traveller of his successes in love — although in fact he had no genuine success with women, who admired, but did not love, the upstart. But this murky atmosphere does not dim his

The Anti-ideological ideologue

---

[1] Max Reinhardt, to whom the original German edition was dedicated. *Tr.*

genius, in fact was the very thing that clears it up, just as a figure can be seen better in diffused light than in full sunshine. And when all is said and done, there is no manner of reasonable doubt that Napoleon was the completest genius the world had ever seen, greater than Cæsar, greater than Shakspere, greater than Goethe. For when one looks at both the intensity and the extent of his gifts, he possessed as much as all three put together: He was a Cæsar in practical oversight and foresight, a Shakspere in creative fancy, a Goethe in knowledge of human nature; and over and above these things he had a power of translating his conceptions into actuality which none of these three possessed in the same measure. One thing only he lacked, that each of the others possessed — idealism. He had no faith in the most real force of the world: namely, human ideals. Altruism, patriotism, piety, were for him available sources of energy to be used and guided, but he did not regard them as of any higher value than cannon, steam-power, or money. It never occurred to him that an *idée fixe* is more and can do more than a hundred thousand bayonets. He did not know that ideas, ideals, ideologies, phantasms, illusions, concepts, are also physical and physiological sources of energy, measurable and effective quantities, ponderable imponderables, so to say; that the consciousness of right, the belief in the Supreme, is just as effective in raising the temperature of an organism as fat, albumen, brandy, and cola-nut. Thus he was not quite so complete an empiricist as he and his supporters thought: He was, paradoxical as it may seem, in this respect, a detached doctrinaire. He had his system of the world and humanity, a philosophical system if you will, but one which, like so many clever and well-constructed systems, was not in tune with, was not *close to,* life. He scorned and despised the " ideologues " and never suspected that he himself was one. He brought the whole world into confusion, drove his masses of men from Sweden to Egypt and from Madrid to Moscow; and he vanished one day as suddenly as he had emerged, went off in smoke like an explosion of gunpowder, leaving nothing behind but startled people and a smell of burning. He mobilized mankind and the forces of nature, wind and water, all the states and towns and peoples of Europe, now on his side, now against him; and when he disappeared, the map of Europe was as it had been twenty years before, with but minor alterations, and the diplomats continued to dispute over revenues, contingents, and princely rights. Napoleon was no dreamer, and *that* is his chief reproach. On that rock he foundered. His conquest could only endure for years and months, for he did not know that in the long run only a dreamer can conquer the world.

CHRONOLOGY

1618	Defenestration of Prague
1619	Ferdinand II, German Emperor
1620	Battle of the White Mountain. Arrival of the *Mayflower*
1624	Richelieu took up the Government. Death of Jakob Böhme. Opitz's *Buch von der deutschen Poeterey*
1625	Death of James I. Charles I. Death of El Greco
1626	Death of Bacon
1628	Petition of Right. Capture of La Rochelle. William Gilbert: magnetism. Harvey: circulation of the blood
1629	Edict of Restitution
1630	Landing of Gustavus Adolphus. Death of Kepler
1631	Storming of Magdeburg. Battle of Breitenfeld
1632	Battle of Lützen: death of Gustavus Adolphus
1634	Murder of Wallenstein. Battle of Nördlingen
1635	Peace of Prague. Foundation of the French Academy. Death of Lope de Vega
1636	Corneille's *Le Cid*
1637	Death of Ferdinand II. Ferdinand III
1640	Accession of the Great Elector. The House of Braganza in Portugal. Death of Rubens
1641	Death of Van Dyck
1642	Outbreak of the English Civil War. Death of Richelieu. Death of Galileo. Tasman sailed round Australia
1643	Accession of Louis XIV. Birth of Newton. Torricelli's barometer
1645	Death of Grotius
1646	Birth of Leibniz
1648	Peace of Westphalia. *Académie de peinture et sculpture*
1649	Execution of Charles I. The Commonwealth
1650	Death of Descartes
1651	Navigation Act. Hobbes's *Leviathan*

1652	Guericke: air-pump
1653	Cromwell becomes Lord Protector
1657	Angelus Silesius: *Cherubinischer Wandersmann*. Pascal: *Lettres provinciales*
1658	Death of Cromwell. Death of Ferdinand III. Leopold I. The first Rheinbund
1660	Restoration of the Stuarts: Charles II. Death of Velasquez
1661	Death of Mazarin. Autocracy of Louis XIV. Boyle: *Sceptical Chymist*
1662	Death of Pascal. *L'Art de penser*. Incorporation of the Royal Society
1663	Guericke: electrical machine
1664	Molière: *Tartuffe*. Trappist Order
1665	Death of Poussin. La Rochefoucauld: *Maximes*
1667	War of Devolution. Milton: *Paradise Lost*
1668	Grimmelshausen: *Simplizissimus*
1669	Death of Rembrandt. Paris Opera-house
1670	Spinoza: *Tractatus theologico-politicus*
1673	Death of Molière. The Test Acts
1674	Death of Milton. Boileau: *L'Art poétique*. New York
1675	Battle of Fehrbellin. Malebranche: *De la recherche de la vérité*. Leeuwenhoek: Infusoria. Death of Turenne. Greenwich Observatory
1676	Death of Paul Gerhardt
1677	Death of Spinoza; *Ethica*. Racine: *Phèdre*. Death of Borromini
1678	Huygens: Undulatory theory. Simon: *Histoire critique du Vieux Testament*
1679	Peace of Nijmegen. Habeas Corpus Act. Abraham a Sancta Clara: *Merk's Wien*
1680	Death of Bernini
1681	Death of Calderon. Occupation of Strassburg
1682	Death of Claude Lorrain. Death of Murillo. Death of Ruysdael
1683	The Turks before Vienna. Philadelphia. Death of Colbert
1684	Death of Corneille. Leibniz: Differential Calculus. Newton: Law of Gravitation

1685	Revocation of the Edict of Nantes. Death of Charles II. James II
1687	Hungary to the Habsburgs. Newton: *Naturalis Philosophiæ Principia mathematica*. Death of Lully
1688	The Glorious Revolution. Death of the Great Elector. La Bruyère: *Les Caractères*
1689	William of Orange, King of England. Accession of Peter the Great. Devastation of the Palatinate
1690	Locke: *An Essay concerning Human Understanding* Papin: steam cylinder
1694	Birth of Voltaire. Bank of England.
1695	Bayle: *Historical and Critical Dictionary*. Death of La Fontaine. Death of Huygens
1696	Toland's *Christianity not Mysterious*
1697	Peace of Rijswijk. Augustus the Strong of Saxony, King of Poland. Battle of Zenta
1699	Peace of Karlowitz. Death of Racine
1700	Death of Dryden. Berlin Academy of Sciences
1701	Prussia becomes a kingdom
1702	Death of William III. Anne. Stahl: phlogiston theory
1703	Foundation of St. Petersburg
1704	Battle of Blenheim. Gibraltar taken by the English
1705	Death of Leopold I. Joseph I
1706	Battle of Ramillies
1708	Battle of Oudenarde
1709	Battle of Malplaquet. Battle of Poltava. Appearance of weekly papers in England. Böttcher: porcelain
1710	Leibniz: *Théodicée*
1711	Death of Boileau. Death of Joseph I. Charles VI
1712	Birth of Frederick the Great. Birth of Rousseau
1713	Peace of Utrecht. Accession of Frederick William I
1714	Peace of Rastatt and Baden. Death of Queen Anne. House of Hanover in England
1715	Death of Louis XIV. Regency. Death of Fénelon Death of Malebranche
1716	Death of Leibniz
1717	Birth of Winckelmann. First Freemasons' lodge
1718	Charles XII killed
1719	Defoe: *Robinson Crusoe*

1720	Collapse of Law's system
1721	Peace of Nystad. Death of Watteau. Montesquieu: *Lettres persanes*
1722	Foundation of the Herrnhut Brotherhood
1723	Death of Philip of Orleans. Rule of Louis XV. Pragmatic Sanction
1724	Birth of Kant. Birth of Klopstock
1725	Death of Peter the Great
1726	Swift: *Gulliver's Travels*
1727	Death of Newton
1728	Voltaire: *Henriade*
1729	Bach: *Matthäuspassion*. Birth of Lessing
1730	Gottsched: *Critische Dichtkunst*
1734	Voltaire: *Lettre sur les Anglais*
1735	Linnæus: *Systema naturæ*
1736	Death of Prince Eugene
1740	Death of Frederick William I. Frederick the Great. Death of Charles VI. Maria Theresa
1741	Handel: *Messiah*
1742	Young: *Night Thoughts*
1743	Death of Cardinal Fleury
1744	Death of Pope. Birth of Herder
1745	Death of Swift.
1746	Gellert: *Fabeln und Erzählungen*
1748	Montesquieu: *Esprit des lois*. Lamettrie: *L'Homme machine*. Klopstock: *Messias*. Excavation of Pompeii begun
1749	Birth of Goethe
1750	Death of John Sebastian Bach. Franklin: lightning-conductor
1751	The *Encyclopédie* begins to appear
1753	Death of Berkeley
1754	Death of Christian Wolff. Death of Holberg
1755	Death of Montesquieu. Kant: *Allgemeine Naturgeschichte und Theorie des Himmels*. Lisbon earthquake
1756	Birth of Mozart. Outbreak of the Seven Years' War
1757	Rossbach, Leuthen
1758	Zorndorf. Hochkirch. Helvétius: *De l'esprit*
1759	Kunersdorf. Death of Handel. Birth of Schiller

1760	Liegnitz. Torgau. Macpherson: *Ossian*
1761	Rousseau: *La Nouvelle Héloïse*
1762	Holstein-Gottorp dynasty in Russia: Peter III. Catherine II. Gluck: *Orfeo*. Rousseau: *Contrat social; Émile*
1763	Peace of Hubertusburg. Peace of Paris
1764	Death of Hogarth. Death of Rameau. Winckelmann: *Geschichte der Kunst des Altertums*
1766	Death of Gottsched. Lessing: *Laokoon*. Goldsmith: *Vicar of Wakefield*. Cavendish's hydrogen experiments
1767	Lessing: *Minna von Barnhelm; Hamburgische Dramaturgie*
1768	Murder of Winckelmann. Sterne: *Sentimental Journey*. Gerstenberg: *Ugolino*
1769	Birth of Napoleon. Letters of Junius. Arkwright: the spinning-machine
1770	Death of Boucher. Death of Tiepolo. Birth of Beethoven. Holbach: *Système de la nature*
1771	Priestley: oxygen
1772	First Partition of Poland. Göttinger Hainbund. Lessing: *Emilia Galotti*. Death of Swedenborg
1773	Dissolution of the Jesuit Order. *Blätter von deutscher Art und Kunst*. Goethe: *Götz von Berlichingen*. Bürger: *Leonore*
1774	Death of Louis XV. Louis XVI. Goethe: *Werther. Wolfenbüttler Fragmente*. Lenz: *Der Hofmeister*
1775	Beaumarchais: *Le Barbier de Séville*. Lavater: physiognomy
1776	Declaration of Independence of the United States of America. Death of Hume. Adam Smith: *Inquiry into the Nature and Causes of the Wealth of Nations*. Lenz: *Die Soldaten*. Klinger: Sturm und Drang. Wagner: *Die Kindermörderin*
1778	Death of Voltaire. Death of Rousseau
1779	Death of Garrick. Death of Raphael Mengs. Lessing: *Nathan der Weise*
1780	Death of Maria Theresa. Joseph II. Lessing: *Erziehung des Menschengeschlechts*
1781	Death of Lessing. Kant: *Kritik der reinen Vernunft*.

455

Voss's translation of Homer. Schiller: *Räuber*. Herschel's discovery of the planet Uranus

1782   Montgolfier's balloon

1783   Peace of Versailles. Schiller: *Fiesco*

1784   Death of Johnson. Death of Diderot. Herder: *Ideen zur Philosophie der Geschichte der Menschheit*. Beaumarchais: *Le Mariage de Figaro*. Schiller: *Kabale und Liebe*

1785   German Fürstenbund. Werner: Neptunism

1786   Death of Frederick the Great. Frederick William II. Mozart: *Figaro*

1787   Death of Gluck. Goethe: *Iphigenie*. Schiller: *Don Carlos*. Mozart: *Don Juan*

1788   The Wöllner Edict on Religion. Death of Hamann. Kant: *Kritik der praktischen Vernunft*. Goethe: *Egmont*. Hutton: Plutonism

1789   Storming of the Bastille. Goethe: *Tasso*. Galvani: animal electricity

1790   Death of Joseph II. Leopold II. Kant: *Kritik der Urteilskraft*. Goethe: *Metamorphose der Pflanzen; Faust* fragment; *Tasso*

1791   Galvani's hook. Death of Mirabeau. Flight to Varennes. Mozart: *Magic Flute*. Death of Mozart

1792   Death of Leopold II. Francis II. September Massacres. Valmy. Rouget de l'Isle: the *Marseillaise*

1793   Execution of Louis XVI. Reign of Terror. Second Partition of Poland

1794   Thermidor. Fichte: *Wissenschaftslehre*. Goethe and Schiller begin collaboration

1795   Directory. Third Partition of Poland. F. A. Wolf: *Prolegomena ad Homerum*. Goethe: *Wilhelm Meisters Lehrjahre*

1796   Babeuf Conspiracy. Death of Catherine II. Bonaparte in Italy. Jenner's discovery of vaccination

1797   Campo Formio. Death of Frederick William II. Frederick William III

1798   Laplace: *Exposition du système du monde*. Malthus: *Essay on the Principles of Population*. Bonaparte in Egypt. Battle of Abukir

456

1799	18th Brumaire. Schiller: *Wallenstein*. Schleiermacher: *Reden über die Religion*
1800	Marengo and Hohenlinden. Schiller: *Maria Stuart*. Voltaic pile
1801	Schiller: *Jungfrau von Orleans*. Gauss: *Disquisitiones arithmeticæ*
1803	Death of Herder. Death of Klopstock. The *Reichsdeputationshauptschluss*. The Code Napoléon
1804	Death of Kant. Napoleon, Emperor
1805	Death of Schiller. Trafalgar and Austerlitz. Beethoven: *Fidelio*
1806	Confederation of the Rhine; end of the Holy Roman Empire. Jena. Continental embargo. Hegel: *Phänomenologie des Geistes*. *Des Knaben Wunderhorn*
1807	Tilsit. Dalton: atomic theory. Fulton: steamship
1808	Fichte: *Addresses to the German Nation*. "*Voilà un Homme*." Publication of the first part of *Faust*
1809	Aspern and Wagram. Death of Haydn. Sömmering: telegraph
1810	Opening of Berlin University. Goethe: *Farbenlehre*. Kleist: *Käthchen von Heilbronn*
1811	Death of Kleist
1812	Russian Campaign. The Brothers Grimm: *Kinder- und Hausmärchen*. Cuvier's Catastrophic Theory
1813	The Battle of the Nations at Leipzig
1814	Death of Fichte. Stephenson's locomotive. Bourbon Restoration. First Peace of Paris. Opening of the Vienna Congress

INDEX

ii

A NOTE
ON THE TYPE IN
WHICH THIS BOOK IS SET

This book has been set in a modern adaptation of a type designed by William Caslon, the first (1692–1766), who, it is generally conceded, brought the old-style letter to its highest perfection. An artistic easily-read type, Caslon has had two centuries of ever-increasing popularity in our own country—it is of interest to note that the first copies of the Declaration of Independence and the first paper currency distributed to the citizens of the newborn nation were printed in this type face.

SET UP, ELECTROTYPED, PRINTED AND BOUND BY THE PLIMPTON PRESS, NORWOOD, MASS.